Decade of Nightmares

DECADE OF NIGHTMARES

The End of the Sixties and the
Making of Eighties America

———

Philip Jenkins

OXFORD
UNIVERSITY PRESS
2006

OXFORD
UNIVERSITY PRESS

Oxford University Press, Inc., publishes works that further
Oxford University's objective of excellence
in research, scholarship, and education.

Oxford   New York
Auckland   Cape Town   Dar es Salaam   Hong Kong   Karachi
Kuala Lumpur   Madrid   Melbourne   Mexico City   Nairobi
New Delhi   Shanghai   Taipei   Toronto

With offices in
Argentina   Austria   Brazil   Chile   Czech Republic   France   Greece
Guatemala   Hungary   Italy   Japan   Poland   Portugal   Singapore
South Korea   Switzerland   Thailand   Turkey   Ukraine   Vietnam

Published by Oxford University Press, Inc.
198 Madison Avenue, New York, New York 10016
www.oup.com

Oxford is a registered trademark of Oxford University Press

Library of Congress Cataloging-in-Publication Data
Jenkins, Philip, 1952–
Decade of nightmares: the end of the sixties and the
making of eighties America / Philip Jenkins.
p. cm.
Includes bibliographical references and index.
ISBN-13: 978-0-19-517866-1
ISBN-10: 0-19-517866-1
1. United States—History—1969–.
2. United States—History—1961–1969.
3. United States—Politics and government—1945–1989.
4. United States—Social conditions—1945–.
5. Social problems—United States—History—20th century.
6. Culture conflict—United States—History—20th century.
7. Conservatism—United States—History—20th century.
8. Political culture—United States—History—20th century.
I. Title.
E839.J46 2006 973.92—dc22 2005020159

1 3 5 7 9 8 6 4 2
Printed in the United States of America
on acid-free paper

To Liz

Contents

Introduction

Imagine a Rip van Winkle who fell asleep in 1970 or 1974 and reawakened in the mid-1980s. Studying the torrent of media images, he tries to make sense of the new world, to understand which side emerged victorious from the social conflicts of his day.

He is startled by how thoroughly conservative interests seem to have triumphed. Ronald Reagan is an immensely popular president who has won a second term by a landslide. Across the political landscape, so many of the controversies of the 1960s have been carried definitively by the right. In foreign affairs, the confrontational anti-Communist rhetoric harks back to the time of John Foster Dulles or Barry Goldwater. Even Goldwater, in fact, is attacking the CIA for going too far in attempting to overthrow the leftist regime in Nicaragua. America's leaders speak the hard-core language of captive nations and slave states, of the need to roll back Communism. The United States is ostentatiously building up its military, with a strong emphasis on nuclear arms, and is contemplating space-based warfare. As in the 1950s, Americans are alarmed by threats from enemies within, and not only from spies and subversives. Islamist terrorists threaten devastating attacks on U.S. soil. Domestically, a ferocious drug war is making dramatic inroads into civil liberties, and few are willing to speak publicly against the simplistic "Just Say No" ideology. Many states have restored capital punishment, which most thought gone for good in the early 1970s. News stories about raids on crack houses are intercut with arrests of domestic terrorist cells. The imagery suggests a nation under siege.

Against this background, our sleeper is puzzled by the survival of liberal gains from his time. The social and political victories won by African-Americans in the 1960s have not been reversed and indeed have permanently changed the nation's cultural landscape. Social movements such as environmentalism still flourish. Women's social position has improved beyond recognition, and the media deal more frankly with sexual issues. Yet at the same time, new threats are dramatically altering sexual behavior: no one laughs anymore at scare stories about the dreadful diseases that can result from promiscuous sex. America believes itself threatened by legions of faceless demons: child abusers and molesters, sex killers and kidnappers, and even satanic murder gangs. Sexual monsters are targeting America's children. Political rhetoric at home and abroad has taken on a religious and specifically Christian tone, warning against the forces of evil that threaten American society. Our imaginary sleeper thinks back to the question Jefferson Airplane had asked about America's near future: "Can you tell me please, who won?"[1] With some obvious exceptions, sixties values went down to defeat. The revolution failed.

Matters would be more ambiguous if our sleeper woke up in 2006. Initially, he might conclude that the radical movements of his own time had succeeded. Everywhere, he sees signs of impressive feminist advances. Abortion is freely available. Women hold senior positions in business and government, and one prominent woman is widely discussed as a likely future president. The extent of racial change is just as evident. Two successive secretaries of state have been African-American, and in a Republican administration. The slightest hint of the kind of segregation that was once commonplace now meets with massive public condemnation, not to mention lawsuits. Openly gay characters proliferate in the media, while gay marriage is a leading political issue. The Democratic candidate in the most recent presidential race was a former leader of Vietnam Veterans Against the War.

Yet, looking closer, the sleeper sees that the tone of political debate is strikingly conservative. In the 2004 presidential election, issues of family and sexual morality, of abortion and gay marriage, proved very contentious, and mobilization around these themes gave conservatives a decisive electoral edge. Even among liberal politicians, few advocate the kind of welfare policies that were popular in the 1960s, and free enterprise capitalism rules unchallenged. It was a recent Democratic president who proclaimed that "the era of big government is over," and boasted of eliminating welfare as we know it.[2] Nor today does one lightly insult the military. In the 2004 election campaign, few attacked candidate John Kerry on the grounds that his dovish protests against the Vietnam War had been too restrained: the most damaging charge was rather that he had exaggerated his credentials as a war hero. And, astonishingly, Communism really has been rolled back, without provoking a global holocaust.

Also conservative is the new social consensus on crime and deviant behavior. Liberals and conservatives vie to impose the harshest penalties on offenders, who are imprisoned with little recourse to the alternative kinds of correction proposed a generation before. In comparison with the late 1960s, this looks like a deeply punitive society, by far the most prison-oriented of any advanced state. And far from drug use having become accepted and normal, an absolute consensus now forbids discussing any relaxation of legal prohibition.[3] Whether dealing with drugs or sexuality, foreign policy or military action, this new society frames its problems in terms of moral absolutes, of dangerous, evil outsiders who can be identified and combated.

The Big Chill

Most would agree that the decade of the 1960s transformed American life, and to that extent, the decade deserves its legendary status.[4] University history departments were already offering courses on the 1960s a few years after the end of that decade. Now "the sixties" carries multiple possible meanings, but usually a speaker is invoking the radical and liberal values of that era, a package of beliefs and ideas that Europeans characterize as "'68ism." These values include personal and social liberation and the imperative need to challenge laws or social mores that restrict those goals. The quest for personal authenticity encompassed sexual liberation, spiritual exploration, and quite likely experimentation with drugs. Embracing ideas of racial and gender equality, '68ism espoused the liberation of historically oppressed and marginalized groups. The sixties inheritance stressed the crucial importance of peace and of changing authoritarian social structures that give rise to war and conflict. Military and corporate business values were rejected as manifestations of racism and sexism. Though all these movements have deep historical roots, in the modern world feminism, pacifism, environmentalism, radical activism, esoteric spirituality, and sexual liberation all have powerful associations with the upheavals of the 1960s.[5]

But just as evidently, the reform currents of the 1960s were challenged and in some important ways reversed in the following years. A modern American transported to the early 1970s would be looking at a radically different society, not just in terms of dress and hairstyles but also in social and political commonplaces. For better or worse, the world of the mid-1980s appears much more familiar. A marked change of the national mood occurred in the mid-1970s, bringing with it a much deeper pessimism about the state of America and its future, and a growing rejection of recent liberal orthodoxies. A conservative social and political movement reached its peak in the early 1980s.[6]

Depending on our values, we can view this movement in different ways. Idealizing the 1960s, many baby boomers see the change in terms of a fading idealism. The elegiac movie *The Big Chill* appeared in 1983, at the height of Reaganism. A similar sense of the decade as a new ice age emerges from Tony Kushner's *Angels in America* (1991–92), in which the onset of AIDS symbolizes the loss of older freedoms. Conservative observers might see the change as a return to common sense, a reining in of the socially self-destructive forces let loose in the years of race riots and Vietnam War protests. For Lee Edwards, this was a key time in the "conservative revolution," a triumphant vindication of traditional values as America emerged from the crises and self-doubt of the 1960s.[7] Whatever the reasons, we have to be impressed by the sheer magnitude of the changes in the decade or so after the end of 1960s turmoil. This later period, these years of containment or counterrevolution, shaped modern American society at least as much as the 1960s did.

Historical eras rarely begin or end at neat or precise points, and decades are highly malleable. The year 1970 is an especially implausible candidate for marking the end of an era, because so much of the unrest of the 1960s was peaking in that year, while critical events we think of as characterizing sixties liberalism actually occurred afterward. Though these historical markers are symbolic rather than real, I will argue that "the sixties" began with the assassination of John Kennedy in 1963 and ended with the resignation of Richard Nixon in 1974. The Watergate crisis was a strictly political affair, but it coincided with epoch-making events in social and economic history, including the OPEC oil embargo and the economic crisis that ensued.[8] Thus redefined, the 1960s now properly include such radical turning points as the Attica prison riot (1971), *Roe v. Wade* (1973), and other key legal cases. I disagree with Bruce Schulman's argument in his important account, *The Seventies: The Great Shift in American Culture, Society, and Politics,* that "if one date delineated the end of the Sixties and the beginning of the Seventies, it was the year 1968," so that much of the ensuing upheaval properly belongs in a "long 1970s," running from 1969 through 1984.[9] There is something eccentric about any version of the sixties that omits Woodstock, Stonewall, the Chicago conspiracy trial, the Weathermen, Kent State, Led Zeppelin, Apollo XI, and Earth Day, not to mention such signature films as *Easy Rider, Zabriskie Point,* and *Five Easy Pieces.*

But if the liberal or radical sixties ended only in 1974, how are we to describe the conservative years that followed? There is no easy or convenient description for the years from 1975 to 1986, since the era does not correspond to any one decade. But the social and political counterrevolution had a logical narrative with its own historical landmarks and a distinctive political dynamic. Trends of the mid-1970s can scarcely be understood or appreciated until we see their outcome in the early 1980s, and without understanding the background in the Carter era, developments of the Reagan years must appear far more innovative then they actually were. The year 1980 offers a tempting dividing line between decades and between political regimes, but in fact that year represents the climax of a story, rather than either an end or a beginning. And this period too has a natural conclusion, around 1986, with the evident mellowing of Cold War antipathies. Also about 1986, a number of political defeats began an era of crisis for Reagan-era conservatism.

All periods of American history involve some degree of change, which is why college teachers grow weary of challenging students who write that a given decade was "a time of transition." Of what decade can that not be said? Nevertheless, some eras stand out because of the unusual rapidity of change and the transformation of values and ideals in a very short time. Examples of such periods would include the 1840s, the years around 1915, and of course the 1960s. But the post-1975 decade was another time when radical changes in politics and culture occurred in just a few years, and in ways that transformed ordinary life, not just the world of political elites.

Because this era so conspicuously defined itself in opposition to the radicalism of the preceding years, we might think of the post-1975 years as the "anti-sixties." This might sound almost blasphemous to someone accustomed to thinking of the sixties as an era of daring and unparalleled cultural creativity, though the post-1975 years certainly have their achievements. It is difficult to think of any period as sterile that produced such amazing technological advances, not to mention the literary, artistic, and cinematic record.[10] These were also the years when the American intellectual world was transformed by "Theory"—by postmodernism, cultural studies, postcolonialism, semiotics, and social constructionism.[11] Of course, most of these authors and scholars defined themselves against the prevailing conservative order, but equally, much of the creative ferment of the late 1960s had arisen in opposition to prevailing political orthodoxies.

So dramatic was the break in American history and culture around 1974–75 that it is difficult to think of "the seventies" as a meaningful period. I take issue here with some excellent recent writers on that decade, including

Bruce Schulman, and also David Frum, whose study of that period is titled *The Decade That Brought You Modern Life—for Better or Worse.*[12] Though critically important changes were under way during the 1970s, I differ about exactly what was happening and, just as important, when it happened.

Only Yesterday

Many accounts of American history trace the history of turmoil and dissent up to the Watergate crisis, and then little of note seems to happen till the Reagan election victory of 1980. It almost seems as if American history, wearied after the daily stresses of the 1960s, took a seven-year vacation after Nixon resigned. In fact, a great deal of substance happens in the late 1970s. The reaction of the 1980s was more than a terrified response to the sudden confrontation with new and more dangerous drugs (mainly crack cocaine) or the newly identified menace of AIDS. The movement was well under way before these menaces appeared on the horizon, and generally before 1980.

One year in particular marks a real turning point in domestic policy, the year in which sixties assumptions were widely challenged. In 1977, we see an assault on permissiveness in sexuality and drug use, a counterattack against gains in gay rights, a sharp new opposition to religious experimentation, and intensifying concern about Communist menaces overseas. At home and abroad, the sixties vision became noticeably grimmer and more threatening. This was far more than just the summer of *Star Wars, Smokey and the Bandit,* and *Saturday Night Fever.* The political transformation of the Reagan years is rooted in the social movements of 1977.[13]

Given their place in modern historical memory, it might seem bizarre to treat the late 1970s as a time of serious political change. These years are largely remembered for their pop culture offerings: airheaded television series, martial arts films, and countless fads, including astrology, streaking, pet rocks, and roller disco. *Saturday Night Fever* left potent images of disco culture—hedonism, casual sex, and outrageous clothes and hairstyles. In a retrospective on the decade in 1979, *Doonesbury* suggested that the nearest thing to bright spots were disco, Watergate books, and a fifties revival. It was "a kidney stone of a decade . . . the worst of times." Peter Carroll's history of the decade is entitled *It Seemed Like Nothing Happened.*[14]

Similar cultural themes have shaped later reconstructions. Among recent films, *Boogie Nights* portrays the southern California porn industry in the late 1970s, when "sex was safe, pleasure was business, and business was booming." The sexual worlds of the time are explored in *The People Versus*

Larry Flynt and *Wonderland*. Other films entranced by the hair, clothes, and disco style of those years include *54* (about the legendary New York disco), *Starsky and Hutch, Austin Powers' Goldmember,* and *Anchorman,* along with the television series *That '70s Show;* kitsch also dominates the stage musical *Mamma Mia!* The films of Quentin Tarantino draw heavily on memories of the 1970s, and his *Kill Bill* is saturated with the martial arts genre. *Lords of Dogtown* remembers the decade for its skateboarding cultures. For Americans under forty, the late seventies are recalled chiefly through the syndicated television shows of the time, most of which—*Man About the House, The Dukes of Hazzard, Six Million Dollar Man, Charlie's Angels*—defy parody. The title of one nostalgic film, *Dazed and Confused,* neatly describes the popular impression of the era. And, however unfairly, many would regard the popular music as not worth preserving, never mind reviving. Grudges left by disco were slow to heal.[15]

Not all retrospectives of the 1970s are vacuous. *Boogie Nights* and *The Last Days of Disco* both offer dark commentary, and Spike Lee's *Summer of Sam* is a hair-raising picture of New York City during the Son of Sam serial murder wave of 1977. But politics rarely surface in pop culture treatments. The 2004 film *Miracle* depicted the sense of looming national crisis in early 1980, but only as a prelude to a fairy-tale treatment of how the U.S. ice hockey team revived national pride by defeating the Soviets in the Winter Olympics. Depictions of the era's radicals—such as *The Assassination of Richard Nixon*—have a freak-show quality.

These treatments stand in marked contrast to films commemorating the 1960s, a mythical time commonly remembered for heroic struggles, titanic individuals, and enduring moral choices. We think of films such as *JFK, Mississippi Burning, X, The Right Stuff, Panther, Born on the Fourth of July,* or *Apollo 13.* The 1960s emerges as an era of civil rights struggles, of passionate debates over Vietnam, of America reaching for the moon; the 1970s was a time of disco and impossible hairstyles, of silly infantilism. In the 1960s, the fictional Forrest Gump was involved in both the Vietnam War and the anti-war movement; in the 1970s, he invented jogging and the smiley face logo.

As yet, the 1980s have not attracted even this level of commemoration, however often VH1 retrospectives may proclaim "I love the eighties," and although eighties styles resurface sporadically in fashion and in toys. From the point of view of cinema and television, this was a decade of AIDS (*Forrest Gump, Angels in America*) and thoroughgoing moral corruption (*American Psycho*). Though the recent song by Bowling for Soup speaks of being "preoccupied with 1985," that does not (yet) reflect the state of national memory.[16]

If a nation defines itself by the history it chooses to remember, then the 1960s will continue to shape events, while the subsequent period seems almost irrelevant. In modern elections, candidates are still confronted by the moral choices they made in the era of Vietnam and civil rights, but not in the conflicts of 1980.

Chain Reactions

But the late 1970s cannot have been simply a time of pop culture triviality: other things must have been happening in those years leading up to the election of Ronald Reagan. Reaganism did not represent a sudden invasion by a mysterious alien force. Conservatism certainly commanded popular support in the 1960s, considerably more than many historians and media outlets might lead us to believe. Through the 1970s too, conservatives were reorganizing and mobilizing their forces. This was the era of the New Right, an effective coalition of groups aroused by both domestic and foreign issues. Conservatives also benefited from a restructuring of liberal opinion, as old-line liberals, alarmed by the nation's international decline, moved to the political right. Neoconservatives—liberals mugged by reality—became a powerful voice in foreign policy, urging firmer stances against Communism and international terrorism. Yet, however important these movements, they were influential only insofar as they found a receptive public. New political alignments mattered because hard-line views were reaching a mass audience, and by no means only among traditional conservatives. Something changed substantially to allow the election in 1980 of not just a conservative but a figure who recently had been widely regarded as too extreme for national office.[17]

In 1991, Thomas and Mary Edsall's book *Chain Reaction* offered a systematic explanation of the shift from liberal hegemony in the sixties to conservative dominance in the eighties. They stress the politics of taxes and rights, but above all of race. In various forms, these issues came to dominate most domestic policy discussions and divided many lower- and middle-class whites from the older New Deal coalition. In this account, conservative policies succeeded in "pitting those who bear many of the costs of federal intervention against those whose struggle for equality has been advanced by interventionist government policies." The conservative coalition that has enjoyed such power since the late 1970s has used a politics of substitution, presenting policies in a socially acceptable form that is free of overt racial references but which nevertheless manipulates racial fears. Complaints about welfare cheats, welfare queens, and freeloaders disguise the older rhetoric of black laziness and fecklessness. Democrats must be blamed for failing to acknowledge the social and political pressures building under them during the 1970s, but the primary culprits were the conservatives, organized in the Republican Party.[18]

The Edsalls' argument appeals to modern liberals, since it allows virtually every aspect of conservative ideology to be dismissed as covert racism. In a similar mode, Thomas Frank's *What's the Matter with Kansas?* argues that issues of morality, family, gender, and "values" seduced working people to support conservative politicians, thereby betraying and sabotaging their own economic interests. Just as the Edsalls highlight race as the critical distraction from authentic issues, so Frank addresses the (spurious) politics of morality. Frank sees "the culture wars [as] a way of framing the ever-powerful subject of social class. They are a way for Republicans to speak on behalf of the forgotten man without causing any problems for their core big-business constituency." Once again, conservative politics are seen as a masquerade, a form of false consciousness, rather than real politics.[19]

Both Frank and the Edsalls present powerful arguments, and the stress on race is especially important. Throughout American history, racial fears have permeated issues that on the surface have no racial content whatever. Debates on welfare, crime, and drugs clearly did, and do, have racial sub-texts. Even when minorities are not the direct targets of the polemic, we find fears that white people themselves will be lured into stereotypically black patterns of violence and sexual immorality, perhaps through the influence of drugs. Indeed, the Edsalls may actually understate a strong case, as they devote so little attention to foreign policy matters. The political shift in the mid-1970s was driven in part by a widespread sense that the white Euro-American world had forfeited its centuries-long global hegemony, a decline symbolized by the loss of the Vietnam War but also by the rise of Arab oil wealth, the Japanese economic boom, and the vociferous demands of radical Third World nations. Foreign news reinforced a sense of racial crisis at home.[20]

But even when we acknowledge these racial agendas, they are not sufficient to explain the political changes that the United States experienced. Race, rights, and taxes contributed to the shift, but so did many other issues, foreign and domestic, in which racial themes are hard to discern. International and military issues also played their role, especially fears of Communism and terrorism. So did concerns about drugs and violence, and so, crucially, did pervasive fears about threats to children and families. Deeply rooted issues of gender and sexuality influenced political behavior as much as did attitudes toward race or class. Neither Frank nor the Edsalls credit conservatives for responding to real or well-grounded concerns or fears in these or other areas.

Understanding the political sea change matters if, as seems likely, we can discern parallels between the America of the 1970s and conditions in the early twenty-first century. Though history does not repeat itself faithfully, there are instructive similarities between the economic situation then and the one that exists now. In both periods, heavy government expenditures combined with lax fiscal discipline to cause serious deficits. The situation was compounded by swelling energy prices and high spending on defense and national security. The result was that America faced then, and faces now, the potential for worrying inflation and a precipitous decline in the value of the dollar. Any solutions would demand stringent fiscal and political measures, potentially damaging to the nation's economic well-being and its standard of living. The last great economic correction, between 1979 and 1982, was an agonizing time.

If America once more faces a crisis like that of the 1970s, we have much to learn from the political conditions of that earlier period. An economic restructuring could not fail to have political consequences, though we can only speculate about their exact shape and wonder if the response to crisis would acquire a left- or right-wing coloring. Depending on circumstances, either side could resort to the populist, the demagogic, and even the apocalyptic. Also recalling the 1970s, political allegiances would be shaped by attitudes toward overseas threats and recent memories of a controversial war. Different ideologies would be in conflict, and the winner would be the side that did the best job of recognizing and shaping public fears, which might or might not express themselves in economic or class terms. Economic woes would encourage the expression of deep-rooted fears and grievances, and pressing issues would likely be defined in the language of morality and virtue, crime and evil, religion and spirituality, and family values. Recent experience suggests that anyone who dismisses these fears as unworthy of serious attention, as a merely symbolic diversion from real politics, has already lost the battle.

In Search of Enemies

Rather than seek any single explanation of the shift away from sixties liberalism, I would instead point to some potent common themes that we find in seemingly disparate concerns at home and abroad. Measured by responses to any one of a range of issues, American sensibilities changed dramatically in the decade after 1975. Whether in matters of foreign policy or war, *views of human nature*   (*)

disorder or terrorism, poverty or urban crisis, crime or drug abuse, many Americans adopted a more pessimistic, more threatening interpretation of human behavior, which harked back to much older themes in American culture. At home and abroad, the post-1975 public was less willing to see social dangers in terms of historical forces, instead preferring a strict moralistic division: problems were a matter of evil, not dysfunction. Ideas of relativism and complex causation were replaced by simpler and more sinister visions of the enemies facing Americans and their nation. And the forces of evil arrayed against us were conceived in terms of conspiracy and clandestine manipulation.

The conspiracy theme is deeply embedded in American political culture, most notoriously in the Red scare years of the early 1950s, but in the post-1975 decade too, a florid imagery of dangerous, conspiratorial outsiders became thoroughly integrated into mainstream political rhetoric. Moreover, these ideas were deployed most consistently to the benefit of socially conservative causes. Political rhetoric was permeated by themes of external threat, national vulnerability, subversion, and internal decadence. These concerns focused on a number of outside enemies, most obviously the Soviet Union, but there were countless enemies within. In the political rhetoric of the time, these diverse groups personified the immorality and outright evil that had arisen in consequence of the moral and political decadence of recent years. Conditions were bad, it seemed, because sixties values had let them get so bad.[21]

An absolutist moral vision reshaped politics. In foreign policy, the vision of the United States and the Soviet Union as competing powers in a perilous world system gave way to a night-and-day conflict between a righteous America and an evil empire. While this looks like a revival of the most confrontational phase of the 1950s Cold War, it was if anything more rooted in grand conspiracy theories. In his 1961 inaugural address, John F. Kennedy appealed to his Communist "adversaries"—not enemies—for a common front against "the dark powers of destruction unleashed by science." In the 1980s, in contrast, the Soviet Union itself was the source and symbol of dark forces.

The change is also manifested in new concepts of terrorism. In the early 1970s, the world suffered a wave of international terrorism, with a huge upsurge in airline hijackings as well as kidnapping and urban guerrilla violence across Europe and the Middle East. In the media and political discourse, this violence was certainly condemned, but it was not seen as part of one global menace, still less one organized from a single source. In different countries or regions, terrorism might have particular causes, arising from local grievances. A decade later, though, the issue was defined in terms of the "terror network," a global alliance directed ultimately from Moscow. The sixties vision of terrorism implied dealing with the political, social, and economic issues that led to violence. The newer concept demanded open confrontation and the destruction of evildoers. On occasion, the narrow focus on one particular enemy diverted attention from other adversaries that were also dangerous, leading to policy choices that would have harmful lasting effects.[22]

A trend toward confrontation was equally marked in domestic matters. In the decade following 1965, a widespread liberal critique challenged many aspects of traditional criminal justice policy and law enforcement. Commonly, poverty and crime were bracketed together as signs of social dysfunction, suggesting that those involved were as little responsible for one as for the other. Solutions were to be found in treatment and therapy rather than punishment: rehabilitation might well work. At the same time, police practices should be strictly regulated in order to prevent abusive behavior against the poor or minorities. Ideas of criminality changed fundamentally from the mid-1970s, as Americans discovered a new range of villains who targeted women and children. The worst criminals were seen as irrational monsters driven by uncontrollable violence and lust. Far from being the product of an unjust society, such criminals (usually deranged men) were nothing short of demonic. Contrary to visions of crime as a curable sickness, the focus now shifted to the offender as a predator, the perpetrator of evil. He could be incarcerated or killed but never cured.[23]

Once conflicts have been personified in terms of predatory outsiders, the range of available solutions narrows dramatically. If social problems arise from structural injustice or inequality, then solutions are complex, requiring social intervention. But if problems and threats can be blamed on specific outsiders, then these hostile groups or individuals can be tracked down, apprehended, and killed or disabled. Personifying an evil allows the possibility of clear-cut victories: when an enemy is captured or killed, the problem ends. This vision easily promotes an imagery of warfare, and military imagery comes naturally to American politics. We recall the wars on poverty and cancer, drugs and crime, child abuse and teen pregnancy. There are also the culture wars, and—most powerfully in recent years—the global war on terror. Problems are painted in terms of identifiable enemies who can be eliminated through a war or crusade, real or metaphorical. Few deny that wars are sometimes necessary, but the metaphor carries weighty implications. Such a war is a zero-sum game in which coexistence is not an option and talk of moral equivalence is not allowed. Americans look to the weighty precedent of Ulysses S. Grant for the belief that the best outcome of a war is unconditional surrender. And fighting wars means cutting legal corners and doing away with the conventional legal niceties that regulate the treatment of ordinary deviance.

The language of external threat lends itself readily to religious interpretations. I have spoken of demon figures, and the warfare analogy often recalls the Manichaean language of battles between light and darkness. Sometimes these images are just a part of conventional high-flying political rhetoric, but we should never underestimate their overt religious content. Throughout American history, movements that initially seem secular tend to develop powerful religious dimensions, and that is true of both left and right. Prophetic and millenarian themes permeated the civil rights movement, and the radical activism of the late 1960s had a strong apocalyptic current. Radicals saw themselves as locked in a death struggle with an imperial militaristic Amerika, the fall of which would usher in an idyllic new age of justice and peace. Perhaps apocalyptic approaches are hardwired into the human mind, since universal experience indicates that great life changes are preceded by traumatic and bloody events, above all by the moments of birth and death. In the post-1975 decade, though, conservative political rhetoric commonly drew on explicitly Christian apocalyptic, with all that implied about the evil and deceitful nature of the enemy and the impossibility of compromise. For many Americans, this was not just war but cosmic war.[24]

Protecting Children

In most societies, the most damning charge that can be made against an enemy is that they threaten harm or destruction to children. Through the post-1975 decade, the pervasive and many-faced threat to children was a dominant media topic, and this ever-present menace was portrayed as unimaginably large and destructive.[25] In 1977, the media discovered the hitherto little-explored topics of child pornography, pedophile rings, and child sexual abuse. In fact, it was exactly in this year that the phrase "child abuse" acquired its modern implications of sexual exploitation. (The phrase "serial murder" entered popular parlance in 1983.) Over the next few years, reasonable and proper concern with child protection spilled over into hysterical campaigns against imagined networks of sexual criminals. The resulting new laws suggested that childhood as a protected sexual category extended up to age eighteen, placing severe limits on the youth rights rhetoric of sixties activism. While fringe religions had once been the vanguard of what one might call a Consciousness Reformation, now they were seen as evil cults preying on children, given to murder, mass suicide, and ritualized child abuse. Again, the turning point came in the late 1970s, as cults became the center of a venomous social mythology. Literally, there were witches out there, and they were out to get our children.

Whether we are looking at drugs, sexuality, or cult activities, much of the cultural shift in domestic affairs involved a new view of threats (plausible or not) against children. Through the mid-1970s, social issues were often viewed in libertarian terms, so consenting individuals were accorded a broad right to err in their own ways. Attacking this principle opened one to charges of intolerance, bigotry, or religious fundamentalism. At the end of the decade, conservative rhetoric successfully challenged this view by stressing dangers to children, who by definition could not give informed consent. This rhetoric resonated with an audience that would define itself as broadly liberal. In the new environment, drugs were attacked on the grounds that angel dust damaged young teenagers, sexual hedonism was denounced because of the dangers from child pornography and child sexual abuse, and religious eccentricities were harmful because cults killed children. Widespread acceptance of these charges gave activists a platform to attack issues that might earlier have been taboo, so that panic responses to lethal "devil drugs" now applied to all illicit substances. One insidious example of issue creep involved child molestation, in which concern about child protection was exploited as a weapon against gay rights.

The idea of child protection does not necessarily lend itself to any political label. In the early 1970s, it was associated with liberal causes, and protecting the young against sexual abuse by predatory males became a critical element of the new feminism. Despite their liberal roots, these ideas proved useful for conservatives engaged in an ideological assault on the 1960s. Between 1983 and 1985, presidential and congressional investigations and public hearings on serial murder, child abuse, and child pornography provided a public forum in which diverse activists presented their agendas in terms of threats to children. Children needed protection, which also implied control and restraint.[26]

We have to choose our words carefully here, and it would be misleading to describe this rhetoric of threat entirely in terms of "paranoia," with its connotation of illusory menace. As we learned on September 11, outside enemies can be all too real, with the capacity to wreak immense damage, and so can domestic villains: sexual predators and criminals do exist. But through the early 1980s, there was a staggering disconnect between the portrayal of menaces and what could plausibly be seen as their objective substance.

Personal and Political

To comprehend the power of the rhetoric of threat and conspiracy, we have to move beyond the common distinction between mainstream politics and social or cultural history. Political historians often ignore social affairs or popular culture, while books on cultural or social matters rarely regard politics as part of their territory. In practice, though, it is impossible to separate these strands, and that is especially true in the post-Watergate years. When deciding how to vote, people draw not solely or even chiefly on political arguments but on social mood and on concerns and fears that ostensibly have little or no "political" content. As one Reagan pollster commented in 1984, "You persuade by reason, but you motivate people by tapping into values that run much deeper."[27]

To give an example, most scholars trying to understand the critical 1980 election would devote little attention to the sensational media stories of this year unless these had specifically surfaced as campaign issues. But that decision would mean missing a great deal—arguably, the heart of the story. Just to take one issue, violent crime was a national obsession of the late 1970s and early 1980s, which is not surprising because actual rates for violent offenses reached a historic peak around that time. Politicians certainly cited the crime problem, but what gave the issue its resonance was that the mass media had saturated the public with images of violence in its most pernicious and sadistic forms. Since 1977, the news media had offered incessant coverage to spectacular crimes and criminals, giving enormous notoriety to names such as Ted Bundy, John Wayne Gacy, and the Son of Sam. In the cinema, new censorship standards permitted a wave of spectacularly violent slasher films, from *Halloween* onward. In turn, these treatments influenced public attitudes toward feelings of safety and risk, gender (the threat of male violence against women), homosexuality (the image of the gay killer preying on boys), and the causation of social ills. Viewers familiar with Bundy or Gacy responded to a rhetoric that blamed crime on individual moral evil rather than poverty and injustice. Tales of violence and sexual abuse helped create a public more sympathetic to conservative social arguments.[28]

Yet many political accounts of the era ignore crime and justice. Partly, this reflects the common focus of political historians on national, federal, and presidential affairs, so that we speak of the "Carter era" or the "Clinton years." Thus an important collection of essays, *The Reagan Presidency*, contains precisely one index entry for crime, nothing on drugs, and just one brief note on children, in the context of child nutrition programs. The preceding volume in the series, *The Carter Presidency*, has no index entries for any of these topics.[29] This neglect is quite proper to the extent that these books concern the presidency, not the whole era, and the vast majority of criminal justice and social welfare issues are dealt with at the state or city level. But a strictly political and federally oriented account of a given era will miss significant issues that, however sensational they might appear, nevertheless do much to shape political allegiances. Few accounts of the pivotal year of 1980 take any notice of the Atlanta child murders, one of the most reported and emotive stories of an action-packed time.[30] Nor should any account of Reagan-era domestic policy omit the war on drugs.

Just as political historians might regard such issues as tabloid fodder unworthy of their attention, so social historians would not normally link their subject matter to national affairs, still less international matters. A scholar studying crime, sexual abuse, or serial murder would rarely draw connections to political events occurring at exactly the same time, even though an ordinary consumer of news would encounter both simultaneously and would assuredly link them.

Equally, domestic and international affairs are closely connected, in the sense that the same audience responds to claims and rhetorical statements about them. A public conditioned to accept conspiratorial and alarmist claims in one area is more willing to listen to similar ideas on other themes, especially when activists try repeatedly to link seemingly unconnected causes. Sensational incidents of child sexual abuse, serial murder, or cult atrocities appeared in the headlines at just the same time as events such as the Iran hostage crisis, the Miami race riot, and the gasoline shortages, and contributed to the sense of pervasive national malaise, decadence, and social failure. Seen alongside international crises and threats, these issues encouraged a sense of imminent apocalypse, a term that can be used with little exaggeration to describe the national mood of 1980.

I Want to Believe

The willingness to accept nightmarish media images in the post-1975 decade suggests the existence of widespread fears and anxieties, which could be readily mobilized. Partly, the depth of concern resulted from rational observation of recent changes in the United States and its position in the world. For a generation that grew up in the 1940s or 1950s, social change had proceeded at an alarming pace, and even liberals sympathetic to social progress were unnerved by obvious threats to the social fabric such as the decay of cities and rising crime. Francis Fukuyama has described what he terms a "Great Disruption" of Western societies, exemplified by crime, family breakdown, and a general loss of trust within society.[31] Internationally, Americans in the mid-1970s saw a world in which U.S. power and prestige stood at historic lows. One did not have to be an alarmist to ask how much further the process of decline would go within the next few years.

But changing social patterns also offered rich opportunities to interest groups making claims about new threats and problems, and any attempt at explaining the redefinition of social problems in these years must of necessity look beyond the realm of purely American politics. When Americans recall the cultural and political shifts that brought an end to '68ism, they usually think in terms of the Reagan revolution, forgetting the quite similar developments that occurred in other nations not subject to that president's authority.[32] Great Britain had its own sixties experience quite reminiscent of America's, and it saw a major cultural and political reversal in the late 1970s, culminating in the election of the conservative Margaret Thatcher in 1979. In this instance, the political influence, if any, ran from Britain to the United States, rather than the other way round. Other countries too elected new and more conservative regimes around this time.[33] Across the advanced Western nations, we see a comparable withdrawal from the more extreme aspects of sixties liberationism. In China, the ultra-radical Cultural Revolution ended in 1976, and in 1978 the nation declared a conversion to the market economy and at least some aspects of capitalism.[34]

Around the world, social reaction often took religious forms, as faith traditions long dismissed as obsolete or irrelevant acquired potent new political voices. The conservative Christian movements that so radically changed U.S. politics in the mid-1970s paralleled similar trends in very different societies. Even in secular Britain, the new conservatism demonstrated a religious quality, with vigorous campaigns to suppress abortion and a notorious attempt to prosecute gay publications under the ancient law of blasphemy. The Indian election of 1977 brought to power the Janata Party, creating the first government in the nation's history to exclude the secular, nationalist Congress Party; the Janata coalition included a Hindu fundamentalist component that soon reshaped itself as the Bharatiya Janata Party. In the same year, Orthodox Jewish forces celebrated the election of Israeli prime minister Menachem Begin and his Likud Party. In 1977 and 1978, the upsurge of Shi'ite Muslim radicalism in Iran would have vast repercussions, initially in Lebanon and Afghanistan, but soon for much of *dar al-Islam*. In 1978, the accession of Pope John Paul II marked a conservative counter-revolution in the Roman Catholic Church, a development with major implications for Latin America. In their different ways, each of these events marked a socially conservative challenge to secular liberalism and to a political consensus that had held for decades. Not just in the United States, the politics of faith mattered immeasurably more in 1979 than they had in 1975.

Citing similar changes in very different societies is not to say that all of these movements grew from the same roots: the upsurge of faith-based politics was not a sign that the planet had passed through the tail of a comet. Political debates and religious changes were shaped by the traditions of individual societies, but both the radicalism and the reaction experienced by these various nations did exhibit certain parallels. Not just in the United States, economic factors played a role. The 1974 economic crisis reverberated across the developed world, and the middle of the decade was marked by social and political explosions. In other countries too, the end of sixties politics and culture can convincingly be dated to around 1974. The economic crash ruined overexposed entrepreneurs in several nations, leading to a wave of corporate scandals and a vigorous populist reaction against capitalism and free enterprise. Whether in Britain or Italy, Japan or Australia, observers in the mid-seventies similarly felt they were "living with an earthquake." As in the United States, political reputations were ruined, regimes collapsed, and old, established parties rethought their whole raison d'être, in their desperation turning to leaders regarded as extreme and confrontational. The growth of socialist or leftist activism at a time of Soviet expansion contributed mightily to the subsequent conservative reaction. In France, former leftists attacked Soviet totalitarianism in terms very similar to those used by U.S. neoconservatives. Economic decline also changed attitudes toward social experimentation and deviance. During a time of prosperity and expanding opportunity such as the 1960s, mainstream citizens were much more tolerant of turbulence and radicalism than they would be in post-1974 austerity.

Common demographic factors also played a role in many nations, ensuring that children would play a central role in social nightmares. When the baby boomers were in their late teens in 1968, many wanted to expand their own rights and rejected official restrictions on sexual activity and drug use. A decade later, the same individuals were starting families and were naturally concerned about the welfare of their own children. Also, a new demographic chasm was emerging. For American boomers, whose cultural experience was defined in terms of youth and adolescence, it came as a shock to realize that there might be later generations of youth, beings so alien that they did not recall where they were when JFK was killed or when Nixon resigned.[35] This new gap became apparent when Generation X children, born in the mid-1960s, entered their teens and were regularly depicted by the media as dangerous and uncontrollable. Intergenerational tensions provided a foundation for political and moral campaigns that were based on threats to the young and which sought to reassert parental authority. Again, the generation that came to political consciousness in 1980, a year when America appeared to be under comprehensive assault, naturally viewed the world differently than did the boomers, who were shaped by 1968.

Equally critical was the social and political emancipation of women, who provided a substantial and receptive audience for claims about sexual threats. In both the United States and Western Europe, post-1968 feminism increased women's political awareness, and many more women were now in the workplace. Women working outside the home were more conscious of dangers such as rape and sexual harassment and were particularly vulnerable to fears about child abuse. Day care was much more commonly used, and for younger children; for all the rhetoric of women's independence, mixed cultural messages ensured that many women felt ambivalent about abandoning their children to the kindness of strangers. In the 1980s, the American public accepted the reality of threats from abductors and child pornographers, particularly in caregiver settings such as preschools and churches. In fact, the post-1975 wave of fears about sex criminals closely recalls the panic of the 1940s, that earlier era when women suddenly entered the workforce in unprecedented numbers. In both Christian and non-Christian societies, the religious reaction of the mid-1970s owed much to the perceived threat to family and gender roles arising from sudden changes in the position of women.

The Trouble with Men

Of the multiple revolutions in progress by the early 1970s, perhaps the most sweeping involved gender roles and traditional notions of masculinity. Apart from the feminist upsurge, gay rights movements also offered startling challenges to older definitions of sex roles. The critique of masculinity was reinforced by the political attack on male images and institutions in the years of Vietnam and Watergate, including the denunciation of government, business, and the military. Feminist writing stressed the linkage between masculine ideologies and sexual exploitation, rape, and child abuse. Running through the domestic threats of these years is the sense that men had to learn to restrain their hedonistic impulses, which posed such a threat to vulnerable women and children. John Wayne symbolized an older, mythical America, while the modern nation produced John Wayne Gacy.

Conservative rhetoric also stressed gender issues, but its theme was masculinity betrayed or compromised. At a time when society was under comprehensive attack from ruthless enemies at home and abroad, America had lost its ability to defend or assert itself, and right-wing critiques drew on a powerful rhetoric of impotence and castration, captivity and restraint. Repeatedly, social dangers were symbolized by the idea of Americans unjustly held captive by evildoers, whether as prisoners of war, hostages to terrorists, or brainwashed inmates held in cult compounds. These themes found stark confirmation in memorable visual images, above all the bound and blindfolded Americans taken captive in Iran in 1979. The obverse of the rhetoric of decadence and captivity was the celebration of manly traditional values, epitomized by concepts such as standing up, standing tall, and fighting back, which were evoked as often in the war on crime as in the international arena. The power of these themes is suggested by the huge success of films and popular culture productions offering strong, manly roles, such as *Rocky* and *Rambo*. Debates over taxes and rights involved themes of masculinity as much as of race, and attacks on excessive taxation and the nanny state clearly deployed a rhetoric of autonomy, individualism, and independence. In politics, Ronald Reagan deployed these images in a masterly way, often by invoking Western mythologies. American party politics still contend with the yawning gender gap that became so evident in those years.[36]

The World the Sixties Made?

Comparing American society and politics in the early 1970s with the situation a decade later, it is natural to think in terms of conservative reaction or a "big chill." For an idealistic liberal, politics had clearly moved in the wrong direction in matters of war and peace, civil liberties, and environmental protection. Undeniably, powerful conservative trends were at work in these years. In some ways, though, we should see these political changes less as a retreat or reaction than as a natural culmination of the earlier liberalism. Some conservative trends of the post-1975 decade grew directly out of the earlier period, and not just in the sense that a radical shift in one political direction inevitably produces a comparable lurch to the other extreme. Thus, for instance, the *Roe v. Wade* decision naturally sparked the creation of a vigorous pro-life movement, and that in turn galvanized the culture war rhetoric of the 1980s and 1990s. Equally, one might expect the boom in drug experimentation to produce a powerful reaction in the following decade. Alternating cycles of hedonism and puritanism have occurred throughout American history, commonly focusing on attitudes toward sexuality and drink or substance abuse. Binge decades are followed by collective hangovers, eras of "clean and sober."

But the inheritance from the 1960s was a follow-through as much as a reaction. In criminal justice, the move toward penal solutions grew out of the prison reform campaigns of the radical years. Liberal reformers had struggled against therapeutic ideologies, demanding that indeterminate sentencing and psychiatric language be replaced with straightforward and predictable sentences for specific criminal acts. When this worthy-sounding reform was duly accomplished, it laid the foundation for the incarceration boom that has been in progress for the last thirty years—exactly the opposite of what its proponents wished.

Meanwhile, the preoccupation with crime and sexual violence in the post-1975 years reflected the growing influence of feminist ideology in the mass media and the academic world. Feminist politics since 1968 had sounded the alarm about sexual dangers to women, by means of anti-rape campaigns, rape crisis centers, and Take Back the Night marches. In the 1970s, this activism increasingly turned its attention to threats against children, especially from within the family. Meanwhile, the possible linkage between pornography and sexual violence encouraged feminist campaigns against sexually explicit materials. Of course, feminist activism was not the only or even the chief motivation for Reagan-era morality campaigns, and feminists were divided over their response to conservative-led movements, not least if it meant a tactical alliance with right-leaning religious groups. Yet the new feminism of the 1970s did promote images of sexual danger, and a line of continuity runs from the radicalism of the late 1960s to the moral activism of the early 1980s.[37]

Equally difficult to assign to either political side is the apocalypticism that surfaces so frequently in the period. Dualistic ideas of good and evil and visions of imminent disaster often took explicitly religious form, and certainly they motivated the evangelical and fundamentalist churches that were so active in the moral counterrevolution of these years. But liberals and secularists had their own powerful apocalyptic tradition in the doomsday environmentalist prophecies of the early 1970s, which entered the political mainstream in the post-Watergate years. Though fundamentalists and environmentalists might have little respect for each other's views, neither held out any great hope that the human race would reach the twenty-first century without facing some appalling global calamity.

To some extent, we can see the post-1975 reaction as the unintended consequence of earlier radical reforms. Much of the political rhetoric in the post-1965 decade urged the expansion of democracy against the interests of elites, with an ever-widening definition of "the people" to enable full inclusion of racial, ethnic, and sexual minorities. After Watergate, American politics saw a powerful revival of populism and anti-elitism, a return to the Jacksonian suspicion of experts and technocrats, whether in the realm of intelligence, foreign policy, or criminal justice. For liberals, though, the problem is that a democracy based on extensive popular participation does not necessarily espouse liberal values. A populist democracy is less likely to rely on expert authority and will prefer commonsense moralistic solutions to social problems such as crime. Such a political community is more willing to speak the explicit language of good and evil, and even to base political actions on religious belief.

An overseas analogy might be useful here. Most observers note that on matters of crime or morality, northern European and particularly Scandinavian states are much more liberal than the United States, and this is undoubtedly true in terms of their legal systems. Opinion surveys, though, repeatedly show that ordinary citizens in those nations hold views more akin to those of Americans, especially on emotive matters such as capital punishment. In matters of religious belief too—if not of practice—ordinary Europeans consistently emerge as rather more like Americans, however strictly secularist the prevailing ideologies of their nations. To adapt Grace Davie's phrase, Europeans believe without belonging.[38] The difference is not so much between liberal Europeans and conservative Americans as between their respective political systems and how far they allow the expression of popular sentiment. With their more compact societies and homogeneous ruling elites, European states operate within a narrower social consensus, in which government and experts make pragmatic decisions on matters of crime and public morality. Europeans have ugly memories of what happens when governments are swayed by mass politics, especially when those are associated with millenarian or apocalyptic beliefs, and accordingly regard such ideologies with suspicion. American political traditions, in contrast, have always been more democratic and populist, and that tendency became even more marked in the 1970s.

One enduring legacy of Americans' deep distrust of government was the tradition of conspiracy theory handed down by Watergate-era liberals and soon appropriated by conservatives. In some form, conspiracy ideas have surfaced every time a populist movement has gained influence, as in the 1830s and 1890s. In the mid-1970s, theories revolving around the CIA were widely disseminated. The package of beliefs included sensational allegations of behavior modification, brainwashing, and programmed assassins. Though that specific wave of panic lasted only a few years, it left lingering echoes in persistent theories about foreign plots and terror networks, child abuse rings and satanic networks. Liberal and populist agitation in the post-Watergate years would have long aftereffects.

The darkening vision was not the result of a deliberate policy of any particular group or agency, whether Reagan Republicans, Christian conservatives, law enforcement bureaucrats, or even liberal feminists. Even if such groups had attempted to manipulate public fears, they could not have succeeded without an audience willing to hear and believe such claims. Rather, we should think of a dynamic process in which shifting public attitudes provided a foundation for activism and claims by a variety of interest groups in a rapidly changing media environment. In the late 1970s and early 1980s, conservatives and traditionalists were the chief beneficiaries of the new attitudes, but this does not mean that they cynically initiated or manipulated the process. No interest group could succeed that brilliantly unless it was playing to an audience already half converted to its point of view.

A closer look at post-1975 cultural shifts and their consequences calls into question the wisdom of thinking about history in terms of party politics and presidential terms. Most writers see a sharp caesura in American history around 1980–81, which they link to the Reagan revolution, and no one should underestimate the symbolic contribution of Reagan's leadership. When Reagan died in 2004, commentators were deeply divided over his legacy, but there was little doubt that the sea change in politics and culture owed everything to Reagan and to presidential leadership. John Ehrman writes of the American 1980s as the "Age of Reagan," and Gil Troy describes "how Ronald Reagan invented the 1980s." Looking at the broader sweep of the post-1975 decade, though, we might question this reading. Reagan's opportunities to impose his particular vision were shaped by a wide variety of developments, social, economic, demographic, and cultural, which were all under way well before the critical 1980 election.[39]

Reagan gave form and direction to powerful social currents, but he did not initiate them. Changes in the realm of partisan politics were accompanied by social transformations that were not confined to Republicans or political conservatives. In the years around 1980, American liberalism was transformed no less than conservatism was, and the complex interaction between those two strands shaped social and political attitudes in the post-1975 decade. Few will deny that Ronald Reagan presided over a revolution, but he was joining a revolution already in progress.[40]

1

Mainstreaming the Sixties

There is no more New Frontier, we have got to make it here.
—The Eagles

Just how sweeping the cultural changes of the post-1975 era were can be appreciated only by contrasting the newer ideas with the commonplaces of the immediately preceding years. The story of American culture in the early 1970s can be seen as the mainstreaming of sixties values, the point at which countercultural ideas reached a mass audience. And though political militancy had little mass appeal after the fall of Richard Nixon, there was still widespread interest in social, sexual, and religious experimentation. So rapid were the changes and so widespread their acceptance that for a while it looked as if the sixties cultural revolution was becoming institutionalized.

Greening?

Often, what historians identify as great or significant events have little impact on the majority of ordinary people. Despite all the changes under way by the mid-1960s, most Americans carried on with their familiar lives, going to the same jobs and schools as they might have done in any other era. By the end of the decade, though, political conflicts and social changes were having a direct impact beyond the political elites and the major cities. At the height of the turmoil, between 1967 and 1971, there were real fears of mass social conflict and even of a collapse of the social order. Following the urban riots of mid-decade, talk of open race war did not seem fanciful. The civil rights and liberationist rhetoric that originated among African-Americans was adopted by a range of groups that felt they suffered a like historic oppression. This was the age of gay liberation, (Latino) Brown Power, (Native American) Red Power, and, most enduring of all, the women's liberation movement. The new radicalism offered a fundamental challenge to American society's assumptions about race, sexuality, and family, and even—through the environmental movement—to the whole basis of industrial civilization.[1]

After 1970, open violence declined. Urban race rioting was no longer a factor after 1968, though there was still a powerful racial agenda in the ongoing violence and street crime that blighted the cities for years afterward. Anti-war fervor shriveled with the end of the draft and the gradual U.S. disengagement from Southeast Asia. The Watergate crisis of 1973–74 helped reunite a splintered country by creating a common cause that brought together not just radicals and liberals but also disaffected conservatives. By this point too, Americans were facing a quite different set of pressing issues, with the oil crisis, the economic downturn, and a plummeting stock market. By 1974, the world of the Kent State shootings and the mass anti-war demonstrations, of Black Panthers and Yippies, was already looking dated. The sixties were becoming history.[2]

At the height of the recent crisis, many Americans hoped or feared that they were living through a revolution of unprecedented scale. But what would be the lasting impact of these events? Perhaps only a small minority truly expected to see the kind of total historical transformation that was termed, vaguely, "the revolution," but '68ism would have long-term effects. Charles Reich's best-seller *The Greening of America* predicted an imminent social revolution that "will originate with the individual and with culture, and it will change the political structure only as its final act. . . . It is now spreading with amazing rapidity, and already our laws, institutions and social structure are changing in consequence. It promises a higher reason, a more human community, and a new and liberated individual. Its ultimate creation will be a new and enduring wholeness and beauty—a renewed relationship of man to himself, to other men, to society, to nature, and to the land." In this view, America was entering an indefinite future of strongly liberal politics, marked by the beliefs of the sixties counterculture but without its stridency or violence. Others foretold a tectonic shift to new spiritualities—a Consciousness Reformation, an Aquarian Revolution.[3]

Partly, this shift from overt politics to personal and cultural values reflected the success of themes pressed by sixties radicals. By the mid-1970s, accumulating evidence seemed to confirm that the Vietnam War had been a disaster from its beginnings, that politicians were corrupt and power-crazy, and that capitalist corporations were bent on profit at all costs, even if it meant destroying the planet. The Watergate crisis weakened respect for traditional authority in general, rather than just a particular leader or political party. Appropriately, this was a golden age for iconoclastic publications that mocked all institutions and orthodoxies, such as *Mad* magazine and its marginally more adult counterpart, *National Lampoon*. Both struggled to produce satire more unlikely or shocking than the realities reported on the nightly news.[4]

Whatever the exact shape of the future, the changes that the sixties had brought appeared irreversible. Surely, no future government would be able to stem the burgeoning interest in chemical experimentation or limit a spreading sexual revolution, and it would be difficult to use scares about crime or subversion to manipulate a public that had come so thoroughly to distrust any statements stemming from its public officials. Initially, the events of the mid-1970s seemed to fulfill these millenarian visions. Proponents of sexual and racial liberation transformed the Democratic Party with their New Politics, seeking to purge the party of the old urban machines. The massive repudiation of the Republicans following Watergate seemed initially to mean not just an epochal shift toward the Democratic Party but a willingness to accept an ever more far-reaching social agenda.[5] After the 1974 elections, Democrats had a two-to-one majority in the House of Representatives. It is in these years that the fundamental political divisions in American life shifted from the older theme of class to newer emphases on gender, ethnicity, and sexual identity.

After the Sixties

Neatly symbolizing the mainstreaming process is the ubiquitous adoption of clothing and hairstyles that a few years earlier would have been daringly countercultural or even badges of gay identity. For men, the long hair, multi-colored clothing, and amazing shirt styles that so easily lend themselves to later parody all represent versions of hippie fashions of the mid-1960s. In 1979, a *New York Times* report on the tenth anniversary of Woodstock noted how sixties style could be seen in the heart of middle America: "In thousands of small, almost imperceptible ways, in the routine trans-actions of daily work, play and family life, Woodstock Nation is alive in Des Moines." Hair, beards, marijuana, and cocaine were among the most notice-able cultural markers, while gay bars and clubs had proliferated, as had natural food stores.[6] Of course, adopting lifestyle trends of itself implied little about political or cultural attitudes. Watching news footage from this era, it is startling to see such post-hippie styles in hair and dress adorning conservative politicians or police officers.

But in other, more substantial ways too, '68ism had its impact. Starting in 1971, when the Twenty-sixth Amendment to the Constitution lowered the voting age to eighteen, politicians had to take account of a larger and significantly younger electorate. Meanwhile, the civil rights movement continued to have its impact in increasing voter registration among minorities. Seventy million Americans cast votes in the presidential election of 1964, while 81 million voted in 1976 and 92 million in 1984. At the same time, many aspects of the Great Society had become thoroughly institutionalized, as government and social agencies continued to expand. Social welfare expenditures by federal and state authorities rose from 11.7 percent of GNP in 1965 to 20 percent in 1975.[7]

Racial attitudes changed rapidly following the collapse of legal segregation, as civil rights leaders moved into mainstream politics. The 1972 congressional elections were victories for rising stars such as Andrew Young from Georgia or Texas's Barbara Jordan, who delivered a historic keynote address at the 1976 Democratic convention. Over the next decade, accounts of such victories would regularly report how candidates were the first African-Americans to hold office in a given southern state since Reconstruction. Outside the South, blacks also won urban offices: in 1973, Coleman Young became mayor of Detroit and Tom Bradley was elected mayor of Los Angeles, and by 1980, Willie Brown was one of the most powerful figures in California politics. Black judges and federal office holders made major advances under the Carter administration. Culturally too, African-American issues achieved unprecedented recognition in mainstream culture. The 1977 television miniseries *Roots* spawned massive interest in black history and the experience of slavery. Another acknowledgment of African-American struggles was the campaign for a national commemoration for Martin Luther King Jr., a holiday comparable to those honoring America's greatest leaders and historic moments. The King holiday was overwhelmingly approved by Congress in 1983, and it was first commemorated in 1986.[8]

Another critical legacy of the 1960s was the idea of diversity, which now became social orthodoxy—the insistence that different ethnic and cultural groups proudly maintain their distinctive identities rather than seeking homogenized assimilation. The whole concept of Americanism and American identity was thus transformed. In 1975, the Indian Self-Determination Act revolutionized the nation's policy toward Native Americans, who were given extensive powers of self-government. The rejection of assimilation would be all the more important given the demographic transformation under way since the 1965 Immigration Reform Act, which vastly broadened the ethnic makeup of the U.S. population.[9]

A New World for Women

The single most important vehicle for new values was feminism. Though the new feminism emerged only in 1968, by the early 1970s the movement enjoyed enormous legal victories in matters of marriage and divorce, child custody, and property law. Through the decade, changes in law and social practice broke down barriers that prevented women from occupying particular jobs, and the media regularly reported new milestones in feminist progress.

Though the story was often trivialized—witness the national obsession with tennis's Battle of the Sexes in 1973, when Billie Jean King defeated Bobby Riggs—the scale of the social transformation was beyond question. The feminist impact was obvious in everyday life through its impact on language and discourse, with the adoption of the title *Ms.* and the spread of gender-neutral language. Just as revolutionary was the change in marital relationships, indicated by women continuing to use their birth names after marriage and giving their children hyphenated surnames. Recording their enormous leaps forward in a very few years, *Time* declared that its Man of the Year for 1975 would be American Women. In 1975, the magazine recorded, "the women's drive penetrated every layer of society, matured beyond ideology to a new status of general—and sometimes unconscious—acceptance." Feminist attitudes and ideology were mainstreamed through their influence in the mass media and also through higher education. Though no women's studies programs or departments existed in 1969, they proliferated over the next decade, and a National Women's Studies Association was founded in 1977.[10]

Women's participation revolutionized the workplace, while the enormous growth of day care transformed family structures. In 1970, about 43 percent of women age sixteen or over were in the labor force, a figure that grew to 52 percent by 1980 and approached 60 percent in the early 1990s. Women made particular advances in high-status professions: they made up just 9 percent of medical students in 1970 but 25 percent by 1980, and in law schools the proportion of women students grew during the decade from 10 to 36 percent. Burgeoning statistics for abortion and divorce illustrated the scale of changes in gender attitudes. Between 1972 and 1980, America's abortion rate roughly doubled. By 1980, there were 359 abortions for every

1,000 live births, a higher ratio than ever before or since. Divorce rates also indicate changed expectations concerning family life. In 1958, there were roughly four marriages for every divorce in the United States; by 1970, the ratio was three to one, and by 1976, it had reached two to one. Married couples with children represented over 40 percent of all American households in 1970 but only 26 percent by 1990.

Together, these shifts suggest disaffection not just with gender roles and family structures but also with the underlying social and religious ideologies. Authors and journalists recorded what seemed to be an escalating gender war, in which familiar institutions were presented as destructive for both men and women. In 1973, Ira Levin's novel *The Stepford Wives* presented traditional gender roles and family structures as, literally, material for a horror story: two years later, the showing of the television movie made the word *Stepford* proverbial for slavish female conformity. Marilyn French's best-selling *The Women's Room* (1977) presented an unflaggingly bleak portrait of a woman's experience in conventional marriage. As the narrator states, to destroy a woman "you don't have to rape or kill her; you don't even have to beat her. You can just marry her."[11] The feminist revolution transformed images of men no less than women, with a new emphasis on values of sensitive masculinity. The United States moved into the era of Alan Alda in *M*A*S*H* and the heroic but clearly non-macho investigative reporters in *All the President's Men*. In the same year as *The Women's Room*, Avery Corman's *Kramer vs. Kramer* approached the crisis from the male point of view, describing a divorced husband trying to fulfill the unexpected role of single parent.[12]

Not surprisingly against this turbulent background, American demographic patterns were very different from what they had been during the baby boom years, 1945 through 1962. In the boom years, the average birth rate was around 25 per 1,000, but that figure then declined sharply, to 18.4 in 1970 and 14.8 in 1975. The rate remained around 15 throughout the 1970s and 1980s, reaching its lowest level between 1973 and 1976. And though the national rate would increase somewhat in later years, much of that growth can be attributed to the new wave of younger immigrant women, while the birth rate for older-stock white Americans remained historically low.

Critically for later debates over issues of crime and justice, feminist activism in these early years focused on issues of violence and sexual exploitation, and charges about the scale of male violence against women transformed perceptions of gender relations. Exposés of domestic violence led to the creation of shelters for battered women, the word *shelter* itself suggesting the need for sanctuaries in which women could be protected from uncontrollable masculine violence. Changing the official response to rape represented another key front for political action. Women Against Rape (WAR) groups appeared about 1972, and in 1973 the National Organization for Women (NOW) created a rape task force. One provocative title from 1974 was *The Politics of Rape,* by Diana E. H. Russell. The idea that a crime such as rape might be a political phenomenon was integral to feminist ideology, but it represented a major departure in public views of sex crime. In 1975, Susan Brownmiller's influential text *Against Our Will* presented rape as a direct counterpart of lynching, a collective act of terrorism by which one social group held another in subjection. Central to the feminist approach was the vision of rape as a crime founded not on sexuality but rather on power and violence, therefore making it an act of oppression.[13]

The issue brought the feminist movement into sharp conflict with the hedonistic and libertarian values of the alternative left culture from which it had originated. For many, sexual liberation was an unqualified good that advanced the revolutionary transformation of society. As Andrea Dworkin noted acidly, "Norman Mailer remarked during the sixties that the problem with the sexual revolution was that it had gotten into the hands of the wrong people. He was right. It was in the hands of men. . . . Fucking per se was freedom per se." For feminists, however, sexual hedonism led to rape and exploitation: "It was the raw, terrible realization that sex was not brother-sister but master-servant—that this brave new radical wanted to be not only master in his own home but pasha in his own harem—that proved explosive."[14]

Anti-rape activists won significant changes in both law and police practice, promoting reforms that assumed the truthfulness of women complainants. Between 1971 and 1975, most states ended the requirement for physical corroboration in rape cases and reduced the defense's ability to introduce evidence about a woman's prior sexual history, while major cities created specialized police units, usually with female officers. Courts expanded their definition of rape to include nonconsensual intercourse inflicted by boyfriends or husbands. The best evidence for the effectiveness of the new laws is the steep increase in reported rapes through the 1970s. Though the actual incidence of sex crimes might have increased in these years, most observers felt that the booming numbers reflected a much higher likelihood of reporting. By the end of the decade, older attitudes about rape were becoming as socially unacceptable as the casual racism of bygone days: one no longer suggested that women invited or invented rape.[15]

Gay Rights

No less subversive of gender attitudes was the change in views of homo-sexuality as gay and lesbian issues gained public sympathy. Gays, obviously, faced more basic legal issues than women in the sense that the first step was to secure a legal right to follow their sexual orientation. Between 1971 and 1976, sixteen states repealed their sodomy statutes, and by 1980, a further six had either undertaken repeal or had their laws declared unconstitutional. In 1973, the American Psychiatric Association removed homosexuality from its diagnostic manual of mental illnesses and rejected attempts to "cure" homosexuals. By the mid-1970s, many jurisdictions were proposing gay rights ordinances that would place discrimination against homosexuals in the same category as racial discrimination.[16]

Though nothing like as ostentatiously as in recent years, gays secured favorable public recognition. When in 1975, *Time* magazine presented a major story titled "Gays on the March," the cover depicted air force officer Leonard Matlovich proudly declaring, "I am a homosexual." Through the mid-1970s, activists struggled against the still-hostile attitudes of the news media. As late as 1975, a *Los Angeles Times* reviewer could still refer dismissively to "faggots," though the usage was now unusual enough to attract attention. And while censorship standards had changed in the cinema, the early consequence of that was to permit the portrayal of homosexuals, but chiefly as perverts, molesters, or sex killers. Only in the mid-1970s did gays start to appear as human and sympathetic. Gay charac-ters appeared in television series, including the police sitcom *Barney Miller* and the 1977 comedy *Soap*.[17]

Gay communities gained visibility in a way that would have astonished even sympathetic observers as recently as the early 1960s. The long-established gay subcultures of cities such as New York and San Francisco were operating far more visibly and proudly than ever before, with a very public network of clubs and bars, while many smaller cities developed their own gay scenes. So public was gay life becoming, in fact, that the community faced divisive debates over just how mainstream it wished to be. In the early post-Stonewall years, gay activism attracted a wide range of sexual sub-cultures, including transvestites and transsexuals, sado-masochists and pederasts. As the decade progressed, though, gay leaders tried to separate themselves from these associations, attracting the anger of the surviving ultras.[18] Respectability had its price.

Much gay cultural influence remained covert, and many who became involved in disco in 1977–78 had little idea that much of this world had originated in urban gay dance clubs. Also at this time, the group Village People enjoyed massive success with their dance songs "YMCA" and "In the Navy." It would be difficult to regard this as any great success for gay rights, since the group's parade of gay images represented almost a freak-show approach. Even so, this was a long way from the early 1960s vision of homosexuality as a debilitating perversion.[19]

Sexual Liberation

Sexual mores changed not just in terms of private behavior but also in public discussion and display. The new sexual frankness can be traced through the pornography industry, which expanded rapidly during the 1970s as censorship standards relaxed. Since the 1950s, the Supreme Court had vastly expanded First Amendment protections over literature and film, and these decisions were consolidated in the 1973 case of *Miller v. California*. While retreating from the most permissive standards suggested by older cases, *Miller* offered a strict definition of material that was "obscene" and therefore liable to criminal action. The decision gave accused pornographers a great many legal loopholes, and most police and prosecutors soon realized that pursuing smut was just not worth the effort. Urban vice squads found that the liberalization of sex laws made their work almost impossible.[20]

Pornography now found a mass audience. Hard-core porn had for some years been generally available in urban stores, but explicit material now reached every convenience store. At the start of the decade, *Penthouse* and *Playboy* took the then daring step of showing their models' pubic hair, but even this seemed tame when compared with the innovations of the brash new magazine *Hustler,* founded by Larry Flynt in 1974. *Hustler* pioneered "pink shots," showing open vaginas in gynecological detail. At its height, the magazine commanded a circulation of three million. To appreciate how shocking these changes seemed, we recall that in the late 1960s, *Star Trek* troubled network censors by its display of female navels and even interracial kisses. As recently as 1972, *The Bob Newhart Show* was considered daring for regularly depicting a married couple sharing a double bed.[21]

In the same years, pornographic films made the transition from clandestine stag performances to the national cinema audience. *Deep Throat* appeared in 1972, *Debbie Does Dallas* in 1976. Meanwhile, the spread of video technology beginning in 1975–76 brought sex films into the home. Much greater frankness about sexual and social issues was now possible in the mass media, especially on commercial television and in the new realm of cable TV. Cable and video brought to mass audiences the once unthinkably daring comedy of stars such as Richard Pryor and Robin Williams, whose every line included a reference to sex or drugs that would been instantly condemned by the networks. While network television could scarcely compete with cable, movie releases were equally frank about themes of sex and drugs. In 1977, the noirish *Looking for Mr. Goodbar* depicted a sexually adventurous woman deeply involved in drug subcultures.[22]

Particularly daring were the explorations of youth sexuality in the popular culture of these years. For many baby boomers, the age of sexual consent made as little sense as the prohibition of marijuana. In the 1960s, activists had demanded full rights for the young, but it was never clear how far the limits of liberated "youth culture" might extend. Clearly, it meant people of student age, and possibly high schoolers, but should younger teenagers have a political voice? And what about experimentation with sex or drugs? In 1975, the popular sex education manual *Show Me!* offered a liberated approach to youth sexuality, so much so, in fact, that today its illustrations arguably fall afoul of the legal prohibition against child pornography. Beginning in the late 1960s, states tried to come to terms with the new situation by lowering the age of sexual majority and easing laws on statutory rape.[23]

By the mid-1970s, highly sexualized images of children and young teenagers proliferated in mainstream popular culture, and the sexual attractions of young teenage girls were praised in rock music. Sexually precocious girls became a regular feature in mainstream cinema during the 1970s, with films such as *Taxi Driver* (1976), in which Jodie Foster played a preteen runaway turned prostitute. In these years, some young teenage actresses became stars by portraying sexually active young women at a far earlier age than would be thought acceptable in either earlier or later epochs. A young Melanie Griffith appeared nude in *Night Moves,* and *Pretty Baby* starred Brooke Shields as a twelve-year-old New Orleans prostitute. In a comic scene in *Animal House,* the hero discovers that his (topless) girlfriend is actually thirteen. In the world of sexual expression, few barriers remained.

Just how far cultural changes were reflected in actual behavior, hetero- or homosexual, is difficult to determine, but we have some indicators. We know that child pornography became massively more accessible between about 1970 and 1977 and was easily available in adult stores at least in major cities. This was not so much a result of social tolerance as of official despair at the prospect of winning any case against pornography. Years of experience had taught police that obscenity prosecutions became suicide missions in the courtroom.[24] Access to pornographic material might well have encouraged acting out, and a number of celebrity scandals and memoirs in mid-decade suggested a vogue for underage sex. In 1977, director Roman Polanski admitted to having had sex with a thirteen-year-old girl.

The only detailed long-term survey we have of any substantial group in terms of sexual misconduct with minors is the 2004 study of abuse complaints against Roman Catholic priests, which compiles complaints for all priests who served in dioceses between 1950 and 2002. The survey found that abuse complaints were certainly not distributed equally over time, as 40 percent of the reports involved acts committed with minors in just the six-year period 1975–80. Overwhelmingly, the acts involved pederastic sex with teenage boys. This finding about chronology might represent a statistical oddity, an accident of reporting or recording, but it is curious that this clerical crime wave should coincide so exactly with such relaxed cultural attitudes toward adult-child sex.[25]

Doors of Perception

When a modern audience watches the films or television programs of the 1970s, most of the sexual references are scarcely shocking, except for the underage content, but the easygoing attitudes to drugs point to a near-revolution in social attitudes. During the 1960s, idealists saw some drugs, especially marijuana and LSD, as the symbol of a coming change of consciousness, an unstoppable phenomenon that would enlighten America's young. In the 1970s, illicit drugs lost virtually all their radical connotations as they became part of the social mainstream. By 1977, about a quarter of Americans admitted to having used marijuana at some point, and 10 percent were using it currently.[26] Surveys of high school seniors showed high usage of illegal substances through the decade, peaking between about 1978 and 1982. In 1979, 54 percent reported using an illegal drug in the previous twelve months. Half reported using marijuana, 12 percent had used cocaine, and other substances such as LSD, PCP, and amphetamines all had their followers. Over a third had used marijuana in the previous thirty days. These figures suggest widespread flouting of the law and the absolute normality of drug use among teenagers; note that they did not take account of alcohol use.[27]

Adults too were consuming serious quantities of illicit drugs. Cocaine gained recognition as what the *New York Times* called in 1974 "the champagne of drugs." Ironically, the drug became popular since it was viewed as a safe and nonaddictive alternative to methamphetamine, which had been the target of intense media campaigns in the past few years. Between 1976 and 1982, cocaine enjoyed a huge vogue among the urban and suburban middle class, and by 1985, some twenty-two million Americans reported having used the drug at least once. Cocaine received wonderful publicity from magazines such as *Newsweek,* which noted the drug's use in high society alongside "Dom Perignon and caviar" and mentioned the use of fourteen-karat-gold coke spoons. The magazine quoted a Chicago anti-drug official who claimed, "You get a good high with coke and you don't get hooked." The disco fad of the mid-1970s popularized cocaine, together with associated substances such as Quaaludes. Another incidental beneficiary of the cocaine vogue was vodka, which offered an ideal accompaniment to the drug. By 1976, American vodka consumption exceeded that of such older staples as gin or whiskey.[28]

For a few years, illicit drugs became an inescapable part of popular culture, particularly in media aimed at teens and young adults. Well-publicized drug use by rock megastars further helped to familiarize drug use, and in 1977, rock artists Eric Clapton and Jackson Browne separately recorded songs entitled "Cocaine." Shel Silverstein's mocking country anthem to Quaaludes celebrated the drug's aphrodisiac qualities ("She's ready for animals, women, or men / She's doin' Quaaludes again"). Drug use was depicted humorously in many films of the late 1970s, including several comedy features by Cheech and Chong. The comedy *Annie Hall* made frequent reference to marijuana and cocaine, while the 1980 film *Airplane* included broad jokes about cocaine, amphetamines, and glue sniffing, not to mention pederasty. Stephen Spielberg's *Poltergeist* (1982) portrays a delightful suburban wife and mother who casually smokes a marijuana joint in moments of giggly intimacy with her husband. The film makes no comment on this drug use except to imply that this relaxed open-mindedness allows her to be on good terms with her sixteen-year-old daughter. Memoirs of the filmmaking world of this time suggest how awash that subculture was in drugs, and the lack of restraint or judgment caused by cocaine use came close to ending some prominent careers.[29]

The existence of a large drug-savvy audience helps explain the popularity of some of the era's most popular television shows and films. Drugs were the subject of countless performances by standup comedians, as well as knowing jokes on network television comedies such as *Taxi, WKRP in Cincinnati,* and (most consistently) *Saturday Night Live,* which debuted in 1975. In a *Taxi* episode, for instance, we see all the characters affected by a hash brownie. In one episode of *WKRP,* disk jockey Johnny Fever responds to a heavy dose of cocaine surreptitiously fed to him by an ex-girlfriend; in another, Johnny is terrified that police searching his desk will find his drug stash. None of these instances, or the many like them, involves social commentary, a chance to condemn the horrors of drug abuse. These are simply comic moments that the audience is meant to relish. Even when drugs are not mentioned overtly, much of the television humor of the time relied heavily on drug-induced sensibility, as in *Taxi, Mork and Mindy,* and the cultish import *Monty Python's Flying Circus.* Sometimes the drug content was visible only to connoisseurs. *One Day at a Time* reputedly owed its youth following to the popular fascination with star Mackenzie Phillips, whose own drug problems visibly affected her performance.[30]

In the face of this respectable drug boom, strict enforcement of drug laws seemed benighted and futile. While few advocated total drug legalization, there was general support for the principle of decriminalizing soft drugs, especially marijuana. Even under the Republican Ford administration in 1975, a presidential task force admitted the impossibility of wholly suppressing drug abuse and urged that official policy shift from law enforcement to treatment and prevention. Eleven states and several cities decriminalized marijuana use, and seventeen more significantly reduced their penalties, suggesting that the drug was on the verge of becoming a mainstream vice equivalent to alcohol or nicotine. Few advocated open tolerance for cocaine, but a remarkable number of respectable experts denied that even this drug caused any significant harm or dependence. For most users, suggesting that cocaine was a dangerous drug recalled the silly anti-drug paranoia of the 1950s.[31]

Turning Within

The mid-1970s marked the height of activity by fringe movements dedicated to exploring inner consciousness, whether through therapy or by overtly religious means. Occult and esoteric themes, which had developed strong roots in the counterculture, now gained a broad national audience. At any point in the twentieth century, believers in reincarnation, psychic powers, channeling, or lost continents could always be found, but they were generally concentrated in limited areas, above all southern California. During the 1960s and 1970s, such ideas went national.[32]

This change reflected the collapse of faith in science, alongside other mainstream institutions. In the 1974 best-seller *Zen and the Art of Motorcycle Maintenance,* Robert M. Pirsig wrote, "I think present-day reason is an analogue of the flat earth of the medieval period." In the same year, responsible media outlets gave respectful coverage to Uri Geller's claims of mystical powers, while one of the nation's best-selling works of nonfiction was Charles Berlitz's *Bermuda Triangle.* The 1977 film *Close Encounters of the*

Third Kind boosted long-standing popular interest in UFOs and extra-terrestrials, while theories concerning human-alien contact and alien abduction flourished. Naturally, the government was believed to be deeply involved in concealing these covert dealings, and at the end of the decade the alleged 1947 flying saucer crash at Roswell, New Mexico, became firmly established in UFO lore. Distrust of conventional science often manifested in popular culture. In *Star Wars,* the hero achieves his greatest victory when he abandons advanced technology and relies on his mystical inner powers ("Trust your feelings, Luke"). Best-selling scientific popularizations such as Fritjof Capra's *The Tao of Physics* presented Western science as a subset of Asian mysticism.[33]

Ironically, a society fascinated by space and other worlds lost interest in supporting the kind of real-world hard science that really would have taken humanity beyond the bounds of earth. The U.S. space program floundered after the end of the Apollo moon-shot program in 1972, so that funding for the proposed shuttle was repeatedly pared back. These cutbacks account for the severe design flaws in the shuttle that actually began flying in the Reagan years, a craft far inferior to what its original inventors contemplated. From 1975, plans to return to space met public opposition and were derided by Senator William Proxmire, whose regular Golden Fleece awards ostensibly exposed public waste. In practice, Proxmire's philistine "awards" made a special butt of experimental science, particularly any work by NASA. Nuclear power also attracted visceral opposition, and in 1976, several state ballots rejected reactor development. What proved to be the last order for a new reactor in the United States was placed in 1978.[34]

Other forms of science were also treated with far more suspicion than hitherto. The enormous success of Robin Cook's novels, such as *Coma* (1977), suggests real concern about the proper limits of medical experimentation and created an alarming stereotype of lethally conspiratorial doctors unconcerned with the lives of their patients. In 1976, a Harvard University proposal to enter the innovative field of gene splicing stirred panic. Establishing an emergency investigative commission, the mayor of Cambridge warned, "God knows what's going to crawl out of the laboratory!" and speculated about Frankenstein monsters. The following year, a symposium on recombinant DNA was stormed by protesters who denounced genetic research, as well as much of modern science. Bitter rhetoric also dominated the debate over E. O. Wilson's book *Sociobiology,* which critics compared to Nazi texts because of its leaning toward genetic determinism. In 1978, Wilson's appearance at a professional conference provoked protests and even physical assault.[35]

In a time of wide-ranging cultural crisis, it seemed natural to turn within, to explore inner resources and needs. It was in 1976 that Tom Wolfe's article in *New York* magazine proclaimed "It's the Me Decade," while Christopher Lasch complained that the times were marked by a culture of narcissism. Lasch argued, "Having no hope of improving their lives in any of the ways that matter, people have convinced themselves that what matters is psychic self-improvement." The quest for self-exploration and personal growth took various forms. Therapy sects offered believers the chance to achieve their full human potential through personal growth and self-actualization, taking total responsibility for one's actions. This was the message of several of the best-selling books of the era, including *I'm O.K., You're O.K.*, but also *Pulling Your Own Strings* and *How to Be Your Own Best Friend*.[36]

The sects, though, taught practical techniques to achieve these goals. The prototypical movement of this kind was est, Erhard Seminar Training, in which grueling sessions forced followers to confront a new view of reality. In addition, more overtly religious fringe movements and cults flourished, including Asian-influenced sects as well as groups growing from sectarian Christianity. Each claimed an inheritance from the movement toward spiritual discovery at the end of the 1960s. Many groups adopted the communitarian ethos of that time and gathered their followers together in communal settlements, often in isolated areas. This movement to separation accelerated with the political crises of the mid-1970s, when withdrawing from an increasingly dangerous world seemed eminently sensible. Also reflecting the crisis of confidence in these years, the new movements claimed to offer absolute certainty and authority, usually symbolized by a charismatic leader, a guru or messianic figure. The fact of being separated from the social mainstream made it easier to exercise this personal authority and to regulate the lives of members. Sect members were in fact being treated as children accepting the discipline of a firm but loving parent, such as "Daddy" Jim Jones, of Jonestown infamy.[37]

A New Age

By about 1974, the fringe religions had become increasingly controversial, and whatever their origins—Christian, Asian, or therapeutic—many were attacked as stereotypical "cults." Principal targets of anti-cult rhetoric included the Children of God, the Unification Church of the Reverend Sun Myung Moon, and the Hare Krishnas (the International Society of Krishna Consciousness), as well as groups such as The Way International, Synanon, the Church of Scientology, and the Divine Light Mission. In 1974, Moon attracted twenty thousand followers to a spectacular event in Madison Square Garden.

Such movements attracted media attention vastly out of proportion to the numbers of their followers. Despite claims that the "cult compounds" might be home to two million Americans at any given time, the real figure was in the tens of thousands. Yet critics were right to point to the upsurge of unconventional religious ideas and more particularly to their spread throughout the country. Though relatively few individuals gave up their lives to cults and therapy movements, millions had some contact with such groups and their ideas. By mid-decade, occult and esoteric ideas were forming a New Age synthesis that would be widely influential. The package was symbolized by California governor Jerry Brown, whose esoteric interests made him the regular target of *Doonesbury* cartoons mocking "Governor Moonbeam."[38]

New Age thought gained strength because of its association with other influential movements, including feminism and environmentalism. The neo-pagan and esoteric upsurge was symbolized by several texts that appeared in 1979–80, all of them growing out of the new interest in feminist spirituality. These titles included Starhawk's *The Spiral Dance,* which revived the worship of the great goddess; Elaine Pagels's *The Gnostic Gospels;* Margot Adler's *Drawing Down the Moon;* and Michael Harner's *The Way of the Shaman.* Each of these books urged the exploration of alternative spiritual paths more closely attuned to the feminine, the intuitive, and the mystical, while encouraging an interest in pagan and primal faiths. Marilyn Ferguson's *The Aquarian Conspiracy* offered a comprehensive manifesto for personal and planetary transformation.[39]

The New Age movement did not generally lead adherents to join communes or even to align formally with a church or sect, but it did encourage interest in spiritualities far removed from traditional religious thought. In turn, the newer spiritualities of the 1970s themselves reshaped cultural and religious orthodoxies, influencing the thought of Christian and Jewish traditions. Campaigns for the ordination of women succeeded in most religious bodies. In the Episcopal Church, the decisive move came in Philadelphia in 1974, when eleven women were ordained, and by the end of the 1970s, women clergy were active in all the major Protestant denominations. Even in the Roman Catholic communion, a powerful movement for women's ordination emerged in these years. Feminist activism was much in evidence in 1976 at the historic Call to Action conference held in Detroit, where leftist, pacifist, and social justice advocates convened to demand a revolutionary transformation of church structures and the overthrow of traditional ideas of hierarchy and priestly privilege.[40] An expansive new politics affected much more than just the Democratic Party.

Whatever the Cost

New approaches to spirituality, together with suspicions about industrial society, produced mass support for a flourishing environmental movement much more aggressive than its predecessors. As in matters of gender and sexuality, support from activist courts ensured that radical ideas would be implemented in the real world, no matter how much they challenged traditional political assumptions.

America's environmental movement was founded on the principle of conservation, urging the defense of natural resources in order to enhance their long-term usefulness for human beings. Meanwhile, environmental health activists stressed the direct danger that pollution posed to humans. During the 1970s, though, activists became more sweeping in their warnings about the dangers of unchecked industrial growth, and more ambitious in their political demands. Several horror stories won popular support for environmentalist claims. These included the revelation of the vast damage caused by a chemical landfill at the Love Canal site near Niagara Falls, a story that first came to public attention in 1976. Love Canal pointed to the long-term effects of dumping hazardous wastes and added the term *PCB* to popular demonology. Also in 1976, the media reported the catastrophic leakage of poisonous dioxin at Seveso, Italy. In 1979, the Three Mile Island disaster showed how uncontrolled technology might feasibly destroy whole cities.[41]

In the same years, newer ecological theories urged the defense of nature and wilderness for their own sake, not just for any possible human benefit. In 1975, Edward Abbey, prophet of the new ecology movement, offered in *The Monkey Wrench Gang* a rationale and a manual for anti-technological sabotage in the defense of nature. The Greenpeace movement, founded in 1971, became a focus for global activism by the end of the decade, and Earth First! appeared in 1980. In keeping with the spiritual trends of the 1970s, many activists saw a distinctly religious quality to environmental defense. In 1979, J. E. Lovelock argued that the totality of life on earth constituted a conscious organism, symbolically termed Gaia, after the ancient earth goddess.[42]

Environmentalists achieved some startling legal and political victories. In 1969, the National Environmental Policy Act provided a foundation for all later environmental law, creating the Environmental Protection Agency. Between 1976 and 1978, the U.S. Congress designated 7.2 million acres as protected wilderness, while a new law in 1980 extended protection to 56 million acres, mainly in Alaska. New legislation also protected wildlife, and not just for hunting. In 1973, the Endangered Species Act sought to limit economic development that might contribute to species extinction.

The Endangered Species law led to a fierce political fight over the construction of the new Tellico Dam by the Tennessee Valley Authority. In 1976, environmentalists demanded that the building of the nearly completed dam be halted because it would lead to the extinction of an obscure species of small fish called the snail darter. In 1977, the Supreme Court agreed "that Congress intended to halt and reverse the trend toward species extinction *whatever the cost,*" and thus the dam should be stopped. Adding to the symbolic force of this case was that the villain, from an environmental perspective, was the Tennessee Valley Authority, which had been a primary symbol of the New Deal's effort to improve the lot of ordinary people and poor communities. Economic growth for its own sake was no longer an unquestioned good.[43]

Ultimately, the controversy failed to stop the Tellico Dam, as in 1979, President Carter signed an extraordinary bill overriding all objections. But the long and venomous controversy indicates a wholly new mood about the limits of government action. Following the disasters of the past decade, the courts—and, often, legislatures—were not prepared to accept traditional claims by government to exercise authority from the top down when this authority interfered with newer concepts of rights and liberties.

Whose Law? What Order?

Through the decade, the federal courts were uniquely powerful engines of social change. In popular memory, the great era of reform in civil rights and individual liberties is thought of as the Warren Court years, which technically ended when Chief Justice Earl Warren retired in 1969. In fact, many of the most memorable examples of liberal judicial activism occurred in the decade following that retirement; *Roe v. Wade* was only one example. Also, some lower-level federal courts were at least as vigorous. Activist courts were the critical forces pushing for school desegregation, even if that meant imposing school busing on deeply reluctant communities.[44]

In the post-1965 decade, matters of crime, delinquency, and deviancy represented the cutting edge of social reform. Here above all, judicial intervention revolutionized official responses to social problems and in the process popularized new approaches to matters as fundamental as human normality and difference, as well as the definition of right and wrong.

In the late 1960s, liberals were deeply concerned about abuses by police and prisons, and some prisoners became popular heroes. The romanticization of the criminal was suggested by the enormous success of Eldridge Cleaver's memoir *Soul on Ice* and by the later fascination with the "Soledad Brother," militant convict George Jackson. Protests following Jackson's violent death in 1971 led directly to the Attica prison riot in which over forty died, making it one of the worst civil disorders of a turbulent period.[45] The courts were sympathetic to radical change, largely as a by-product of the judiciary's sensitivity to racial justice. Historically, police, courts, and prisons in southern states had symbolized racial oppression at its harshest, and it was not surprising that reforming criminal justice should be seen as a natural next step in desegregation. During the 1960s, a number of epoch-making court cases revolutionized police procedure, demanding that arrested offenders be read their rights and offered full legal assistance while being protected from improper interrogation. By the 1970s, the due process revolution reached the prisons, to the extent that the penal systems of whole states (mainly in the South) were deemed to be inflicting cruel and unusual punishment. These prison systems were placed under judicially appointed masters, who supervised reform efforts that often stretched over decades. In 1972, the U.S. Supreme Court struck down all existing capital punishment laws while declining to rule that execution in itself constituted cruel and unusual punishment.[46]

But reform efforts went beyond demanding that the state's agents exercise authority without partiality, racism, or brutality. From the late 1960s, radicals challenged the fundamental right of the authorities to reform or cure criminals, and the federal courts supported this activism. Newer policies stressed the rights of the individual against authority and challenged any notion that the values being imposed were in any sense natural or correct. It was as if the courts were trying to maintain an even-handed balance between two equally flawed forces, between crime and the justice system.

These ideas received powerful support from influential sociologists and criminologists who had been exposed to the currents of 1960s radicalism. Ideas of interactionism, labeling theory, and deviancy theory taught a generation of students the relativism and thoroughgoing suspicion of power that would later be associated with postmodernism, and authors were already drawing on Michel Foucault. Scholars studied "deviance"— the nonjudgmental term included not just crime but also mental illness and political dissidence. According to a common view, all societies had individuals who differed from the norm, and depending on the particular society, these people might be seen as criminal, lunatic, or heretical. The individuals in question were not inherently ill or evil, but classifying them in this way reflected the values and interests of the social groups possessing the power to impose the deviancy label. Calling someone an addict or a mental patient, a criminal or a sex offender, had little to do with any qualities of the individual so described.[47]

Radical criminology noted how often the criminal justice systems of various states had enforced laws that were subsequently regarded as evil, obvious examples being the race laws of Nazi Germany, South Africa, or the segregationist South. From this point of view, criminals might have a moral legitimacy higher than that of the police or courts, especially in a society ruled by unchecked capitalism. Watergate and the ensuing corporate scandals offered wonderful ammunition for such a critique. Theorists chiefly focused on so-called victimless offenses, acts that harmed nobody except the culprit and other willing participants, yet which attracted so much public alarm. Drug use and homosexuality were cases in point, and both were notoriously likely to spawn public panics, yet neither type of conduct was in this view inherently wrong, any more than witchcraft had been in the seventeenth century.[48]

Mainstream legal reformers drew on these approaches in their attempts to liberalize official responses to sexuality and substance abuse. Even the term "victimless crime" constituted a potent argument for removing criminal penalties. If an act harmed only willing participants, why should society trouble to penalize it? By the early 1970s, liberal judges were skeptical about the potential harmfulness of most minor sex crimes, including offenses against children. America faced what Sanford Kadish called a "crisis of over-criminalization."[49] Until that overarching problem was resolved, most inmates of American prisons and reformatories were assumed to be victims of unjust laws founded on social and racial prejudice. Even at their best, such institutions must of necessity force inmates into servile conformity.

By the early 1970s, penal ideas were under fierce attack, as exposés such as *Struggle for Justice* and Jessica Mitford's *Kind and Usual Punishment* reached a mass audience.[50] Apart from condemning the casual brutality of American prisons, these polemics denounced the whole theory of reform and rehabilitation that had been central to penal thought through much of the previous century. In its purest form, the whole theory of rehabilitation was founded on a medical model of crime, which treated the offender as a sick individual in need of correction. Just as a doctor committed a patient to a hospital until cured, so a court should send a convict to an institution until reformed, rather than allotting a specific sentence. Indeterminate sentencing meant that an offender might be sent to prison for "two to twenty years," with the actual release date to be decided by a parole board.[51]

For radical critics, though, institutions as flawed as the prisons could scarcely hope to reform anyone. Even if they could, they had no right to impose the standards of upper- and middle-class white America on the poor and minorities who made up the vast bulk of inmates. Total pessimism about the chance of reform was summarized by Robert Martinson's powerful article in *The Public Interest,* which examined the practical effectiveness of a huge sample of rehabilitative programs. Martinson's study found that "with few and isolated exceptions, the rehabilitative efforts that have been reported so far have had no appreciable effect on recidivism." The article's message was epitomized by the simple phrase "Nothing works." Central to any effective social reform movement was deinstitutionalization, freeing those people labeled as deviant or criminal. In Massachusetts, a new director of youth services closed the state's Dickensian reform schools, replacing them with community-based programs and inspiring imitators nationwide. Deinstitutionalization was the declared goal of the federal Juvenile Justice and Delinquency Prevention Act of 1974.[52]

The radical attack succeeded in dismantling the established structures of criminal justice and corrections, and in making rehabilitation a dirty word. If prisons were so oppressive, then one solution was to limit their discretion by insisting that courts impose strictly determinate sentences. Instead of trying to reform, courts should inflict what Andrew von Hirsch called just deserts, a specific sentence for a specific offense.[53] The goal of punishment should change from rehabilitation to deterrence, and even to the ancient concept of retribution. In response to these new ideas, most states passed new determinate sentencing codes. Many went further to eliminate discretion by removing the power of judges to adapt their sentences to particular individuals. Under new mandatory sentencing laws, a conviction for, say, robbery would mean a two-year prison term, not a day more or less. Under the Supreme Court's *Gault* decision of 1967, the principle of limiting judicial discretion was applied to the juvenile courts, which henceforward had to treat accused delinquents according to strict rules of due process. In 1975, the principle of curbing official discretion was extended to high school students when the U.S. Supreme Court ruled in *Goss v. Lopez* that even suspension from school without due process constituted a violation of the Fourteenth Amendment.[54]

The courts were seeking to eliminate the race and class biases that apparently made the justice system so oppressive. Most criminologists felt that the reforms would drastically reduce the scale of the prison population;

Martinson himself thought his findings would lead to a massive reduction in the use of prisons, since these institutions failed so abysmally. As sentencing commissions met around the country to shape the new laws, experts initially tried to avoid imposing severe prison terms for any but the most severe and violent offenders, leaving most minor criminals to be dealt with by probation or other noncustodial means. The benefits would be all the greater when combined with the legal moves to decriminalize drug use as well as many consensual sexual acts. Without petty criminals, drug users, homosexuals, and other minor sex offenders, no one would be left in the prisons except the murderers, rapists, and robbers, the ones who really belonged there. Or such was the goal.

Whose Normality?

No less sweeping were the new approaches to mental illness. Prior to the 1960s, there was no question that the mentally ill, no less than criminals, needed to be confined for the public good, and ideally they should be brought to accept the standards and behaviors of the mainstream society; "normality" was non-negotiable. This attitude changed fundamentally as the works of Thomas Szasz and R. D. Laing denounced psychiatric practice. Szasz's books attacked "the psychiatric dehumanization of man," debunked "the myth of mental illness," and offered comparisons between "the Inquisition and the mental health movement."[55]

Radical sociologists saw mental illness as a label arising from unjust power relations rather than any objective condition. These approaches were popularized through fictional treatments such as the 1975 film version of Ken Kesey's *One Flew Over the Cuckoo's Nest*. From this perspective, mental patients were dissidents rather than victims of pernicious illness, and hospitals in practice differed little from Soviet-bloc institutions that similarly tried to impose official ideologies upon their particular deviants. Society needed to respect "the right to be different," to use the title of Nicholas Kittrie's influential 1971 study of "deviance and enforced therapy."[56] Deviance meant being different, not being wrong.

Federal and state courts asserted the need for due process safeguards to be applied to all offenders on the borderland of insanity, no less than to criminals and convicts. In just a few years, the courts undermined the whole legal foundation on which the mental health system had operated for over a century. By the mid-1970s, involuntary commitment to a mental institution was no longer a routine matter largely entrusted to medical authorities. Now the patient was entitled to the full range of due process protections that a criminal suspect might enjoy, including the right to counsel. Even if they claimed to be working for the patient's own good, doctors must be restricted in their potential ability to inflict injustice. Courts assumed that institutionalization should be avoided where possible and that the authorities must always employ the "least drastic alternative" available. In the wake of multiple court decisions, extended involuntary commitment became difficult to impose except where individuals posed a grave and immediate danger to themselves or the community, and that became ever harder to prove. Between 1965 and 1975, the number of resident mental patients in state and county institutions fell from 460,000 to 190,000, and to 110,000 by 1985.[57]

During the daily traumas of Watergate, it was difficult to feel much optimism about the American political system. In mid-decade, though, liberals had much to celebrate in domestic affairs, more in a general change of social sensibility than in any specific new policy. If feminists and gay rights activists had not achieved all their goals, at least they had made incalculably large progress in a short time; also, issues of race and ethnicity were being treated with acute new sensitivity. In economic matters, reformers saw real hope of changing the long-standing American obsession with growth for its own sake, whatever the cost to social ethics and the environment. At the same time that the courts were extolling the interests of an endangered species over economic development, legislatures were attempting to ban the use of bribery by American corporations at home or overseas.

By 1976, America was liberalizing its attitudes in matters of deviancy and difference, becoming less willing to condemn those who violated social and sexual norms. The limits of social tolerance were to be expanded enormously, and far less reliance should be placed on prisons or other institutions. The age of mass incarceration was surely dead, alongside such historical bygones as drug panics and wars on crime. In so many ways, perhaps the nation could fulfill many of the idealistic hopes of the 1960s, as liberal and radical ideas began a long-term hegemony.

To say the least, many of these hopes went unrealized, and the 1980s were anything but a decade of limitless tolerance. For most modern observers living after that cultural transformation, some of those failures should not be lamented. But however we assess the gains and losses, we can see that the triumph of social liberalism in the mid-1970s contained the seeds of the later reaction.

2

Going Too Far: Bicentennial America

Nixon, Watergate, Patty Hearst, the Bicentennial. The Media got bored with 1967, so they zapped it. . . . I mean, what's left? There's not a single fucking place where it's still 1967.
—A San Franciscan voice, recorded by Armistead Maupin

As the twenty-first century opened, the United States stood at an apex of wealth and power in an era of hectic, triumphant globalization. Commentators discussed the nation's position as the world's sole hyperpower, the last empire standing. So powerful was this image—at least before the disasters of September 11, 2001—that it is difficult to recall how radically the world had changed since the mid-1970s, roughly over the life span of the World Trade Center itself. When the Trade Center was dedicated in 1973, the towers rose in a city in the midst of deepening uncertainty, in a troubled and divided nation facing the imminent prospect of steep international decline. So enormous is the contrast in perceptions of American wealth and power between 1973 and 2001 that it demands an effort of will to recall just how parlous the nation's prospects seemed such a very short time ago.

In media portrayals of modern American history, the turmoil of the 1960s is often presented as ending with some unforgettable events of the mid-1970s. One was the resignation of Richard Nixon in August 1974. Another convenient terminal point is the fall of Saigon in April 1975, with its images of the last Americans fleeing the U.S. embassy and of helicopters being pushed off the decks of aircraft carriers. However painful these images, at least they represented a kind of closure, an opportunity to begin afresh. As Gerald Ford said after Nixon resigned, "Our long national nightmare is over." Looking back on the era, though, these moments seem rather to mark the beginning of a new phase of social crisis and a long period of political instability in a world even more perilous than today's.

Crisis of Faith

In 1974, the film *Godfather II* drew unfavorable comparisons between "legitimate" politics and business, on one hand, and the Mafia, on the other. Seated at a conference table in Havana, the only difference between Michael Corleone and the heads of America's corporations is that at least Don Corleone operates according to some rudimentary sense of honor and loyalty. This scene suggests the cynical attitude toward crime and law in these years, the lack of public willingness to claim overarching moral superiority over the criminal and antisocial, the right to condemn.

In these same years, attitudes of moral equivalence dominated approaches to other traditional foes, especially in foreign affairs. For many, the United States that carried out the war in Vietnam and supported Third World dictatorships could claim no moral superiority to the Soviet Union or China. Soviet imperialists suppressed freedom in Czechoslovakia; American imperialists suppressed freedom in Chile. Just as the language of evil could hardly be applied to domestic crime, nor could it be used seriously of overseas adversaries, whether Communist or Third World nationalist. In this area too, the United States was less sinned against than sinning.

In its utter condemnation of the American establishment, *Godfather II* is a classic Watergate-era movie, one of a whole genre of films and novels united by themes of distrust and paranoia. Though Watergate is today recalled chiefly in terms of the scandalous misdeeds of one president, together with his loyal henchmen, the scandal had enduring effects on American views of government.[1] The affair brought into the social mainstream a critique of American society more radical than anything since the Popular Front days of the late 1930s. In 1975, former presidential candidate George McGovern declared that the time had come to pursue the logic of the revolution that had created the United States, "by replacing and by repudiating the tyranny of the war-makers. What has happened to us is not a random visitation of fate. It is the result of forces which have assumed control of the American structure—economic royalists as oppressive as the Crown two hundred years ago. These forces are militarism, monopoly and the maldistribution of wealth." The following year, David Wise published the book *The American Police State: The Government Against the People*.[2]

The emphasis on corruption at the highest level began an era of furious efforts to root out the appearance of misconduct in public life. Though this began with the federal government, the moral crusade soon extended into intelligence and criminal justice agencies, state and city governments, and the corporate world. So passionate was the zeal to purify public life that it ran the risk of sabotaging the effective operation of government, as the challenging of authoritarian structures spread to the rejection of authority as such. The weakening of government in the mid-1970s contributed to a growing economic debacle—and to a real sense of despair about the nation's future, as each new revelation seemed to confirm the apocalyptic view of systematic corruption. Uncomfortably, this perception of approaching ruin was reaching its peak around the time that the United States celebrated its bicentennial in 1976.

Crimes of the Powerful

Though Watergate is remembered as a bizarre burglary scheme, what John Wayne dismissed as a glorified panty raid, the scandal led to the exposure of widespread misdeeds by political leaders and the intelligence community. Through the 1960s, law enforcement agencies enjoyed vast discretionary powers to bug, infiltrate, and sabotage leftist, liberal, and anti-war movements. Meanwhile, the White House ran its own intelligence and operations unit to plug leaks, and these "plumbers" undertook the actual Watergate burglary in 1972. The arrested burglars had ties both to the White House and to a baroque underworld of CIA agents and anti-Castro Cuban activists. Journalists investigating the plumbers uncovered a vast illegal financing operation employed by the Nixon White House to fund covert operations, and the term *money laundering* now entered mainstream parlance.[3] Ensuing investigations resulted in the prosecution of many high-placed officials, including several White House aides, U.S. attorney general John M. Mitchell, and FBI director Patrick Gray. But issues of corruption and high-level malfeasance certainly did not go away with Nixon's resignation. Watergate controversies were revived by the film of *All the President's Men* in 1976, and again by the appearance of Nixon's memoirs in 1978.[4]

Between 1973 and 1978, public corruption was never far from the headlines. In 1976–77, the Lockheed Corporation was under fire for paying bribes and kickbacks to officials in Japan and several European nations as part of the accepted way of doing business in the armaments industry.[5] In the same months, a number of congressional figures lived in dread of the ongoing Koreagate investigation. This affair grew out of the ambitions of the Reverend Sun Myung Moon, founder of the Unification Church, whose emissaries spread a good deal of money around among congressional figures. Some thirty representatives were implicated, as well as several senators. Complicating the matter, Moon was tied to the KCIA, the intelligence agency of South Korea, which wanted to secure its political influence at a time when the United States was reassessing military commitments in Asia. From 1976 to 1979, the Korean scandal suggested the powerful influence of money and foreign influence on American politics.[6] The term *Koreagate* suggests how contemporaries now viewed official malfeasance; it also implies the likelihood that illegalities would be traced to vast and sinister networks, linking government, intelligence, and corporate elites. While Watergate revelations hammered the executive branch, Congress fared little better: by the summer of 1979, public approval of Congress was running at an abominable 19 percent.[7]

Meanwhile, other scandals suggested that American big business was not only corrupt but actively homicidal. In the Ford Pinto case, the company admitted that it had not taken steps to correct the car's vulnerability to explosion if involved in certain types of crashes. Based on a risk-benefit analysis, it was cheaper to face lawsuits for the resulting deaths rather than to spend the money correcting the faults. Another ongoing scandal focused on Karen Silkwood, who had been in conflict with the Kerr-McGee Corporation over safety issues at an Oklahoma nuclear plant. Her mysterious death in 1974 led to her portrayal as a martyr at the hands of bloodthirsty corporate America. Apart from the corporations, labor unions endured years of scandal, as the disappearance of Jimmy Hoffa in 1975 resurrected earlier revelations of mob ties. In 1974, the president of the United Mine Workers was convicted of organizing the murder of a reforming rival. Both national and local scandals—such as the 1976 murder of Arizona reporter Don Bolles—seemed to prove intimate alliances between organized crime and legitimate politics and business.[8]

Putting these stories together created as sinister a vision of capitalist America as the far left had ever suggested, and a whole genre of corporate crime horror stories now appeared in print. Indeed, modern scholarship on white-collar and corporate crime dates from precisely these years.[9] And unlike earlier eras of scandal, such as the 1930s, the press was now much more enthusiastic about exposés, as the investigative journalist became a popular hero.

Corporate scandals left a critical institutional heritage in the form of much more aggressive approaches to litigation. Seeking to limit the power of overly mighty corporations, new legal arrangements now made it vastly easier to sue organizations and to reap rich rewards in the process. The level of legal damages had been rising since the 1960s, when punitive awards became more common, but the trend accelerated following a series of product liability cases, such as the $125 million award in the 1978 Ford Pinto affair.

The American legal profession abandoned older restrictions on actively seeking clients or fomenting lawsuits, while contingency fee arrangements made litigation both more likely and more profitable. Court decisions of the 1960s and 1970s made it easier to launch class action suits. In the same years, the civil rights revolution had transformed attitudes about the role of courts and law and promoted the view that litigation might be a healthy and socially desirable means of redressing injustice. "Litigating for rights" was appropriate when cases were fought on behalf of classes of hitherto unrepresented victims opposing powerful corporations or institutions. By the start of the 1980s, asbestos-related litigation drove the giant corporation Johns Manville to seek Chapter 11 bankruptcy protection.[10]

Particularly threatening was the application of RICO, the Racketeer Influenced and Corrupt Organizations law, originally passed in 1970 to combat organized crime activity. Once an organization was deemed to fall under the provisions of RICO, it faced devastating sanctions, including triple damages in lawsuits and the pretrial forfeiture of assets. As the law was interpreted, the RICO label was increasingly applied to mainstream businesses, even giants such as Shearson Lehman/American Express. Civil RICO suits revolutionized the corporate legal environment.[11]

Taken together, these reforms produced what Peter Huber described as a liability revolution, based on the fundamental assumption "that most accidents have preventable outside causes that can be effectively deterred by litigation." Problems did not just happen: they were perpetrated, and finding conspiracies could be lucrative. Though the litigation explosion was initially a response to corporate wrongdoing, it contributed mightily to the way in which all manner of social problems were understood. Civil cases involving gender relations and the maltreatment of families and children were now much more likely to come before the courts, and by the early 1980s, lawsuits challenged the doctrine of charitable immunity, which had hitherto protected churches, hospitals, and schools. The constant threat of litigation gave a powerful element of economic self-interest to recent social reforms, ensuring that they remained a permanent part of the social scene.[12]

Guarding the Guards

Even more than the large corporations, intelligence agencies were principal targets of the culture of exposé in these years. Evidence that the FBI and CIA participated in Nixon-inspired cover-ups provoked investigations of those agencies and uncovered scandals dating back decades. In the case of FBI, the main skeleton in the closet was its extensive counterintelligence program, COINTELPRO, which targeted anyone the agency deemed subversive. Contrary to its charter, the CIA had engaged in domestic surveillance and law enforcement in the 1960s, while overseas it had destabilized and overthrown hostile regimes. From 1974 through 1978, congressional investigations provided a steady stream of sensational stories, many sounding like the more outrageous elements from a James Bond film. Appropriately, the CIA's domestic surveillance operation, CHAOS, took its name from the evil global conspiracy in the television comedy show *Get Smart*, co-written by Mel Brooks.[13]

The sequence of investigations began in late 1974, when the *New York Times* revealed the CIA's domestic surveillance operations as well as its involvement in the previous year's Chilean coup. In early 1975, President Ford created an investigative committee chaired by Nelson Rockefeller. This body described Operation CHAOS and the CIA's vast mail intercept operations. However, allegations were now coming so thick and fast that the committee could touch only briefly on some of the most embarrassing issues, notably CIA involvement in the JFK assassination.[14]

Meanwhile, both the House of Representatives and the Senate initiated their own inquiries, the Senate's committee being headed by Frank Church of Idaho. The Church committee provided wonderful copy with its examinations of U.S. involvement in coups and assassination plots overseas. Just as fascinating as the deeds themselves were the means by which they were carried out. Through 1975 and 1976 investigators heard about incredible weapons that the agency had hoped to deploy, including poisons, explosives, hidden firearms, and even an exploding seashell designed to eliminate Fidel Castro as he walked along a Cuban beach. The committees also examined CIA efforts to achieve mind control, to create a programmed assassin on the lines of the fictional Manchurian Candidate using behavior modification techniques and also drugs such as LSD.[15] The array of inventive CIA dirty tricks entered popular culture through its official code name, MK/ULTRA, which symbolized a fantastic science fiction world of mad scientists, robot assassins, and all-embracing conspiracy theories, in which deception and betrayal were the norm. Illustrating public curiosity about how far these inquiries might lead, it was about this time that a popular button proclaimed, "I was a UFO pilot for the CIA."

This political generation was dominated by the memory of its own September 11—the day in 1973 when a U.S.-supported military coup overthrew the democratically elected regime of Chile's Marxist president, Salvador Allende. The coup was long cited as proof of the agency's sinister and homicidal activities. Anti-CIA activism was boosted by the work of Philip Agee, a former agency officer who in 1975 published the muck-raking *Inside the Agency*. Agee's revelations stirred efforts to uncover agents in order to sabotage future CIA activities. Across Europe, radical and leftist newspapers published the names and identities of CIA agents in their respective countries, while the magazine *Counterspy* named three hundred agents.[16]

The resulting danger to personnel was thought a fair price to achieve the greater goal of defeating a clandestine U.S. power that appeared to be the most dangerous force in the modern world. Preventing another Chile—another September 11—demanded extraordinary measures. The campaign reached a turning point in December 1975 when Greek leftists murdered CIA official Richard Welch, who had recently been outed in one of the post-Agee revelations. Welch's death briefly slowed the anti-CIA frenzy and provoked legislation banning the naming of active CIA agents. But for years afterward, the agency occupied a prime place in liberal demonology. Between 1974 and 1980 Congress placed increasing restrictions on the activities of both the CIA and the FBI, gravely restraining their capacity for effective action.[17]

Government by Gunplay

Some of the revelations about intelligence misdeeds appeared farcical, but one question arising in all these hearings, whether overtly or covertly, was anything but humorous: had the CIA or any government agency been involved in the assassination of public figures within the United States, especially President John F. Kennedy? Now, to argue for conspiracy is not necessarily to venture into paranoia or hysteria. To assert that a conspiracy killed JFK need not imply that more than a few individuals were implicated, and certainly not large sections of the military or intelligence community. Genuine assassination conspiracies have occurred in American history: Abraham Lincoln fell victim to one, while Harry Truman was the planned target of another. In the 1970s, however, conspiracy acquired quite different connotations, as theorists argued that the JFK assassination and others were the work of a sinister alternative government, a far-flung "assassination network." For a few years, Assassination became reified as a free-standing menace, much as Terrorism has since 2001.[18]

Assassination theories boomed during 1973 following the release of the film *Executive Action*, a far-left speculation that blamed JFK's death on a military-corporate network of cartoonish malevolence. The underground worlds of Watergate figures such as Howard Hunt pointed to the interlinked subcultures of intelligence and organized crime in south Florida and New Orleans. The CIA revelations showed that the agency genuinely had been discussing assassinations (albeit overseas); they had been interested in carrying out violence through untraceable cut-outs, usually in organized crime. By 1974, media outlets that previously would have had no sympathy for conspiracy theories were openly speculating about official involvement in the deaths of not just John Kennedy but also Robert Kennedy, Martin Luther King Jr., and Malcolm X, as well as in the 1972 attack on George Wallace. Had Lee Oswald and Sirhan Sirhan been programmed assassins, part of an MK/ULTRA operation to generate "lone nut" killers?[19]

Conspiracy theorists argued that such clandestine plots had repeatedly shaped American politics, so much so that the constitutional government was little more than a façade for powerful hidden forces. At the height of the Watergate affair in 1973–74, rumors were rife about splits within the administration, with actual threats of coups and military intervention. When charges surfaced that the Joint Chiefs of Staff were operating a spy ring within the White House, a congressional investigation of the affair was popularly known as "Seven Days in May," after the novel imagining a military coup in Washington. One well-publicized rumor in 1974 claimed that Nixon proposed a coup to hold on to power. Another story, reported in military circles, told of a proposed counterplot to install Barry Goldwater as interim president until elections could be held.[20]

Fears that "dirty tricks" were still in progress reached their height in September 1975, when President Ford was the target of two separate attacks by women in California, both apparent lone nuts. In the first instance, in Sacramento, the attacker was Lynette "Squeaky" Fromme, an alumna of Charles Manson's cultish family. In San Francisco just seventeen days later, the attacker was Sara Jane Moore, who had floated on the fringes of the radical underworld and associated with the Symbionese Liberation Army.

In such a fantastic world of cults and conspiracies, anything seemed possible. In 1976, Sidney Blumenthal edited a collection of wild and wonderful assassination theories under the title *Government by Gunplay*, with an introduction by Philip Agee. The plethora of assassination theories made it inevitable that yet another congressional investigation would be spawned. From 1976 through 1978, the House Select Committee on Assassinations examined the deaths of JFK and Martin Luther King Jr. In its final report, the committee concluded that the killing of President Kennedy did in fact constitute a conspiracy, though the evidence on which this finding was based was much criticized. The committee also reported strong evidence of conspiracy in the King murder.[21]

The Age of Conspiracy

The influence of conspiracy theories can be seen in countless Hollywood films, including some of the classics of the era. *The Parallax View* (1974) uses a fictionalized version of the Robert Kennedy murder to show how a sinister intelligence agency used programmed assassins to eliminate public figures and then mobilized media and political connections to put the blame upon innocent patsies. But assassins were almost obligatory figures in films that ostensibly lacked any serious political content. *Taxi Driver* shows how urban squalor, loneliness, and sexual frustration drove one troubled man to the point where he is prepared to kill a political candidate. (The film was based on the true-life story of Arthur Bremer, who had attempted to kill George Wallace.) The assassination of a celebrity singer marks the climax of Robert Altman's *Nashville*, a gallery of Americana in the time of the bicentennial. More generally, the films of this era stress the central theme of paranoia: even the person closest to you might be part of Them, one of the sinister groups out to destroy you. We see this powerfully in Francis Ford Coppola's *The Conversation*, a film dominated by Watergate images of bugging and secret surveillance.[22]

The repertoire of possible military-industrial-corporate villains seemed limitless. It included the businessmen who grabbed southern California's water supplies (*Chinatown*, 1974), executives of nuclear power companies (*The China Syndrome*, 1979), and Pentagon villains plotting to seize Middle Eastern oil (*Three Days of the Condor*, 1975). In 1978, *Capricorn One* introduced the theory that the space program was a gigantic fraud, using films faked in the American Southwest. This vision of modern life as the product of sensational media, the triumph of image over reality, starred O. J. Simpson. Appropriately, a science fiction book best captures the political mood of these years. In 1975, the massive *Illuminatus* trilogy by Robert Shea and Robert Anton Wilson was predicated on the simple assumption that all conspiracy theories, left and right, were in fact literally true.

The wave of conspiracy politics began to subside only at the end of 1976, partly because the public was tiring of the theme: what else remained to be said? Also, the election of Jimmy Carter raised the prospect of a new and, ideally, cleaner political era. Liberals had little more to gain by rehashing scandals that primarily tarnished the Republican Party, which was now safely out of office. Yet although conspiracy themes faded from the center of political life, they would have lasting consequences for politics, law enforcement, and intelligence. However much the conspiracy culture of the 1970s looks like a carnival of the bizarre, it had long-term effects. Up to the present day, Americans have showed a powerful predilection for exposé politics, for attempts to unravel the sinister manipulators supposedly responsible for grave social threats, foreign and domestic. And conservatives would show themselves at least as deft as liberals in deploying the rhetoric of conspiracies and "enemies within." Many features of mid-1970s paranoia had a lengthy afterlife. Even sinister notions of mind control and programming would surface in theories of child abuse, sex rings, and debates over recovered memory, not to mention attacks on cults and deviant religions.

The Terror Noncrisis, 1974–77

The near-total focus on abuses by government and law enforcement meant that political leaders and the media did not pay attention to pressing political dangers of a kind that in any other political environment would have demanded an urgent response. To that extent, the radical critique of the Watergate era was a self-limiting process: the more the United States appeared unable to respond to threats of attack at home and abroad, the more that perception of weakness would arouse calls for national revival and reconstruction. The extreme liberalism of the mid-1970s naturally generated the conservative reaction of the following decade.

The powerful focus on evils committed by the state diverted attention from subversives or revolutionary threats, however well documented those dangers. In popular culture, American Communism was vindicated and wildly romanticized. While the cinema of the 1950s had depicted Communist spies and villains, the new image even questioned whether Communists existed, at least in the United States. Newer portrayals of American Communists depicted well-intentioned radicals who sought to improve the condition of the masses but were falsely smeared with the "Red" label. This was the message of films such as The Way We Were (1973), Fear on Trial (1975), and The Front (1976), all based on the blacklisting era of the 1950s, and the biographical treatment of Woody Guthrie in Bound for Glory (1976). As Richard Gid Powers writes, "The Hollywood blacklist took on mythic status as a roll call of cultural heroes." To point to an authentic Communist menace was Red-baiting or McCarthyism, and henceforth even the most dedicated Communist Party activists were cited or memorialized as "radicals." Conversely, Gerald Ford and Ronald Reagan were both damned by the fact that they had supplied information to the FBI, which was portrayed as a repressive Gestapo.[23]

Another related area of near-blindness involved terrorism. In terms of the scale and frequency of attacks, America during the mid-1970s was suffering one of the worst waves of terrorist violence in its history to that point. Of course, no attack in this era came close to later mega-terror episodes such as Oklahoma City or September 11. Yet even by the standards of contemporary Europe, America had a lot of deadly urban guerrillas, and political violence hit various parts of the country, not just New York and Washington. For a few years, bombs were a familiar part of extremist political culture. A 1975 bombing at LaGuardia airport killed eleven, more even than the first World Trade Center attack in 1993. (The LaGuardia attack is generally attributed to Croatian extremists.) Yet for all the mayhem, few observers bemoaned a "terrorist crisis." This curious silence is largely explained by the utter confusion besetting the intelligence agencies in these same years.[24]

Some of the most active domestic militants of these years were veterans of the late 1960s, the peak years of antiwar protest and black extremism. During the mid-1970s, the survivors of this era formed a loose confederation, drawn from the Weather Underground, the Black Liberation Army (BLA), and Puerto Rican nationalist movements. The Weather Underground attacked the U.S. State Department in 1975, and the BLA murdered several police officers. In 1973, BLA member Joanne Chesimard (Assata Shakur) killed a New Jersey police officer, and following her escape from prison some years afterward, she found sanctuary in Cuba. Particularly effective were Puerto Rican groups such as the Armed Forces of National Liberation (FALN) and the Macheteros. In 1976 alone, the FALN claimed over thirty bomb attacks in New York, Chicago, and Washington. A 1975 bombing at New York's historic Fraunces Tavern killed four and injured sixty, providing news footage reminiscent of contemporary Northern Ireland.[25]

The extent of organized violence by African-American militants remains controversial. In the Zebra murders of 1973–74, the Death Angels, apparently influenced by Black Muslim ideology, carried out a series of racial murders against whites. (A similar murder series occurred in Chicago some years later.) Bloody internal fighting among African-American groups sometimes ventured into overt terrorism. One conflict in Washington, D.C., in 1973 left five dead. This battle in turn led to a sectarian Muslim takeover of the B'nai Brith headquarters in Washington in March 1977 and a siege in which hundreds of hostages were taken. Fearing a replay of the Attica massacre, the government negotiated, and bloodshed was limited.[26]

By no means did all the violence stem from the domestic left. The numerous movements from the anti-Castro Cuban exile community were firmly on the right. Miami became the heart of a flourishing terrorist and guerrilla subculture, and by the 1980s, anti-Castro Cuban groups had been involved in hundreds of violent actions in many nations. In 1975, a veteran of the botched Bay of Pigs invasion launched a bombing campaign in the Miami area, hitting thirteen government targets over the course of two days. The following year, Cuban exiles were involved in a political assassination in Washington, when they helped Chilean authorities murder a prominent leftist exile from that country, Orlando Letelier.[27] In 1976, Miami-based anti-Castro extremists bombed an aircraft belonging to the Cuban national airline, killing seventy-three. Apart from such active militant groups, other movements carried out political violence on U.S. soil. Some political murders can also be traced to radical Arab groups, including the Libyan and Iraqi governments and Palestinian terrorist movements.[28]

Reading such a catalogue of attacks, it is astonishing that it registers so little in popular memory and that as late as 1995, writers on Oklahoma City were still remarking that finally "terrorism had come to the United States." But the response to the 1970s terror wave can be understood in light of the political conditions of the time. Since the FBI was in such disarray following the Nixon scandals, it was poorly prepared either to prevent violent acts or to mobilize public concern. Infiltration and surveillance of the sort that once would have been commonplace was now highly unpopular, and supervisors were much more reluctant to grant permission for such activity.

Meanwhile, terrorist incidents attracted nothing like the attention they should have done. Individual episodes were reported, and some became famous. The most celebrated terror group of these years was the Symbionese Liberation Army (SLA), which was active in California. With a brilliant eye for the American cult of celebrity, the SLA's kidnapping of heiress Patricia Hearst won them global attention, all the greater when Hearst converted to their cause (more evidence, it seemed, of the power of mind control). The SLA was all but destroyed in a bloody siege in Los Angeles in May 1974, in which six terrorists were killed.[29]

But Americans paid strikingly little attention to terrorism as a phenomenon, as a systematic threat to political order. Terrorism as such—as opposed to particular movements—was the subject of no presidential commissions or congressional hearings, no television documentaries or even true crime books. Foreign terrorists provided villains for occasional thriller stories, as when Thomas Harris's 1975 book *Black Sunday* portrayed a Palestinian-led attempt to wipe out the spectators at the Super Bowl (a film followed in 1977). Domestic groups seldom appeared, though the SLA appeared in jokey form in *Network* and again as pathological villains in Clint Eastwood's *The Enforcer*. These rare examples must be set against the dozens of contemporary treatments of government conspiracies and homicidal rogue CIA agents.

In mainstream discussions of terror incidents, we seldom hear charges that would certainly have arisen a few years earlier, namely, that domestic subversion was directed by Soviet or other Communist forces. Such charges plausibly could have been made given the strong evidence that leftist militants were using Cuba as a sanctuary and that FALN leaders were allied with Cuban intelligence. In the context of 1976, such allegations would have been greeted with scorn and denounced as Red-baiting. Reinforcing liberal concerns, Ronald Reagan was one of the very few political leaders to make domestic terrorism a political priority and to urge more intense surveillance; in the left's view, anything Reagan stood for had to be wrong. If there was a "terror international," then for liberals it was the far-right network founded by the CIA and most clearly manifested in the anti-Castro Cuban groups. The political aspect of the Death Angel killings received minimal attention, presumably because police and media feared charges of inflammatory stereotyping. Certainly the FBI's record in racial matters gave it no credibility in discussing such a charged case. But in any case, serious conspiracies evidently stemmed from government and the political right: there could be no enemies on the left.

But though the interpretation of terrorism remained a thorny topic, the extensive violence had its impact. The frequency of attacks contributed to the pervasive sense of general weakness and disarray, as well as a feeling that America had become a banana republic, with foreign spies settling scores on Washington's Embassy Row. U.S. ineffectiveness stood in painful contrast to the achievements of other countries, especially Israel, which won such a telling victory against terrorism with the Entebbe raid of 1976. News of this determined military action arrived just as Americans were celebrating their own bicentennial, amidst such political uncertainty.

Innocents Abroad

The domestic political crisis of the mid-1970s had enormous repercussions internationally. Already by 1973, the executive branch was in so much disarray that it was difficult to imagine a president being able to act decisively against foreign threats. U.S. military power was discredited by the experience of Vietnam, and it was obvious that no Congress would authorize military activity overseas for the foreseeable future. The War Powers Act of 1973 raised grave constitutional questions about the powers of the presidency to intervene overseas without the full authority of Congress. These lessons were reinforced by America's first post-Vietnam military venture, the attempt in May 1975 to recapture the ship *Mayaguez* from its captors, the Cambodian Khmer Rouge. The operation was successful but costly in American lives. Even when responding to a direct attack by such a minuscule statelet, the United States was unable to act effectively.[30]

From a liberal standpoint, the greatest dangers internationally were from the political right, in terms of U.S. militarism and interventionism, and the contempt for human rights by U.S.-backed right-wing and military regimes. Liberal opinion largely accepted a diluted form of the Marxist theory that states operate for the benefit of aggressive corporate interests and that wars generally reflect these interests. The media served wider corporate purposes by exaggerating foreign menaces and inventing evil villains. From this radicalized perspective, the growing threat of Communist and Soviet power was no longer on the political map, except as a bogeyman to draw an ill-informed nation into military adventures. Political liberalism and anti-interventionism now dominated groups that had once been committed to the Cold War cause, including much of the Catholic hierarchy and large sections of the clergy. The Chilean experience encouraged support for liberationist and anti-imperialist policies in Latin America. In 1976, the Catholic bishops condemned the use of nuclear weapons and added that even the threat to employ them was illegitimate, flatly attacking the existing theory of deterrence.[31]

Acknowledging America's political plight, the nation's foreign policy in the mid-1970s stressed accommodation and coexistence with the Communist world. The policies that conservatives would protest so strenuously originated in Republican administrations, especially in the State Department under Henry Kissinger. (Kissinger served as national security adviser from 1969 through 1975 and as secretary of state from 1973 to 1977.) For Kissinger, all powers should be encouraged to accept their role in a balanced world order, which took account of their competing interests and recognized their legitimate security concerns within their own particular spheres of influence. Like the Americans, the Soviets had their proper place in the global picture. Though the two nations would never achieve the complete peace and harmony of an entente, they could aspire to détente, to an agreed understanding to reduce tensions. Détente found a spectacular visual symbol in the joint Apollo-Soyuz space mission in 1975.[32]

A critical part of this vision was arms limitation and an end to the swelling of nuclear arsenals. Looking at the First World War, as popularly interpreted, diplomats feared that the unchecked expansion of armaments would itself create a dynamic that would lead to war, regardless of what individual governments thought or wanted. The United States and the Soviet Union worked together to promote the Strategic Arms Limitation Treaty (SALT), and a first agreement was signed in 1972. In 1975, the Helsinki Conference recognized existing borders in Europe and sought increased East-West cooperation and cultural contacts. In the same year, the United States and the Soviets agreed on the broad principles of a SALT II agreement.[33]

But détente had enemies. The process abandoned the moral boast of Western superiority over Communism that had been so often proclaimed since 1945, as well as definitively forfeiting claims to liberate peoples subjugated by Communism. In the new realpolitik, the idea of eliminating or rolling back Communism was nowhere on the agenda, even as a distant dream. Worst of all, perhaps, was the long-term prospect for the United States. In 1976, the hawkish Admiral Elmo Zumwalt claimed that in 1970, Kissinger had declared that the United States was already in decline. The nation "has passed its historic high point like many earlier civilizations . . . He states that his job is to persuade the Russians to give us the best deal we can get, recognizing that historical forces favor them." Though Kissinger denied the charge, his actions seemed to fit the analysis.[34]

Détente assumed a parity between the United States and the USSR, if not precisely in terms of nuclear weaponry, then broadly in diplomatic status and prestige. And by agreeing to limit U.S. power, America was ignoring the danger that the Soviets would cheat on any agreements, raising the imminent danger of Communist military hegemony. SALT II offered the Soviets a great many loopholes in the means of counting its nuclear launching systems, allowing it, for instance, not to count certain nuclear armed bombers, while equivalent U.S. aircraft were included. By 1980, the USSR deployed three times as many warheads as it had ten years previously. Labor leader George Meany complained, "Détente means ultimate Soviet military superiority over the West."[35]

The Fall of America

U.S. weakness was all the more dangerous given the radicalism emerging across much of the globe. The cultural and political activism of the 1960s had been boosted by opposition to the Vietnam War and was further advanced by the economic crises following the oil shock of 1973–74.

Anti-Western forces were winning striking victories in the Middle East. In 1973, the Yom Kippur War came close to threatening the existence of Israel, causing real alarm among many Americans, especially Jews. The confrontation saw the U.S. Navy outnumbered and outgunned by the Soviets in the Mediterranean.[36] Meanwhile, the oil crisis vastly enhanced the wealth and power of the Arab nations, which spent lavishly in an attempt to build their political influence. Over the next two years, the global community, as represented in the United Nations, became ever more hostile to Israel. In 1974, PLO leader Yasser Arafat came to New York to address the UN General Assembly. Though Third World and Eastern-bloc nations received the speech enthusiastically, Americans still regarded Arafat as a ludicrous thug. In 1975, the Palestine Liberation Organization acquired observer status at the UN, short of the governmental recognition it sought, but still a major step. The nadir of American isolation at the UN came in November 1975, when the General Assembly's Resolution 3379 proclaimed Zionism a form of racism. Such diplomatic moves led Americans to believe that they were alone and vulnerable in a deeply hostile world.[37]

Matters seemed perilous even in Western Europe. By the early 1970s, some radical groups were openly moving toward urban guerrilla and terrorist warfare, a trend encouraged by the Chilean lesson that capitalism could not be ended by elections and parliaments alone. By 1976–77, domestic terrorist violence was reaching alarming heights in Italy, Turkey, Spain, and West Germany, not to mention the ongoing savagery in Northern Ireland. With Communist parties seeking inclusion in several European governments, the future of NATO and the Western alliance seemed shaky. Could the United States share military and political secrets with France, Italy, and Spain if those governments had Euro-Communist cabinet ministers? Even in Britain, the political right warned of crypto-Communist influences in the Labour government, and coup talk rumbled in that nation's military and intelligence circles. Perhaps the whole of Europe would go the way of Finland, retaining a free market economy while forfeiting the right to military self-defense or a "provocative" anti-Soviet foreign policy. The West would be politically and militarily castrated. In the summer of 1977, it did not seem far-fetched to imagine a systematic collapse of U.S. influence much along the lines of what actually befell the Soviet bloc in 1989.[38]

The Soviet Union benefited enormously from the spread of radical movements around the globe, though that point was not readily conceded in the America of the time. Given the experience of Vietnam, Americans were suspicious of claims that left-wing movements were tools of Moscow or that the KGB was active globally in subversion and violence, though it evidently was. Already in 1973, Soviet leader Leonid Brezhnev gave an ominous speech, warning, "Come 1985, we will be able to extend our will wherever we need to." Supporting his words was the dynamic work of Admiral Sergei Gorshkov, then engaged in building the Soviet Navy into a potent blue-water fleet capable of global intervention. When American forces abandoned their Vietnamese naval bases at Da Nang and Cam Ranh

Bay, the Soviets wasted little time moving in, offering an evocative symbol of one empire supplanting a declining rival.[39]

By 1975, U.S. power was in such decline that the Soviets were emboldened to act in ways that would have been inconceivable a few years earlier. The catalyst was the leftist military coup that occurred in Portugal in 1974 and which over the following year seemed likely to produce Western Europe's first fully fledged Communist state. Portugal itself was a minor player on the international scene, but it retained a troubled colonial empire, chiefly in Angola and Mozambique. The fall of the Portuguese government ignited civil wars in those regions, in which Soviet-backed leftist organizations rose to power.

Other nations became involved, including South African forces on the anti-Soviet side. That fall, Cuban forces began a major military intervention in Angola, which would ultimately draw in some fifty thousand Cuban troops. Cuban forces also appeared in Mozambique and in Ethiopia, where another Communist-linked regime was establishing itself. Much of the motivation for these movements stemmed from Castro's long-standing personal devotion to Third World revolution, though at the time, the U.S. government saw the Cubans simply as direct surrogates for the Soviets. Whatever the reasons, the Angolan intervention had immense consequences for southern Africa, counterbalancing South African military strength and weakening white power in Namibia and Rhodesia. It also offered an example of resistance to the moribund liberation struggle in South Africa itself. The new balance of power stimulated the popular youth uprising that began in the township of Soweto in 1976, and it stirred the black consciousness movement. But while most Americans sympathized with the weakening of apartheid, the Cuban presence encouraged black movements to identify with Communist and pro-Soviet causes, raising the likelihood that a black revolution in southern Africa would be an anti-Western upsurge.[40]

In any earlier period, this kind of African adventurism certainly would have generated a confrontation with the United States, and probably a nuclear standoff, but this was simply not plausible in the political circumstances of the time. Besides the generalized opposition to U.S. intervention, American liberals were repelled by any alliance with apartheid South Africa, an ultimate pariah. In their view, the anti-Communist side in southern Africa must inevitably be aligned to racism and apartheid. In December 1975, the House of Representatives passed the Tunney Amendment, terminating covert assistance to anti-Communist forces in Angola. The lack of U.S. response encouraged further Soviet-bloc activism and political intervention, ultimately creating the conditions for the new Cold War atmosphere of the 1980s. In the emerging world order, America's allies needed to rethink their reliance on failing U.S. power, either by making deals with the Soviet bloc or by improving their own defenses. In 1979, South Africa probably tested a nuclear weapon, likely produced in alliance with Israel.[41]

Looking back, we know that Soviet audacity overseas concealed the weaknesses of its system, its decrepit economy, and the growing tensions among its subject peoples. In Eastern European nations such as Czechoslovakia, dissidents appropriated the human rights language of the Helsinki accords as ammunition for their own attacks on local Communist regimes. At the time, though, Western commentators were impressed by how decisively the Soviets had moved beyond the Cold War stalemate to advance their position around the globe: in Southeast Asia, in southern Africa, in Europe itself. While nobody was imagining Communist revolution in the United States, the Soviets conspicuously seemed to be winning the post-1945 standoff. Perhaps some shrewd analyst contemplated writing a book on the approaching "end of history," describing how the old ideological struggles had ended in the global victory of state socialism.[42]

The Fall of the Cities

While affairs in Italy or Angola had little direct impact on ordinary Americans, economic decline at home daily reinforced a sense of weakness and decay. Far from the 1960s revolutions having "made America livable"— as Reich's *Greening of America* had promised—they seemed to have had the opposite effect. Also, the specific forms that economic troubles took suggested close linkages with developments overseas. This gave the potential for a conservative analysis that would present foreign and domestic crises as part of a coherent whole, which integrated concerns about moral decline.

The global economic crisis was itself shaped by American policies during the Vietnam era, when enormous military expenditures had spurred inflation. Inflation was further promoted by the collapse of the postwar Bretton Woods financial system and the 1971 decision to let the dollar find its own level on international currency markets. By late 1973, a perception of terminal weakness in the U.S. administration encouraged the oil-producing nations to launch a massive price increase, coupled with boycotts against the United States and other nations thought too supportive of Israel. The action provoked the most substantial interruption yet to post-1945 global growth, giving a frightening new push to inflationary pressures. In the short term, gas prices soared. Conditions were aggravated by a ten-day truckers' strike in February 1974, a politicized conflict that led to serious violence. The affair raised alarming questions about the whole basis of America's industrial civilization. From 1945 through 1973, U.S. productivity had grown steadily at 2.5 percent a year, and incomes grew accordingly; after the oil shock, though, productivity growth dropped to less than 1.5 percent annually and remained at that level for two decades. Real income growth slowed accordingly.[43]

The oil issue was inescapable to any American who was not actually a hermit. For over a decade after 1974, the federal government encouraged fuel economy by enforcing a national speed limit of 55 mph. Though troublesome everywhere, this policy had a vast effect on rural areas, and travel times lengthened intolerably in the Plains and the West. The national speed limit had a potent foreign policy resonance: in the popular mind, the oil shortage resulted from America's failure to stand up to the loathed oil sheikhs. Though Nixon considered military action to seize Arab oil fields, such a response was politically impossible at this time. (A second invasion plan that surfaced in the media in 1975 was likely a trial balloon to test public reaction, or perhaps a diplomatic device to put pressure on oil producers.)[44]

In fact, the oil crisis subsided as some of those sheikhs, especially the Saudis, were appalled by the enormous damage they had inflicted on the global economy, which threatened to promote instability and radicalism. But enormous damage had already been done. The Dow Jones index reached a historic high of over 1,000 in late 1972, but the gains were wiped out in the brutal bear market of 1973–74, when the Dow plunged to a low of 577. Not until the fall of 1976 did the index again rise over the 1,000 mark. By the end of 1975, Republican Party advisers were alarmed about the possible impact on the forthcoming elections: "Over half of the people mention one of these two issues [inflation and unemployment] as their leading issue concern. They are obviously the cause of the strong negativism and pessimism in the data. A large majority of people in the country are, or think they are, hurting financially."[45]

The condition of American cities promoted a sense of economic decay. Though the economic storm made matters worse, the main problem was a longer-term shift of retailing and manufacturing activity away from the traditional city centers. Ever since the 1940s, growing numbers of city residents had been moving to suburbs, a process accelerated by fears of crime and urban violence and by the decline of public schooling. Philadelphia's population fell by 25 percent between 1950 and 1990, though surrounding suburban counties boomed. In just eight years in the 1970s, New York City lost half a million private sector jobs. As downtowns deteriorated, new malls and suburban shopping centers flourished, revolutionizing concepts of social space.[46]

One element forcing urban change was the aggressive desegregation policy demanded by federal judges, who saw school busing as a means of ensuring racial equity. When implemented, busing policies provoked violence among white working-class communities, most notoriously in Boston between 1974 and 1976. The rioting acquired a shocking memorial in the spring of 1976 when a celebrated photograph of the era depicted a white protester using a flagpole to try to impale a black rival. The photo stood in deadly contrast to all the benevolent red, white, and blue images that proliferated that bicentennial season. Apart from underlying racial hostility, protesters were infuriated by the perceived threat to their communities and especially to their children. In the longer term, busing controversies helped drive middle-class children out of urban schools and often pushed white families out of the cities altogether. By 1976, the conflict had reduced the number of children enrolled in the Boston school system by some twenty thousand, and the system never regained its precrisis size.[47]

As tax bases collapsed, cities found it ever more difficult to survive, and some faced open default on their debts. This story was most famously demonstrated by New York City, which reached fiscal meltdown in October 1975. When the U.S. government refused to prevent insolvency, the city's *Daily News* headlined, "Ford to City: Drop Dead." In 1978, Cleveland became the first U.S. city since the 1930s to default on its bonds. Unable to pay police or public employees, city governments faced repeated strikes and cuts in public services, which made the cities look shabbier and more dangerous. Even police officers joined the labor militancy of the era, through unofficial work stoppages and sick-outs ("blue flu"). In 1974, Baltimore's police strike led to serious looting. The July 1977 blackout in New York City was accompanied by massive and widely reported looting, in sharp contrast to the more sedate response to the earlier blackout of 1965.[48]

Far from being showplaces, American cities seemed dirty, dangerous, and locked in a cycle of continuing decline. Deinstitutionalization policies threw tens of thousands of former mental patients onto the streets, where they swelled the ranks of the homeless and the nuisance offenders. Worries about urban violence and racial conflict focused on youth crime and gangs; this was a perennial American theme, but it acquired special force in the bicentennial years. In a major 1975 feature, "The Crime Wave," *Time* offered alarming headlines and subheads: "Statistics: All Trends Are Up," "Criminals: Young and Violent," "The Cities: Canyons of Fear." Through the 1970s, the South Bronx became a recurring symbol of an urban area so devastated that it almost ceased to be part of the civilized world, having reverted to brutal gang rule. The local police precinct was famous as "Fort Apache."[49]

Urban decline had implications for debates over sexual morality, since American cities were, metaphorically as well as literally, far dirtier than they had ever been. Big cities had always had their red-light districts, but the decline of property values and the plague of vacancies made it easy for adult establishments to operate in what had once been prime retail areas. Also, changing moral and legal standards meant that adult businesses were offering services that were franker and more outrageous than in years gone by. By the mid-1970s, child pornography and bestiality materials were easily accessible in any major metropolitan area, while adult bookstores, massage parlors, and strip clubs made prostitution overt and readily available. Repeated media reports turned New York's Times Square and 42nd Street into a global symbol of commercialized vice and moral decadence. Here, as in other cities, the booming sex business catered to what was obviously widespread interest in underage prostitutes, male and female. In 1975, *Time* magazine claimed, "Male prostitutes who are teen-age or younger are greatly in demand, particularly by older married men. Robin Lloyd, a Los Angeles writer-producer, . . . estimates that more than 100,000 American boys between the ages of 13 and 16, mostly runaways from working-class or welfare families, are actively engaged in prostitution. Neither the Los Angeles nor the San Francisco police find his figure too high. . . . [A] national guide to the trade, *Where the Boys Are,* has sold 70,000 copies at $5 each." Finding a startling range of sexual services required only a few blocks' walk from city hall or an old civic center—or, in Washington, from the White House itself. Drug sales were equally blatant.[50]

Police agencies were in no position to suppress these developments. Understrength and underfunded, with plummeting morale, most urban forces could barely cope with their backlogs of unsolved murders and robberies, let alone with what were now commonly called victimless offenses. And who even knew which behaviors would continue to be criminal in a few years? Why, for instance, should police continue to arrest organized gamblers and numbers racketeers if cities such as Atlantic City were already legalizing casinos in the hope of achieving urban renewal and states were organizing legal lotteries? Even if police wished to act against sexual vice, legal and constitutional changes made it difficult to prosecute such cases, to convince a jury that seized films were obscene. Far better, then, to leave the adult businesses alone, and if that was to be the policy, why should officers not take gifts and bribes? In drug matters too, shifting public attitudes gave little support to any official zeal against traffickers, not to mention ordinary users. Through the 1970s, police forces suffered repeated corruption scandals, usually arising from these sensitive morality offenses.[51]

Though clarity demands that historians treat events separately, such an approach fails to convey the cumulative effect of news stories as they are reported within a short period. In order to reconstruct the mood of Americans entering the bicentennial year, we should think of the combined effect of the barrage of disasters reported in the last few months of 1975. September brought the twin presidential assassination attempts, October the New York fiscal crisis. November was the month of the United Nations resolution against Zionism and also of the war in Angola, while the sensational hearings of the Senate's Church committee produced daily revelations from September through December. The debate over action in Angola continued through December, while the CIA exposé led to the murder of Richard Welch. And terrorism again made headlines that same month, with the Miami bombing spree and the carnage at LaGuardia. To say the least, hopes that the national crisis had ended with the fall of Saigon that past April looked decidedly optimistic.

Happy Days

In the 1976 film *Network,* deranged news anchor Howard Beale launches a hysterical denunciation of the agonies and frustrations in contemporary America and urges his viewers to shout at their neighbors that they are mad as hell and they are not going to take it anymore. Many thousands of viewers follow his advice, joining his shrieks of rage at collapsing cities, a fraying society, and a falling economy. Overnight, Beale becomes a messianic leader, as desperate people see him as the one public figure who understands their sufferings. Ultimately (and inevitably, given the film's date), he is assassinated during a live broadcast.

Network remains a fascinating film, not least for its prophetic vision of the trash sensationalism that would dominate the mass media during the 1980s. But it also expressed a genuine public mood of frustration about the directions that the nation was pursuing. How could one survive in a society with such awful prospects? For some, the answer lay in political activism to reverse the process of decline, but others sought refuge in simpler times, in either an idealized past or an imagined present. Through the decade, we often find a puzzling paradox: the same people who idealized liberation and self-exploration also sought a return to traditional authenticity, if possible rooted in a simpler bygone world. The "desolation of reality" can be an uncomfortable place to live. The fictional political candidate in *Nashville* proclaimed, "What this country needs is some one-syllable answers," but in the America of 1975, that goal seemed unattainable. But the thirst for such an approach would often surface in popular culture, and even more strikingly in the politics of nostalgia, exemplified so differently by Jimmy Carter and Ronald Reagan.

This cultural nostalgia took different forms. During the depths of the Watergate mess, the smash hit in movie theaters was *That's Entertainment,* a compilation of dance numbers from the Fred Astaire era. The decade of the 1950s also inspired escapist longings as the last good era in American history before the dual curses of the JFK assassination and Vietnam. *American Graffiti* (1973) was set in a small California town in 1962, on the eve of national catastrophe. The film inspired other paeans to the era, including the television series *Happy Days* and *Laverne and Shirley.* Across the country, the historical research and reconstruction projects of the bicentennial year generated new interest in community roots, and genealogical research boomed. Many younger people sought idealized pasts that long predated the United States, and the 1970s proved a golden age for pseudo-medievalism, with a proliferation of creative anachronists and reenactors, along with Tolkien-inspired sword-and-sorcery novels. The game Dungeons and Dragons appeared in 1974. Even the film *Star Wars,* supposedly set in a far distant future, was a world of knights and quests, sabers and sorcerers. In the real world, the yearning for traditional certainties underlies the appeal of old-time religion in these same years. Though that trend is most familiar from the renewed upsurge of evangelical religion, we also see the popularity of strictly observant forms of Judaism, including Orthodoxy.

Quests for American authenticity often focused on regions that had supposedly maintained the older sense of community and American values, including traditional gender values. In *Rocky* (1976), the idealized community is an ethnic neighborhood of Philadelphia. Typically, the film shows sport as a paramount expression of both community pride and gutsy masculinity. In the real world too, the greatest heroes of professional sport were firmly linked to tough traditional cultures. The Pittsburgh Steelers, winner of four Super Bowls in the 1970s, were symbolically associated with the virile steel culture of western Pennsylvania, while the Dallas Cowboys cultivated a Texan image of sturdy footballers and unimaginably sexy cheerleaders. The 1979 meeting between the two in Super Bowl XIII is widely regarded as a high point of NFL history, an area of American life in which heroic drama and clear victory still seemed possible. In 1980, a hit song by the Charlie Daniels Band used the Steeler fan as an icon of American patriotism.[52]

Commonly, the nostalgic vision turned to a mythicized South or West. The rejection of the troubled present helps explain the revival of country and western music through the mid-1970s, which manifested in the country rock style of the Eagles and culminated in the urban cowboy phenomenon at the end of the decade. Southern bands playing distinctively southern themes to a national audience included Lynyrd Skynyrd and Charlie Daniels. One beneficiary of this boom was Burt Reynolds, star of the amazingly successful *Smokey and the Bandit*. Through the decade, western values were epitomized by the films of Clint Eastwood, including his Dirty Harry cop series, but also by populist country-oriented comedies such as *Every Which Way but Loose*. Another pop culture fad glorified the independent trucker, who emerged as a rugged cowboy figure rebelling against officialdom and gasoline shortages. The 1975 hit song "Convoy" began a fad for the CB radios that promised a new kind of spontaneous western community based on populist technology. Even *Roots* was a manifestation of nostalgia, in this case for an idealized African past. And despite its depiction of the evils of slavery, it still portrayed a rural southern society that was truly a community, although the focus of nostalgia now had shifted from the great mansion to the slave quarters.[53]

The political potential of the nostalgia boom was unmistakable, though it was not clear which party might ultimately benefit. Distaste for national politics encouraged a search for populist leaders outside the current elites, who might be hoped to speak truth to power—a real-life Howard Beale. George Wallace was too divisive on racial issues, but other southerners repeatedly inspired hope. In 1973, North Carolina senator Sam Ervin briefly became a Capra-esque cult figure when he chaired the committee investigating Watergate: T-shirts proclaimed him "Uncle Sam." Jimmy Carter's appeal in 1976 was that he was not connected to Washington power circles and could not be blamed for the horrors of recent years. Recent events gave enormous force to his declaration that "I will never lie to you." To the last, his greatest strength, and ultimately his greatest weakness, was that he remained "a stranger in a strange land" in Washington.[54]

No Future

If matters seemed bad in bicentennial America, there was little sense that this was just a transient phase: things were going to get worse. Already in the late 1960s, growing social disorder and international tensions encouraged widespread pessimism about the long-term future of civilization, and perhaps of humanity itself. This was another aspect of the utter loss of confidence in Western and specifically American destiny. The sense of foreboding took many forms, many overtly religious, others not.

Doomsday ideas were popularized by the rise of environmentalism, with its dire warnings about the effects of ecological degradation and human overpopulation. Since the late 1960s, threats of disaster had been discussed by books such as Paul Ehrlich's *Population Bomb* and *Famine 1975!* In 1972, the Club of Rome report *The Limits to Growth* envisaged the late-twentieth-century world as a desperate and impoverished place, a scene of mass starvation and political chaos. As Paul Ehrlich warned, the world was facing a sickness that might well be terminal: "A cancer is an uncontrolled multiplication of cells; the population explosion is an uncontrolled multiplication of people."[55]

Science fiction writers and filmmakers exploited these visions of a dreadful near future. Films such as *Soylent Green* and *Silent Running* depicted different versions of environmental and social ruin, usually through overpopulation and resource exhaustion. *Logan's Run* imagined a future in which everyone over thirty suffered euthanasia. John Brunner's novel *The Sheep Look Up* remains perhaps the most convincing account ever written of how terrorism and ecological decline might conspire to destroy the United States. One of the best-selling mainstream novels of 1973 was Allen Drury's *Come Nineveh, Come Tyre*, about the descent of a near-future United States into political chaos and dictatorship, leading ultimately to Soviet occupation. Nightmares about the urban future are reflected in the 1982 film *Blade Runner*, in which the Los Angeles of 2019, violent, polluted, impoverished, and overcrowded, looks like a ramshackle city in Southeast Asia. *Escape from New York* (1981) imagined a future Manhattan as a convict colony.[56]

As long as prophecies of demographic ruin focused on the Third World, Americans could afford to find them merely disturbing. It was ugly to think that Mexico or India might be forced to lose half or a third of its people, but that was no more than Malthusian inevitability. Beginning in 1973, though, the oil shortages raised immediate fears of what the United States itself might look like without the advanced technology made possible by traditional energy supplies. The resulting forecasts were sobering. Since the "energy balloon" was evidently finished, Americans must become used to living in a new age of scarcity, in which they would need to rediscover their puritan traditions of frugality. For the United States, Robert Heilbronner predicted that "scarcity and ecological barriers" would produce "a drift toward public control over production and consumption" under powerful governments, "maybe left wing, maybe right wing." In 1974, Paul and Anne

Ehrlich warned readers that "in ten or fifteen years—twenty or twenty-five at most—you will be living in a world extremely different from that of today—one that, if you are unprepared for it, will prove extraordinarily unpleasant." By that measure, the 1990s should have been one of the menacing decades in American history, apt preparation for the general ghastliness of the twenty-first century. In 1976, the media respectfully reported a theory that the world's harvests would soon be devastated by global cooling and an incipient ice age.[57]

In 1977, *Time* asked science fiction writer Isaac Asimov to project a future America without fuel, and he did so with gusto. Describing the horrific year of 1997, Asimov sketched a society without cars, in which trains run only one day in five, where people suffer frigid cold through the winter, and in which population is regulated by soaring infant mortality. Fortunately, employment opportunities can be found in demolition, as "the fading structures of a decaying city are the great mineral mines and hardware shops of the nation. Break them down and reuse the parts." Another benefit is the end of military resources, since only the United States and USSR can afford "to maintain a few tanks, planes and ships—which they dare not move for fear of biting into limited fuel reserves." "Work, sleep and eating are the great trinity of 1997, and only the first two are guaranteed." This new Dark Age would soon return society to a preindustrial world. Not in the romantic way the creative anachronists hoped, the future would be medieval.[58]

Pessimism was reinforced by further energy crises, aggravated by new turmoil in the Middle East. In 1980, alarmism became something like official federal policy, when a presidential commission tried to prophesy the state of the world in 2000. The report concluded, "If present trends continue, the world in 2000 will be more crowded, more polluted, less stable ecologically, and more vulnerable to disruption than the world we live in now. . . . Despite greater material output, the world's people will be poorer in many ways than they are today."[59]

In some respects, the report proved accurate, but the image of a world starving and shivering was far from correct. The problem with the report's conclusion, and other such projections, lay in the words "If present trends continue," as of course they did not. Like *The Limits of Growth* before it, *Global 2000* made no acknowledgment of the vast productive resources that would be released by surging technological advances, coupled with increased economic globalization and freer trade. In reality, the proportion of the world's people living in dire poverty would roughly halve between 1981 and 2001, from 40 to 21 percent. At the time, though, such qualifications seemed unthinkably optimistic, and the media reinforced the report's jeremiads. Headlines spoke of "gloom and doom quantified," while *Time* found the "global outlook extremely bleak." The magazine imagined "Earth, a desolate planet slowly dying of its own accumulated follies."[60] If these were the futures imagined by secular and scientific leaders, who supported their views with what seemed solid evidence, it is scarcely surprising that religious believers in the late 1970s so easily accepted warnings of imminent doomsday and judgment, with all that implied for political activism.

Societies such as those confidently predicted for near-future America would be nasty, brutish places, in which anything like contemporary liberal democracy would be untenable. Some speculated that something like the dragooned anthill society of Chinese Maoism might be the only possible means of survival. So awful were the prospects that through the decade, and especially after 1975, writers imagined various responses to apocalypse, whether through overt revolution or withdrawal from a dying Babylon. Paul Callenbach's *Ecotopia* imagined a utopian society in the Pacific Northwest, though one created only by an act of separatism enforced by threats of nuclear terrorism. The book influenced William Pierce's *The Turner Diaries* (written under the pseudonym Andrew MacDonald), the story of a racial apocalypse, from which would emerge a Nazi-dominated white world. Though the book remained little known to the general public before some devotees tried to implement its vision in Oklahoma City in 1995, *The Turner Diaries* is firmly rooted in the conflicts of 1975. Gerald Vizenor's *Bearheart* imagined white Americans fleeing from a collapsing society to take refuge in Indian reservations.[61] One 1977 best-seller, *Lucifer's Hammer,* used the disaster format to deliver a socially conservative message. After the world has been devastated by a giant meteor strike, some farsighted Americans survive because they have withdrawn to remote rural fastnesses, from which they hope to restore the old society by high technology and nuclear power. They are challenged by a neo-Luddite army fanatically opposed to technology, a murderous cult bound together by ritual cannibalism.[62]

In the real world, fears of social collapse drove survivalist believers to flee the doomed cities and move to remote compounds or settlements. The idea of survivalism owes much to the work of science fiction writer Robert Heinlein, who pointed out in the 1950s that ordinary citizens had an excellent means of surviving nuclear war, namely, by being somewhere else when the bombs hit. Survivalism became a popular movement in the doomsday atmosphere of the mid-1970s, when it merged with a paramilitary culture based in the anti-Communist right, a movement pledged to maintain aggressively traditional concepts of manhood. From its first appearance in 1975, the magazine *Soldier of Fortune* developed a sizable following among paramilitary buffs and armchair mercenaries. Religious belief also led many out of the cities, as fringe religious movements and cults relocated to rural settlements.[63] When the 1960s ended, the model alternative settlement was the utopian hippie commune, the idyllic haven depicted in *Easy Rider*, potentially the nucleus of a new cooperative society. A decade later, the popular image of the remote retreat was the cult compound or the survivalist fortress.[64]

In *Nashville*, a country song celebrating the bicentennial includes the chorus "We must be doing something right to last two hundred years." In 1976, it was difficult to think just how such a troubled nation could have come so far, or how, realistically, it could survive much longer. But the very depth of the national crisis also meant real opportunities for any political voices that could provide alternative analyses to the conventional wisdom and offer real hope.[65] Only by understanding the thorough pessimism of these years can we understand the amazing appeal of Ronald Reagan a few years later, when a national leader actually gave the impression of believing that the United States might indeed have a future worth living in.

3

Against the Grain

*Our struggle is not against enemies of blood and flesh but against
the rulers, against the authorities, against the cosmic powers of this
present darkness, against the spiritual forces of evil in the heavenly
places.*

—Ephesians 6:12

The problem with writing modern history is that surprise endings are out
of the question. Everyone knows that Ronald Reagan won the presidency in
1980, and his coattails swept many key liberals from Congress. During the
1980s, American politics shifted substantially to the right, and many of the
liberal commonplaces of the bicentennial era fell out of favor. But hindsight
can also suggest a sense of inevitability. During the eulogies that followed
Reagan's death in 2004, it was rarely recalled just how widely he was once
regarded as unacceptably extreme. In 1966, the *New Republic* argued
that "Reagan is anti-labor, anti-Negro, anti-intellectual, anti-planning,
anti-20th Century," while during the 1970s, he was commonly bracketed
with George Wallace as the electoral face of the ultra-right.[1] The fact that the
Republicans won the presidency is scarcely surprising: even in 1976, with
Watergate and the Nixon pardon constantly in the background, Gerald Ford
came surprisingly close to victory. But the success of a leader as militantly
conservative as Ronald Reagan indicates the scale of the political shift that
had occurred since the mid-1970s.

Through the years of liberal social policies in the 1960s, a substantial share
of the electorate showed itself deeply unhappy with the ongoing cultural
revolution, though it could rarely make its voice heard in mainstream
political debate. The winner-take-all nature of the American political
system obscures the existence of minorities, even if they run into the tens
of millions. One constant in American political life is the 40-percent rule

—namely, that it is difficult for even the weakest presidential candidate from a major party to win much less than that proportion of the electorate. On the Democratic side, the party suffered electoral massacres in 1972 and 1984, and in each case the losing candidate was mocked as unelectable. Yet in each year, the Democratic standard-bearer—respectively George McGovern and Walter Mondale—earned around 40 percent of the popular vote. Even amidst the horrors of 1980, 41 percent of Americans voted for Jimmy Carter. On the Republican side, the equally "unelectable" Barry Goldwater took 39 percent of the popular vote in 1964.[2]

We can scarcely describe the Goldwater vote as a conservative hard core, since the meaning of conservatism would change so much over the next decade or two, but at least that figure indicates a sizable population skeptical of liberal rhetoric. Over the following decade, that conservative base would be swelled by alienated recruits from traditional Democratic constituencies. Goldwater united the historic currents of the American right with newer, emerging concerns and fears.[3] Conservatives made enormous gains within the Republican Party, based partly on new forms of organization and voter mobilization. But their victories would not have been possible if they were not able to appeal to a mass public ready to respond to a message radically different from the liberal orthodoxies of the time. Popular anger and fear were aroused by perceptions of military weakness and international decline, but these issues were intimately linked to threats to the most basic realities of life: family structures and gender roles, neighborhood and community.[4]

In each case, conservative victories were assisted by the extremism of their opponents. In mid-decade, liberals obstinately refused to accept that enemies might exist on the left or overseas, and acted as if they saw the U.S. government as the source of evil. Liberal politicians showed little willingness to take seriously fears of national decline or Communist subversion, giving the impression that they regarded such concerns as cynical flag-waving, intended to distract from real-world economic matters. Within the United States too, liberal policies seemed to assume that mainstream white opinion was automatically racist and demanded to be overridden. Portraying people constantly as deadly enemies is scarcely a way of winning their sympathy, and to that extent, liberal complaints about the backlash of the late 1970s are disingenuous. Conservatives were not so much peddling fear as taking seriously fears that were already widespread, and doing so in a way that encouraged acceptance of other parts of their agenda.

Conservatives effectively intertwined the traditional themes of "high" politics with social issues, applying to both a familiar moralist and religious rhetoric. Exponents of sixties liberationism had stressed that the personal was political. Conservatives accepted this equation and carried it much further: the realm of personal moral choice was indistinguishable from that of national politics, law and order, defense and diplomacy. And in each of these areas, good and evil mattered.

Silent Majorities

Steven Hayward has traced the theme of the progressive administrative state through twentieth-century American history. Beginning in the Progressive Era, the idea that government should intervene vigorously to promote social progress was revived massively in the New Deal of the 1930s and again in the Great Society envisioned by Lyndon Johnson. In each case, the proper activity of politics concerned economic management and the removal of obstacles that kept social or racial groups from participating fully in American prosperity. Of course, government dealt with other issues as well, such as foreign threats or internal security, but in domestic affairs, economic matters prevailed. To paraphrase James Carville, it's always the economy, stupid. Though democratic values must be respected, administration was ultimately an affair for highly trained experts, technocrats qualified to understand the complicated issues involved. To suggest that the practice of government offered easy answers was foolish or demagogic.[5]

For liberals, politics was a profoundly moral endeavor, but morality was defined in terms of public affairs, of the quest for social justice and—increasingly—for racial justice. Issues of personal morality, gender, or family were not within the proper scope of government, except insofar as they reflected the broader economic agenda. That definition became problematic during the 1960s, as rapid social change threatened basic moral assumptions. In an important article in 1967, James Q. Wilson remarked how public opinion showed time and again how concerned ordinary people were by moral issues, defined in terms of the decline of values and threats to family. Unfortunately, these were simply not things that political parties could or should try to do anything about, since "public debate over virtue is irrelevant or dangerous." As Daniel Patrick Moynihan wrote in this same year of cultural revolution, "Family is not a subject Americans tend to consider appropriate as an area of public policy."[6] Of course, we can reasonably ask which Americans he was writing about. Though much elite opinion saw appeals to public morality as harking back to the censorious world of *The Scarlet Letter,* many ordinary people actively sought public and political intervention to combat social decay.

The strength of this sentiment was suggested by the 1968 presidential campaign of George Wallace, with his populist themes of patriotism, anti-elitism, and hostility to cultural radicalism. Wallace's forthright attacks on hippies, anti-war protesters, anarchists, "pinhead" socialist theorists, and treacherous intellectuals suggests how easy it would be for conservatives to force a wedge into the Democratic coalition.[7] Wallace's central point was that political elites in both parties had fallen badly out of touch with the values and concerns of ordinary people. One of the best arguments in favor of his position was the widespread media consensus that he was a racial demagogue pure and simple and that his issues were entirely based on the manipulation of racial fears. In some ways that analysis is fair; in others it is not. The charge of demagoguery surfaced particularly when he highlighted street crime, a concept that seemed to be political code for the racial threat posed by African-Americans. Yet most urban residents, white and black, had a thoroughly justified fear of rising violent crime rates and doubted that the problem would be dealt with by Great Society economic reforms. Repeatedly over the following years, liberals argued that because conservative protests must be rooted in racist bigotry, they did not need to be treated as serious arguments. So paramount was the rhetoric of race that little respect was accorded to the language of community, values, and family. Apart from the crime issue, similar contempt was accorded to the community concerns that led to the anti-busing movement, while attacks on evangelical schools antagonized religious conservatives. In each case, heavy-handed official action made grassroots opposition even more determined.

Wallace himself earned 13 percent of the popular vote in 1968, nearly ten million votes, which was more than enough to swing the election to Richard Nixon. Nixon successfully adopted Wallace's populism, first in 1968 and again in 1972, when Spiro Agnew tarred the Democrats as the party of cultural subversion, of "acid, amnesty [for draft dodgers], and abortion." Though conservatives and Republicans suffered dreadfully as a result of Watergate and the related scandals, the underlying cultural concerns never wholly vanished. In fact, they gained strength due to the actions of the Democratic Party. With the Republican Party in ruins, the Democratic left took the electoral successes of mid-decade as a mandate for radical change, or at least a statement that such changes would not meet significant opposition. That led voters to see the far-reaching social changes of recent years in party political terms and associate them with the Democrats. The further and faster the social revolution advanced and sixties values become mainstream, the more potential there was for something like the Nixon coalition to become a permanent part of the U.S. political landscape.[8]

New Foundations

Conservatives benefited from long-term trends in the structure of American society. Gender issues were critical, given the increasing disaffection of male voters from traditional Democratic constituencies. The 1980 election first drew attention to the gender gap that has since become such a familiar component of electoral affairs. In that year, Ronald Reagan won the support of 54 percent of men but only 46 percent of women, the largest such disparity recorded since data were compiled in the early 1950s. Jimmy Carter attracted the votes of 45 percent of women but 37 percent of men. George H. W. Bush would win the 1988 election with a 7 percent gender gap, and the underlying trend has often reappeared in later years. In both 1996 and 2000, an 11-point gender gap divided the presidential candidates, as Democrats Clinton and Gore massively outpolled Republicans among women voters. The gender gap in itself does not necessarily benefit either party: provided the votes are there, the sex of the voter scarcely matters. But the split was especially damaging for what had, since the 1930s, been an overwhelmingly powerful Democratic alliance.

Regional alignments also shifted. Since the 1930s, Democratic Party power had been based on an unlikely alliance between white southerners, northern urban voters (especially from newer ethnic stocks), and liberal intellectuals. By the 1970s, the southern side of the coalition was dissolving, which was all the more alarming because of demographic shifts in these years. In 1975, Kirkpatrick Sale's prophetic book *Power Shift* warned of "the rise of the southern rim and its challenge to the eastern establishment." The proportion of Americans living in the statistical regions known as the South and West rose from 46 percent in 1960 to 58 percent by 2000.[9]

As Sunbelt states grew, they acquired steadily more electoral votes, while those of their northern counterparts contracted. Between 1952 and 2002, the combined electoral strength of New York, Ohio, and Pennsylvania slipped from 129 to 93 electoral votes. In the same years, Texas, Florida, and California grew from 66 votes to 116. As people moved to those regions and electoral votes gradually moved with them, American politics would be shaped by the different patterns characteristic of the Sunbelt. Among other things, the West had a long tradition of resentment of eastern domination and suspicion that an effete and socialistic East Coast was trying to restrict western independence and initiative. During the 1970s, this hostility found political expression in the so-called Sagebrush Rebellion, hostility to excessive environmental regulation and federal control of vast western lands.[10]

Increasingly too, white southern voters abandoned the Democratic Party, or as they saw it, the party abandoned them.[11] Conservatism had powerful roots in this region, partly but not exclusively because of racial conflicts. Democratic allegiance cracked irreparably with the civil rights movement. When in 1964 five southern states favored Goldwater, racial resentments undoubtedly dominated their decision. But other issues also became prominent, including gun ownership. Though gun owners and hunters had long been represented by political pressure groups such as the National Rifle Association, these were not traditionally partisan. In the 1960s, though, concern about urban violence inspired new federal restrictions on gun ownership, most controversially a comprehensive 1968 law. During the liberal hegemony of the mid-1970s, activists sought even stricter controls: Handgun Control Inc. was founded in 1974. Cheap, easily accessible weapons—so-called Saturday-night specials—were the initial targets of political wrath and media exposés, but the ultimate goal was evidently the prohibition of all private handgun ownership. Gun rights advocates saw an alarming portent when the District of Columbia enacted the nation's most stringent control measures, prohibiting the possession of any handgun acquired or registered after the start of 1977. Gun ownership was a sensitive theme in many rural areas and was especially symbolic in the South and West, where it connoted a whole mythology of outdoor culture and masculine camaraderie. Gun laws also focused fears about crime and the sense that governments were forbidding law-abiding private citizens from exercising means of self-defense. The history of handgun control suggests the divergence of political attitudes. An early advocate was Pete Shields, whose son had fallen victim to the Zebra killers. While Shields felt that reducing access to guns would help solve America's violence problem, conservatives argued instead for the effective suppression of predatory criminals and terrorists.[12]

When concerns about crime were taken alongside issues of gender and sexuality, America was facing pervasive cultural conflicts in which the South became a conservative bastion. Republicans commanded a solid South in the presidential contest of 1980 (except for Carter's home state of Georgia) and swept the region in 1984 and 1988. In 1984 also, Reagan drew on an absolutely solid West, and a Reagan campaign official could boast, "We have built an electoral fortress in the South and West. We can withstand anything in this campaign—any mistake, anything at all, and still win." The nation's modern political divisions—red and blue, retro and metro—were taking shape. By 2004, Republicans held eighteen of the twenty-two Senate seats from the states that had made up the old Confederacy.[13]

The one exception to this record of Republican success was itself significant, since in 1976 Jimmy Carter won all southern states except for Virginia. Carter was of course a southerner, but as a very public Baptist, he attracted a large evangelical vote that was conservative on social issues.[14] Carter was the first president to speak openly of being "born again," a term that baffled the national news media but struck an instant chord across the South. Southerners responded enthusiastically when he urged, "We should live our lives as though Christ were coming this afternoon." The electoral force of the Sunbelt encouraged a greater prominence for explicitly religious factors in national public life. This rising conservatism also linked domestic and foreign issues in a way that now seems absolutely commonplace but which was then not seen as quite so inevitable. In Barry Goldwater's time, a conservative could be extremely hard-line on issues of foreign policy, defense, and anti-Communism while liberal or libertarian on moral and sexual issues, but the southernization of American politics made such an ideological profile untenable.

If not quite so thoroughly, white ethnic and working-class voters were also detaching from automatic Democratic allegiance. These groups were repeatedly hit by the conflicts of the 1960s, the fear of urban rioting and crime, a patriotic reaction against the anti-war movement, and concerns over changes in sexual morality. Industrial workers were also deeply involved in growing disputes over affirmative action. And the growing crisis facing older industries during the 1970s weakened the unions that were the traditional mainstays of Democratic organization and fund-raising. Successful newer industries often sprang up in states with strong right-to-work laws, and in 1977, the manufacturer-supported Council on Union-Free Environment was created to coordinate anti-union activism. The proportion of the workforce enrolled in unions shrank from a historic high of 35 percent in 1954 to 23 percent in 1980 and just 12.5 percent today. Taking just the private sector, the proportion of unionized workers has contracted from around a third in 1955 to barely eight percent in 2006.[15]

Religion played its role in political change, since Catholics made up an increasing share of the white urban population. As Catholic communities had invested so heavily in buildings and institutions, it was far more difficult for them to uproot and move to the suburbs than it was for Jews or white Protestants. This placed white Catholics in the forefront of resistance to racial change in old ethnic neighborhoods. In the long term, Catholics did not become a Republican constituency as firm in their loyalty as the old Democratic monolith, but they demonstrated a greater willingness to vote for parties or candidates on selected issues, and in many cases it was Republicans who benefited. White voters who moved to the suburbs worried that the ills that characterized the cities could spread to their own communities and, above all, to their own children. Though fears about urban problems might be well grounded, they were reinforced by racial stereotypes. Most obviously, drug use was symbolically associated with urban minority cultures. Seen from the suburbs, gangs represented another inner-city curse that should not be allowed to spread.[16]

Meanwhile, disputes within the Democratic Party set the radical exponents of the new politics against the old urban ethnic machines, which were portrayed as corrupt and racist. At the end of the 1960s, the left viewed Chicago mayor Richard Daley's efficient Democratic machine as an adversary almost as pernicious as the Nixon White House itself. In Philadelphia, hard-line police chief Frank Rizzo became a hate figure for liberals, though this opposition did not prevent him from serving as Democratic mayor from 1972 through 1980. In 1972, a new set of rules devised by George McGovern radically changed the composition of the Democratic convention, demanding much greater representation of women and minorities and limiting the power of traditional political leaders. In a massive symbolic defeat, an Illinois delegation headed by Mayor Daley was rejected in favor of a group headed by the Reverend Jesse Jackson. Democratic Party conventions became increasingly representative in the sense that organized feminist and gay groups were much in evidence, as were ethnic minorities, but the traditional urban machines that spoke for "white ethnics" were not to be seen. Inclusiveness had its limits.[17]

Urban tensions made white voters far more amenable to conservative arguments about the roots of social problems. Poverty was seen as a matter of personal failings and irresponsibility, rather than as a product of a flawed economic order. The fecklessness that supposedly created such social dysfunctions as illegitimacy, unemployment, and welfare dependency was itself the product of overly generous government and the Great Society. From this perspective, not only did government fail to recognize the importance of personal morality and responsibility, but it actively fought against it by offering disincentives to work. By destroying character, anti-poverty programs directly promoted poverty and blighted communities, while the welfare trap visited the social curse on new generations. And far from being a response to poverty, crime was simply a product of personal immorality or evil. Government could indeed help solve social problems, but through emphasizing policing and deterrence, rather than sinking more money into welfare policies.

The Politics of God

While social and ethnic changes were creating a potential power base for conservatives, so also was the Protestant religious revival then gaining momentum. When discussing religion in the post-1965 decade, academic commentators and journalists usually focused on the mainstream churches that were then experiencing such divisive debate over accommodating secular liberalism. The Roman Catholic Church was absorbing the full impact of the second Vatican Council, while liberal mainline churches such as the Episcopalians and Lutherans were divided over the ordination of women. The future of the churches seemed to lie in still greater liberalization, with a greater emphasis on social activism in the secular city.[18]

In reality, the religious bodies enjoying the greatest success in these years were at the opposite end of the theological spectrum, among the evangelicals and fundamentalists. Between the late 1960s and mid-1980s, liberal denominations such as the Episcopalians, Methodists, and Presbyterians suffered an alarming drop in membership, losing 20 or 30 percent of their faithful in two decades. In the same years, conservative churches such as the Southern Baptists and Assemblies of God were recording increases of 50 or 100 percent. (Meanwhile, Orthodox and Hasidic groups enjoyed impressive growth, representing an ever-larger proportion of American Jews.) In a time when all human institutions and orthodoxies were crumbling and the world might be facing terminal crisis, people naturally sought firm teachings and definitive answers. Alongside the much-touted drift to cults and therapy movements was a vastly larger and more enduring movement toward evangelical religion, manifested in the rise of new Christian denominations, para-church networks, and megachurches. The vast Willow Creek congregation, near Chicago, was founded in 1975. In 1976, the Calvary Chapel movement spawned the congregation that would soon become the Vineyard denomination, one of the fastest-growing religious organizations in modern America. The rising evangelical movement found an organizational focus in the televangelism ministries of pastors such as Jim Bakker, Oral Roberts, Rex Humbard, and Pat Robertson, who exploited the opportunities opened by cable television. As early as 1977, Robertson's Christian Broadcasting Network (CBN) built its own satellite earth station. Evangelicals reached local communities through Christian bookstores and publishing ventures as well as the churches. The Evangelical Christian Publishers Association dates from 1974.[19]

The denominational shift was accompanied by a revived emphasis on traditional theological orthodoxies and biblical literalism. In 1979, a leadership coup within the Southern Baptist Convention placed the sixteen-million-strong denomination firmly in the hands of strict conservatives. Beyond the organized churches, we can also see a widespread taste for ideas of supernatural evil and the demonic: the furor over the 1973 film *The Exorcist* was accompanied by a substantial revival of beliefs in spiritual warfare and exorcism. A wave of devil films followed in mid-decade, as *The Omen* and its sequels popularized the idea of the Antichrist. In 1975–76, the nonfiction best-seller lists were headed by Billy Graham's *Angels: God's Secret Agents.*[20]

Unlike their predecessors, who scorned and feared worldly politics, the newer churches were more activist, interpreting secular matters in prophetic and apocalyptic terms. The evangelical political constituency first stirred in opposition to the Supreme Court's school prayer decisions of the 1960s, but the new gender politics provided many incentives to activism. One key influence was Francis A. Schaeffer, whose *How Should We Then Live?* and other books encouraged a generation of seminary students to explore secular philosophy and literature and to appreciate the Christian roots of an imperiled Western civilization. (*Newsweek* called Schaeffer the "guru of fundamentalism.") For Schaeffer, abortion and secular humanism represented an evil perversion of this tradition, which future generations would dismiss as equivalent to the horrors of the Nazis. The book discussed "the rise and decline of Western thought and culture." Also crucial was the apocalyptic strain derived from Hal Lindsey's 1970 book, *The Late Great Planet Earth.* From such books, evangelicals acquired an abiding interest in "signs of the times," moments in secular politics that might portend the great religious changes foretold in the Christian scriptures, especially in the Books of Daniel and Revelation. The re-creation of the state of Israel in 1948 signified that the prophetic clock was now ticking, that the countdown to doomsday had begun: for believers, any remaining doubts about this timetable were dispelled by the Israeli reunification of Jerusalem in 1967. As read by Lindsey and others, the critical moment would come when the forces of Communism launched their inevitable assault on the state of Israel. Middle Eastern crises, the formation of the European Economic Community, the growth of Soviet power, and the likelihood of nuclear confrontation were all read into this schema.[21]

The growing churches largely accepted premillenarian theories, that is, the idea that dreadful conflicts and persecutions would ravage the world before the final vindication of God's rule and the thousand-year reign of Christ on earth. In the immediate future, believers could expect the rising power of diabolical forces on the earth, the subversion of morality, and a frontal satanic attack on the churches, leading to the temporary triumph of an Antichrist figure. These ideas were popularized in the 1972 film *Thief in the Night,* one of the most widely viewed films of all time. Its enthusiasts claim a total audience of some three hundred million since its release. Secular politics thus had a potent religious dimension. According to this worldview, America was disarming morally at a time of desperate confrontation with the literal forces of evil, symbolized by the Soviets and their radical Middle Eastern allies. In their attacks on the traditional family and gender roles, their advocacy of abortion and homosexuality, liberals were subverting the most basic components of Christian morality.[22]

From this perspective, children were the main targets of liberal propaganda, making the public schools a critical theater for a moralist counterattack. Through the 1980s, opinion polls regularly suggested that around half of all Americans believed firmly in the biblical creation as taught in the Book of Genesis, dismissing evolution as a secularist fad, and most wanted to see creationism taught or at least acknowledged in the public schools. Federal courts, though, sternly resisted any infusion of religion into public education. School textbooks were another sensitive issue, as local campaigns tried to remove radical or sexually explicit materials from classrooms and school libraries around the nation. A Texas couple, Mel and Norma Gabler, pioneered effective textbook campaigns that were imitated across the United States. From the evangelical point of view, school busing was feared not so much because it promoted racial mixing but because it deliberately removed children and the educational process from the community and from any element of family control.[23] The times demanded comprehensive political activism. And given the role of federal courts in implementing an unwelcome cultural revolution, the political response must of necessity be directed toward taking power at national level, and ultimately to controlling the presidency.

Gender Politics

With the departure of Richard Nixon and the end of the Vietnam War, cultural issues became paramount in American politics, with a wholly new urgency in light of the liberal triumphs of the past few years. Just how rapidly political assumptions were changing is suggested by the history of the federal Equal Rights Amendment (ERA). This amendment, passed by Congress in 1972, declared, "Equality of rights under the law shall not be denied or abridged by the United States or by any state on account of sex."

The ERA needed to be ratified by thirty-eight states in order to obtain the three-quarters majority demanded by the U.S. Constitution. At first, passage seemed straightforward, and thirty states had agreed by the end of 1973. Gaining the remaining eight seemed like an easy formality, a matter of months rather than years. Initially, the ERA stirred strikingly little opposition, even in conservative states. Support for the amendment was part of the Republican Party platform through 1976, and both Gerald Ford and Ronald Reagan were supporters.[24] At this stage, gender issues scarcely divided the parties, which remained focused on matters of "real" politics, economic affairs, law and order, war and peace, and attitudes toward Communism.

But the popular reaction provoked by the ERA signaled a critical change in the definition of national politics. Horrified opponents claimed that the ERA might provide a constitutional basis for abortion, for homosexual rights, including marriage, and for the military conscription of women. The pioneering conservative activist was Phyllis Schlafly, who prior to 1972 was best known for her concern with national defense issues and her opposition to the SALT I agreement. In that year, however, she formed a STOP ERA campaign, which won a series of victories that contradicted the common media assumptions about the overwhelming support for political feminism. (STOP ERA later morphed into the Eagle Forum.) Four more states ratified the ERA in 1974 and 1975, none in 1976, and one in 1977. ERA supporters remained three states short of the required total, while battles raged in statehouses around the nation. Meanwhile, several states that had ratified in the early years of enthusiasm now tried to withdraw their support, despite doubts about the constitutionality of rescission. ERA supporters faced failure, since the ratification process was approaching its 1979 expiration date, and a three-year extension failed to win any more states.[25]

The anti-ERA movement reflects the new regional alignments in American politics, as resistance to ratification was concentrated largely in the South and Southwest. Of the fifteen states that held out against ratification, nine had been members of the old Confederacy, leaving only Texas and Tennessee in the column of supporters. The remaining holdouts included Oklahoma, Missouri, Arizona, Utah, Nevada, and—in this curious company—Illinois. The list of anti-ERA states becomes even more solidly southern and western when we included such rescission states as Kentucky, Tennessee, Idaho, and Nebraska. With some obvious exceptions, such as Illinois, a map of opposition to ERA foreshadows the electoral geography of modern-day Republicanism.

ERA brought to the center of American political life fears about changing gender roles, the fate of the family, and the state of masculinity. These fears were summarized in George Gilder's assault on feminism in his 1973 book *Sexual Suicide*, which would powerfully influence moral conservatives. Gilder saw ERA and legalized abortion as part of an explicit revolutionary assault on the most basic features of humanity as known hitherto, an assault that would literally destroy civilization. Wrote Gilder, "There are no human beings; there are just men and women and when they deny their divergent sexuality, they reject the deepest sources of identity and love. They commit sexual suicide." Meanwhile, he argued, feminism caused untold social damage, most immediately to men: "The feminist program thus usually consists of taking jobs and money away from men, while granting in return such uncoveted benefits as the right to cry." But more worrying agendas threatened the whole society. The attack on the family would ultimately benefit only the state, which was seeking the right to shape the values of children. Gilder asked, "Will the scientists and women's liberationists be able to unleash on the world a generation of kinless children to serve as the Red Guards of a totalitarian state?" Gilder also used another argument that would become powerful among conservatives: that the reactionary views of ordinary people over gender roles, sexuality, and abortion represented authentic popular wisdom against elite faddery. Most people "still instinctively recognize that preservation of the sexual constitution may be even more important to the social order than preservation of the legal constitution."[26]

Gender controversies mobilized religious organizations in a way that had not been seen for decades. The most effective attacks against ERA generally came from religious groups, including evangelicals and particularly Baptists, who reasserted traditional gender roles; so did Mormons in the West. Another powerful voice was the Roman Catholic Church, which ever since the New Deal had been closely tied to the Democratic Party and had generally supported organized labor and liberal social causes. In the civil rights era, the church was clearly on the side of racial equality. By the 1970s, though, as gender issues came to the fore, the church increasingly found itself cast on the conservative side of the political divide. In the ERA debates, the Catholic hierarchy opposed ratification because of fears that the law might provoke attacks on single-sex education or inspire federal courts to mandate the ordination of women.[27]

The ERA campaigns coincided with the Catholic reaction to the *Roe v. Wade* decision of 1973. Catholics were the leading promoters of the National Right to Life Committee, founded that year, with affiliates in each state. Over the next few years, anti-abortion campaigns provided a common platform for religious activists who once would have felt little in common, as Catholics worked closely with evangelicals. *Roe v. Wade* was a pivotal moment in the redefinition of right and left, conservative and liberal, in the American political system.[28]

Apart from the immediate detonator issues of abortion and the ERA, other moral crusades beckoned through the middle of the decade. One issue was pornography, which was becoming so readily available. Following the example of ERA, this issue seemed to demand local organization through a kind of citizen initiative. The Supreme Court opened the way to this activism by allowing community standards to be a criterion for assessing whether a work was obscene. But how was "community" to be defined when a magazine or film was widely circulated? A magazine might not be obscene by the standards of Los Angeles, where it was produced, but it might shock a less liberated community in which it was bought and viewed. Obscenity battles raged through 1976 and 1977. In one instance, the city of Wichita prosecuted the New York–based magazine *Screw,* which was mailed to local subscribers, while Memphis prosecuted an actor from the film *Deep Throat* after that was shown locally. In 1976, Cincinnati prosecuted Larry Flynt's *Hustler.*

Unsettling urban legends indicated popular alarm about pornography. One concerned the "snuff film," portraying the actual murder of a victim. Though such products might have existed, the vast majority of alleged instances of snuff films prove to be fictitious, and the tale can usually be traced to a friend of a friend. The genuine cinematic release *Snuff* (1976), which appeared to justify all the public outrage, was in fact a straightforward exploitation film based on a Manson-like cult. None of the principals suffered any actual violence, apart from the damage inflicted on their careers. Equally spurious was the porn film alleged to be forthcoming through 1976–77, *The Sex Life of Jesus Christ.*

Yet for all the myths, enough truly unsettling material was circulating to generate real qualms even among liberals who previously would have had nothing to do with campaigns against smut. Even some convinced libertarians denounced *Snuff,* as did many feminists, and anti-rape activists denounced porn for promoting violence against women. As activist Robin Morgan wrote, "Pornography is the theory, rape is the practice." Susan Brownmiller declared, "If the porno houses were devoted to the lynching of blacks or the gassing of Jews, you would not find so many civil libertarians rushing to their defense." In 1976, pornography featuring bestiality, violence, and adult-child sex attracted protests in New York City. Responding to the protests, *Time* devoted special coverage to "The Porno Plague," warning that "America is deep into its Age of Porn. . . . How will the current avalanche of porn change America? Many who oppose censorship now wonder if the mounting taste for porn is a symptom of decay, of corrosive boredom, of withdrawal from social concern for obsessive personal pleasures." "The worst conceivable outcome of the porno plague" would be "a brutalizing of the American psyche that turns U.S. society into the world portrayed in *A Clockwork Orange.*" Through the decade, Kubrick's classic film would frequently be cited as a dreadful prophecy of the nihilistic social order that could emerge if social restraints collapsed, as they appeared to be doing in the mid-1970s.[29]

The Present Danger

Also in the mid-1970s, conservatives were winning support for their attacks on Communism and for their urgent calls for the United States to acknowledge the Soviet danger. Some activists were old Goldwater stalwarts, such as Phyllis Schlafly, but by the mid-1970s, anti-Communism was acquiring a quite different constituency, since many of the most vocal activists described themselves as Democrats. In this instance too, New Deal alignments were fragmenting. From the earliest days of the New Deal, Democrats had been divided over how far their coalition could extend to the left and how far it might form a tactical alliance with Communism. That issue was thought settled in the mid-1940s, when the Democratic Party became a comfortable home for anti-Communist liberals, who shared many assumptions with working-class ethnic and Catholic voters. But by the early 1970s, the anti-Communist front was fractured by the rise of pacifism, anti-war radicalism, and the furious conspiracy theories surrounding the U.S. intelligence agencies. If not actually Communist—since that party had faded to insignificance—the foreign policy stance of many liberals made them passionately anti-anti-Communist. The Communist issue drove some old liberals to highly conservative positions.[30]

The end of the Vietnam War allowed a new perception of the Communist threat, as Communist conduct in the months following the fall of Saigon seemed to justify the discredited domino theory in both Asia and Africa. Communist atrocities were now described in sources far removed from the traditional domestic far right. The brutality of Communist rule was illustrated by the harrowing accounts of the Khmer Rouge regime in Cambodia and by the visual evidence of the exodus of boat people from Vietnam. Though Alexander Solzhenitsyn's *Gulag Archipelago* (1974) told academics little they had not already known about Soviet history, the publicity surrounding the book gave a new emphasis to the Communist legacy of repression and mass murder. Its lasting legacy was the word *gulag* itself, which reminded Westerners that the Soviet system was based on concentration camps much like those of the Nazis.[31]

But this perspective on the evils of Communism ran contrary to the policies of successive U.S. administrations, which moved away from any prospect of confrontation. At the same time, liberals could expect no improvement from any conceivable Democratic administration. In 1972, facing a party in the hands of McGovernite radicals, anti-Communist liberals formed their own pressure group, the Coalition for a Democratic Majority, which found its natural leader in hawkish Washington senator Henry "Scoop" Jackson. Democratic divisions intensified when a radicalized party went down to crushing electoral defeat, while the 1973 oil crisis raised troubling questions about the United States' capacity to defend its interests worldwide. For the old liberals, soon to be known as neoconservatives, the radical emphasis on the evils of the U.S. government and the CIA was not only absurd but extraordinarily dangerous in a world at risk from an aggressive and expansionist Soviet Union. Far from being willing to confront the new dangers, U.S. elites seemed to accept a Spenglerian view of the ongoing decline of the West, and an ever-shrinking Western role in the Third World.[32]

Jewish issues played a major role in the political realignment. American Jews were traditionally among the most liberal of communities, but by the late 1960s, urban Jews often found themselves in conflict with radical minority activists, who sometimes espoused anti-Semitic rhetoric. In the academic world, meanwhile, Jewish students and faculty were especially likely to suffer from affirmative action policies favoring African-Americans. During the 1970s, Jewish allegiance to liberalism was severely tested by the growing threats to the existence of the state of Israel. Attacks on Israel at the United Nations aroused anger at the Soviet-bloc nations—which were arming the Arab powers—and against their Third World allies. Also, the USSR was home to several million Jews, most of whom wished to emigrate to Israel or other nations. Though the Soviets staunchly refused permission, American hawks felt that they could be forced to change their attitude by a combination of threats and enticements. In 1974, the Jackson-Vanik Amendment made the extension of trade benefits to the USSR conditional on that nation's emigration policies.[33]

Reinforcing Jewish alarm about international threats was the new emphasis during the 1970s on the Holocaust not just as a historical tragedy but as a unique defining moment in Western civilization, a transcendent manifestation of moral evil. Extensive new research and writing fostered awareness of the event, which reached a mass audience with the 1978 miniseries *Holocaust*. As Peter Novick argues, by the 1970s the civil religion of most American Jews had at its core the Holocaust and the state of Israel. Together, these two historical facts offered a powerful mythical narrative of the near-annihilation of a people, followed by national resurrection. Studying the Holocaust contributed to a sense that supernatural evil might be manifested in present political realities as much as in historical events. To this extent at least, quite liberal Jews shared the mind-set of evangelical Christians, who sympathized with Zionist aspirations. These historical connotations gave added power to contemporary complaints of anti-Semitism. As the Israeli ambassador to the UN noted, the "Zionism is racism" debate occurred on the anniversary of Kristallnacht.[34]

The Entebbe crisis of 1976 contributed to these fears and stereotypes, and again had a special impact on Jews. The story began when hijackers seized an Air France jet, with the specific goal of seizing large numbers of Israeli hostages. (By this time, El Al aircraft were so heavily defended that attacks on them generally resulted in bloody defeats for terrorists.) The Air France attack was undertaken by a combined team of Palestinian Arabs and German militants, immediately linking the diverse terrorist menaces worldwide and placing them in an anti-Zionist and anti-Semitic context. The aircraft then flew to Uganda, where the terrorists were allied with a black Third World dictator who notoriously compared himself to Hitler. The hostages were divided between Jews and non-Jews, a moment that inevitably recalled the Holocaust era, when Jews were selected for extermination. In the television movies arising from the event—*Victory at Entebbe* (1976) and *Raid on Entebbe* (1977)—the specifically German context of the anti-Semitism is heavily stressed, with the German terrorists portrayed almost as reincarnated concentration camp guards. Terrorism, Third World radicalism, and anti-Semitism merged symbolically. The dazzling Israeli rescue mission proved, triumphantly, that armed force could and should serve as the proper response to such menaces. It did not take great imagination to extend these lessons to the confrontation with Communism.[35]

One focus of neoconservative hope was Daniel Patrick Moynihan, who in 1975 served as ambassador to the United Nations. Though Moynihan's credentials were socially liberal, he denounced the UN's chronic anti-Western and antidemocratic biases. (The organization's secretary general, Kurt Waldheim, criticized the Entebbe raid as a violation of Ugandan sovereignty.) Moynihan's furious response to the 1975 anti-Zionism resolution made him a hero in the United States. The outpouring of popular support indicates the desperate hunger for someone who would visibly stand up for America and its values in an international forum. The British representative to the UN condemned Moynihan's confrontational speeches, complaining, "Whatever else the place is, it is not the OK Corral, and I am hardly Wyatt Earp." The remark suggests an enduring gap between U.S. and European cultures. In Europe, cowboy imagery suggests boyish immaturity. In a U.S. context, though, it continues to imply toughness, virility, and the sort of attitude that many felt appropriate in the international setting of the time. Moynihan's "cowboy" approach propelled him to overwhelming victory in the 1976 New York contest for the U.S. Senate.[36]

Through 1975 and 1976, conservative and neoconservative critics denounced American weakness in the face of the USSR. Kissinger was blamed for urging President Ford not to be photographed with Solzhenitsyn in order to avoid international embarrassments. Protests reached new heights at the end of 1975, just as Congress intervened to cut off aid to anti-Communist forces in Angola. In December, Kissinger's aide Hal Sonnenfeldt appeared to state a troubling foreign policy doctrine: "So it must be our policy to strive for an evolution that makes the relationship between the Eastern Europeans and the Soviet Union an organic one." Though the administration denied the exact wording of the remark, the new "doctrine" was a convincing portrait of U.S. actions and goals.[37]

For many ordinary Americans—and certainly not just on the far right —these ideas were anathema. An obvious analogy came to mind. If the Nazi empire still existed, would the United States still seek coexistence of this kind, still strive to avoid provocations, while respecting the legitimate interests of the Reich? For policy makers and liberal media outlets, the analogy was absurd, since the Communists, however misguided, were utterly different from the absolute evil of the Nazis. For conservatives, though, the distinction between Nazis and Communists was a mere matter of terminology—both were totalitarian and genocidal. One could not bargain with the Soviets any more than FDR's generation could have compromised with the Nazis. The notion of moral equivalence never won mass support among a population quite prepared to believe that the Soviets were, like their Nazi predecessors, evil and tyrannical. By 1976, warnings about American weakness were having their effect. That spring, worried about his conservative base, President Ford banned the word *détente* from administration usage.[38]

Growing anti-Soviet feeling had its impact within the administration and the intelligence community, which was already staggering in the face of post-Watergate scandals. From 1973 through 1976, the CIA was headed by William Colby, who purged anti-Soviet hard-liners. Throughout Colby's tenure as director, détente was repeatedly attacked by hawkish figures within the intelligence and defense establishment, including Donald Rumsfeld and

Richard Cheney. Conservatives denounced the CIA and State Department's analysis of Soviet capabilities and intentions, which they were accused of underestimating for political ends. Though Colby rejected criticisms, the hawks won the sympathy of his successor, George H. W. Bush.[39]

In 1976, the CIA established an alternative group of experts, Team B, to analyze all available information on Soviet strengths and intentions. The members of Team B included some well-known hard-liners, including Richard Pipes, Paul Nitze, and Paul Wolfowitz. Predictably, this group offered a much harsher interpretation of Soviet intentions, warned of the USSR's high defense expenditures, and urged much greater Western caution in entering into future arms agreements. Central to the Team B analysis was its view of aggressive Soviet intentions, a quest for victory and domination, which stood in a line of continuity from tsarist times. The Soviets were depicted as predators biding their time before they could strike at a weakened West. If these views were correct, any U.S. concessions over SALT II would simply be encouraging aggression.[40]

The Team B approach has been criticized for its exaggerated view of Soviet power and for its "ideological" approach, though the mainstream intelligence community was no less politicized or ideological in its way. As we now know, the Soviets were nothing like as strong as they appeared in 1976, and their economy was already showing alarming signs of strain. But whatever the value of its ideas, the Team B effort had lasting consequences. Individual team members published extensively and were quoted by journalists, and their views carried weight because they were substantiated by such (apparently) solid insider information. Anti-Soviet positions were popularized by such pressure groups as the bipartisan Committee on the Present Danger, which included Reagan-era luminaries Richard Allen, Jeane Kirkpatrick, George Shultz, William Casey, and Richard Perle. In a statement issued in 1976, the committee warned, "The principal threat to our nation, to world peace and to the cause of human freedom is the Soviet drive for dominance based upon an unparalleled military buildup. . . . The Soviet Union has not altered its long held goal of a world dominated from a single center—Moscow." The committee's alarms about the Finlandization of America, its subordination and emasculation, reached a mass public through books such as Norman Podhoretz's *The Present Danger*.[41]

The New Right

On many issues, then, a number of different constituencies could potentially be drawn into a broad coalition alarmed at the vision of national weakness and social decadence, whether or not members were prepared to accept the label "conservative." The diversity of themes means that such an alliance was anything but inevitable. There is no intrinsic reason why a feminist ERA supporter should not advocate military expansion, or why a gay rights activist should necessarily oppose the right to carry a handgun. The fact that the Catholic hierarchy stood on the political right in the abortion debate did not prevent the church from espousing liberal positions on many other core issues. In terms of the political labels that would become standard in the 1980s, Gerald Ford and Ronald Reagan were quite liberal on social and gender issues.

In practice, though, these different political strands came together at mid-decade in a new right-wing coalition. The symbolic detonator for a new movement occurred in 1974, when the new president, Gerald Ford, chose as his vice president Nelson Rockefeller, the personification of the eastern liberal tradition in the Republican Party. From the opening days of his presidency, then, Ford would meet stiff opposition from his party's infuriated conservatives, who had not forgiven Rockefeller's deadly opposition to Barry Goldwater in 1964. In 1975, conservatives were appalled to find just how liberal First Lady Betty Ford herself was on key issues: she favored handgun control and ERA, saw little harm in marijuana, and thought *Roe v. Wade* "a great, great decision." Conservatives in 1975 feared Betty Ford's behind-the-scenes influence in the White House much as they would dread the power of Hillary Rodham Clinton twenty years later. Even so, matters could still get much worse. The right was alarmed by the prospect of a radical leftist administration, and the nightmare of an Edward Kennedy presidency became the most powerful organizing and fund-raising tool for the hard right. One ugly slogan circulating sub rosa in mid-decade was "Release Sirhan for '76," referring to the imprisoned assassin who had already killed one Kennedy brother.[42]

Already in 1975, Kevin Phillips was describing a New Right, "a new coalition reaching across to what elite conservatives still consider 'the wrong side of the tracks.' " This movement found its home in the Republican Party, a fate that was anything but certain at this time. Some activists felt that the Republicans were too discredited to have any future and that a new third party should be formed, based on solid conservative principles. In 1975, William Rusher advocated just such a party, which would run Ronald Reagan and George Wallace as their dream ticket in the next election. Rusher was wrong to the extent that his ideas would be expressed not in a third party but in the Republicans, who became the main vehicle of conservatism.[43]

The realignment on the right owed much to new tactics of political mobilization, demanded by massive changes in the electorate. The population of potential voters was expanding rapidly at a time when long-standing party loyalties were crumbling, traditional means of getting out the vote were declining, and new legal structures demanded much greater sophistication in fund-raising. Post-Watergate legal changes to campaign financing had been largely counterproductive. Intended to curb the influence of big-money donors, the laws actually ensured that much power passed to political action committees (PACs), which coordinated the donations of a particular industry or interest group.

Conservative thinkers adapted happily to the new environment, most famously Paul Weyrich and Richard Viguerie. Wealthy angels such as Joseph Coors funded a loose confederation of national foundations and think tanks, such as the Heritage Foundation, the Committee for the Survival of a Free Congress, and the National Conservative Political Action Committee (NCPAC). By the end of the 1970s, this network would provide conservatism with an institutional framework that would be the despair of Democratic rivals. Direct-mail fund-raising allowed money to be produced rapidly for diverse conservative causes and permitted rapid lobbying of candidates on an unprecedented scale. Viguerie was the master of this new political form, building on his extensive lists of contributors to the Goldwater and Wallace campaigns. Again in 1975, that great year for conservative organization, a list of names supplied by Viguerie allowed Howard Phillips to launch his Conservative Caucus.[44]

Conservative activism was so important because the difference between the electoral bases of the two parties was so relatively small. Recent history suggested that each party had a solid core of around 40 percent of the electorate, with elections being decided by shifts among the remaining minority. In 1976, Carter won with a mere 50.1 percent of the popular vote, while Reagan won 51 percent in 1980. In both years too, polls suggest that many voters made up their minds within the last days of the campaign, so determined campaigning by either side easily could have shifted the result. Moreover, the proportion of eligible voters who troubled to cast ballots had fallen steadily, reaching a historic low of 55 percent in 1976. The new methods of fund-raising and voter mobilization promised to transform American politics.

The Election of 1976

The electoral campaigns of 1976 illustrated the transformation of old political labels. On the Democratic side, the successful candidate was Jimmy

Carter, one of the most conservative of the likely contenders, and the target of a prolonged effort to choose "anyone but Carter." A symbol of the new sensitive masculinity, Carter also presented himself as a symbol of an older America, rural and communal. His victory owed much to his appeal to the emerging evangelical constituency, especially in the South—which on this occasion backed the Democrats.[45]

Even so, the new politics was still much in evidence at that year's party convention. The Democrats produced a sweepingly liberal platform, promising "full and vigorous enforcement of all equal opportunities laws and affirmative action." While recognizing that abortion troubled some Americans, nevertheless "it is undesirable to attempt to amend the U.S. Constitution to overturn the Supreme Court decision in this area." The platform also declared, "Handguns simplify and intensify violent crime. Ways must be found to curtail the availability of these weapons." And while Soviet expansionism was acknowledged, the primary foreign policy grievance was human rights violations by rightist dictatorships. Great space was devoted to opposing the South African regime, virtually none to the new Soviet spheres of influence in the region (though "efforts should be made to normalize relations with Angola"). In his acceptance speech, Carter himself lurched surprisingly toward radical populism, complaining, "Too many have had to suffer at the hands of a political and economic elite who have shaped decisions and never had to account for mistakes, nor to suffer from injustice."[46]

In the Republican Party too, ideological battles raged around social issues. That spring, Ronald Reagan won a series of important caucuses and primaries, to the horror of the mainstream party, which looked to Gerald Ford. Reagan won five states in a row, in different regions of the country, confirming his national appeal. In the 1960s, Reagan's opponents had accused him of serving as "the spokesman for a harsh philosophy of doom and darkness," but that approach seemed exactly right for the circumstances of the United States in 1976. He was most successful when exploiting fears of international decline, citing the Panama Canal Treaty, détente, and the policies of Henry Kissinger. In explaining Reagan's success, Ford's followers noted the organizational impact of the New Right movement.

> Turnout is very high, the people coming to vote or to the caucuses are unknown and have not been involved in the Republican political system before; they vote overwhelmingly for Reagan. A clear pattern is emerging; these turnouts now do not seem accidental but appear to be the result of skillful organization by extreme right wing political groups in the Reagan

camp operating almost invisibly through direct mail and voter turnout efforts conducted by the organizations themselves. Particularly those groups controlled by Viguerie hold a "rule or ruin" attitude toward the GOP. They are deeply interested in their particular issues, they will work to support their positions, they will turn out to vote in larger numbers than party regulars.

Among these "highly motivated right wing nuts," Ford's advisers singled out NCPAC, the Right to Work, the NRA-linked Gun Owners–Campaign 1976, the Heritage Foundation, and the right-to-life movement.

So determinedly ideological was Reagan's support that he lost critical followers when he chose a northeastern liberal as a potential running mate, and Reagan narrowly forfeited the nomination. Yet as Steven Hayward has remarked, "Reagan failed to capture the nomination, but his capture of the party's soul was nearly complete."[47]

The defeat of the Reagan insurgency left conservatives with no option but to support Ford, though with little enthusiasm. Ford himself made a disastrous mistake in the presidential debates when he proclaimed, bafflingly, that "there is no Soviet domination of Eastern Europe, and there never will be under a Ford administration." This cost him the support of ethnic voters in important swing states and may have lost him the election. The party divisions of that year make it difficult to describe 1976 as a decisive victory for either liberals or conservatives, yet the election did show how large socially conservative constituencies were, and how powerful they could be if they ever united their forces.

In a 1976 episode of *All in the Family*, a recurrent bugbear of the conservatives, Archie Bunker made the then seemingly ludicrous prophecy that while the liberals were celebrating, they would change their minds when they got Ronald Reagan in 1980. In many ways, the 1976 election boded well for the New Right, for which Reagan was now clearly the champion. It was even a blessing that the Republicans were no longer in office, since conservatives no longer had to fight internal party battles against an administration deemed insufficiently conservative. Now conservatives could unite against a liberal Democratic administration, and the new emphasis on social issues promised much sharper polarization between the parties. Meanwhile, the experience of power made it impossible for the Carter administration to hold on to its evangelical supporters, who were gravely disappointed by its failure to deliver the kind of moralist policies they sought. Detached from the administration and feeling betrayed, evangelicals made natural allies for the conservatives, whose structure and tactics had been honed in the recent election.

The Carter Years

Jimmy Carter took office at a time when underlying social forces were running powerfully against liberalism. Moreover, his reputation suffered heavily from the character of the U.S. presidential system, in which the incumbent inevitably becomes the symbol of national hopes and expectations. The president thus becomes the focus of national pride in good times, but also a scapegoat during crises and disasters, even ones for which he has little personal responsibility. This symbolic role makes huge demands on the incumbent's ability to convey strength and confidence, though this will be successful only if it can build upon an existing national mood. The Carter administration suffered the worst of all possible worlds, being buffeted by international economic and diplomatic disasters while never convincing the public that it was trying to resolve them. Both at home and abroad, the administration projected an image of weakness and ineffectiveness, and seemed consistent only in its inconsistency. Carter's easygoing populism made his administration a natural scapegoat for the prolonged economic woes.[48]

Inflation and endemic crisis allowed depression and misery to be associated with a Democratic regime, in contrast to the generation-old tradition that laid the Great Depression at the feet of the Republicans. The economy remained in the doldrums, with the Dow Jones index stagnant in the '80s through much of 1978 and 1979, a time when the inflation rate was reaching alarming levels. The consumer price index rose by 4.9 percent in 1976, 6.7 percent in 1977, 9 percent in 1978, and 13.3 percent in 1979. The combination of economic weakness with inflation, "stagflation," baffled orthodox economists. Like his immediate predecessors, Carter suffered from critical energy problems that were largely beyond his control. He saw energy policy as "the moral equivalent of war" and did his best to achieve victory. Yet while he made important moves toward conservation and encouraged alternative sources of energy, his policy of deregulating the price of oil and natural gas produced in the United States contributed to inflation. And most Americans were not ready to share his willingness to adjust to the diminished expectations that permanently reduced energy supplies might demand.[49] Economic problems also limited the administration's ability to shore up popular support by progressive social spending, despite the campaigns by officials such as Joseph Califano, secretary of health, education, and welfare, who wanted a revival of Great Society–style intervention. But government too had to live with diminished expectations.[50]

Attempts to get economic life moving once more commonly used the language of gender and virility, of allowing people to make their own adult decisions rather than depending upon a maternal state. Jude Wanniski's influential text *The Way the World Works* (1978) called for a strict classical approach to supply-side economics, with all that meant for tax cuts, spending cuts, and reducing state intervention. In 1978, the Kemp-Roth proposals aimed for a substantial cut in federal tax rates. This was also the time of a radical populist assault on taxation policy as it had been known in the United States for decades. In 1978, the passage of California's Proposition 13 reduced assessments and made it more difficult to pass new taxes in the future. The proposition was wildly popular, passing by a two-to-one margin, and the tax revolt pushed other states to reduce or curb their tax burdens over the next two years. Even so, the movement's immediate effects were less important than what it suggested about the approach to authority and the idea of trusting the state. As Carter pollster Pat Caddell warned, "This isn't just a tax revolt, it's a revolution against government." Or to quote the *Washington Post* headline, "California to Liberal Government: Drop Dead."[51]

Underlying social and racial resentments made it easier to stir anger against taxation and the expansive role of government: just what did they actually want the money for? Through the 1970s, popular suspicion of organized labor focused on public sector unions, which grew spectacularly at a time when most older unions were in decline. By 1975, the American Federation of State, County, and Municipal Employees (AFSCME) was 680,000 strong, and over the next five years, it attracted the allegiance of several independent associations of public employees: the union passed the million-member mark in 1978. By definition, the organizations with which the booming public sector unions were bargaining were themselves funded by the general public through taxation, and strikes or work stoppages had a direct and painful impact upon ordinary citizens. In Pennsylvania in 1975, fifty thousand unionized state employees struck the state government in the largest public workers' general strike in American history. Popular hostility also had a racial component, since public unions recruited especially among minority workers, potentially bringing together issues of high taxation, big government, and affirmative action. The resulting resentments contributed to the tax revolt, as conservatives tried to de-fund government and the unions that flourished at public expense.

Activist government was tolerable so long as it was not acting against one's own interests, and for many white middle-class people, that was the issue raised by affirmative action. Race-based policies seemed, prima facie, to violate the rhetoric of color-blind equal rights, and they were especially contentious during a time of diminished resources. These issues came before the courts in 1975 and 1976, after the U.S. Supreme Court held that affirmative action was needed both to "bar like discrimination in the future" and to "eliminate the discriminatory effects of the past." However, subsequent cases in federal courts rejected some race-based programs as unlawful reverse discrimination. The proper limits of affirmative action would be decided in the case of Allan Bakke, a white student who was refused admission to the University of California's medical school despite his having achieved better academic scores than minority students who actually were admitted. He persuaded the liberal California Supreme Court that this rejection constituted a violation of his rights, leading the court to reject race-based admissions as racially discriminatory. Through 1977, affirmative action was hotly debated as the Bakke case was considered before the U.S. Supreme Court. In 1978, a divided Court upheld the use of racial factors in the process of college selection, explicitly approving affirmative action policies.[52]

Though the Carter administration had no direct responsibility for the Bakke case, it became the target for anger among even moderate whites worried at what they saw as pro-minority discrimination. Also, the administration included many representatives of the rights-based liberalism then in the ascendant in the Democratic Party, and some policies succeeded in galvanizing opposition more effectively than New Right activists could have hoped. In 1976, the Supreme Court determined that the ban on racial discrimination extended to private institutions, including schools. Building on this principle, new IRS guidelines issued in 1978 tried to remove the tax-exempt status from many of the new independent Christian schools that had arisen over the previous decade. The assumption was that such institutions represented a new form of covert racial discrimination, rather than disdain for the secular public school system. "A prima facie case of racial discrimination" would be presumed where Christian schools had been created around the time of the desegregation of public schools and had insignificant number of minority students.[53]

The measure was easily presented as a deliberate attempt to suppress Christian schools, a declaration of war on the evangelical community, especially in the South. It focused religious anger on the IRS and on the politicized use of tax policy to achieve liberal social goals. And by targeting children, the action confirmed the most alarmist prophecies about the ambitions of secularist government. Anger at this policy helped mobilize right-wing activism among evangelicals, which found expression in the

Moral Majority, established in 1979.[54] For conservatives, such conflicts sent the message that government could not actively help society by promoting economic progress, but it could harm by threatening communities and families. Government was the enemy.

No More Pinochets

Between 1977 and 1979, foreign policy controversies and administration blunders contributed mightily to growing political conservatism. As president, Carter initially appeared fairly hard-line in international matters, taking the Soviets to task for their human rights policies and appointing veteran hawk Zbigniew Brzezinski as national security adviser. Brzezinski was a prestigious analyst and critic of totalitarianism, especially in its Soviet manifestation. However, Carter's secretary of state, Cyrus Vance, saw little hope that the United States could reverse Communist advances, especially in southern Africa: "We can no more stop change than Canute could still the waters." A number of 1960s-era activists were prominent in the new administration. As assistant secretary of state for human rights and humanitarian affairs, Patricia Derian pursued a radical human rights agenda that ran into conflict with the traditional diplomatic establishment. Conversely, Carter alienated neoconservatives by refusing to choose appointees from the Coalition for a Democratic Majority.[55]

In May 1977, Carter gave a speech at Notre Dame in which he seemed almost to proclaim a unilateral end to the Cold War. "Democracy's great recent successes . . . show that our confidence in this system is not misplaced. Being confident of our own future, we are now free of that inordinate fear of Communism that once led us to embrace any dictator who joined us in that fear. . . . We can no longer separate the traditional issues of war and peace from the new global questions of justice, equity, and human rights." Carter denied "that we can conduct our foreign policy by rigid moral maxims." Shortly afterward, he canceled the proposed B-1 bomber while ignoring apparent Soviet attempts to evade the SALT treaties. In mailings to potential donors, the Conservative Caucus warned that SALT II "will mean the permanent surrender of the United States of America to the military superiority of the Soviet Union." Carter's new director of central intelligence demonstrated the administration's distaste for covert operations by slashing the CIA's Operations Branch, firing hundreds of experienced officers in what became known as the Halloween Massacre. The purge would have long aftereffects around the world, but especially in the Middle East.[56]

By 1978, Daniel Moynihan was declaring, "Our foreign policy already portrays symptoms of a nation which knows it has been outmatched by the Soviet Union." One sign of this outmatching was the furor over the so-called neutron bomb, a weapon designed to stop Soviet armies invading Western Europe by inflicting high levels of radiation. Ideally, the weapon would kill soldiers while minimizing damage to infrastructure. There were good grounds for questioning the weapon, but the Soviets successfully launched a global propaganda campaign against the "ultimate capitalist weapon," which would kill people but preserve property. In 1978, Carter delayed deployment. Carter's China policy also angered the right. In 1979, the United States granted full recognition to the People's Republic while abandoning its defense treaty with Taiwan.[57]

Carter's emphasis on negotiation and peacemaking won important victories, above all the breakthrough peace agreement between Israel and Egypt brokered at Camp David in 1978, which marked the high point of his presidency. But the administration repeatedly faced problems with the human rights policy that was central to its approach to foreign affairs. In itself, this policy was neither foolish nor utopian, though it did make assumptions about the roots of political violence and conflict. Liberals felt that repressive regimes tended to stir up dissent that could not be expressed in legitimate political channels and therefore spawned violence and terrorism. Worse, that violence would be directed against the United States, as the sponsor and puppetmaster of the loathed dictatorship. On a global level, the United States had to defend corrupt client states, losing its moral advantage in the ideological struggle with the Communist bloc. In the long run, persuading a repressive state to respect human rights and democracy could be good for U.S. interests as well as for the nation in question. Carter's watchword was "No more Pinochets" as much as "No more Vietnams."[58] States would be persuaded to respect human rights through linkage, as the United States granted or withheld its support to a given regime depending on its progress toward democracy. Perhaps the best illustration of the Carter policy occurred after his presidency, when the 1986 revolution in the Philippines overthrew an unsavory tyrant and reestablished an authentically popular democratic regime. The left made little progress, and the political skies did not fall.

The problem with the Carter formula was that it assumed that violence and unrest were a reaction to injustices within a particular country, as opposed to being manipulated by some external force hostile to the United States. That view might have been correct in some instances, but it was not accurate in others. Also, as it was easier to pressure allies than foes, enforcing human rights looked like a means of punishing traditional friends. By putting pressure on a friendly government, even a blatantly repressive one, the United States ran the risk of destabilizing it and perhaps seeing it overthrown by a much more dangerous hostile regime. From a conservative perspective, used to stressing the Soviet hunger for expansion, the Carter administration's human rights policy weakened America's global position in the name of unworkable idealism. According to this view, dictators such as the shah of Iran or Ferdinand Marcos of the Philippines might be villains, but they were infinitely superior to any likely left-wing replacement, a point made abundantly by the recent transition in Cambodia. However despicable, the right-wing military elite in that country was not remotely in the same league of violence as their genocidal Khmer Rouge successors, who massacred a quarter of the population in just four years. By 1978, even George McGovern was calling for U.S. military action against the Khmer Rouge.

Conservatives argued that Communist states were qualitatively different from mere dictatorships. The first were totalitarian and could never change through internal reform, while dictatorships were authoritarian and would reform themselves in time. The best arguments for the reformist dynamic of rightist and authoritarian states were Greece and Spain, which during the mid-1970s had shaken off years of dictatorial rule and evolved impressively toward democracy. In retrospect, the fall of the Soviet Union disproves the argument about the unchangeable nature of left-wing totalitarianism, but at the time it seemed convincing.[59]

Furthermore, Carter was applying his policies at a time when anti-Communism was regaining influence it had lost during the Vietnam years, and even becoming voguish. Anti-Communism gained important new public faces. The accession of Pope John Paul II focused attention on the oppression of his home nation of Poland and made the Catholic Church once more a platform for anti-Communist activism. Within the United States, he also provided a unifying symbol for all shades of Christian conservatives, amazingly so given the long evangelical suspicion of the Roman church. The election of the "Iron Lady," Margaret Thatcher, in the United Kingdom in 1979 gave U.S. conservatives a stirring example of militant anti-Communism abroad coupled with unapologetic right-wing fiscal policies at home. In the Soviet Union itself, the evils of Communism were symbolized by heroic dissidents such as Andrei Sakharov. Such images suggested that Communism could be successfully challenged. In the United States itself, new research dented the heroic image of domestic Communism. Allen Weinstein's 1978 book *Perjury* proved beyond a reasonable doubt that Alger Hiss had indeed been spying for the Soviets and that the much-maligned Whittaker Chambers had been telling the sober truth through the whole controversy. Weinstein's work undermined liberal mythology and suggested a more sinister and conspiratorial view of Soviet Communism.[60]

Just as Carter appeared soft on Communism, so he seemed unwilling to stand up to Third World despots. For many Americans, the assumption of pretentious military finery by dictators almost represented self-parody. In recent memory, these figures included Idi Amin, Muammar Qaddafi, Yasser Arafat, and (by the end of the decade) Nicaragua's Daniel Ortega. Such images had a racial subtext, suggesting that such primitive creatures were at best masquerading when they adopted the uniforms of advanced nations and races. Treating these cartoon figures according to their pretensions was a sign of how far America had fallen. Carter's UN ambassador, Andrew Young, demonstrated his sympathy for Third World liberation movements, including some that were clearly anti-American. Young explained the Cuban interventions in Africa in terms of that nation's "shared sense of colonial oppression and domination."[61]

Third World issues remained in the headlines because of the administration's desire to sign a treaty returning control of the Panama Canal to the nation of Panama. Militarily, the decision made sense, in that the canal had nothing like the strategic importance it had had in the days before airpower, while politically, returning the canal would be an excellent way of showing U.S. respect for Latin American sensibilities. For critics, though, the treaty wantonly gave away a major American asset to a pipsqueak Third World nation. For many on the New Right, the deal seemed like a literal sellout, reputedly for the benefit of New York banks, those traditional targets of populist suspicion. By the time the treaty was being readied for ratification in the fall of 1977, polls showed two-thirds of Americans in opposition, and this proved an important mobilizing issue for the Reaganite right. When the treaty was ratified in 1978, the outcome showed the chasm between public and elite attitudes.[62]

Thinking About Vietnam

America's Vietnam syndrome would for many years make the nation reluctant to face military entanglements, especially in the Third World. Even so, attitudes toward Vietnam and the wider Cold War changed noticeably during the Carter presidency. Throughout the war years, despite massive political opposition, a sizable number of Americans had always been prepared to support the Vietnam effort. What changed during the Carter years was that public and popular depictions of the conflict became noticeably more sympathetic to the American cause, and especially to the ordinary Americans who had fought and suffered in that conflict.[63]

The war issue revived over the question of amnesty to draft evaders. In early 1977, Carter issued an amnesty to those who had avoided the draft either by not registering or by traveling abroad. The president wanted chiefly to end national divisions and to begin his term with a clean slate. But just as he hoped the Vietnam issue would subside, it returned to the public consciousness through popular-culture depictions of the war of a kind that had been too sensitive to be made while fighting was in progress. In film, one of the greatest successes of the era was *The Deer Hunter,* with its savage portrayal of Communist forces and its loving images of the ethnic working-class Americans who fought them: in a moving conclusion, the surviving characters sing "God Bless America." *Apocalypse Now* presented American soldiers as confused innocents lost in a phantasmagoric hell. On television, *M*A*S*H* offered idealized glimpses of the military experience, camouflaged in the safely distant guise of the Korean War. Meanwhile, scholarly works such as Guenter Lewy's *America in Vietnam* challenged the older liberal mythology about the war, dismantling, for instance, the lurid charges of U.S. war crimes floated by the Winter Soldier movement. Publishers began to present what would soon become a vast genre of Vietnam War memoirs written by ordinary soldiers. Guilt about the treatment of U.S. soldiers and veterans found expression in tales that veterans had been spat upon as they returned home. Though such incidents might have occurred, the image of spitting protesters was largely an urban legend, and the story's popularity reflected public guilt about extreme anti-war activism.[64] The more understanding vision of the U.S. experience found a material symbol in the Vietnam Veterans Memorial, built in Washington in 1981–82.[65]

From 1975 too, conservative views of Vietnam received support from the POW/MIA issue. All wars produce MIAs, soldiers missing in action, whose fate cannot positively be determined. Usually, their bodies were destroyed beyond recognition or were left behind enemy lines, while a handful of soldiers might have defected or deserted. After 1975, though, relatives and friends of America's Vietnam MIAs increasingly came to believe that hundreds were still alive and in captivity. Indeed, it became common to speak of the issue as the POW/MIA problem, suggesting a refusal to write off the missing as dead. The POW/MIA flag became the widespread patriotic symbol that it remains to this day. In these years as well, the National League of Families developed a much more critical anti-administration tone, with a special animus against Henry Kissinger and the "deceitful lies" emanating from the diplomatic establishment.[66] It was charged that the U.S. government knew of the existence of live POWs but was engaged in a cover-up, a systematic betrayal of its fighting men.

From the late 1970s, the issue inspired activism and even led to some private paramilitary rescue actions. A subculture of true believers emerged, with more than a few confidence tricksters peddling suspect information and sightings. The POW theme offered a political message for successive campaigns to restore American strength and self-respect. According to one legend, prisoners were displayed to visiting anti-American fighters from around the world, to prove that the U.S. military was a paper tiger.

The POW/MIA issue helped assuage American feelings of guilt, instead focusing blame on evil Vietnamese Communists and cowardly U.S. politicians. Above all, the prisoner theme reversed the rhetoric of bullying and aggression that had been so powerfully deployed against the U.S. intervention, with its images of advanced Western technology failing to suppress a poor peasant force in black pajamas. In the new reconstruction of memory, it was the Americans who were weak, impotent, and victimized by heartless Asian slave masters and torturers. The most powerful scenes in *The Deer Hunter* depict the brutal treatment of American prisoners. New views of Vietnam did not translate to active support for military intervention overseas, but the image of the starving, tortured American soldier rotting in a jungle cage offered powerful support to interpretations of the U.S. failure in Vietnam as a stab in the back, a liberal betrayal. In 1980, Ronald Reagan would proclaim that in Vietnam, "ours was, in truth, a noble cause."[67]

By 1978, conservatives were proving effective at mobilizing against the administration, however odd these tactical alliances sometimes appeared. As supply-side enthusiast David Stockman wrote, "I didn't give two hoots for the Moral Majority, the threat of unisex toilets, the school prayer amendment and the rest of the New Right litany." He did not relish being aligned with "Jerry Falwell, the anti-gun control nuts, the Bible-thumping Creationists, the anti-Communist witch-hunters and the small-minded Hollywood millionaires to whom 'supply side' meant one more Mercedes." Reagan himself was "antediluvian." But despite Stockman's disdain, the various causes had more in common than he might have acknowledged, in their critique of government, their emphasis on individualism and self-reliance, and their harking back to older values. And the ideological package was attractive to many. As the Edsalls wrote, "Conservative populism gave the Republican Party . . . a coherent response to the anguish of the white patrolman, the night worker, the nurse, and the Catholic land-lady." Republicans made major gains in the 1978 congressional elections, and the party was well funded for the next presidential election.[68]

But more important than any single policy was the emphasis on themes of family, gender, morality, and virtue as the proper subject of politics—indeed, as primary issues of social concern. Commonly, these concerns were expressed through the rhetoric of children and child protection, a powerful force for social mobilization that mainly benefited conservatives.

4

The Politics of Children: 1977

*I am here to protest against child molesters. For as surely as
there are those who lure children with lollypops in order to rape
their bodies, so, too, do these lure children with candy-coated lies
in order to rape their minds.*

—Rabbi Maurice Davis

Accounts of the 1960s often focus on the single year 1968 as the symbolic date
when the forces of insurrection and cultural upheaval reached their climax.
Though it is far less celebrated, the year 1977 also demands attention as
a time of intense political activism and conflict over fundamental moral
values. Domestic politics in 1977 were dominated by questions of gender
roles and relationships and of sexual exploitation and restraint, by concepts
of normality and perversion, by the definition of masculinity—in short, by
exactly those issues of virtue and morality that not long before had seemed
inappropriate for mainstream political discourse. It was in this year above
all that the modern culture wars flared.

The beginning of the Carter presidency marked a transition for both
liberals and conservatives. Liberals and feminists had high expectations of
an administration that included some conspicuous radical sympathizers,
while Democrats held a convincing majority in Congress. For just the same
reasons, though, conservatives were impelled to act, to halt the advance
of social liberalism. The fact that liberalism was now so identified with
the administration meant that official failures in any area, in economics
or foreign policy, would damage Democratic credibility in all aspects of
domestic affairs. The worse Carter did in any area, the more conservatives
would benefit in debates over gender and morality.

For a decade, feminist and gay rights advocates had made repeated legal
gains, and although some attempts had been defeated, new legal rights had

never been rolled back. Once the ratchet had turned, it seemed impossible to reverse it, and the best that conservatives could hope for was to delay the next victory. In 1977, though, conservative activists hoped to reverse rather than merely to slow liberal advances. They would do this by local activism of the sort that had already derailed ERA ratification, involving campaigns at the state and city levels. The impact of these moral campaigns indicates serious discontent about the direction that America had taken over the previous decade, into immorality and sexual exploitation.

Though campaigns were diverse, what they had in common was a new focus on children's issues and the threats posed to children by relaxed attitudes toward sex and drugs. Obviously, this belief was not the prerogative of either liberals or conservatives, and initially most activism over child protection issues stemmed from the liberal and feminist left. But once the children's issue was in play, conservative activists adapted it to their own ends. The clearest example of the shift was in the politics of abortion, which supporters viewed entirely in terms of the interests of the woman and her ability to "control her own fertility." Anti-abortion activists stressed that the act involved the destruction of a human life: it's not a choice, it's a child. Anti-abortion appeals freely used the term "baby killers" and stressed that "abortion means killing a living baby, a human being with a beating heart and little fingers . . . killing a baby boy or girl with burning deadly chemicals or a powerful machine that sucks and tears the little infant from its mother's womb."[1]

Throughout American history, morality campaigners have often warned against drug pushers, child molesters, and smut peddlers. In the late 1970s, though, these issues proved alarming to the same people who had previously resisted moralist rhetoric.

Gender Wars

Anti-feminist campaigns that had been in progress for some time reached a new peak in 1977, winning victories that startled a liberal movement long used to victory. One area of setback was abortion. In 1976, Representative Henry Hyde introduced an amendment to the appropriation for the Department of Health, Education, and Welfare, forbidding the use of Medicaid funds for abortion except where the mother's life was at stake. The Hyde Amendment was the subject of impassioned hearings in the opening months of 1977, and not only did it pass, but it was upheld by the U.S. Supreme Court. In 1978, the principle of banning federal funds was extended to other appropriations bills, including medical provision for military personnel. In addition to encouraging conservatives, the success of the Hyde Amendment damaged the Democratic coalition. Feminists were incensed by Jimmy Carter's pallid response to the Supreme Court decision and his remark that while cutting medical aid for poor women might seem unfair, "there are many things in life that are not fair, that wealthy people can afford and poor people can't."[2]

In the same months, the struggle for the ERA was becoming desperate. Supporters had won no new ratifications over the previous two years and were painfully aware of the approaching 1979 deadline. Ratification battles raged in several states. In January, the ERA secured its last victory, in Indiana, leaving only three states needed for success, but the measure failed in Virginia, Nevada, and Florida. Meanwhile, several states were voting to rescind their earlier approval of the ERA, which threatened to destroy the whole process. By the end of the year, ERA supporters launched a damage control operation, seeking a congressional extension of the time limit and a clear declaration against the right of any state to rescind ratification. In each case, the U.S. Justice Department supported the legality of the move, and both were passed by early 1978. The effort to save ERA generated new activism, and a demonstration in Washington attracted a hundred thousand supporters, but even so the amendment failed.[3]

Women's rights and gender issues were the theme of the National Women's Conference held in Houston in November 1977. Feminists fondly recall the affair as a moment of solidarity and rededication, but it also attracted conservative attacks. The right condemned governmental funding of feminism, suggesting the same kind of official alliance that was apparent from the Justice Department's attempt to keep the ERA alive. The Women's Conference grew out of the United Nations' designation of 1975 as International Women's Year. President Ford established a commission to celebrate Women's Year, which called for a national meeting preceded by state conventions. For the right, organized feminism was now associated with every possible evil: federal power, taxpayer money, the Democratic administration, and the ultimate bugbear, the United Nations. The right found easy ammunition for attacks on "the one-world, humanist, feminist socialist philosophy."[4]

Feminists dominated the national convention itself, which produced a far-reaching plan of action that supported the ERA and homosexual rights, as well as calling for federally funded child care. But anti-feminists also had a strong presence, representing some 20 percent of delegates, and with vocal activists such as Phyllis Schlafly in attendance. Schlafly asserted, "The American people do not want the ERA. And they do not want government-funded abortion, lesbian privileges, or the federal government to set up institutions for universal child care." Adding to the impact for conservative purposes was the media coverage of the event, which highlighted the activities of radical feminists. Lesbian activists were much in evidence, with banners declaring, "We are everywhere," and anti-religious slogans were publicized. Guaranteed to infuriate was "Jesus was a homosexual." However moderate the proceedings of the event, television news naturally focused on the more outrageous and anti-male aspects of the proceedings, such as banners suggesting, "A woman needs a man like a fish needs a bicycle." Together with the conflicts over ERA, the Women's Conference stirred debate about the future of family structures, the social tolerance of homosexuality, attacks on conservative religious beliefs, and the role of government in encouraging radical changes in lifestyle and gender relations.[5]

Discovering Child Abuse

In effect, if not in official title, 1977 was the year of the child. Attitudes toward children and their rights changed radically, especially in matters of sexuality, as sexual abuse and molestation appeared quite suddenly on the political agenda.

To speak of a discovery of child abuse may sound odd from a modern standpoint, but the revolutionary nature of the change can be appreciated only in light of conditions immediately preceding 1977. The fact that adults were performing sexual acts with children has been recognized throughout human history, and men were being punished for this kind of behavior in colonial America. Yet different societies vary enormously in how seriously they regard this kind of conduct, and also in what constitutes a "child." As late as the 1880s, the age of consent for American or British girls was as young as ten. In some eras, sexual threats to children have stirred enormous public concern and even panic, and molesters, pedophiles, and sex fiends have become demon figures. Historians speak of such a sex offender panic in the America of the 1940s. By the 1960s, however, attitudes had become much more relaxed, largely in reaction to the earlier hysteria.[6]

In the twenty years or so before 1977, attitudes toward childhood sexuality were so radically different from those prevailing today that we seem to be visiting a different planet. Reading the most authoritative experts on what we would now call child abuse or molestation, most modern readers would be amazed by how lightly the behavior was viewed and how at every stage the prevailing assumptions were diametrically opposed to those of today. In this earlier period, the persistent belief was that molestation occurred quite rarely, and incest virtually never. Pedophilia was such a rare condition that it was scarcely mentioned in the professional literature, even in tomes on arcane sexual deviations. In the 1950s, prominent psychiatrist Manfred Guttmacher characterized molesters as "so often essentially passive, non-aggressive individuals, who can be dealt with leniently with minimal super-vision." Light therapy was recommended for such minor, noncompulsive offenders. The language of predators and sex fiends was dismissed as hyper-bole, fit only for sensationalist media.[7]

According to the common interpretation of the offense, molestation usually involved some degree of guilt by the child herself, while the act involved little harm or trauma. In 1960, criminologist David Abrahamsen wrote, "Often a woman unconsciously wishes to be taken by force. . . . We sometimes find this seductive inclination even in young girls, in their being flirtatious or seeking out rather dangerous or unusual spots where they can be picked up, thus exposing themselves more or less unconsciously to sexual attacks." Wardell Pomeroy, one of the original Kinsey team, argued that incest between adults and children could be "a satisfying and enriching experience," giving rise to "many beautifully and mutually satisfying re-lationships between fathers and daughters . . . they have no harmful effects." Little of the expert writing on child abuse published between about 1955 and 1976 can be read today without embarrassment.[8]

Parents were warned that reporting an act of molestation was a risky venture, since the actions of police and courts might cause the kind of emotional damage that the act itself did not. A leading criminologist of the time, Paul Tappan, argued that little lasting harm *need* be caused by the experience of "rape, carnal abuse, defloration, incest, homosexuality or indecent exposure": "In some instances the individual does carry psychic scars after such an experience. Characteristically the damage is done far more, however, by the well-intentioned associates of the victim or by public authorities than by the aggressor." The Kinsey researchers agreed that "the emotional reactions of parents, police officers and other adults who discover that the child has had such a contact may disturb the child more seriously than the sexual contacts themselves." Such was the therapeutic orthodoxy prevailing through the early 1970s.[9]

This trivializing view of adult-child sex meshed well with the radical cultural ideas of the 1960s, when young people were rebelling against tra-ditional sexual codes. Older ideas about the dangers of rape and sexual assault were also undermined by changing racial ideas. For prefeminist liberals, a plethora of controversial rape cases suggested that sexual charges were often falsely made, commonly against African-American men. Memories of the Scottsboro Boys case lingered, reinforced by *To Kill a Mockingbird*.[10]

But the same social ferment that caused such widespread questioning of sexual mores prompted a reevaluation of threats to children. In 1962, the problem of "child abuse" entered the popular vocabulary, not in its modern sense of sexual exploitation but in the context of physical violence, of baby battering. As feminist and other critics of the nuclear family held, the benevolent image of the patriarchal household concealed extensive exploitation and violence, which needed to be investigated and confronted. By the mid-1970s, these perceptions were disseminated in the media, demanding a prompt official response.[11]

All political persuasions could agree with a measure to protect vulnerable children, but liberals especially supported a campaign against authoritarian family structures. In 1974, Walter Mondale sponsored the federal Child Abuse Prevention and Treatment Act, which mandated the reporting and investigation of abuse allegations and promised matching funds for states that identified abused children and prosecuted abusers. The act created a new federal agency, the National Center on Child Abuse and Neglect (NCCAN). This measure in turn justified the creation of state and local agencies whose existence depended on the investigation and exposure of child maltreatment. Mandatory reporting swelled abuse statistics, including cases in middle-class households. A number of public and private agencies now emerged. Private groups formed between 1970 and 1975 included the Children's Defense Fund, the National Committee for the Prevention of Child Abuse, Parents Anonymous, Parents United, and the Society for Young Victims.[12] The booming child protection issue attracted activists and journalists who would long dominate media discussions of threats to the young. Kenneth Wooden's book *Weeping in the Playtime of Others* offered an exposé of the nation's juvenile justice system, while Judianne Densen-Gerber's Odyssey House sought to help at-risk children and offered drug rehabilitation services. In New York City, Father Bruce Ritter founded what would become an influential national ministry to homeless and runaway young people.[13]

In these same years, concern about child protection shifted from physical violence to sexual exploitation, largely as an offshoot of feminist campaigns against the rape and sexual assault of adult women. The rape crisis centers that had become such a mainstay of feminist organization were reporting surprisingly large numbers of very young victims, who usually had been molested by family members. Radical feminists saw sexual violence and molestation as essential components of patriarchal society. Linking this approach to the common perception of domestic violence, it was no giant leap to formulate the modern concept of child sexual abuse as a pervasive and immensely damaging threat that could strike what on the surface were the happiest and most normal families. By 1977, *Ms.* magazine asserted that "one girl out of every four in the United States will be sexually abused in some way before she reaches the age of eighteen." Given the growing institutional structure of child protection, it was only a matter of time before child sexual abuse became a powerful social issue.[14]

Exposé

In 1977, child molestation made headlines in a way it had not since the 1940s. The pioneer was youth advocate Judianne Densen-Gerber, who campaigned against commercial sex operations involving the young and worked with New York social workers, religious leaders, and community improvement groups to demand an official crackdown. In early 1977, police responded with a crackdown on the startlingly open vice culture that had emerged around Times Square, where child pornography films and magazines were readily available, as were young teenage prostitutes. Activists exposed the widespread youth prostitution of this "slimy underbelly of Manhattan," which was known as the Minnesota Strip because of the reputed midwestern origins of many of its young runaways. Bruce Ritter suggested that passers-by here were constantly barraged with offers of underage sex. In a typical sales pitch reported by Ritter, a pimp's runner offers potential clients a choice of young teenage sex partners: "You can have any one you want for $20. . . . Take this one. You'll like this one. His name is Nandy. He's eleven." The Times Square campaign was all the more influential because it seemed the first successful blow against an urban vice culture that appeared to be beyond any hope of redemption. The new movement against underage vice was imitated in other major cities.[15]

The child pornography issue attracted headline coverage in newspapers, as well as in print sources such as *Redbook, Parents, Newsweek, U.S. News and World Report, Ms., Time,* and most major newspapers. Television documentaries plunged enthusiastically into the topic. In May, a report on NBC television news stated extravagantly, "It's been estimated that as many as two million American youngsters are involved in the fast-growing, multi-million-dollar child pornography business." That same month, a much-quoted series in the *Chicago Tribune* described the harrowing subculture associated with child pornography and prostitution, introducing readers to terms such as "chicken hawks," that is, men with a taste for young boys or "chickens." The series connected child pornography with the actual abuse and seduction of runaway children: "Child pornography is a nationwide multi-million-dollar racket that is luring thousands of juveniles into lives of prostitution." According to Densen-Gerber, child models were "emotionally and spiritually murdered."[16]

Political action followed swiftly. That spring, a bill was proposed to prohibit the manufacture, distribution, and possession of child pornography, and congressional hearings on the sexual exploitation of children followed through May and June. Witnesses included Densen-Gerber, Wooden, and Lloyd Martin, from Los Angeles' new Sexually Exploited Child Unit. This core of child advocates became the most quoted experts in the swath of stories about child exploitation that became obligatory for major media outlets in these months.[17] Activists offered ambitious charges of conspiratorial activity. Martin alleged that a national pedophile ring was linked to "widespread infiltration of adult suspects into all types of national youth groups and youth-oriented organizations . . . There is nationwide mobility, interaction and communication among adults involved in child exploitation." Michigan prosecutor Robert Leonard agreed that "the tentacles of this illegal activity form an underground network stretching from New York to California and Michigan to Louisiana. Prosecutors in cities across the country have uncovered and compiled information pointing to a high degree of exchange and communication among those who prey on our children. Seemingly isolated cases of such deviancy reveal a frightening set of sophisticated intercommunications upon closer scrutiny."[18]

Based on such evidence, the child protection movement attracted near-unanimous support, as the bill passed the House of Representatives by a vote of 401 to 0. The rock-solid public sentiment needs little explanation. Liberals and feminists naturally supported a measure to defend innocent children and teenagers. Moral and political conservatives used the child porn issue as a means of discrediting the whole pornography industry and the lax laws that allowed it to flourish. For police and prosecutors, the new legislation promised to create an environment in which it would once more be possible to assert public morality. Conversely, child pornographers had next to no public defenders, even among convinced civil libertarians. As Densen-Gerber remarked, "There is no such thing as a child consenting to be photographed sexually: it is an act fundamentally of exploitation."[19]

The obvious popularity of the cause also made it difficult to criticize even the most extravagant claims about the alleged scale of the dangers threatening children, all the emerging tales of multi-billion-dollar child porn industries, and hundreds of thousands of exploited victims (Densen-Gerber was especially creative in inventing awe-inspiring numbers). Even if someone doubted these vast figures, if only on commonsense grounds, expressing skepticism ran the risk of appearing sympathetic to the smut peddlers and abusers and failing to sympathize with traumatized child victims. The 1977 campaign began a vogue for outrageous figures about child exploitation that were scarcely even challenged until the mid-1980s and not laid to rest for years afterward. Such figures helped to transform public perceptions of child abuse. Within the space of a few months, the term shifted dramatically in meaning, from physical to sexual endangerment. In 1976, an "abused child" had been battered; by 1978, he or she had been raped or molested.

Believing

The sudden shift of attitudes demands explanation. This was not a case where experts and professionals made some revolutionary discovery that transformed social policy. In fact, few of the claims now made about child sexual abuse were terribly new. The same ideas had been discussed widely at least since the 1890s, when one child protection pioneer argued that "rape of children is the most frequent form of sexual crime." Even in the years of greatest skepticism about the harm caused by molestation, at least some children's advocates had continued to complain that rape and assault were real social dangers. The idea that a quarter of girls faced sexual molestation was originally taken from the (deeply flawed) Kinsey study *Sexual Behavior in the Human Female*, published in 1953. What changed in the mid-1970s was not that new ideas were being expressed but that they acquired a new degree of credibility. People were prepared to believe that children were uniquely endangered in a way that had not been true ten or twenty years previously.[20]

The audience for claims had changed in critical ways. One involved the social and political emancipation of women, who provided a substantial and receptive audience for claims about sexual threats against themselves and their children. The more women were in the workplace, the more concerned they were about threats of personal violence and sexual assault against themselves or their children. The concept and terminology of sexual harassment emerged alongside that of child sexual abuse, and at exactly the same time.

Though campaigns against harassment are founded on the 1964 civil rights law, only in 1976 did the issue attract major media attention, and not until 1977 did the courts decide that this was a pressing form of discrimination comparable to racial oppression. (The word *harassment* is taken from black activism of the 1960s.) In a landmark case, Paulette Barnes claimed that "she became the target of her superior's sexual desires because she was a woman, and was asked to bow to his demands as the price for holding her job," until her job was ultimately abolished. In 1977, a federal court agreed, for the first time, that sexual harassment was a form of discrimination. Sexual harassment law now became a powerful weapon against not just misbehaving supervisors but also employers, who had a mighty incentive to curb any such behavior in the future. Once publicly acknowledged, the sexual harassment problem attracted a swelling literature, and just like child abuse, the definition of the behavior expanded rapidly. Though next to nothing was available on the harassment problem in 1976, by 1980 activists could refer to a series of well-known works, such as *Sexual Shakedown* and *The Secret Oppression*, and the topic was often treated in magazines and news programs.[21] Harassment, like rape and child abuse, was added to the catalogue of systematic male violence against women.

Also promoting belief in the gravity of child abuse were demographic factors, especially the aging of the baby boom generation. Imagine someone born at the height of that boom, say in 1954. That person would have been in his or her mid-teens in 1969 and might well have sympathized with demands for sexual liberation and lowering the age of consent. Tales of widespread abuse and molestation would likely have been dismissed as part of the scaremongering with which the authorities of that era condemned youthful experimentation with sex and drugs or outlawed consensual offenses such as homosexuality. But by the mid-1970s, that same person would be starting a family and thinking more seriously about parental roles and the issue of threats against children. That would become even more true over the next few years as the baby boomers' children entered day care, went to school, and ventured off on their own.

Recognizing a new social attitude, Hollywood films of these years increasingly addressed the plight of parents and families, in films such as *Kramer vs. Kramer* (1979). Parent-child relationships were central to other films of these years, including *Ordinary People, Breaking Away,* and *The Great Santini.* At least for a few years, filmgoers were assumed to share the attitudes of parents or even to be parents themselves, rather than to observe parents as the twisted and hypocritical figures of the sort found in 1960s films such as *The Graduate.* In 1979, *Hardcore* had as its hero a distraught father trying to rescue a wayward teenage daughter from pimps and pornographers, including homicidal makers of snuff films. The film draws heavily on the John Wayne classic *The Searchers,* though this time urban vice districts serve as Indian country, literally the badlands. And the story is told from the perspective of the desperate father rather than the rebellious teenager. The child abuse issue often surfaced in popular culture. In an episode of the police sitcom *Barney Miller*, detectives strongly suspect that a middle-aged man ostensibly doing charitable work among runaway youths has immoral intentions. Even in the 1978 epic *Superman*, the villainous Ursa is so evil that her "perversions" did not spare the children of the planet Krypton. There is no further reference to this theme, which is utterly removed from the atmosphere of the original comic book, but at the time, this was the ideal way of associating a character with the worst thing in the world.

A literature on child sexual abuse now appeared, just as works on rape had mushroomed a few years earlier. While in 1977 little on child sexual abuse was available in book form from either the professional or activist perspective, an explosion of research and publishing was soon in progress. The year 1979 marked America's first-ever national conference devoted to the theme of child sexual abuse. Between 1978 and 1981, pathbreaking books appeared such as *The Sexual Assault of Children and Adolescents*, *Sexually Victimized Children*, *Betrayal of Innocence*, *The Best-Kept Secret*, and *Father-Daughter Incest*. In 1980, the child abuse literature adopted the theme of post-traumatic stress disorder, a condition recently publicized by the Vietnam veterans' movement. In this view, childhood abuse represented a devastating form of captivity, torture, and terrorism, to which victims responded by repressing memories that could be recovered only during therapy. This new approach underlay the controversial recovered-memory movement of the next two decades. At the same time, a growing literature on the molester or pedophile emphasized the compulsive and dangerous quality of the behavior: these were not harmless nuisance offenders. By the end of the decade, child sexual abuse was firmly part of the cultural landscape.[22]

Whose Problem?

The child protection movement made some excellent points. Child pornography of a harrowing kind had become widely available in American cities, underage prostitution was quite commonplace, and most professionals were understating the extent and severity of child molestation. But establishing a sexual abuse problem did not necessarily establish what kind of problem it was, and the earlier neglect was arguably followed by a panicked overreaction. Once the gravity of child abuse was established in the popular imagination, activists could use the issue to draw attention to their own particular cause. If child abuse was, by common consent, an ultimate evil, then any other theme that plausibly could be connected with it acquired a similar taint.

The child abuse issue can be presented in different ways, each carrying a distinctive set of policy outcomes, and interpretations depend largely on one's ideological preference. For a feminist such as Susan Brownmiller or Diana Russell, the most pervasive and dangerous form of sexual abuse occurred in the home. It was incest, father-daughter rape, and could be eliminated only by social transformation. As pioneering activist Florence Rush argued in 1971, "The sexual abuse of female children is a process of education that prepares them to become the wives and mothers of America." In 1975, Brownmiller's *Against Our Will* included a section on the frequency of father rape as part of "the absolute dictatorship of father rule," that is, of patriarchy. During the 1977 child porn crisis, *Ms.* magazine published an article titled "Incest: Sexual Abuse Begins at Home."[23]

But more conservative views were possible, and they were much in evidence during 1977. According to this view, sex crimes could be traced to the libertine heritage of the 1960s and the deformation of gender roles. The apparent wave of sex abuse resulted from men deserting traditional masculine roles and women abandoning their role as protectors of children and family. Also, much of the concern about abuse focused not on fathers but on strangers, molesters, commonly organized in gangs or sex rings. A public grown used to assassination rings was quite prepared to see the child abuse issue in terms of networks of like-minded deviants, seducing and filming the young. The Watergate-era image of intrusive surveillance segued easily into theories about perverts making pornographic images of the nation's children. In this view, child abuse was a menace, like drug trafficking or organized crime, that could be fought only by the criminal justice system.

The tougher new view of child abuse justified action against other kinds of sexual deviants whose behavior could be linked rhetorically to the menace facing children, including pornographers. Historically, child protection panics had awful consequences for adult homosexuals, who were persistently confused with pedophiles and molesters. Not surprisingly, given the passion of debates surrounding gay rights in the 1970s, the upsurge of concern about children also found a target in gay men, and it offered a rhetorical weapon of great power.[24]

At first sight, the gay-pedophile link seems spurious, a despicable form of guilt by false association. Nobody today wants to reinforce the alleged linkage between adult homosexuals and child molesters, still less the association with sexual crime and violence; but much depends on issues of definition and language. A thirty-year-old man who has sex with other men over the age of eighteen is a homosexual. If a man has sex with boys below the age of thirteen, he is a pedophile. But what about the intervening category, involving boys in their mid-teens, say fifteen or sixteen? The best available word is *pederast*, though that is rarely used today. In gay cultures through the centuries, men have had relations with teenage boys, just as heterosexual men have had sex with girls in their mid-teens. But just where should the legal age limit be? Since 1969, mainstream America showed itself willing to grant much greater legal rights to homosexuals, but the issue of the age of consent was, and remains, contentious.[25]

In the liberated atmosphere of the mid-1970s, there was widespread sympathy for lowering the age of consent, whether gay or straight. Gay publications and pressure groups freely discussed lowering the male age of consent. Radicals were encouraged by the example of post-Stonewall legal changes concerning homosexuality, which showed how rapidly familiar sexual standards might be transformed. And if homosexual acts were to be legalized, what about pederastic acts between men and boys or teenagers? That does not mean that gay activists were advocating pedophilia, but as for heterosexuals, the notion of sexual liberation was being extended to younger teenagers. At the fringes of the gay movement, some voices were pushing for much more radical changes, including the abolition of the age of consent, and were extolling "man-boy love." During 1977, anti-gay activism focused effectively on themes of child molestation and abuse.

Save Our Children

Jeffrey Escoffier has written that 1977 and 1978 "were watershed years for the gay movement, analogous to 1968 on the Left."[26] Political conflict ignited in January 1977 when Dade County, Florida, voted to prohibit discrimination on grounds of "affectional or sexual preferences." Though similar ordinances had become common, the Dade measure infuriated singer Anita Bryant, who now began a career as a conservative activist. Bryant complained, "What these people really want, hidden behind obscure legal phrases, is the legal right to propose to our children that there is an acceptable alternate way of life. I will lead such a crusade to stop it as this country has not seen before." Though condemning discrimination, the measure itself had just that effect, she argued, in that "you would be discriminating against my children's right to grow up in a healthy decent community." Bryant demanded a referendum to repeal the ordinance, the vote to be held in June 1977.[27]

Bryant's critique of gay rights was chiefly religious, based on scriptural condemnations of homosexuality, and she attracted religious believers to her cause. She herself was a Southern Baptist, with a natural outreach to evangelicals and fundamentalists who had recently mobilized to elect Jimmy Carter, while the local Roman Catholic community also condemned the Dade ordinance. Bryant's appearance on the evangelical programs *700 Club* and *PTL* made her a conservative heroine who also spoke on such other key issues as the ERA. She enthusiastically quoted George Gilder's *Sexual Suicide*, which saw the upsurge of homosexuality as an "escape from sexual responsibility, and its display as a threat to millions of young men who have precarious masculine identities." The organized gay movement was a pernicious, conspiratorial foe: she was fighting "militant homosexuals who are highly financed, highly organized, and who were able to ramrod the amendment through in our city."[28]

Bryant's campaign was above all based on the issue of child protection and charges that homosexuals posed a unique sexual threat to the young. As the slogan claimed, "Homosexuals aren't born, they recruit," and recruitment took the form of child molestation and abuse. As Bryant declared, "Homosexual acts are not only illegal, they are immoral. And through the power of the ballot box I believe the parents and straight-thinking normal majority will soundly reject the attempts to legitimize homosexuals and their recruitment plan for their children." As she said in an appeal to potential donors, "I don't hate the homosexuals! But as a mother I must protect my children from their evil influence. . . . They want to recruit our school children under the protection of the laws of the land." Bryant's movement took the name Save Our Children, and the molestation theme pervaded its propaganda materials. Leaflets offered a series of headlines from the spring of 1977: "Teacher Accused of Sex Acts with Boy Students," "Police Find Sexually Abused Children," "Homosexuals Used Scout Troop," "Senate Shown Movie of Child Porn," "Ex-Teachers Indicted for Lewd Acts with Boys." The litany concluded, "Are all homosexuals nice? These are the actual stories in the nation's press. Judge for yourself. THERE IS NO HUMAN RIGHT TO CORRUPT OUR CHILDREN." Also valuable were statements by some gay organizations themselves, however far removed from the movement's mainstream, with their calls for the abolition of age-of-consent laws.[29]

Save Our Children drew powerfully from the contemporary exposés of sex rings involved in pornography and prostitution. The movement quoted "the Los Angeles Police Department" (that is, Lloyd Martin) to the effect that "25,000 boys seventeen years old or younger in that city alone have been recruited into a homosexual ring to provide sex for adult male customers." In the congressional hearings on the child exploitation bill, Robert Leonard cited a case of several men who recruited runaway teenage boys as "male prostitutes to serve wealthy homosexuals." The *Chicago Tribune* series tracked "a nationwide homosexual ring with headquarters in Chicago [that] has been trafficking in young boys." Kenneth Wooden asserted that "most agree that child sex and pornography is basically a boy-man phenomenon."[30] By the end of 1977, the media were reporting estimates that perhaps a million boy prostitutes were active in the contemporary United States. For Bryant and her allies, gay rights were dangerous because homosexuals molested children or patronized the kind of prostitution and pornography that was being exposed in the nation's cities. Relaxing legal sanctions would make the situation worse.

The Dade County referendum became a critical battlefield for gay activists, who believed that "Miami is our Selma." Some tried to phrase their own cause in terms of children's interests, asserting that Bryant wanted "gay women and men . . . [to] join a conspiracy to pretend we don't exist, so that other people can lie to children." Even so, Bryant's cause won massively in June, by 69 to 31 percent of the vote, provoking anti-gay rhetoric in the media.[31]

That victory spawned other local activism against gay rights, and additional referenda followed over the next year: in St. Paul, Minnesota, in Eugene, Oregon, in Wichita, and in Seattle. Gay rights opponents won most such contests easily. The most significant contest occurred in the state of California in November 1978, when the Briggs initiative sought to prohibit the advocacy of homosexuality in public schools. Its sponsor, state senator John Briggs, believed that "one-third of San Francisco teachers are homosexuals. I assume most of them are seducing young boys in toilets." Under the proposed law, any teacher found to be "advocating, imposing, encouraging or promoting" homosexual activity could be dismissed. Briggs symbolically launched his campaign in San Francisco, calling it "the moral garbage dump of homosexuality in this country." Though early polls showed a substantial majority in favor of Briggs, as high as two to one in some polls, the measure ultimately failed by a million votes.[32]

Although Bryant succeeded in mobilizing moral conservatives, the Briggs referendum also indicates the limits of what they could achieve. Indeed, later gay activists cited the Bryant campaign as a decisive moment in stirring gay activism, and a spur to later legal victories. Media accounts of the time often presented Bryant's followers as fanatical and intolerant, and discredited more moderate opponents of legal change. The immediate reaction to the referendum result was a spontaneous demonstration in San Francisco's gay community, which contributed to political organization. Some months later, Harvey Milk won election to the city's Board of Supervisors. His standard stump speech began with a jab at Bryant: "My name is Harvey Milk and I'm here to recruit you." Nationally, Bryant's success "resurrected a slumbering activism and converted apathy into anger and action. It inspired spontaneous demonstrations by thousands in the streets of New York, Los Angeles, Chicago, Houston, New Orleans, San Francisco, and other major cities. It gave birth to a host of new organizations and programs to counter the threat of an anti-gay backlash. It elicited new support from national leaders, organizations, and the press. And it opened many closet doors." Mobilization for the referenda also contributed to national political structures, which were powerfully in evidence during the gay and lesbian march on Washington in October 1979. At this point, the prospects seemed excellent for major gay political advances during the 1980s.[33]

Sex Rings

But such later victories seemed distant and improbable in 1977 and 1978, when the child abuse issue was turned against aspects of adult sexual liberation. The media focus on child pornography now generated support for measures against pornography in general, and even in San Francisco, a new anti-porn bill encouraged police crackdowns against gay bookstores and theaters. The traditional perception of gays as pedophiles heavily influenced the practices of police and prosecutors investigating sexual deviance and of the news media reporting their activities. The discredited vice squads now resumed their careers as "pedo squads," ostensibly targeting not homosexuality in general but underage sex. Accounts of sex rings proliferated. Of course, the fact that such tales were coming to light may indicate not that such groups were suddenly becoming widespread but rather that police forces were now more likely to apply conspiratorial interpretations to cases that came to light—whether or not the charges would withstand closer examination.

In Boston in 1977, police and media proclaimed the exposure of a vicious sex ring based in the suburb of Revere. According to initial reports, hundreds of boys were "drugged and raped" by a sex ring of perhaps dozens of men and forced to make pornographic films. These images of rape and abduction are recalled by the opening sequence of the film *Mystic River*, which is set in the Boston of that era. The Revere case was rather more complex than early reports suggested. In fact, the case involved not a "ring," with all its implications of hierarchy, centralized control, and division of labor. More accurately, the case involved a pederastic subculture, or milieu, of individuals who had only tenuous connections with one another. The men were involved with teenage boys who were selling sex. To draw this distinction is not to deny that sexual exploitation was occurring, but this was not the world of predatory molestation suggested by the press. Nor were reports of child pornography substantiated.[34]

The Revere case angered gay activists, who were already radicalized by the Florida referendum fight. At first, the prosecutions were seen simply as an anti-gay witch-hunt, on the lines of the notorious cases that occurred in Boise, Idaho, in the 1950s. (That affair was commemorated in John Gerassi's book *The Boys of Boise*, a classic case study of political homophobia.) Confirming this perception of witch-hunting, Boston police clamped down on familiar gay cruising areas such as the public library, arresting hundreds. A Boston-Boise Committee coordinated protests, deploying visible spokesmen such as Allen Ginsberg. When these events turned into raucous rallies against Anita Bryant, the Revere campaigners confirmed their credentials as part of the gay rights cause. In 1978, the Boston protests spawned an authentic pedophile activist movement, the North American Man-Boy Love Association (NAMBLA): "boy love" translates the Greek-derived *pederasty*. NAMBLA claimed to be in the tradition of an earlier gay rights movement, the Mattachine Society, which had been intolerably controversial in its day but was now seen as an honored forerunner of mainstream gay activism. For several years, NAMBLA enjoyed a turbulent relationship with the gay rights movement, participating in protests and demonstrations.[35]

But Revere and NAMBLA proved divisive for sexual activists. The cases endangered the gay rights movement at a time of frequent referenda on political and legal rights, in which charges of child molesting were made so easily. The more enthusiastically the Revere arrests were portrayed as a homophobic purge, the more easily the gay cause was linked to that of child molesters.[36] Revere and its aftermath raised delicate questions concerning relationships between adults and youngsters and the limits of sixties rhetoric about sexual freedom and experiment. As they focused on issues of rape and harassment, feminists defined sexual exploitation in terms of unjust power relationships. Prima facie, that imbalance certainly applied to cases in which an adult man paid a fifteen-year-old boy for sex, and the point became still more glaring when activists pressed for abolition of the age of consent. Feminists largely refused to condemn the Revere prosecutions; this included state legislator Elaine Noble, who had attracted national attention in 1974 when she became the nation's first openly lesbian elected official. Feminist debates over the following years led to an ever stricter definition of acceptable behavior, even among consenting adults. In its Delineation of

Lesbian Rights Issues, released in 1980, NOW resolved that pederasty was "an issue of exploitation or violence, not affectional/sexual preference/ orientation." Not just for the political right, child protection was a trump card in morality debates.[37]

Death Drugs

In drug-related matters too, a rhetoric of child protection succeeded in stemming what seemed to be limitless social tolerance. Threats to children inspired a surging anti-drug movement that gained force in 1977, at exactly the time of the anti-child-abuse campaign. Of course, denunciations of illicit drugs had been a familiar part of the American scene for many years, especially during the flower power era of the 1960s. This new movement, however, was different since it generated mass mainstream support, including among those who might have been sympathetic to substances such as marijuana or even cocaine. A generation accustomed to scoffing at charges about the extreme menaces posed by illicit drugs themselves proved willing to believe those very claims, especially when they were directed against a new "teen drug."[38]

When the Carter administration came to power in 1977, the question seemed to be when, rather than if, marijuana would be decriminalized. Carter himself believed that "penalties against possession of a drug should not be more damaging to an individual than the use of the drug itself; and where they are, they should be changed." In March, the House of Representatives held hearings on decriminalization, at which the chief of the criminal division of the Department of Justice testified that the federal government no longer made marijuana prosecution a priority, "nor do we, under any conceivable way, in the federal government have the resources to do so." In August, Carter asked Congress to remove federal criminal penalties for possession of less than one ounce of marijuana, suggesting instead the imposition of minor fines. The administration was broadly sympathetic to reform, especially the president's chief adviser on drug matters, Peter Bourne. In 1978, however, Bourne's relaxed attitudes to drug matters led to scandal. He was accused of writing a false prescription for Quaaludes, and of using cocaine and marijuana at an event organized by the National Organization for the Reform of Marijuana Laws (NORML). While he denied the cocaine use, it is amazing enough in retrospect to contemplate a federal official working so amicably with NORML. In 1979, White House chief of staff Hamilton Jordan was accused of snorting cocaine at New York's Studio 54 disco (he was later acquitted).[39]

But high-level drug scandals were not the only obstacles to liberalization. The reform movement had its enemies, and by no means solely from the old anti-drug activists centered in the federal law enforcement bureaucracy. Instead, the new opposition stemmed from a novel grassroots movement speaking the rhetoric of parents' rights. Initially, as in the case of sexual abuse, concern initially focused on young people around the age of puberty, say between eleven and fourteen—those too young to have participated in the earlier teenage revolution but still indirectly affected by its reverberations. As the years went on, though, the new stringency would broaden to include older teenagers and young adults, and, in the case of drugs, to a rigid policy of prohibition that would extend across the whole of society.

When the anti-drug movement reached its height during the Reagan years, supporters looked back to an event in 1976 that acquired mythical significance. One night that summer, an Atlanta couple named Ron and Marsha Keith Schuchard hosted a party for their thirteen-year-old daughter. After the event, they were appalled to find massive evidence of marijuana use, and as Keith Schuchard wrote, "We had a sense of something invading our families, of being taken over by a culture that was very dangerous, very menacing." Both articulate professionals, the Schuchards began campaigning against teenage drug and alcohol abuse, initially among fellow parents in their upscale Atlanta neighborhood. They believed that their actions reversed the tide, creating a community of drug-free children "truly normal in their high spirits, open communication, and eager participation in family and school activities."[40]

Reasonable observers can disagree about the plausibility of what the Schuchards were describing. According to their own account, drug use provided an instant explanation of "subtle, but vaguely disturbing personality changes" they had witnessed in their daughter. Though previously a happy and outgoing child, as she approached thirteen she had become withdrawn and even hostile: " 'Yuk!' 'It would be so embarrassing!' 'There's nothing to do here'—these were her explanations as she bolted out the front door to meet her friends somewhere else."[41] To most parents in modern America, those comments sound highly characteristic of young teenagers, not least pubescent girls. In 1976, even more than today, young teenagers often were deeply alienated from their parents. However, the Schuchards determined that these problems were drug-related, an explanation that would prove highly attractive to distraught parents over the coming decades.

Whatever their interpretation of the problem, they seemed to have won an important victory. By early 1977, the group they founded became concerned about forthcoming congressional hearings that were widely expected to herald an era of decriminalization. One of the group, a self-proclaimed "mad mom," approached Robert DuPont, the director of the National Institute on Drug Abuse (NIDA), who responded to these appeals. He visited the community, opening lines of communication between parent activism and the federal public health bureaucracy that would prove critical in making drug policy over the following years.

The pace of anti-drug activism accelerated dramatically during the summer of 1977, with the national furor over PCP, or phencyclidine. PCP gained popularity during the 1970s, especially among teenagers, who knew it as "angel dust." By 1977, perhaps seven million Americans had tried the drug, and the following year, 13 percent of high school students said they had used PCP on at least one occasion. PCP was accessible and familiar for a generation thoroughly accustomed to marijuana. Users saw the drug as at most a mild escalation from pot, and the substance appeared as an adulterant in much of the marijuana sold in this period. The association between the two drugs was a valuable weapon for contemporary anti-drug campaigners, who argued that seemingly benevolent pot might often conceal this far more dangerous ingredient.[42]

Allegedly, PCP was a uniquely dangerous substance, though the vast majority of users reported no long-term harm. The anti-PCP crusade recalled the most extreme charges made against marijuana in the 1930s and against heroin and other hard drugs during the 1950s. Even more markedly than in those earlier scares, the emphasis was almost entirely on teenagers and children. As one book claimed in its title, this was the "number one teen killer." The PCP panic erupted in exactly the months that concern over sexual threats to children were at their height, and often from the same activists: Judianne Densen-Gerber was as visible an enemy of angel dust as she was of kiddie porn.[43]

Media reports presented PCP almost in terms of demonic possession. Among the press headlines from this period were "Schizophrenia Epidemic Here Linked to Youths' Use of PCP" (Washington Post) and "Angel Dust: The Devil Drug That Threatens Youth" (Woman's Day). As the Detroit Free Press wrote, "A little bit of this angel dust can bring on a whole lot of hell." Reputedly, the drug turned a user into a savage and primitive monster, and racial rhetoric implied that such atavistic reversion was especially likely for African-Americans. Throughout, the paramount danger was that savage "jungle" habits would be transmitted to the white middle class, especially its children. Todd Strasser's Angel Dust Blues (1979) was a successful young adult novel telling how a respectable white teenager lost everything by dabbling with PCP, bringing the minority world of the South Bronx into his respectable suburb and literally going over to the dark side.[44] The most deadly accusation against the drug was that it drove users to acts of irrational violence against themselves or others. Horrifying reports of users tearing out their own eyes circulated as urban legends. Atrocity stories accumulated during the panic atmosphere of 1977, when the *Washington Post* declared that PCP could "turn a person into a raging semblance of a cornered wild animal." Whenever a sensational crime of violence occurred, the media were swift to stress any evidence that the perpetrator was a PCP user. The Los Angeles media suggested that a demented PCP user might be responsible for the ongoing Hillside Strangler serial murder case.[45]

The cumulative effect of such reporting was damning. In congressional hearings during 1978, witnesses testified that "PCP is dynamite. It can do to the brain what TNT can do to a building." It was "a threat to national security . . . children were playing with death on the installment plan." Baby boomers who regarded *Reefer Madness* as one of the great comic productions were quite prepared to believe that PCP was "the King Cobra of all hallucinogens . . . [it] should be better known as hellfire." As Robert DuPont declared in 1977, "[PCP] is a real terror of a drug. Everything people used to say about marijuana is true about angel dust." From 1977 through 1984, PCP was the ultimate death drug, the maker of monsters and urban predators.[46]

The PCP scare stemmed the easygoing social tolerance of drugs, at least among the young, as some of the angel dust stigma now adhered to marijuana. As one witness told the 1978 congressional hearings, in drug matters "right now, it seems to me that the pendulum has swung back to support law enforcement." Parents' groups did much to change social attitudes, and the start of the 1977–78 school year witnessed a series of anti-drug campaigns in schools across Georgia. One typical campaign, in Dublin, Georgia, began as a response to PCP use but soon spread to condemn other, milder kinds of substance abuse. At the same time, ad hoc groups protested the merchandising of the drug culture through head shops, stores selling "space-gun marijuana smokers, toy cocaine kits, 'practice grass' sets, Quaalude candies, and LSD comic books."[47] Local ordinances prohibited the sale of drug paraphernalia; the measures would prove legally contentious but soon would drive underground the most overt manifestations of the drug culture.

This activism had a long and influential aftermath, as parents' and teachers' groups adopted hard-line anti-drug policies. By 1979, the movement reached the state level, when H. Ross Perot led a Texans' War on Drugs project, a first draft of the national movement of the 1980s. Meanwhile, DuPont asked Schuchard to write a text, *Parents, Peers, and Pot*, which ultimately sold over a million copies. The book presented every traditional anti-marijuana argument, rarely based on any significant scientific literature: the drug was said to create physical dependence, it interfered with sex hormones, it irreparably damaged the brain, and it was a precursor to more dangerous drugs. In this view, the whole notion of "soft" drugs was simply false: they were simply less immediately lethal than the more notorious chemicals. The book scoffed at the concept of " 'mere' marijuana."[48]

Parents, Peers, and Pot became the manifesto for a national parents' movement. The Schuchards formed Families in Action, which developed excellent contacts in the Carter administration. In turn, the National Federation of Parents for Drug-Free Youth was founded in 1980, and it gained enormous influence in the Reagan years. The emerging movement presented a rhetoric of "drug-free youth" that seemed cranky and puritanical in 1977 but by the 1980s would achieve the status of social orthodoxy. The whole notion of "just say no" can be traced precisely to the circumstances of 1977.

Cults

According to the common media images offered during 1977, children and teenagers were stalked by sex rings, seduced by drug dealers . . . and ensnared by evil cults. In each case, the imagined threat represented a perverted manifestation of some kind of freedom preached during the 1960s, respectively sexual liberation, chemical experimentation, and spiritual exploration. By 1977, however, each seemed to have gone terribly awry.

Concern about cults grew during the mid-1970s, especially about the means through which young people were initially recruited or converted into fringe movements. The stereotype held that recruits were not consciously or knowingly joining a particular sect but were pulled into it unwittingly through a deceptively titled front group. The Unification Church used such fronts to draw potential converts into ever-closer social and emotional ties with existing members. Once fully converted to the new sect, recruits were cut off from the outside world except in stringently controlled circumstances, their lives virtually owned by the movement. Some movements renamed their converts, signifying their absolute removal from their old lives. Appalled parents saw their teenage and young adult children utterly torn from their families.[49]

Trying to explain this rejection, parents eagerly adopted theories that cult leaders exercised some form of forcible mind control or brainwashing.

With its origins in the Korean War, the brainwashing theme was firmly associated with Asian villains, and this linkage attracted new concern when U.S. prisoners of war returning from Vietnam reported torture. The Korean origins of the Moon organization gave credibility to charges that sect leaders might use "Oriental" tactics against American youngsters. The idea was reinforced by the experiments recently reported by Stanley Milgram, who showed how ordinary people could be persuaded to commit cruel or harmful actions if they believed that they were obeying an established higher authority. Also in the news since 1973 was Stockholm syndrome, a psychological condition that induced hostages to identify with their captors. This phenomenon confirmed parents' beliefs that their children really were prisoners and captives, no matter how fervent their protestations of love and devotion to the cult and its leaders.[50]

As surely as mind-altering drugs, cult mind control allegedly turned American youngsters into robotic servants, even programmed assassins. One articulate critic of cult advances, Rabbi Maurice Davis, explicitly compared the new cults to German Nazism. In his view, a group such as the Unification Church was "1, a totally monolithic movement with a single point of view and a single authoritarian head; 2, replete with fanatical followers who are prepared and programmed to do anything their master says; 3, supplied by absolutely unlimited funds; 4, with a hatred of everyone on the outside; 5, with suspicion of parents, against their parents . . . I tell you, I'm scared." And statistics seemed to bear out this fearsome analysis. In 1979, a Senate inquiry was told that "since the early 1970s, more than ten million Americans have embraced cult activities." Rabbi Davis spoke of "two million victims and four million parents, and a country bewildered and frightened and ashamed." The news media eventually settled on a consensus figure of two million to three million cultists.[51]

These charges are open to doubt. Even if the membership of cults was as large as rumored, which is wildly unlikely, young recruits did not succumb to the kind of seductive mind control techniques that parents and professional anti-cult activists affected to believe. Just as parents of unhappy teenagers found convenient villains in drugs, so families whose children strayed to religious extremism liked to believe that they had not left of their own accord. Whatever the reason, an anti-cult movement was soon thriving. Like the anti-drug campaign, it specifically used the rhetoric of parents' rights, but this time with the more immediate goal of "freeing" children supposedly held captive in sects and compounds. Among the first of the emerging groups was the Parents' Committee to Free Our Sons and Daughters from the Children of God Organization (later FREECOG).

Others used names such as Love Our Children or Citizens Engaged in Reuniting Families. A national network now pressured the media and political leaders.[52]

But as families soon found that converts rarely wanted to be saved from their new sects, they became ever more convinced that cult recruits had indeed been subjected to brainwashing or "psychological kidnapping." They were what one book termed "hostages to Heaven." If that was the case, then families thought themselves justified in using like countermeasures. Brainwashing would be defeated through deprogramming: mind control fought mind control. By the mid-1970s, enterprising individuals were advertising their services as professional deprogrammers, who would, for a substantial fee, kidnap the convert and reconvert him or her to social and religious normality. Deprogrammers became visible experts on cult affairs, widely quoted in the news media, though such "experts" had a vested interest in making the cults appear as predatory as possible, in order to justify their own existence.[53]

In addition to families, deprogrammers, and therapists, religious groups joined the anti-cult crusade, as Christian and particularly evangelical groups challenged the "culting of America." Jews were especially concerned, since Jewish youngsters formed a disproportionate share of the population at risk from cult recruitment. An added danger from this perspective was the rise of messianic movements such as Jews for Jesus, which appeared to be seducing Jewish youth from its religious roots. This was dangerous at a time when Jews were felt to be under threat around the globe, especially in Israel and in the Soviet Union. In the United States itself, in 1977 and 1978, neo-Nazis were seeking permission to march through the heavily Jewish suburb of Skokie, Illinois. While reluctant to attack Christian evangelism directly, Jewish groups successfully framed their denunciation of proselytism in terms of protecting the young and gullible from cultish sects on the religious fringe.[54]

These diverse attacks on fringe religions gained media support, making cults as familiar and pervasive a social danger as drug dealers and child abusers. In 1976, *Time* exposed "the darker side of Sun Moon," charging him with massive personal corruption, megalomania, and the practice of ritual sex. Over the next two years, anti-cult exposés and sympathetic accounts of deprogramming appeared in mass-market magazines such as *Seventeen*, *Woman's Day*, and *Good Housekeeping*. These accounts commonly told how some young person escaped or was rescued from the clutches of an evil or destructive cult and reunited with a loving family. Parents were left in no doubt that cults were targeting their children. Cult horror stories featured in all kinds of films and television programs, including fictional dramas of rescue and defection. Even in a comedy such as *Mork and Mindy*, the heroes fight to discredit an exploitative guru.[55]

The volume of cult-related scandals grew rapidly. The Church of Scientology was engaged in bitter controversies with the U.S. government over its claims to tax-exempt status. The conflict reached the point of guerrilla war when church members purloined thousands of documents from the IRS and Justice Department, and in 1977 FBI agents raided Scientology headquarters in Los Angeles and Washington. But Scientology was only one controversial group among many. In the fall of 1978, congressional hearings into the Koreagate scandals linked the Unification Church to a bewildering network of influence peddling and political corruption. The Synanon movement offered another classic example of a cult movement prepared to strike back forcefully at critics and enemies—in one legendary instance, with a four-foot rattlesnake left in the mailbox of a lawyer who had won an action against the group. The group's leader, Chuck Dederich, once warned, "Don't mess with us—you can get killed dead, physically dead." In 1978, he pleaded nolo contendere to charges of conspiracy to murder. In Philadelphia, meanwhile, police fought a bloody battle with the "back-to-nature cultists" of the MOVE sect, which had fortified its urban headquarters.[56]

Some of the oddest anti-cult stories were very poorly substantiated, but this did not prevent them from enjoying a hair-raising currency on the conspiracy-minded fringe. Through the early 1970s, tales of cattle mutilations surfaced sporadically across the West, the crimes being variously attributed to vandals, UFOs, and sinister government experiments. In 1974–75, however, respectable regional newspapers took up the story, blaming cults and satanists. The *Denver Post* reported suspicions that "devil worshipers or cultists" were using the animal parts in bizarre rituals, while police feared that the same satanic gangs (apparently traveling in black helicopters) might soon turn their attention to dismembering people. Such stories—under headlines such as "Satanism in Kiowa?"—prefigured the obsession with satanic and ritualistic killers that would become so disreputable a feature of news reporting in the mid-1980s.[57]

In late 1978, the Jonestown murder-suicides in Guyana disarmed any skepticism that people might have felt about anti-cult rhetoric and warnings of violent extremism. Some nine hundred people reputedly killed themselves at the behest of megalomaniacal cult leader Jim Jones, many of the victims leading their families to drink poisoned Kool-Aid; hundreds of children were among the dead. Jonestown naturally spawned a number of exposé books, as well as TV movies.[58] The incident also prompted Senator Bob Dole to hold congressional hearings on the cult phenomenon, at which anti-cult critics and deprogrammers depicted a comprehensive and lethal danger to America's young people.[59]

In a media-saturated society such as the United States, social problems have their own life cycle. They begin with clamorous exposés that hit the headlines, often accompanied by sensational revelations at political hearings. Gradually, the reality of the problem is accepted, and then it enters the cultural mainstream, as what was once regarded as bizarre or outré comes to be seen as familiar. At this stage, social issues enter common parlance through their portrayal in cinema, television movies and documentaries, true crime exposés or thriller fiction, popular manuals and self-help books, and situation comedies and cartoons. By such means, within the space of two or three years, popular attitudes toward a given issue shift from "Is this really a problem?" to "How can anyone be so callous as to doubt the sufferings of the victims?"

In the late 1970s, the various threats to children—sexual, chemical, criminal, and religious—made their first impact together, most acutely during the first half of 1977, and were mainstreamed together over the next two years or so. By the end of the decade, not only were threats to children a familiar concept, but so was the imagined form of the danger: clandestine rings and secret organizations, evil predators seeking to seduce or capture them. The answer to such threats lay not in social reform nor in legal liberalization: it was a matter of war.

5

Predators

Nothing happened to me, Officer Starling. I happened. You can't
reduce me to a set of influences. You've given up good and evil
for behaviorism, Officer Starling. You've got everybody in moral
dignity pants—nothing is ever anybody's fault. Look at me,
Officer Starling. Can you stand to say I'm evil? Am I evil?
—Dr. Hannibal Lecter,
in Thomas Harris, *Silence of the Lambs*

In the late 1970s, American attitudes toward crime and justice became
significantly harsher and more punitive. Criminals were seen as motivated
by evil and beyond hope of rehabilitation or cure. In the model that now
achieved dominance, crime was the product of individual moral choice.

The basic proposition was expressed simply by James Q. Wilson, writing
in 1975: "Wicked people exist. Nothing avails except to set them apart from
innocent people. And many people, neither wicked nor innocent, but
watchful, dissembling and calculating of their opportunities, ponder our
reaction to wickedness as a cue to what they might profitably do. We have
trifled with the wicked, made sport of the innocent, and encouraged the
calculators."[1] We see analogies here with the views of the contemporary
right on international affairs, in which the United States confronted a
malevolent rival power while lesser nations calculated carefully how many
liberties they could take with American interests. In both cases, domestic
and foreign, deterrence worked. So did incapacitation, that is, ensuring that
offenders were not in a position to repeat their misdeeds.

Driving new interpretations of crime was a rash of spectacular offenders
whose careers made nonsense of conventional liberal interpretations.
Throughout these cases, we find much the same themes that motivated the
contemporaneous scares over children and child protection, and indeed,
children featured as the special targets of these terrifying predators. If these
criminals were in fact the menaces facing society, this fact demanded a

fundamental rethinking of the official response. Rather than being confused social rebellion, crime was the work of ruthless social predators, commonly habitual offenders with long records. Contrary to radical beliefs, punishment could and did prevent crime. Enforcing the criminal law and inflicting punishment was essential for the preservation of society and was in no sense an imposition of middle-class values upon the insurgent poor. Conversely, theories emphasizing social or psychological causation were derided as effectively making excuses for morally wrong behavior.[2]

Punishing

Through the 1960s, liberal approaches to crime stressed the importance of social reform and anti-poverty campaigns. In 1967, an influential presidential commission produced a report titled *The Challenge of Crime in a Free Society*, which rejected traditional visions of a repressive "war on crime." Instead, it argued that "warring on poverty, inadequate housing and unemployment is warring on crime. A civil rights law is a law against crime. Money for schools is money against crime." Some years later, though, writers such as Wilson attacked what had become the orthodoxies of criminal justice. In his book *Thinking About Crime*, Wilson noted the obvious paradox. Since 1960, the United States had experienced a massive war on poverty, with the dramatic expansion of social welfare and various Great Society programs. If in fact crime resulted from poverty, then it should surely have declined, or at least got no worse. Instead, crime rates had risen to historic highs since 1963, "the year . . . that a decade began to fall apart." Just in terms of murders, Los Angeles experienced the equivalent of a St. Valentine's Day Massacre every weekend, though such atrocities had become too commonplace to attract much concern.[3]

Wilson's views and conclusions were socially conservative, but they meshed well with the liberal reforms of the post-1965 decade, and specifically the rejection of rehabilitation. By the mid-1970s, prison reformers believed they had achieved significant victories by ending indeterminate sentencing and curbing discretion in courts and penal institutions. They looked for a steep reduction in prison populations, but it was precisely during the determinate sentencing wave of the mid-1970s that U.S. prison populations began to soar. Ironically, the authoritarian criminal justice system of the last thirty years grows directly from post-1965 libertarianism.[4]

The beginnings of America's modern punishment boom can be dated to the mid-1970s: indeed, histories of modern prisons and criminal justice often take as their baseline 1974 or 1975. Looking back at the dreadful era of the Attica riot, it comes as a shock to realize that prisons then stood as empty as they had for many years previously, and far emptier than they would soon become. Combining state and federal prisons, together with jails, America's inmate population in 1974 was under 300,000. But that figure grew to 540,000 by 1980 and would soar during the following decade.

By other measures too, the mid-1970s marked a shift toward punishment as a solution for social ills and as a symbolic assertion of social values. In 1976, the U.S. Supreme Court approved the reintroduction of capital punishment, upholding death penalty statutes as they had been revised by a number of states. Though at first executions were rare—just four between 1977 and 1981—during the 1980s the death penalty would once more become a familiar part of law enforcement practice, especially in southern states. By 2000, a total of 683 prisoners had been executed, two-thirds in just five states (Texas, Virginia, Florida, Missouri, and Oklahoma). Ninety-eight executions occurred in 1999 alone. Nationwide, support for the death penalty stood at 42 percent in 1966, showing that conservative approaches still retained a mass base, even at a time when political leaders and the mass media were widely hostile to capital punishment. The level of support rose to 67 percent by 1976 and to a crushing 79 percent by 1988.[5]

Wild in the Streets

Why did initial hopes of reform go so badly wrong? The most obvious reason for the pressure to punish was steeply rising rates of violent crime, which were linked to demographic changes. The baby boom generation was now passing through its most crime-prone age, and it would have been amazing if violence had not increased during the 1970s, regardless of changes in drug use or police practices. In 1961, the most serious crimes were recorded by police at a rate of 145.9 for every 100,000 Americans, a figure that by 1981 had increased fourfold, to 576.9. The FBI's statistics for index crimes jumped by 17 percent between 1973 and 1974, the highest ever increase for a single year.[6] Property crime rates rocketed, reaching a historic peak around 1981. And suburban and rural areas were as likely to record dramatic increases as were major urban areas.

Official crime statistics can be easily criticized, but the overall picture is confirmed by other, more reliable indices, especially studies that ask large samples of people about their encounters with crime. Victimization studies confirm that the years from 1978 through 1981 were among the most dangerous in modern American history, with more violent crime than in any more recent period. Index crime rates "exploded" in 1980, with a 10-percent nationwide increase in reported serious offenses just in the first half of that year. If we look at statistics for robbery, one of the most reliable indices for the actual incidence of violence, then the rate in 1981 was five times what it had been twenty years before. Though not ideal as a statistical measure, the homicide rate was also suggestive. In 1965, around 10,000 Americans were murdered, which already gave the United States a murder rate eight or ten times higher than that of most comparable western societies. But there were 20,000 murders by 1980, approaching 25,000 in the early 1990s. Several cities vied for the title of murder capital of America, the usual candidates including Houston, Detroit, Atlanta, and Washington, and media accounts of these cities encouraged perceptions of crime lurching out of control. Houston in 1979 was reportedly "like Dodge City of the 1880s." By 1981, Chief Justice Warren Burger denounced the "reign of terror in American cities," asking, "Are we not hostages within the borders of our own self-styled enlightened civilized country?"[7]

Not only was there more crime, but it appeared to be becoming more sadistically destructive. In 1981, *Time* claimed that crimes were becoming "more brutal, more irrational, more random—and therefore all the more frightening." Ominously, the new generation of younger criminals was extremely prone to wanton and sadistic bloodshed. In 1977, *Time*'s cover story on the "youth crime plague" argued that the United States was facing "a pattern of crime that is both perplexing and appalling . . . A new remorseless mutant juvenile seems to have been born, and there is no more terrifying figure in America today. . . . Youthful criminals prey on the most defenseless victims." The following year, Charles Silberman argued that "street criminals are more lethally armed, and they appear to be a good bit readier to use violence of any sort . . . random, senseless violence is more widespread now than in any time in the recent past, and that younger and younger boys are involved . . . sometimes, in fact, murder seems to be just a form of recreation." Some of the worst horror stories he recounts involved younger teens, usually boys of fourteen or fifteen. In 1978, ABC News offered a feature entitled *Youth Terror: View from Behind the Gun.*[8]

Crime fears found a focus in the national panic over youth gangs in the mid-1970s. Gang activity in New York peaked in 1976, when some two hundred to three hundred gangs claimed a reported seventeen thousand members. In 1976, organized criminal activity by Detroit's gangs was so extensive as to be labeled "urban terrorism." The most notorious manifestation involved a rock concert at which a hundred gang members attacked and robbed concert-goers, committing at least one rape. Recalling *Clockwork Orange*, this was termed a "clockwork riot." In 1977, *Newsweek* noted that while Americans no longer worried about urban riots, the gang culture of areas such as the South Bronx left them suffering "a constant urban riot—a year-round ever-spreading conflagration in many of our cities." In contrast to the legendary time of "long hot summers" in the 1960s, now "it's always hot in the city."[9]

The gang threat was popularized in sensational films such as *Assault on Precinct Thirteen* and *The Warriors*. Both depicted gang members as inconceivably numerous, soldiers in vast armies capable of virtual human-wave assaults, and devoid of any normal restraint. *The Warriors* begins with a phantasmagoric gang convention in which gang overlord Cyrus tells the assembled faithful how easily they could rule the city if they ever wished. The film's publicity blared, "These are the Armies of the Night. They are 100,000 strong. They outnumber the cops five to one. They could run New York City."[10]

Crime really was growing worse at a time when most liberal political leaders tended to dismiss concern about violent crime as coded language for racial hatred and white supremacy. At the same time, federal judges were enhancing the rights of criminal suspects and defendants, apparently hampering the effective workings of the criminal justice system. The gulf between popular and official perceptions of crime was reflected in popular culture and in the rapturous public response to films that showed a no-nonsense response to brutal criminals, such as *Dirty Harry* (1971). In the most famous scene, a professional criminal is seen as a rational "calculator" of the precise sort described by Wilson. A wounded robber has to decide whether grabbing a gun is more likely to lead to immediate escape or violent death ("You've got to ask yourself a question: do I feel lucky?"). He makes his calculation and is deterred from violence. The film's central theme, though, involves the pursuit of an evil serial killer who cannot be deterred and must be destroyed. Even so, the forces of justice are hampered at every stage by the deluded liberalism of courts and officialdom, who have no realistic sense of the iniquity they are facing. In 1974, liberal commentators worried about the public reception of *Death Wish* as audiences literally cheered the frustrated white vigilante who executes street criminals. A public terrified of violent offenders demanded that its elected officials respond with sharp punishments. Even if "nothing worked," at least criminals could be kept off the streets. Perceptions that crime was careening out of control gave added urgency to combating other problems that could be linked to this menace, especially illicit drugs such as PCP.

Desperate concern over youth crime encouraged the search for unorthodox solutions that stressed individual responsibility and promised a back-to-basics approach based on simple deterrence. This willingness to clutch at straws explains the enormous success of the "scared straight" phenomenon at the end of the 1970s. According to media reports, juvenile authorities in New Jersey had taken a group of young offenders on the verge of entering careers of serious crime and subjected them to a prison-based program in which they were confronted with convicts serving life sentences. In their interactions, the youths learned to their horror the fate that awaited them if and when they entered adult prisons: the routine of brutality and sexual exploitation, all described in harrowing street language. The appalled teenagers learned the risks they were running and resolved to mend their lives. This was the story recounted in newspapers and in an Oscar-winning documentary widely seen on national television in 1978.[11]

As it stands, the "scared straight" story is myth. The "young criminals" used as subjects were in fact a cross section of average teens rather than serious delinquents, and claims about the program's effectiveness were never substantiated. The popular impression, though, was that the solution to youth crime lay in a short, sharp shock that would turn lives around and force young offenders to make the right moral choices. Applied promptly and sternly, deterrence worked. The enormous popularity of the "scared straight" approach apparently gave a solid professional basis to popular assumptions about the straightforward moral choices underlying crime. Only a few months later, in early 1979, the media reported yet another cure-all for crime in the form of the urban vigilante movement, New York City's Guardian Angels.[12]

The increase in violent crime encouraged a greater use of incarceration, but this was not the only explanation for swollen prison populations. The fact that incarceration rates kept rising so steeply after the peak of violent crime had passed shows that other forces were at work. Also, the people being imprisoned were by no means the violent hard core, the murderers, rapists, and robbers. A distressing number were sentenced for nonviolent offenses, usually involving drugs. The escalation of penalties was partly a consequence of handing sentencing reform directly to legislators during the determinate sentencing wave of the 1970s. Though administrators and criminologists might be skeptical of the usefulness of punishment, such concerns did not deter elected officials from racking up prescribed sentences in order to prove their samurai credentials in the struggle against crime. By enforcing tough policies, they could show themselves responsive not just to traditional law-and-order constituencies but also to feminists, who demanded tough penalties for sex offenders, rapists, and abusers.

The conflict between administrators and legislators recurred time and again in the sentencing debates. Criminologists and correctional administrators might propose that a given crime merited a sentence of, say, one year, which would provide both adequate deterrence for the offender and protection for the public. A political bidding war would then ensue, and the final recommended sentence might be eight or ten years. Moreover, in the new environment, judges would have no option but to impose that term, however inappropriate it might appear for a given case. Mandatory sentences were particularly tempting for legislatures responding to real or imagined crime waves. Whether the issue was drug trafficking, carjacking, or stalking, it was politically popular to threaten an impressive mandatory sentence for the crime du jour.

Monsters

The shift to punishment per se also reflects a sea change in concepts of the nature of crime. The much-maligned older model of treatment and rehabilitation was based on a vision of the offender as in some sense a victim, someone whose crimes grew out of social or psychological pressures. Criminology was a subset of sociology or psychiatry. Radicals attacked this medical approach, which denied individual responsibility and made the criminal less than fully human. But once the therapeutic model was gone, how could one realistically explain the misdeeds of a criminal, especially one whose deeds seemed so disturbing? If the offender had full responsibility and chose to rape or kill repeatedly, what explanation could one advance except for archaic ideas of personal wickedness? This view was aptly expressed by Gary Gilmore, who in 1977 became the first American to be executed following the reintroduction of the death penalty. Explaining his refusal to delay his execution, he said, "Weak bad habits . . . have left me somewhat evil. I don't like being evil and . . . desire not to be evil anymore." In its 1977 special issue on the "plague" of youth crime, *Time* attacked the linkage claimed between crime and poverty, suggesting that the sheer sadistic brutality of the acts represented "expressions of what moral philosophers would call sheer evil."[13]

The textbook illustration of the criminal as monster was Willie Bosket. In 1978, Bosket, then age fifteen, was arrested for murdering two passengers on New York subway trains as part of a series of violent robberies. He had been committing crimes since the age of nine and claimed involvement in some two thousand offenses. He looked convincingly like the homicidal demon-child imagined in the contemporary hysterias over PCP and evil cults. The affair was all the worse because his extreme youth made effective punishment impossible. Since Bosket was too young to be treated as an adult criminal, he was subject to the juvenile system, which meant that he could be incarcerated only until he was twenty-one. (In fact, a series of assaults that he later committed while in prison would lead to prolonged incarceration.) The case provoked draconian legal reform, allowing offenders as young as thirteen to be tried and punished as adults for serious crimes. Through the 1980s, this principle of sending certain juvenile cases to the adult system would cause an ever-growing number of teenagers to face serious criminal sentences, as the boundaries once separating the juvenile and adult justice systems all but vanished. The dream of deinstitutionalization faded.[14] The Bosket affair also focused attention on the roots of crime. Bosket himself demonstrated that at least some criminals were "born bad" and stood no chance of being reformed. The fact that Bosket's own father was a career criminal ensured that old theories about the bad seed were freely cited. As Willie Bosket's trial proceeded through 1978, the news media presented daily images of the criminal as irredeemably evil and predatory.

We might ask how the Bosket affair could have been interpreted otherwise, but abundant examples from the recent past suggest how alternative images would have been available in a different political or cultural setting. A sensational crime may lead to the offender being represented as a "monster," but that it is not the only image that might be offered by the media or popular culture and which will live on in popular memory. In the 1940s, Chicago serial killer and sex offender William Heirens was remembered not as a monster but as a tragic case study of Freudian theories about the compulsive nature of crime (he left a pathetic plea at a crime scene urging police, "For heaven's sake catch me before I kill more. I cannot control myself"). In the 1950s, serial rapist Caryl Chessman earned worldwide fame as a martyr to the brutality of capital punishment.[15]

A telling counterpart to the Bosket affair occurred in New York City itself in 1964, when Kitty Genovese was murdered. The affair attracted worldwide notoriety because neighbors had refused to respond to the victim's cries for help, causing soul-searching about urban anomie and alienation, collective selfishness, and the callous refusal to help one's neighbor. Commentators suggested that the case showed how public apathy permitted political evil to flourish, whether in Nazi Germany or the segregationist South. The case became the subject of television dramas and documentaries, nonfiction books, folk songs, poems, and artworks, and it was featured for years afterward in college lectures and religious sermons. Society, in short, murdered Kitty Genovese.[16]

All but forgotten in this fervor of penitence was the actual killer, Winston Moseley, who confessed to two other murders and who claimed "an uncontrollable urge to kill . . . I chose women to kill because they were easier and didn't fight back." Even the judge at his trial announced, "When I see this monster, I wouldn't hesitate to pull the switch myself." Though he was at least as plausible a candidate for monster status as Willie Bosket, that was never how he appeared in cultural representations, and Moseley's name soon fell into oblivion. Accounts of the Genovese murder refer generically to "the man who killed her" without bothering to provide details. Moseley, in fact, was forgotten as thoroughly as the victims of Willie Bosket or the victims of later serial killers would be in their day. We read into criminal cases those lessons that we want and need to find. The contrasting responses to Moseley and Bosket indicate a transformation of popular attitudes to crime.

The Hard Core

In part, this shift grew out of new trends in academic criminology. Since the 1920s, American criminologists had stressed the social factors that gave rise to crime and deviance, but such studies tended to overexplain crime, in the sense that by no means all children born in slum areas became violent criminals. During the 1970s, a growing body of research reported that the great bulk of crime, and especially dangerous violent crime, was in fact the work of a tiny group of chronic offenders. As criminologist Marvin Wolfgang asserted, "We know who he is by the time he is thirteen or fourteen," and Wolfgang's evidence powerfully influenced James Q. Wilson. One influential study published in 1980 described violent crime as stemming from the "violent two percent," though in fact only a fraction of 1 percent of the population would ever be involved in the most serious acts of robbery, rape, and murder. This tiny hard core was very prolific. Willie Bosket was one example of a significant, and dangerous, phenomenon. In the late 1970s, one notorious family of four New York brothers was reportedly connected with between two thousand and three thousand serious crimes. Contemplating such individuals, sober academic criminologists used the moralistic language of "restraining the wicked."[17]

While not denying the role of social causation, such studies raised the question of what other factors might drive one individual rather than another to commit extreme or outrageous crimes. They also favored certain official responses. While rehabilitation was out of the question in such cases, so was deterrence. The only real grounds for punishment was incapacitation, that is, putting offenders behind bars for very long stretches.

Academic studies did not have an immediate impact on popular opinion, though they influenced legislators and professionals. More effective in shaping public perceptions of crime were portrayals in popular culture, which in many ways echoed the findings of sober scholarship. Images of the killer as the embodiment of evil began to appear in the early 1970s, partly as a result of the Charles Manson affair, but it was from mid-decade that such images acquired unprecedented notoriety, as the serial killer came to epitomize violent crime in the popular imagination. Soon we can speak of serial murder as a whole mythological system, with its repertoire of heroes and demon figures.

Psycho Killers

As in the case of drugs or child abuse, what was new was not the scale of the serial murder menace but the lethal seriousness with which it was now seen. Cases of serial homicide were first recorded in the United States in the nineteenth century, and they occurred quite frequently in the first half of the twentieth. It was in the decade after 1974, however, that they became part of public legend.[18]

Just how celebrated the cases of these years became can be illustrated by asking an average consumer of news to identify the following individuals: Chester Dewayne Turner, Efren Saldivar, Charles Cullen, Robert L. Yates, Lorenzo Gilyard, Ted Bundy, and John Wayne Gacy. Unless the respondent is a crime buff, it is unlikely that he or she would recognize the names of some of America's most prolific serial killers until the names of Bundy and Gacy are reached. These two cases remain legendary, while the others are relatively obscure—surprisingly so, since one would expect the more recent incidents to remain within the horizon of popular memory. (All of the first five names are contemporary, in the sense that all have been tried or convicted since 1998.) Nor are cases remembered because some individuals claimed a particularly high number of victims: Saldivar and Cullen both were allegedly connected to more victims than either Bundy or Gacy.[19]

The celebrity attached to a multiple killer has little to do with any intrinsic qualities of the particular case. On average, major serial murder cases are reported somewhere in the United States every three or four weeks, and many offenders claim ten or more victims. Even so, most cases attract no more than local notoriety, and only a few instances become sufficiently well known to become the subject of a gaudy true crime book. But no case in the last decade has acquired anything like the legendary quality of the cases of the 1970s. Bundy and Gacy are so well remembered because they provided faces to what was quite suddenly—between 1976 and 1978—perceived to be a national threat. This phenomenon attracted such attention because it gave a visible and comprehensible focus to intense fears about violence, specifically directed against women and children.[20]

Also crucial, if unstated, was the racial dimension of the multiple-murder issue, namely, that the public could express its nightmares about violent crime without being accused of race baiting. Throughout modern political history, the politics of law and order have often become conflated with the language of race, and at least notionally, politicians deplore racial panic-mongering. Through the gang panics of the 1970s, racial tensions were difficult to avoid. It is not easy to discuss groups such as Detroit's Black Killers or Chicago's Black Gangster Disciples without being accused of linking race to gang violence. Serial homicide, though, initially *seemed* to offer a race-free issue. In reality, African-American and other minority serial killers are a well-known phenomenon. Blacks make up about as large a proportion of serial murderers as they do of homicide offenders as a whole, and some minority killers have claimed large numbers of victims: Coral Watts was one notorious example from the 1980s. Most, though, have been neglected in popular culture, allowing nonspecialists to believe that serial murder is a distinctively white offense. Sensational accounts of multiple killers such as Ted Bundy can use all the familiar rhetoric of subhuman savagery, animal brutality, and monstrous atavism without venturing into the controversial realm of race. Serial murder is one of the rare types of crime in which polemical law-and-order rhetoric can be used and widely accepted without the possibility of giving racial offense.[21]

The Age of Murder

Through the early 1970s, several cases of extreme serial murder made national headlines, all of which attracted national and international attention. In 1973, the Houston case of Dean Corll offered the spectacle of a pederastic killer torturing and massacring teenage boys. By 1974, true crime studies concerning such cases began to proliferate, becoming a whole genre by the end of the decade. Partly, this was a response to the phenomenal success of best-selling books on the Manson case, which clearly tapped into an enthusiastic mass audience.[22] People wanted to read about the most extreme instances of criminal evil.

Soon, journalists and true crime writers found sensational new material, especially with cases that occurred in major metropolitan areas readily convenient for the media. Spectacular cases in 1977 included the Son of Sam killings, committed by David Berkowitz in New York City, and the Hillside stranglings in Los Angeles. Both stories dominated the headlines for months, and coverage surged with each new victim, every new lead or suspect. The Berkowitz case gained added force from the killer's celebrated letters to the newspapers, published that spring. These contained evocative passages linking random violence to social dysfunction and urban decay: "Hello from the gutters of New York City, which are filled with dog manure, vomit, stale wine, urine and blood. . . . Thirsty, hungry, seldom stopping to rest; anxious to please Sam. Sam's a thirsty lad and he won't let me stop killing until he gets his fill of blood."[23] In each case too, discussion and comment was kept alive for several years afterward by true crime books, television documentaries, and television movies. The Son of Sam case was commemorated in rock music through the 1977 Talking Heads song "Psycho Killer," while the cartoon *Doonesbury* used the case to attack the sensational tone of New York tabloid journalism.[24]

The best-known villain from these years was Ted Bundy, perhaps the most notorious serial killer since Jack the Ripper. The affair first came to light in 1974 with a series of murders in Washington state and Utah. Bundy was arrested in January 1977, but a daring prison escape earned him a place on the FBI's Ten Most Wanted list. Bundy was already a figure of national notoriety when he made his second jailbreak in December 1977 and traveled to Florida to commit his final series of murders. His televised trial, together with some prison interviews, left an impression of a handsome and articulate individual with a sense of humor, a figure whom observers found striking and even likable—though he may have killed thirty women and girls.[25] He emerged as an effective popular villain who could epitomize evil without being a simple mindless brute. The story provoked several television movies and numerous true crime books.

While the stories of Bundy and Berkowitz were making national headlines, many lesser-known murder series were drawing regional attention. Just during 1977, multiple murder cases occurred in Oakland County, Michigan; Columbus, Georgia; and Wichita, Kansas, while early 1978 brought the gruesome Vampire killings in Sacramento. Meanwhile, the California Freeway killings claimed the lives of over forty young men between 1976 and 1980, allegedly the work of one prolific offender. (Subsequent prosecutions would show that the crimes were actually the work of at least two unrelated serial killers.) Through 1977 and 1978, it was difficult to avoid finding news stories about not just one such case but several in progress concurrently somewhere in the nation.

The multiple-murder issue acquired a terrifying new focus at the end of 1978 when Chicago police were investigating the disappearance of a teenage boy. Searching the house of contractor John Wayne Gacy, police found twenty-nine bodies buried in his crawlspace, and he was subsequently connected to thirty-three killings of boys and young men, though the actual total may have been far higher. Apart from the number of victims, Gacy owed his uniquely evil reputation to his image as the "killer clown." As a public-spirited citizen, he had entertained local children by donning a clown suit, and the shocking juxtaposition with his career of murder proved unforgettable. One photograph showed him posing alongside First Lady Rosalynn Carter. The lethal clown face came to symbolize the multiple-murder threat just as effectively as the handsome talking head of Ted Bundy.[26]

Slashers

A successful wave of film treatments ensured that multiple murder remained in the popular imagination. Since the early days of the cinema, stories based on Jack the Ripper had appeared regularly, and treatments reached new heights during the noir years of the 1940s. In the 1970s, however, serial murder stories enjoyed a new popularity, due in part to the near-collapse of cinema censorship. The worldwide success of *The Exorcist* in 1973 demonstrated the commercial potential of ultra-violent horror films, and two 1974 cult films would spawn dozens of slasher successors. *The Texas Chainsaw Massacre* introduced the idea of the killer as a deranged monster wielding bizarre weapons and thoroughly depersonalized by his use of a mask. *Black Christmas* (also released under the title *Stranger in the House*) was a pioneering tale of attractive young women being stalked and slaughtered by a faceless (male) killer. Also demonstrating the commercial power of bloody horror was the 1976 Brian De Palma film *Carrie*.[27]

These themes coalesced in the 1978 film *Halloween*, which tells how Michael Myers slaughters several suburban teenagers. Michael appears as a thoroughly inhuman monster, voiceless and masked, and his only function is to serve as a relentless killing machine. *Halloween* was not directly based on any specific case, but the concept of the multiple murders of young women over a single night owed something to Ted Bundy's rampage in a Florida sorority house. The film's director, John Carpenter, had an excellent sense for public nightmares, as his previous venture was the 1976 gang film *Assault on Precinct Thirteen*. *Halloween* swiftly became "the most profitable independent film in Hollywood history." The film's influence was soon seen in a wave of derivative films that came to be known as slasher or slice-and-dice movies, which were at their height in 1980 and 1981.[28]

These films differed radically from their predecessors in the abandonment of any pretense at subtle interpretation of the homicidal offender.

They are studies of pure evil, not psychiatric disorder. In 1960, the film of *Psycho* ends with a psychiatrist explaining the Freudian conflicts that drove Norman Bates to become an irrational killer, a process for which he had little direct responsibility. In *Halloween*, the psychiatrist who has escaped from the clutches of Michael Myers explains that yes, Michael was indeed the bogeyman. The regularity with which slasher villains resurrected after their apparent deaths gave them a distinctly supernatural or demonic quality. Supernatural evil motivating a serial killer was also a theme of a serious mainstream film, *The Shining* (1980).[29]

The boom in slasher movies coincided with a revival of interest in horror themes in popular culture. During the 1970s, the horror genre was resuscitated by the work of authors such as Stephen King and Peter Straub, who used extreme and violent images. The success of such writing encouraged many imitators in search of new themes, especially as traditional villains such as vampires and werewolves had become so hackneyed.[30] Authors were attracted by the serial murder stories then occupying such a prominent role in the media. Stuart Woods's *Chiefs* portrayed a Gacy-inspired multiple killer burying boys in his secret cemetery. The most influential of the new wave was Thomas Harris's *Red Dragon*, which created a whole mythology of brilliant and utterly evil serial killers and the preternaturally skilled FBI agents who combat them. (The better-known sequel to *Red Dragon* is *The Silence of the Lambs*.) Like John Carpenter, Harris had an excellent eye for public nightmares, and his 1975 novel *Black Sunday* described an Arab-sponsored attempt to carry out a terror attack against the Super Bowl.

Agendas

The deep public interest in multiple murder needs some explanation. In any typical year, serial murders account for perhaps 1 or 2 percent of all homicides, a minuscule number compared with the victims of domestic violence, though the latter type of crime rarely features in popular studies of violence. Nor do acts such as robbery or burglary, which are far more likely to impinge on the lives of ordinary people than the highly infrequent acts of a Ted Bundy. The popularity of the serial murder theme must rather be sought in the mythical quality of the narratives, the moral and political messages they convey.

At first sight, it seems odd that people would respond so enthusiastically to the hyperbolic images of serial murder offered in popular culture, whether in films, novels, or true crime stories. The abundance of treatments gave the impression that a new Bundy or Gacy could strike at any time and that the reader or viewer could be the next victim. One might think that such images would intimidate a potential media audience, but the approach can be explained if it is placed in the context of the underlying mythology of the genre. Extremely dangerous and threatening individuals undertake dreadful crimes, but in some ways they are perhaps less threatening than "everyday" criminals, since they can be personalized and individualized. Violent crime is attributed to a handful of evil individuals, and understanding this menace is less difficult than comprehending the diverse social factors that drive the faceless robbers, rapists, and murderers of real life. Once a monster has been identified, he can be defeated and captured. Nothing like the same confidence can be attached to the truly faceless robbers or burglars that one is far more likely to encounter. As the ever-quotable Bundy himself remarked, "For people to want to condemn someone, to dehumanize someone like me, is a very popular and effective way of dealing with a fear and a threat that is just incomprehensible."[31]

But political messages were more complex, given the controversies of the time. It did not take great imagination to see the army of serial killers as products of the sexual permissiveness of the 1960s and its perversion of proper manhood. Following the exposés of sexual abuse and exploitation during 1977, Bundy and the Hillside Strangler could easily be read as manifestations of specifically male violence against women. They also symbolized the consequences of unchecked sexual stimulation, given the easy availability of explicit pornographic material. Most of these cases were not just murders but sexually motivated rape-murders. Bundy would attribute some of his criminal tendencies to early exposure to pornography.[32]

Such cases gave ammunition to the growing feminist movement against pornography and sexual violence. Already in 1975, Susan Brownmiller's anti-rape text *Against Our Will* both analyzed serial murder as a subset of sexual crime and denounced the media romanticization of the killer, and by the end of the decade, this type of crime was featuring increasingly in feminist analyses. Feminist theorists found abundant support in the radically misogynist remarks of arrested offenders themselves. Following his arrest in 1979, the Hillside Strangler, Kenneth Bianchi, summarized one of his killings thus: "She was a hooker. Angelo [Buono] went and picked her up. I was waiting in the street. He drove around to where I was. I got in the car. We got on the freeway. I fucked and killed her. We dumped the body off and that was it. Nothing to it."[33]

Also reflecting the concerns of 1977, much of the serial murder activity was directed against children or young teenagers. Teenage boys represented the main victims of several of the most publicized villains of the period, including Dean Corll and John Wayne Gacy, and the Trash-Bag and Freeway killers. Such stories highlighted the danger of homosexual predation directed toward boys and young men. The media rhetoric of "gay serial killers" confounded homosexuals with both pedophiles and child killers, a powerful political weapon at the time of anti-gay reaction. Again, this linkage between homosexuality and unpredictable violence was well cultivated in the popular media. A strong fictional tradition associated multiple murder with homosexuality or transvestism, an idea central to *Psycho*. In 1977, a deranged homosexual killer claimed the life of the (female) central figure in *Looking for Mr. Goodbar*. The 1980 film *Cruising* depicted New York's gay leather and sado-masochistic subcultures in chilly terms, portraying a sex-obsessed world inherently prone to savage violence. Though the ending is ambiguous—it is never quite clear who carries out a particular murder —the film implies that exposure to this poisonous environment might so corrupt even a straight police officer that he becomes a sadistic killer.[34]

The Insanity of Insanity

The surging interest in extremely violent offenders, fictional and real, had its impact on debates over criminal justice policy. At the core of the new controversies was the issue of individual responsibility for crime, as theories stressing free will and personal choice supplanted determinism. This transformation was epitomized by changing attitudes toward the insanity defense. Since the beginning of the twentieth century, this defense had provided a critical means of expanding the role of psychiatry and medicine in the courtroom, while diminishing older legal ideas of strict individual responsibility. Under the *Durham* rules of 1954, a defendant was not criminally responsible if the unlawful act was "a product of mental disease or defect," a formula that allowed expansive latitude to psychiatric expert witnesses.[35]

Over the next twenty years, conservatives challenged the insanity defense for apparently letting flagrantly guilty offenders escape punishment. Critics of medical and therapeutic views of crime gained new ammunition from the assassination controversies of the 1970s. Repeatedly, psychiatric experts proposed implausible-sounding "lone nut" theories, tracing the roots of an assassination to the individual makeup and experience of the offender while ignoring any political context. In the case of Sirhan Sirhan, psychiatrists were accused of brainwashing the arrested assassin in order to make him sound irrationally obsessed with killing Bobby Kennedy. Such medical experts, it was claimed, were playing supporting roles in the larger official conspiracy.[36]

During the late 1970s, the insanity defense came under renewed challenge, but this time in an environment deeply suspicious of any attempt to evade personal responsibility for crime. Within a few weeks at the end of 1978, a series of shocking events proclaimed the sheer power of moral evil and, by implication, the bankruptcy of therapeutic approaches to crime. That November, global news headlines were dominated by the story of Jonestown, as Jim Jones proved the astonishing charismatic power of evil, of a psychopathic god. The language of the demonic was widely used in news reporting and in the congressional hearings on cults that ensued in early 1979. The case recalled images of Charles Manson and Hitler and even aroused fears that America's social chaos could produce a Jim Jones-style demagogue. Reporting on the film *The Warriors, Time* magazine drew analogies between Jones and the charismatic gang leader Cyrus, who dreams of mobilizing his followers to control New York City. Such speculations were sufficiently widespread to provoke a *Doonesbury* parody about the fanatical sect threatening the country, the "Liberal Cult," and its charismatic compound-dwelling leaders, the Kennedys ("'What sort of sway does "Ted" have over his followers?' ... 'I would do anything for him'").[37]

A few days after the Jonestown catastrophe, Americans heard of yet another instance of political assassination when disaffected conservative politician Dan White assassinated two of San Francisco's leading liberal politicians, including gay leader Harvey Milk.[38] The fact that these killings occurred so soon after Jonestown stimulated conspiracy theories, not least because Jim Jones had been so close to San Francisco's liberal elite. (Jones's followers had already assassinated a northern California congressman.) Some days after the White murders, headlines announced the discovery of the secret graveyard under John Wayne Gacy's Chicago house. All three of these grotesque cases occurred within the space of barely three weeks, and in different ways each story presented troubling messages about the state of contemporary society—the tendency to random and sadistic violence, the presence of dangerous psychopaths, the vulnerability to fanaticism, and the need to explain what appeared to be pure moral evil. The careers of Jones and Gacy also pointed to the savage consequences of unchecked sexual exploitation and suggested that these various elements often combined to victimize the young: children made up a large proportion of the Jonestown victims.

The White and Gacy cases both raised questions about the ability of the justice system to cope with evil. In the spring of 1979, White stood trial for what appeared to have been a carefully planned assassination. However, defense psychiatrists persuaded the jury that White was suffering from an untreated depressive condition, which had contributed to his crime. One piece of evidence for this was that the previously fastidious White had recently shifted to a diet of junk food, including Twinkies. On the basis of the depression argument, White was convicted only of manslaughter, a decision that enraged liberal and gay forces in San Francisco, and a major riot ensued. For the debate over criminality, the actual decision was less significant than what urban legend reported about the case, namely, that White's lawyers had convinced a gullible jury that junk food had actually *caused* his homicidal action. The legend of the "Twinkie defense" boosted efforts to reform or abolish the insanity defense and to reassert the responsibility of the individual for criminal acts.

Demands for reform were further energized when Gacy went on trial in 1980, again a hugely publicized event. His lawyers too pressed an ambitious series of psychiatric defenses that to a lay audience appeared contrived and implausible. This case again demonstrated the massive theoretical and linguistic gulf separating psychiatrists for the prosecution and defense, who seemed unable to agree on even the most basic terms and concepts. As legal scholar Norval Morris remarked, the insanity defense had become "witches and warlocks, ritual and liturgy."[39] Each side appeared to be operating as hired guns rather than objective experts. In media reporting, the Gacy case further discredited the already battered therapeutic model of crime, particularly when at one point the defense seemed likely to win a reduced sentence on grounds of mental disorder. The response was predictable: could the courts not even protect American children from a John Wayne Gacy?

Though they are rarely treated together, obvious parallels exist between the new constructions of America's foreign and domestic problems in the late 1970s, between predatory states overseas and predatory individuals at home. In both cases, urgent problems were viewed in terms of identifiable stereotyped enemies, rather than underlying social and economic tensions. Answers were to be found in a straightforward assertion of traditional moralities and a clear demarcation of the lines separating right and wrong. At home and abroad also, the rhetoric of evil condemned the naïveté and weakness of existing institutions and ideologies, especially of those liberal views stemming from the moral relativism of the 1960s. Whether protecting its interests overseas or its children at home, American society needed to adopt more aggressive and confrontational attitudes toward its enemies. By 1979, these ideas had become mainstream, and they would be far more central given the dramatic political events that unfolded in the next year.

6

Captive America: 1980

The absence of alternatives clears the mind marvelously.
—Henry Kissinger

The year 1980 was one of the most frightening in modern American history. The sense of national weakness and dissolution that had been gathering through the decade found a focus in a massive international crisis, which reverberated in domestic politics. For the first time in decades, ordinary Americans were wondering whether they would have fuel to run their cars and heat their houses, whether society could continue in its familiar patterns. Through 1980, American media were reporting events that were depressing or frightening in their own right, but which became worse because of their cumulative quality. The hostage crisis in Iran was bad enough by itself, highlighting American military weakness and portending oil shortages and gas lines, but it was aggravated by the memories that it inevitably conjured up: the fall of the U.S. embassy in Saigon, American prisoners in Vietnam. Such connections arose spontaneously, without the need for political activists to drive them home.

Against this chaotic background, America by 1980 was a society ripe for conspiracy interpretations of problems, whether these clandestine threats involved terrorism, serial murder, or hate crimes. What had changed since 1976 was that now, the most potent claims of threat and conspiracy came from the political right rather than the liberal left. Global events gave the lie to recent hopes that the superpowers could achieve some rational sense of balance, suggesting instead a stark moral choice between the forces of right and wrong. The most pessimistic conservative interpretations seemed justified. The United States was clearly involved in a global confrontation from which it might not emerge victorious. The Cold War might yet be lost. This atmosphere of threat and crisis gave enormous importance to the critical presidential election of that year.

Iranian Prelude

When Americans recall the horrors of 1980, they are not thinking of events that observed a neat chronological limit. The crisis began in earnest with the seizing of the Tehran embassy in November 1979 and reached a kind of resolution with the election of Ronald Reagan almost a year to the day later. But problems had been growing steadily over the previous year, as the Carter administration encountered more and more difficulties, especially with its foreign policy and its insistence that friendly nations obey U.S. concepts of human rights. As conservatives had asked, though, what happened when these troubled nations were under revolutionary threat?

The most critical target for radical change was Iran, which under its dictatorial shah had been America's closest ally in the region, apart from Israel. Iran had refused to join in oil boycotts against the United States, and it served as a stabilizing force on world oil markets. It was also an exemplar of rapid economic growth, plausibly hoping to reach European standards of living within a generation. However, Iran had a repressive police state apparatus, with its notorious secret police, SAVAK, and human rights abuses caused friction with the Carter administration. Reportedly, U.S. assistance to the Iranian regime included techniques of surveillance and interrogation, encouraging the exposure of new CIA horror stories. American liberals recalled that the shah's regime owed its power to the 1953 coup engineered by U.S. and British intelligence agencies. Congressional Democrats, including allies of Vice President Mondale, made no secret of their loathing of the shah and promised to make it harder for him to receive arms and other support. The United States progressively discontinued military and intelligence support, including its long-standing efforts to mute Islamist rhetoric by co-opting or buying off firebrand preachers.[1]

By 1978, the Iranian regime was facing growing popular hostility with the rising power of radical Shi'ite Islam under its charismatic leader, the Ayatollah Khomeini. The harder the regime tried to suppress the turmoil, the more American liberals denounced repression and campaigned to cut off support. By February 1979, following a winter of growing instability, the regime collapsed. The shah fled the country, and Khomeini took power in a new Islamic republic. U.S. military and intelligence personnel were forced to leave Iran under chaotic circumstances in which important secret materials were allowed to fall into revolutionary hands.

These events baffled American policy experts, who were accustomed to seeing the world's conflicts in terms of secular political issues such as Communism and nationalism; they had utterly failed to take the Islamic challenge seriously. Walter Mondale was not the only Washington policy maker asking pathetically, "What the hell is an ayatollah anyway?" Khomeini failed to follow the familiar East-West divide, condemning both Americans and Soviets equally as two sides of one Western secular coin. Worse, the new force of political Islam spread rapidly: in November, radical insurgents seized the Grand Mosque in Mecca, Saudi Arabia. The United States was facing something much like the discredited notion of the domino theory, with the media speculating nervously about which country would be next. *Business Week* devoted a special issue to "the decline of U.S. power," with a cover image of the weeping face of the Statue of Liberty. Declaring Khomeini its Man of the Year in early 1980, *Time* noted, "Already the flames of anti-Western fanaticism that Khomeini fanned in Iran threaten to spread through the volatile Soviet Union, from the Indian subcontinent to Turkey and southward through the Arabian Peninsula to the Horn of Africa."[2]

For nonspecialist Americans, the medieval figure of Khomeini was alternately ridiculous and alarming, but the timing of the revolution allowed disturbing domestic parallels to be drawn. With his legion of fanatical devotees, the demagogic Khomeini looked like nothing so much as an American-style cult leader, of the sort so recently in the news from Jonestown. The news from Iran came in exactly the same weeks that congressional inquiries into domestic cults were making daily headlines. Had a cult taken over a once-powerful country? If so, could the new regime possibly be worse than the old SAVAK state that the media had loved to hate? In fact, the new Iran proved much more brutal than the shah's, entirely reversing his economic gains and achieving a general decline of living standards on a scale rarely paralleled in modern history. In exchange for a dictatorship friendly to U.S. interests, the administration had obtained a far more ruthless despotism thoroughly hostile to the West.[3]

At this point, foreign policy issues came home to the American people with a vengeance, as disruptions in global oil supplies produced gas shortages in the United States. This second oil shock was not as immediately dangerous as the boycotts of 1973–74, nor did it arise unequivocally from the actions of Arab or Muslim states, but it hit consumers hard, especially in certain regions. By May, California was the scene of lines of several hundred cars queuing for gasoline, with fights and minor riots erupting. In June,

OPEC raised prices by 50 percent. In real (inflation-adjusted) terms, oil prices now reached their all-time high, of around $90 a barrel in modern-day terms. In the popular view, the new oil crisis seemed to be another example of the U.S. failure to assert its power. Graffiti and bumper stickers urged, "Nuke Their Ass and Take Their Gas" and "Send the Marines for Oil Now." One ultra-right poster showed a grinning American soldier standing over a dying Arab, with a mushroom cloud in the background; the caption read, "How much is the gas now?"[4]

Making matters worse was the near-meltdown that had occurred in March in Pennsylvania's Three Mile Island nuclear plant. Initially, the disaster spurred enormous support for environmentalists and liberals, who denounced the capitalist greed that had produced such a potential disaster. In the long run, though, the disaster removed nuclear power as a plausible alternative to other sources of energy, which led to greater emphasis on fossil fuels.[5]

Facing these accumulating disasters was a president with sharply declining popularity and grave image problems. Some commentators, then and since, have discussed this growing sense of crisis in terms of the character of Jimmy Carter himself and his inability to represent the conventional stereotypes of manliness expected of a national leader. To quote one observer in the Wall Street Journal, "Once in office, he lost no time revealing his true feminine spirit. He wouldn't twist arms. He didn't like to threaten or rebuke. . . . We've already had a 'woman' president: Jimmy Carter." He "did not project the image of being a real man." The perception of weakness achieved farcical proportions in the spring of 1979 when what was originally a lighthearted filler story escalated to a full-scale report that the president had had a confrontation with a killer swamp rabbit. The Washington Post headlined, "President Attacked by Rabbit," while a cartoon mocked the menace of "Paws." By this point in Carter's term, the story verged on the credible. The following year, in its reporting of a Carter speech, the Boston Globe accidentally used a headline that had circulated as a private newsroom joke: "Mush from the Wimp." His administration looked like an interregnum, a trusteeship presidency.[6]

Confronting a sharply worsening public mood, Carter himself acknowledged a sense of national failure and impotence, what an aide termed "malaise." In a speech on the energy crisis in July 1979, he identified "a crisis that strikes at the very heart and soul and spirit of our national will. We can see this crisis in the growing doubt about the meaning of our own lives and in the loss of a unity of purpose for our Nation. The erosion of our confidence in the future is threatening to destroy the social and the political fabric of America." Carter's speech, with its lament about selfish individual-ism, was influenced by Christopher Lasch's best-selling book *The Culture of Narcissism: American Life in an Age of Diminishing Expectations*. The sub-title resonated with Carter's growing pessimism about the retrenchment that the nation would have to face, which would demand a new degree of Spartan cooperation and sacrifice.[7]

Politically, though, the speech raised questions about just why expec-tations were diminishing. At least in the case of Iran, disaster had not just happened but had been promoted by the United States' failure to support its friends. For conservatives, the national weakness Carter was bemoaning was his own creation, the direct consequence of his personal weakness. Liberals too attacked Carter's incompetence, and it became clear that Carter would face an electoral threat from Edward Kennedy in 1980. By the fall of 1979, polls were showing Kennedy thirty points ahead of Carter for the presidential nomination. Jimmy Carter succeeded brilliantly in making himself the ideal symbol for malaise, personifying failure. *Time* recorded that Carter "was perhaps most bitterly resented for shrinking [the nation's] hopes down to the size of a presidency characterized by small people, small talk and small matters. He made Americans feel two things they are not used to feeling, and will not abide. He made them feel puny and he made them feel insecure."[8]

Toe to Toe

Just as Americans were beginning to ask who had lost Iran, the adminis-tration was also under assault for its failures against more traditional enemies, as a potentially alarming revolution occurred in Central America. Though Nicaragua was of negligible economic significance, it was much closer to home and a well-established part of the U.S. sphere of influence. Since the 1930s, the nation had been ruled by a spectacularly corrupt regime headed by the Somoza family, which was closely allied with the United States. In 1977, the Carter administration withheld aid from Nicaragua and other Central American dictatorships until and unless the human rights situ-ation improved. Over the next two years, leftist radicalism grew rapidly in Nicaragua, with the unabashed support of sections of the U.S. media. In 1978, though, even the liberal *Washington Post* was warning of the rise of a "second Cuba in Central America."[9]

By the spring of 1979, the challenge from the leftist Sandinista National Liberation Front was threatening to overthrow the regime, but Carter refused to intervene. The dictatorship's image was further damaged when its soldiers were filmed executing an American television cameraman. In July, the Somoza regime collapsed just as thoroughly as the shah's had, and Central America had a new left-wing regime clearly sympathetic to Cuban and pro-Soviet policies. Inspired by this victory, similar revolutionary movements gained force in El Salvador and Guatemala. Coupled with the Panama Canal issue, the Nicaraguan revolution showed U.S. reluctance to assert influence even in its backyard.[10] Initially, American media did not project concern about the growing force of revolution in Central America. The existing regimes demonstrably were corrupt and repressive, while the rebels fitted into a well-known romantic stereotype that had been familiar to North Americans at least since the time of Zapata. Also, large sections of the Roman Catholic Church in the United States were sympathetic to radical change, and the new Nicaraguan regime included some well-known exponents of liberation theology.

Still, other events now raised worrying questions about the administration's weakness in the face of Soviet and Communist challenges, making the spread of radicalism in Latin America look doubly dangerous. That summer, conservatives made great play of the presence of a Soviet combat brigade stationed in Cuba, apparently a direct violation of the pact that had ended the 1962 missile crisis. In fact, a Soviet force had been present since the 1960s, though it only now came to light, but the suggestion of a new deployment stirred speculation about imminent Soviet aggression. Even Frank Church, nemesis of the CIA, used the issue to try to build his patriotic credentials with moderates. *Doonesbury* mocked the congressional hearings into the affair as "Operation Manhood," led by Senators Jackson and Howard Baker. ("In another development, the senators also pledged to investigate new evidence linking Russian saboteurs with the sinking of the *Maine*.") Though the affair failed to ignite a confrontation, it again showed a reluctance to confront the Soviets. As Senator Baker said, using a telling cowboy analogy, "We stood toe to toe with the Soviet Union and unlike 1962, we blinked instead of the Russians." Worry about American weakness doomed the administration's cherished proposal for a SALT II agreement, which was to come up for Senate ratification in 1979. Even though he promised a substantial increase in defense spending, Carter recognized that the ratification was doomed.[11]

Hostages

An already stumbling administration was dealt a potentially lethal blow on November 4, 1979, when thousands of students and activists occupied the

U.S. embassy in Tehran. They took hostage all fifty-two Americans inside as a means of pressuring the United States to return the shah for trial and, presumably, execution. (The shah had been admitted to the United States for cancer treatment.) The Tehran affair produced one of the most memorable and influential images of modern American history, of the blindfolded hostages being led by their captors. In illustrating American impotence, this was quite as powerful a picture as those of the fall of Saigon. It also recalled other pathetic images of the American POWs believed to be languishing in Southeast Asia, not to mention the captives and slaves of deviant cults. The Tehran crisis boosted popular belief in the existence of live MIAs, and in 1980, surveillance photos taken over Southeast Asia showed what appeared to be the number 52 written on the ground. This suggested that surviving prisoners had somehow heard about the Tehran hostages and also sought release. Whatever the truth of the story, what mattered was that it was believed.[12]

The Tehran affair was important for what it did not produce, namely, a massive U.S. military response. Partly, the administration did not want to forfeit the lives of the hostages in a general attack on Iran, but the United States was also keenly aware of the international implications. Both the United States and the USSR wanted to avoid any chance of the Iranian crisis becoming a superpower conflict. After all, Iran shared a long border with the USSR, and in late 1978, the Soviets had sternly warned Carter against intervening militarily to save the shah. But if the reasons for caution were excellent, the effects were appalling. For over a year, Iran got away with having defied U.S. power so blatantly, trampling all known rules of diplomacy. As the months went on, Iranian behavior became even more outrageous, as the regime threatened to try the Americans as spies, with the obvious hint that they would be killed. In face of this challenge, the U.S. secretary of state, Cyrus Vance, consistently behaved the way a stereotypical ultra-liberal politician might have done in a simplistic morality tale drafted by the far right: at every stage favoring negotiation in the face of extortion, and resisting attempts to grant the shah asylum in the United States. Even the prospect that U.S. personnel might be subjected to espionage trials scarcely seemed to arouse him enough to consider direct action.[13]

Though ordinary Americans remained reluctant to consider outright war, the administration's failure to respond adequately was generating public fury by the end of 1979, and not just among the traditional right wing. American frustration was manifested in extravagant celebrations at the slightest positive signs or any suggestion of international friendship.

When it was learned, for example, that the Canadians had helped six U.S. diplomats escape Iran, pro-Canadian sentiment boomed and citizens of that nation were fêted.

New events overseas raised the prospect of East-West confrontation. That Christmas, while the United States was focused on the plight of the Tehran hostages, the Soviets occupied Afghanistan. Technically, this was not exactly an invasion in the sense of the wanton occupation of a hitherto anti-Communist power, since the Soviets were defending a Communist client regime, and Afghanistan had been drawn ever closer to the Soviet orbit since its monarchy had been overthrown in 1973. Through the decade, Islamist unrest had been mounting, receiving a powerful boost from the Iranian revolution. Beginning in the spring of 1979, armed resistance began to spread across the nation, threatening the destabilization of Communist rule. That summer, the Carter administration made the historic decision to support the Islamic resistance, a force that Zbigniew Brzezinski viewed as a potent surrogate against the Soviets. Nor was the latest Soviet move the daring strategic coup de main that many claimed. Much of the new concern in the United States arose from the popular assumption that Muslim Afghanistan must somehow be connected with the oil-rich lands of the Middle East. The nation's proximity to Iran also seemed frightening, although if the Soviets ever did choose to invade that nation, they already had a comfortably large border from which to do so. In terms of its implications for Soviet military power, the Afghan invasion was arguably less troubling than the earlier move into Angola. But a shaken Carter administration saw a potential challenge to the oil of Iran and the Gulf and responded as if a direct East-West military confrontation was imminent.[14]

In his State of the Union address on January 21, a somber Carter catalogued the various menaces. "At this time in Iran, fifty Americans are still held captive, innocent victims of terrorism and anarchy. Also at this moment, massive Soviet troops are attempting to subjugate the fiercely independent and deeply religious people of Afghanistan. These two acts— one of international terrorism and one of military aggression—present a serious challenge to the United States of America and indeed to all the nations of the world." He addressed "the steady growth and increased projection of Soviet military power beyond its own borders" and condemned "this latest Soviet attempt to extend its colonial domination of others." He also warned Iran, "If the American hostages are harmed, a severe price will be paid." Raising the prospect of war, Carter proposed his distinctive presidential doctrine: "An attempt by any outside force to gain control of the Persian Gulf region will be regarded as an assault on the vital interests of the

United States of America, and such an assault will be repelled by any means necessary, including military force."[15]

Moving Right

In the space of a few weeks, the Afghanistan crisis moved American politics substantially to the right. The Soviet invasion appeared to settle once and for all the argument as to whether the United States was endangered more by external Soviet threats or by domestic forces such as corporate power and the intelligence agencies. Also, the fortuitous linkage between the twin crises in Iran and Afghanistan enhanced the level of threat perceived by ordinary Americans. Soviet misdeeds were now directly linked to oil supplies and thus to issues of America's everyday needs and even its survival.

Cold War politics were definitively back in vogue. In January, Carter formally asked the Senate to delay the ratification vote for SALT II, though both sides agreed to operate as if the treaty had been signed. In a powerful symbolic move, he restored registration for the Selective Service, a system abandoned at the end of involvement in Vietnam. Carter specifically called for both men and women to register, attracting furious bipartisan opposition. He declared that his decision "confirms what is already obvious throughout our society—that women are now providing all types of skills in every profession. The military should be no exception." Though the attempt to have women register failed, it killed any remaining hope for ERA ratification, since if the amendment did pass, it would conceivably force young women to fight in Iran or Afghanistan.

Also symbolic of Carter's new outlook was the United States' withdrawal from the Olympic Games scheduled to be held that summer in Moscow. The Soviets had invested heavily in making this event a political advertisement for Soviet strength and for an ascendant USSR. Western backers of a Moscow boycott drew the comparison to the Berlin Olympics of 1936, explicitly linking Nazi and Soviet totalitarianism and drawing parallels between Hitler and Soviet leaders such as Leonid Brezhnev.

In this new mood, the explicit rhetoric of good and evil was once again fashionable. Since the mid-1960s, American leaders had been accustomed to see the United States and USSR as competitors in a global power system, and reasonable people understood the need to rise above empty propaganda. Now, the language of right and wrong was returning to popular currency, and in contrast to perceptions during the mid-1970s, it was difficult to see the United States as so evidently in the wrong. Though it was left to Ronald Reagan in 1983 to coin the phrase "evil empire," the rhetoric was in the air three years previously.

Though the administration's hard line was a simple response to new realities, it placed Carter in a nearly impossible situation, since the right was much more comfortable with Cold War politics and symbols. Carter himself was plainly unhappy with the kind of stern anti-Communist rhetoric that the situation demanded, and his harshest words came across as petulant and ill-tempered. Even after expressing fury with the Soviets, Carter blighted his own cause when he declared, "My opinion of the Russians has changed [more] drastically in the last week than even in the previous two and a half years before that." While the remark showed a new awareness of Soviet power, it startled moderate Americans, who had never doubted that the Soviets were expansionist and militarist.[16]

Time and again, Carter failed to follow the logical implications of his new stance toward foreign dangers. Conservatives demanded to know why, if in fact the Soviets were so expansionist, the administration was so unconcerned with resisting further leftist gains in Central America. Carter refused to reach out to the right-wing Democrats who had an impeccably anti-Soviet record, the group mobilized in the Coalition for a Democratic Majority. Infuriated neoconservatives moved ever closer to the Reagan Republicans. Yet while Carter could not move far enough right to win some supporters, he had already swung so far toward Cold War positions that he had alienated his liberal base, which looked to Kennedy. Conservatives themselves demanded still more action. Ronald Reagan explicitly compared Carter's policies to "the sorry tapping of Neville Chamberlain's umbrella on the cobblestones of Munich."[17] In February, Reagan won the New Hampshire presidential primary, and he dominated the Republican primaries thereafter.

In the short term, Carter won support for his new (relative) determination, and like most incumbents, he benefited from a patriotic reaction during a national crisis. In the early months of 1980, the U.S. media acquired an anti-Soviet tone that they had not demonstrated so consistently since the earliest days of the Vietnam War. A new mood was obvious that February with the U.S. hockey victory over the Soviets at the Winter Olympics in Lake Placid, the "miracle on ice." This event marked the renaissance of flag-waving patriotism, as supporters chanted, "USA, USA" and "USA all the way." The response is easier to understand when we know the other events making news at the time. The *New York Times* report of the sports sensation was flanked by headlines announcing, "Price Index Up 1.4%, the Most Since 1973; Prime Rate at 16.5% . . . Energy a Big Factor" and "Anti-Soviet Rioting Brings Martial Law to Afghan Capital." Good news, in other words, was in very short supply. The flamboyant mood was sustained when the hockey team—wearing cowboy hats—drove through Washington to be fêted at the White House; some spectators hanged Soviet figures in effigy. Patriotism now returned as a theme in popular culture. Charlie Daniels's song "In America" asserted the unshakable unity of "the cowboys and the hippies and the rebels and the yanks."[18]

But even given the new political assertiveness, American options were limited, whether in Afghanistan or Iran. The Iranian crisis was the more pressing, as months of diplomacy proved fruitless. Only the following spring, on April 24–25, did the United States attempt a commando-style rescue, and the disastrous failure of Desert One left more awful images of burned-out helicopters, inevitably recalling the abandonment of Saigon. Eight servicemen died. A telling joke at the time suggested that if Jimmy Carter had been president in 1945, the United States would have dropped the atomic bomb on Honolulu.[19]

The failure was all the more telling when set against successful hostage rescues undertaken by the special forces of other countries around this time—by the Israelis in 1976 or by the Germans and the Dutch in 1977. Only ten days after the Desert One fiasco, the British Special Air Service carried out a spectacular hostage rescue during a siege at the Iranian embassy in London. Comparison was scarcely fair, in that it was vastly easier for the British to organize such a raid on their home territory than for the United States to project its power halfway around the globe. But the experience of foreign powers reinforced the apparent lesson that everyone could protect their citizens except for the United States. From November 1979 through January 1981, for 444 days, the hostages remained in captivity, their experience brought home daily to Americans by the yellow ribbons tied on trees and the ringing of bells from churches and college campuses. Just as the foreign menace escalated, so the U.S. ability to respond collapsed.[20]

Redefining Terrorism

At the same time, right-wing activists enjoyed great success in promoting a new and more threatening vision of the menaces facing the United States, suggesting that matters were even worse than they appeared. The United States faced two quite distinct foreign foes: the Communist Soviet Union and an Islamist regime in Iran. Though the two made an improbable pairing, the coincidence of time and place drew them together in American eyes. The two crises developed within a few weeks of each other and in neighboring countries, while Carter and other administration figures discussed the two issues in the same breath. In the popular media, the Ayatollah Khomeini became a symbol of menace at least as potent as Brezhnev. Also,

Carter's description of the Tehran hostage taking as international terrorism contextualized it with well-known hijackings and bombings from the previous decade. This was a more powerful linkage than he might have suspected, since just at this time conservatives were tracing the roots of that worldwide terrorist activity to Moscow and the KGB. Putting these different elements together—Soviet expansion, international terrorism, and the emerging presence of radical Islam—transformed a series of distinct and separate phenomena into a vast and troubling international menace, with a huge potential for future attacks on American interests.

In the first half of 1980, an effective campaign deployed conspiracy concerns on behalf of the political right. In magazines and books, conservatives now presented their sweeping new interpretation of the wave of terrorism that had affected many nations over the previous decade. According to this view, global terrorism was a tactic organized and directed by the Soviet Union, often through subsidiaries such as Czechoslovakia and Bulgaria, in order to destabilize the West. Though terrorist actions might seem to arise from separate local circumstances—as in Ireland, Palestine, or Spain—the underlying reality was the hidden hand of the KGB, operating through its proxies and subsidiaries. This theory first gained currency at the Jerusalem Conference on International Terrorism in 1979, and it reached a worldwide audience through writers such as Claire Sterling, Paul Henze, and Michael Ledeen.[21]

The primary example cited for state-sponsored surrogate terrorism was Italy, which since 1976 had been under siege by competing paramilitary organizations. Though some spectacular incidents were linked to neo-Nazi groups, conservative theorists focused their attention on ultra-leftists, especially the Red Brigades. In 1980, a defector from the Czech intelligence service indicated that his agency and other Eastern-bloc forces had created and armed the Red Brigades and that leftist terrorism in modern Europe was a well-planned Soviet strategy to destabilize the West. The case was spelled out at length in Claire Sterling's 1980 exposé, *The Terror Network*. Though Sterling described the recent terrorism of the 1970s, calling it "Fright Decade I," she warned explicitly that things would grow much worse in the 1980s, "Fright Decade II." The prospect that terrorists might acquire weapons of mass destruction made such warnings still more alarming. Discussions of possible nuclear terrorism became more frequent after the magazine *The Progressive* in late 1979 published details of how to make a hydrogen bomb.[22]

The KGB-sponsorship theme received its widest publicity in the 1980 best-selling novel *The Spike*, by conservative journalists Arnaud de

Borchgrave and Robert Moss. *The Spike* depicted the machinations of Soviet spies and their U.S. puppets being exposed by investigative reporters struggling against the corrupt and Communist-infiltrated Western media. The spike of the title refers to the means by which controversial stories are disposed of before troubling the public, especially anything that would disturb their bland illusions about the peaceful intentions of the USSR. The plot concerns highly placed Soviet agents and friends in the U.S. administration, including the vice president, the director of the CIA, and the principal negotiator of "SALT IV." (Moss was a veteran of recent campaigns to unmask the alleged Soviet subversion of Britain's Labour government.) Pro-Communist opposition to U.S. intervention assists the Soviets in an audacious scheme to dominate Middle Eastern oil while neutralizing the NATO allies through terrorist surrogates. The heroes include a senator based on Daniel Moynihan, who ultimately purges traitors from the administration. Just as transparent are the villains of *The Spike*. One Washington think tank caricatured in the book as a vital KGB front is easily identifiable as the liberal Institute for Policy Studies, while CIA whistleblower Philip Agee is presented as a reptilian KGB stooge. The book built successfully on existing worries about violence and clandestine warfare undertaken by intelligence agencies, except now the villains were the KGB, not the CIA.[23]

The terror network theory had powerful implications for Middle Eastern conflicts. Since the mid-1960s, the Palestinians had successfully used terrorism and guerrilla violence as a means of making the world aware of their cause. If Western nations viewed Israel and the Palestinians as rival forces with equal moral claims, then it made sense to try to force a settlement between the two, presumably by advancing Palestinian political causes. But if the Palestinian guerrilla groups were tools of Moscow, as Sterling and the rest argued, then they were simply on the wrong side of a polarized global conflict, and the United States had no alternative but to give wholehearted backing to its ally Israel. The Palestine Liberation Organization featured centrally in most of the charts of linkages used to portray the network. Pro-Israel writers enthusiastically espoused the new interpretation of global terrorism as a prime argument for their cause.

Contextualizing Middle Eastern and Communist issues offered other rewards for the right, which found opportunities to link the Carter administration to the global terror network. In 1979, Andrew Young was dismissed after holding controversial secret meetings with PLO representatives. Even though he was fired, suspicions lingered that the administration's more radical members were friendly to Third World extremism, and Young's conduct stood in contrast to Moynihan's ringing rejection of Third World rhetoric. This affair was especially damaging for Democratic prospects among Jewish voters, a key voting bloc.[24]

Even more embarrassing was the president's brother, Billy, who was involved in kickback scandals involving the sale of aircraft to Libya, for which nation he acted as a lobbyist. When his activities first came to public attention, Billy was regarded as a joke, a caricature redneck on the make. In 1980, though, more disturbing charges surfaced, as Carter's attorney general was accused of covering up Libyan connections in what became known as Billygate. Together with other recent debacles—the malaise speech, Andrew Young, the drug charges against Hamilton Jordan, and a financial scandal looming over Treasury secretary G. William Miller—Billygate reinforced the impression of an administration falling apart. Worse, the White House was linked to the most deranged and violent terrorist sponsor state in the Middle East. (Defending his friends, Billy asserted that "a heap of governments support terrorists and [Libya] at least admitted it.") In June, the still unexplained crash of an Italian airliner off Sicily probably resulted from a chaotic dogfight between NATO and Libyan aircraft, suggesting that the Mediterranean might be on the verge of a shooting war. The more Jimmy Carter tried to mobilize the nation against foreign threats, the more those foreign threats were used against his administration.[25]

These new and more threatening visions of international conflicts did reach a mass public. In 1979, one of the most popular nonfiction books was *The Third World War: August 1985*, an imaginative pseudo-history. Of the ten top-selling novels of 1980, four were works of realistic conspiracy or near-apocalypse, featuring the predictable cast of nightmare figures, Arab or Soviet. Apart from *The Spike*, Robert Ludlum's *The Bourne Identity* dealt with brainwashed (leftist) assassins and real-life pro-Palestinian terrorists, including the legendary Carlos the Jackal. *The Fifth Horseman*, by Larry Collins and Dominique Lapierre, featured Muammar Qaddafi in a plot to destroy New York City with a thermonuclear device (the "horseman" of the title invokes the Book of Revelation). Frederick Forsyth's *The Devil's Alternative* described a near-future Soviet Union plunged into famine and stumbling toward nuclear confrontation with the West. Another novel of this year, *The Last President*, imagined nuclear terrorism in Washington, D.C., as part of a domestic coup attempt. Charles McCarry's *The Better Angels* foresaw a corrupt liberal president exploiting terrorism fears in order to steal an election. (He ensures his victory by manipulating electronic voting machines.) Meanwhile, a fanatical Islamist sect called the Eye of Gaza deploys nuclear suicide terrorism against the American homeland.[26]

hilarious

Though the Afghan and Iranian events remain strongest in popular memory today, a series of quite distinct crises through the spring and summer of 1980 increased the odds of imminent global confrontation. Three simmering crises deserve special mention, namely, the events in Korea, Yugoslavia, and Poland. The potential meltdown in South Korea began in late 1979 when the head of the Korean CIA assassinated the nation's president, initiating a wide-ranging process of political transformation and liberalization. However, ensuing riots and massacres aroused fears of a war between the two Koreas, which could well turn nuclear. In May 1980 also, the long-expected death of Yugoslav leader Marshal Tito generated alarm, as a breakup of the Yugoslav federation could easily spawn a European war. Recognizing the extreme sensitivity of the situation, every leading nation chose very highly placed political leaders as representatives to the funeral. The exception was the United States, as Jimmy Carter dispatched his *mother* as envoy. Following so shortly upon the Desert One affair, this decision reinforced an impression in international circles of the president's ignorance of global affairs and his scandalous inadequacy to lead in dangerous times. Finally, in August, a labor protest in the Polish shipyards spawned the Solidarity movement, which looked like the vanguard of an anti-Communist political revolution. Through 1980–81, the diplomatic world nervously awaited a likely Soviet invasion and the resulting European crisis. By December, the U.S. government believed that twenty-four Warsaw Pact divisions were preparing to crush Poland.[27]

Or perhaps the world was so close to obliteration that no specific cause was needed. The atmosphere of near-panic was enhanced by two episodes in which U.S. early warning systems mistakenly signaled a major Soviet missile launch, one in November 1979, the second in June 1980. Though both were correctly identified as technical malfunctions, U.S. officials briefly had to consider the option of firing their own missiles in response and detonating a third world war. This period had nothing to teach the early 1950s about nuclear paranoia. Anyone who believed the United States might actually reach the year 1984 sounded like Pollyanna.

Coming Apart

Quite separate from the twin dangers of Islamism and Communism, American society in 1980 was showing signs of unraveling. Underlying other problems was a looming economic crisis, as the oil shock boosted inflation. The inflation rate hit 18 percent in the first quarter of 1980 and was still around 13 percent at midyear. These were the sort of figures that, if sustained for any length of time, portended hyperinflation and currency collapse. In fact, the Federal Reserve Bank had already taken measures to deal with the crisis: in October 1979, Chairman Paul Volcker announced his "Saturday night special"—policies intended to tighten the money supply dramatically. This monetarist response to inflation would work, but the solution could take a grueling two or three years.[28]

Americans faced a brutal credit crunch. The prime rate had remained in single digits from 1975 through 1978, but it reached 10 percent in October 1978. The rate rose to 15 percent in October 1979 and briefly hit 20 percent in April 1980. (To put this in perspective, the figure from 2001 through 2004 fluctuated between 4 and 6 percent.) In some states the rates demanded by legitimate banks threatened to trip usury statutes designed to curb loan-sharking. Banks became reluctant to issue credit cards to new users, a serious blow in a society increasingly oriented to plastic money. The crisis was a menace to businesses, since it simultaneously dried up demand and prevented investment. New financial stresses accelerated the ongoing collapse of the steel and auto industries and inflicted further damage on urban economies. Long-term prospects were no better, given the strong likelihood that confrontation in the Middle East would generate yet another oil shortage. Doomsday predictions for the U.S. economy proliferated. In 1979, Howard J. Ruff's *How to Prosper During the Coming Bad Years* became a bible for survivalists, while Douglas R. Casey's *Crisis Investing: Opportunities and Profits in the Coming Great Depression* was a nonfiction best-seller in 1980. Ezra Vogel's *Japan as Number One* (1979) created the vogue for books seeking to predict which other society would replace what was evidently a collapsing United States.[29]

Domestic events too recalled the nightmares of the late 1960s, but without the countervailing sense of utopianism. While racial conflict was a familiar American theme, the urban riots of the 1960s had at least a claim to political content: to some extent, they were social protests. In 1980, though, several racial struggles stood out for their nihilistic and bloodthirsty quality. In February, a hostage situation at the New Mexico state penitentiary in Santa Fe produced more grisly violence as inmate gangs took over the institution. Though the media underplayed the racial angle of the violence, the worst violence was the work of white supremacist gangs, who tortured and executed dozens of informers and political enemies. The eventual death toll was reputedly thirty-three, somewhat less than the Attica riot of 1971. Nor was this the only manifestation of violence from the far right. The previous November, Ku Klux Klansmen and neo-Nazis killed five leftist demonstrators in Greensboro, North Carolina. Responding to the New Mexico horrors and the implications for American society, the liberal *New Republic* suggested, "At least in regard to cruelty, it's not at all clear that the system of punishment that has evolved in the West is less barbaric than the grotesque practices of Islam."[30]

The other great racial confrontation occurred in May 1980, when a riot erupted in Miami's Liberty City after a jury acquitted white police officers of murdering a black civilian. In many ways, the riot followed the familiar pattern of past outbreaks, though with some highly contemporary elements: mobs were inflamed by charges that whites were murdering black children. But the degree of violence was greater than in most previous events and was expressed in pure race-based hatred, in which whites and Latinos were casually murdered and mutilated. The riot left eighteen dead and caused $100 million in property damage. These were the worst urban race riots since the violence following the assassination of Martin Luther King Jr. in 1968, and as in that time, the media offered pictures of military units patrolling American streets. As in the worst days of the 1960s, armed white civilians defended their barricaded neighborhoods.[31]

The depth of Miami's violence reflected growing fury among African-Americans, not just against improper police behavior but against a huge influx of Cuban migrants. Facing internal dissent, Fidel Castro told his subjects that if they were not happy in Cuba, they would be allowed to leave for the United States. Seizing the chance to escape, Cubans began a mass exodus that would ultimately number 125,000, mainly from the port of Mariel. Though Castro soon reimposed travel restrictions, the damage was done, and south Florida especially found itself with a major influx of impoverished immigrants. In other circumstances, the Mariel affair should have represented a giant ideological victory for the West: Cuba showed itself such an oppressive and impoverished dictatorship that its residents would risk their lives to escape. But the resulting exodus had a seriously destabilizing effect on the United States. At a time of economic crisis, blacks feared that they would yet again miss their chance to climb the social ladder, displaced by white and Latino newcomers. But whatever the roots of the Miami savagery, and however localized, the harrowing images suggested a vision of urban America in dissolution. Days after the riots subsided, a neo-Nazi assassin tried to assassinate civil rights leader Vernon Jordan, with the goal of accelerating the nation's looming race war.[32]

Nor was Miami the only city in which stories about corruption, decadence, and conspiracy dominated news coverage in early 1980. Over the previous two years, federal agencies had undertaken some long-term undercover investigations that now reached fruition. Among the most notorious was ABSCAM (for "Abdul scam"), in which an informant disguised as an Arab sheikh let it be known that he wished to invest in Atlantic City casinos and was prepared to pay for political influence. The resulting scramble for bribes ensnared a number of prominent politicians from Pennsylvania and New Jersey, including a U.S. senator from the latter state, Harrison Williams. As a bonus for conservatives, it showed liberals anxious to sell out U.S. interests to wealthy Arabs. Incidentally, the whole scheme indicates that Arabs were exempt from the otherwise sweeping ethnic sensitivity of this era, and casual racism directed against them was commonplace. Beyond the terrorist stereotypes, cartoon treatments of Arabs were commonly harsh caricatures of plutocratic oil sheikhs. In *The Blues Brothers*, released about this time, the John Belushi character, wishing to shock a family, pretends to be a wealthy Arab seeking to buy their pubescent daughter.[33]

Shortly after ABSCAM, a Miami pornography investigation, MIPORN, exposed the corporate network through which powerful organized crime figures dominated the nation's booming pornography industry. For conservatives, the investigation proved an incontrovertible link between sexual decadence and the most dangerous forms of violent gangsterism, making nonsense of liberal assertions that pornography was a harmless indulgence.[34]

Just as the carnage in the Miami riot was being reported, another news story was competing for the headlines. On May 18, Washington's Mount St. Helens volcano erupted spectacularly, causing several deaths. Not even his most dedicated critics could blame Jimmy Carter for such a natural disaster, but in the context of the time, the event offered a bizarre confirmation that in 1980, anything that could go wrong in American life was going to do so. Apart from its Murphy's Law quality, Mount St. Helens attracted attention from believers in Christian apocalypticism, who knew that the end times would be heralded by wars and rumors of wars, civil conflicts, and great natural disasters that would darken the skies. That seemed an accurate description of America's year up to that point.

The Evidence of Things Not Seen

Through the spring and summer, tales of savage random violence permeated the news headlines. The ongoing "plague" of violent sexual crime was evidenced by the litany of serial murder cases publicized during the year, several of which claimed forty or fifty victims. The media were full of the Sunday Morning Slasher, the Sunset Strip murders, the Freeway killings, and two lengthy murder series attributed to Gerald Stano and Gerald Gallego, while the Gacy trial daily publicized the full horrors of that case.[35]

Crime stories attract headlines when they focus generalized fears and concerns. In that sense, one of the most "successful" crime stories in modern America was the Atlanta child murders, which became a much discussed domestic news story that summer and fall. Apparently beginning in late 1979, someone was killing dozens of black children in Atlanta, and police were unable to solve the crimes. Now, later investigation has cast grave doubt on the reality of the murder series, still more on the guilt of Wayne Williams, the reputed culprit. While some young people were murdered, the notion of a distinct series connected to one individual probably arose from the way in which Atlanta authorities recorded and tabulated suspicious cases, often using very broad criteria. A case that arose from the disappearances of "children" was soon counting teenagers and young adults among the victims, and Williams was eventually convicted for killing two men in their late twenties.[36]

In the summer of 1980, though, such caveats did not interfere with the main thrust of a simple and frightening story: someone was slaughtering the black children of Atlanta. Each new disappearance led the headlines on national television news. Through 1980, liberal and African-American commentators saw the case as a horrifying epitome of the victimization of black America. James Baldwin made the murders the subject of his book *The Evidence of Things Not Seen*. As the murders continued unchecked, observers speculated about just why the Atlanta child-killer remained at large, and conspiracy theories surged: were the police themselves involved? Many urban blacks attributed the crimes to a racist sect dedicated to exterminating black youth. Some argued that the crimes were the work of a clandestine satanic cult, perhaps linked to a pedophile network. The perceived menaces of cults, predators, conspiracies, threats to children, and racism effectively combined to sustain this nightmare story. By 1981 it was alleged that the Atlanta deaths were "sacrificial murders" by "a cult involved with drugs, pornography and Satanism," which marked its ritual sites with inverted crosses.[37]

What would soon become a national panic over satanism, cult sacrifice, and ritual abuse can be traced precisely to this time. Several ongoing investigations were already focusing attention on the violent or criminal activities of real or supposed satanic cults. In 1980, the San Francisco police department issued a circular warning of itinerant satanic groups involved in "animal mutilations and ritualistic homicides of human beings wherein internal organs are removed from the victims and used in church baptisms and rituals." Just at this time, Maury Terry's journalistic investigation of the Son of Sam killings in New York City was arguing that the murders were the work of a national satanic cult, perhaps linked to the earlier career of Charles Manson. Also in 1980, former FBI agent Ted Gunderson claimed a breakthrough in the notorious case of Jeffrey MacDonald, a Green Beret whose family had been gruesomely murdered in 1970. Though MacDonald himself was convicted of the crimes, new evidence purported to prove that the murders were the work of Manson-style cult members.[38]

For some influential investigators and journalists, the worlds of satanism, cults, child abuse, and multiple murder were merging. Kenneth Wooden's book *Children of Jonestown* pioneered the notion of cults "ritualistically abusing" young people and perhaps engaging in the murder of small children. Also pivotal was the 1980 book *Michelle Remembers*, ostensibly a memoir of how a therapist helped a young woman remember her ghastly sufferings at the hands of a satanic cult in Vancouver during the 1950s. Cult members caged, molested, and tortured children and sacrificed animals, culminating in a grand Feast of the Beast, a witches' Sabbath. Though the book has no apparent basis in reality, *Michelle Remembers* became the template for all subsequent tales of ritual abuse and for most "recovered memories" purporting to reveal cult atrocities.[39] At home and abroad, the idea of evil had a currency and a plausibility that it had not had for many years past. Not just in the Middle East, terror networks were in the air.

There You Go Again

If Jimmy Carter thought the nation was suffering from a national malaise in mid-1979, he would have been shocked to see how far that mood would advance over the next twelve months. By July 1980, an ABC-Harris poll showed that 77 percent of Americans disapproved of Carter's performance as president, the worst figure in the history of polling. Even Nixon attracted more support during the depths of Watergate.[40] Having said this, polls do not decide elections, and the political disasters of 1980 did not rule out a chance of a Carter victory in the fall. Even after Desert One, many Americans were pleased that the president had at least attempted a military solution, while Reagan still alarmed moderates. In a world as unstable as that of 1980, a hair-trigger response to crisis might ignite a global thermonuclear war, and there was a widespread popular expectation that Reagan, if elected president, would launch prompt military action against Iran and, conceivably, the USSR. Liberal Republicans were so convinced that Reagan could not or should not be elected that in March, Gerald Ford offered to come out of retirement to rescue the party. Through the summer, the party dabbled with the notion of a Reagan-Ford ticket, in which Ford, as vice president, would virtually rule as co-president, thus serving as a rein on the cowboy president. Though the scheme collapsed, it suggests once more the nervousness about an unchecked Reagan.

During the summer, though, Carter failed to restore his position. One factor was his barely disguised pessimism about current events and the longer-term future of the country. Carter was visibly shaken by a report he had commissioned on the state of the world in the near future, *Global 2000*, which warned of global ruin.[41] Believing that the nation is on the eve of destruction does not create a sunny or positive presidential candidate. The more pessimistic and wavering he seemed, the sharper the contrast with Ronald Reagan, whose denunciations of present realities were accompanied by rosy optimism about what the nation could achieve in the future. Critically, Reagan denied that America had to accept its current crisis of "a disintegrating economy, a weakened defense and an energy policy based on the sharing of scarcity." In his acceptance speech at the Republican convention that July, he dismissed liberal pessimism: "They say that the United States has had its day in the sun, that our nation has passed its zenith. They expect you to tell your children that the American people no longer have the will to cope with their problems, that the future will be one of sacrifice and few opportunities. My fellow citizens, I utterly reject that view."[42]

At the same time, Carter's newfound toughness on foreign challenges posed its own dangers. Democratic liberals were already multiply alienated by Carter's views on abortion, his environmental policy, and now his apparent militarism. Time and again, Carter demonstrated his unique gift for alienating both sides at once. In March, the administration initially supported and then repudiated a United Nations resolution demanding Israeli withdrawal from "occupied Arab territories," including East Jerusalem. Failure to follow through on the resolution won the United States no new friends overseas. At the same time, the apparent betrayal of Israel infuriated Jewish voters and ensured Ted Kennedy's victory in the New York primary. (In November, Reagan would do better among American Jews than any Republican before or since.) By the fall, alienated liberals were defecting to the third-party candidacy of John Anderson, a liberal Republican who supported gun control, the Panama Canal treaty, and federal funding of abortions. Anderson ultimately attracted 6.6 percent of the popular vote.[43]

Carter's new foreign policy attitudes removed one of his strongest arguments against Ronald Reagan: the charge of war-mongering. As Reagan argued in his debate with Carter that October, the problem was not adopting a hard line but inconsistency: "We can get into a war by letting events get out of hand, as they have in the last three and a half years under the foreign policies of this administration of Mr. Carter's, until we're faced each time with a crisis." War resulted not from strength or assertiveness but from a perception of weakness, a lack of manly resolve. Equally successful was Reagan's attack on Carter's failure to understand the evil nature of totalitarian systems, which had led him to sacrifice America's own friends who "didn't meet exactly our standards of human rights." In Iran, Nicaragua, and elsewhere, the United States had "aided a revolutionary overthrow which results in complete totalitarianism, instead, for those people. I think that this is a kind of a hypocritical policy when, at the same time, we're maintaining a détente with the one nation in the world where there are no human rights at all—the Soviet Union." While his arguments carried conviction, more important was that Reagan emerged as a sober and cool-headed leader, rather than the drooling fanatic depicted by liberals. He evidently was not a demagogue on the lines of *Network*'s Howard Beale.[44]

Reagan won in 1980 because events in that year had done so much to justify the right-wing analysis of the menaces and external enemies confronting the United States. To a striking extent, Jimmy Carter himself shared that analysis. Once it was agreed that the Soviets genuinely did pose an imminent threat to the United States, that the United States needed to rearm to resist that aggression, charges of being a cold warrior no longer counted, and debate could then turn to other social and economic themes. Reagan scored a point in the debates when he asked, "Are you better off than you were four years ago? Is it easier for you to go and buy things in the stores than it was four years ago? Is there more or less unemployment in the country than there was four years ago? Is America as respected throughout the world as it was? Do you feel that our security is as safe? That we're as strong as we were four years ago?" For many, the questions answered themselves. Reagan scored again when he said, "Recession is when your neighbor loses his job. Depression is when you lose yours, and recovery is when Jimmy Carter loses his."[45]

Though Reagan took 51 percent of the popular vote to Carter's 41 percent, he won a massive ten-to-one majority in the electoral college. Carter carried only six states plus the District of Columbia. In addition to the obvious Republican realms in the West and South, Reagan also won such later true-blue states as California, Washington, Massachusetts, Connecticut, Pennsylvania, and Illinois. Moreover, Republicans now controlled the U.S. Senate for the first time in decades, in a victory that ejected some of their most hated liberal rivals, including George McGovern, Frank Church, John

Culver, Warren Magnuson, and Birch Bayh. McGovern and Church both represented the most extreme liberal faces of the mid-1970s. Republicans gained an impressive twelve Senate seats, giving the party their first majority since 1952, and they won an additional thirty-three seats in the House.

Many excuses could be found for the scale of the Democratic defeat. Carter himself blundered by conceding defeat before 10 p.m. Eastern Time on election day, when polls were still open in the West. This encouraged Republicans to vote in still greater numbers, while disheartened Democrats stayed home, boosting Republican victories in congressional races. Also, some Democratic senators were defending seats they had picked up in the very untypical circumstances of 1974, in the immediate aftermath of Watergate, when the party had made advances that it could not defend in normal circumstances. Finally, Republicans made excellent use of their new political networks, and groups such as NCPAC and the Moral Majority proved invaluable in organizing voters.

But nothing could disguise the scale of the political transformation, especially since both parties had moved so far toward conservative assumptions, particularly in foreign policy. As the *Washington Post* remarked, "Nothing of that force and size and sweep could have been created over a weekend or even a week or two by the assorted mullahs and miseries of our time." Morton Kondracke argued that Reagan Republicans offered voters a "consistent alternative world view to that of the Democrats, and the public decided to try it. It is a simplistic world view, a John Wayne view, but it is thoroughly American and of obvious appeal: the United States can do anything it wants, if it has the will. . . . Carter and the Democrats told people that the United States was caught up by forces beyond its control. Reagan came along to tell them they could control the future, all of it, if they wanted to."[46] This was a mandate for fundamental change.

Counterfactual

At first sight, the personal contrast between Jimmy Carter and Ronald Reagan could hardly be greater. Carter is recalled as a well-meaning but ineffectual liberal devoted to human rights; Reagan is seen as the confident cold warrior dedicated to making America strong. Obviously, we think, the new decade, the Reagan era, bears the mark of this dynamic new president. Yet while the two leaders differed in their approaches, perhaps the Carter and Reagan presidencies were not quite as radically distinct as sometimes appears. This must make us ask how important the change in Washington was in setting the cultural tone for the coming decade. Assuredly, America in the 1980s looked very different from what it was in the 1970s. But did the political leadership preside over those changes, or did it follow currents already under way?

Carter and Reagan had much in common. Carter was more conservative than is often recalled, and Reagan more liberal. On issues of gender and morality, Reagan had a distinctly moderate record, having endorsed the ERA and opposed the anti-gay Briggs initiative. His two terms as governor included liberal measures on abortion rights and no-fault divorce, not to mention a fairly progressive tax policy and a respectable environmental record. At times, he looked like the kind of politician the Reaganites were warning about. The two men also shared an idealistic moral vision and a religious sense of national purpose. Both explicitly saw national problems in moral terms, as issues of the human heart. Neither was reluctant to invoke moral justifications for policy or to see a divine hand in political destiny, and both were attacked for religious sentiments that the secular-minded regarded as naive or hypocritical. Reagan would have echoed Carter's remark that "you can't divorce religious belief and public service. I've never detected any conflict between God's will and my political duty. If you violate one, you violate the other."[47]

In their different ways, both Carter and Reagan drew on powerful aspects of the Christian political tradition.[48] Where the two parted ways was in their respective visions of the godly state. The biblically based idea of the nation specially chosen to fulfill a divine purpose is often misunderstood: it does not (or should not) imply a simple assertion that God is on our side and will conveniently eliminate any enemies. The idea also implies, indeed demands, special responsibility, with the warning that God will inflict a heavy punishment on a wayward or disobedient nation. For Carter, with his Baptist roots, the moral understanding of social problems was pervasive. In foreign policy matters, the United States could succeed only by eliminating its inner faults, its tradition of making expedient alliances with oppressors. But the moralistic theme extended to explaining inflation and energy issues in terms of American selfishness and materialism. Our country has sinned and can advance only by repenting and making amends. This sense of national sin helps explain Carter's controversial postpresidential career, with his heavy-handed diplomatic interventions overseas, often working against the official U.S. policy of the time.[49]

For Carter, the problem was us. For Reagan, on the contrary, the problem was them. While he agreed that the United States had gone astray, he asserted that its worst sin was to weaken the godly nation in the face of its numerous external enemies, which threatened to bring down the shining city. This image of national chosenness was central to Reagan's vision, the foundation upon which stood his entire political philosophy. He had "always believed that this blessed land was set apart in a special way, that some divine plan placed this great continent here between the oceans to be found by people from every corner of the Earth who had a special love for freedom and the courage to uproot themselves . . . to come to a strange land."[50] Though the rhetoric was different, in practice both men could respond quite similarly when faced with political crises.

We might reasonably ask just how different the America of the eighties would have been if Jimmy Carter had won the 1980 election, and that could have happened quite easily.[51] Any number of events might have transformed the political landscape of that year. The Tehran hostage rescue might have succeeded in April 1980, while through the summer, Reagan supporters worried that Carter might arrange an "October surprise," a last-minute diplomatic breakthrough that would bring the Tehran hostages home in time for the election. The euphoria produced by such an event would have returned Carter quite comfortably. But based solidly on the actual events of 1980, we can make some likely predictions about the course of a second Carter term.

After all, the new phase of the Cold War was already in progress following the Afghanistan crisis. Apart from Afghanistan, areas of crisis in the early 1980s would certainly have included Poland and Central America, while the United States would have had to respond to the recent Soviet missile deployments in Europe. It would have been natural for any U.S. administration to try to weaken the Soviet bloc through proxy forces, who would receive clandestine support or training from the United States. Well before the 1980 election, Carter began U.S. support for Afghan mujahideen. It was in 1980 that the United States flatly charged the Soviets with extensive use of chemical warfare, the "yellow rain" allegation that liberals would later criticize as a disreputable piece of Reagan-era Red-baiting. Closer to home, the Nicaraguan experience could not be allowed to spread across Central America or the Caribbean. In the last days of his presidency, Carter was sufficiently alarmed by the imminent collapse of the Salvadoran regime to restore U.S. military aid, which stemmed what the guerrillas vaunted as their final offensive. In December 1980, he directly warned the Soviet government against military intervention in Poland. Throughout 1980, we can discern the stark anti-Communist mood of the Reagan years, the renewed patriotic upsurge. Carter's administration began the pro-Iraq tilt following that nation's invasion of Iran, and the United States would shortly have no choice but to respond to Libyan provocations in the Mediterranean.[52]

Given the different political emphases of the two leaders, the global confrontation might have worked out quite differently. Carter never stood a chance of convincing the nation's foes of his steely determination, while Reagan's reputation for tough inflexibility benefited hugely from the "mad bomber" image painted by his foes. Arguably, war would have been far more likely under an indecisive Carter regime. Much also would have depended on the outcome of the 1980 congressional races. Quite feasibly, Carter might have won the presidency but faced a hostile Senate aching for an excuse to impeach. The recent history of the hard right suggests that charges of Soviet infiltration in a Democratic administration would have flown more freely then than at any other time since the 1950s. But whatever the political coloring of the new administration, it is difficult to see how some kind of East-West face-off would have been avoided.

In domestic affairs too, Carter pioneered the fiscal conservatism commonly associated with Reagan, and likewise applied a powerful moral agenda to economics. Carter, as much as Reagan, believed firmly that "government cannot solve our problems," and he was repeatedly in conflict with liberals over drastic cuts to social programs. To quote Bruce Schulman, President Carter was already "slouching toward the supply side." On his watch, the Federal Reserve had taken the steps necessary to cut inflation, and a second Carter administration likely would have both suffered a deep economic crisis in 1981–82 and benefited from some kind of subsequent recovery, though scarcely on the Reagan scale.[53] Conversely, Reagan was nothing like the thoroughgoing ideologue of the caricature. He raised taxes more frequently than he cared to admit, and he negotiated with both terrorists and the states sponsoring their activities.

Much social policy of the "Reagan years" had its origins before Reagan took office. By 1980, all the foundations were already laid for a much more hard-line approach to crime and justice, most aspects of which had little to do with the federal government. A drug war was already under way, with all the attendant rhetoric, and was likely to be extended to substances apart from PCP. Sooner or later, any government would take drastic steps against the vast imports of cocaine then overrunning U.S. borders. Also by 1980, as we will see, so many of the cultural factors that would shape later conservatism were already in place, in the form of new generational conflicts, developments in the presentation of news and popular culture, and new technological breakthroughs. Quite independently of the national administration, child protection rhetoric was already being used to attack sexual immorality, pornography, drug abuse, and cult atrocities. In each case, well-founded concerns about social dangers provided the basis for popular scares and nightmare stories, which supported broader attacks on moral and sexual irresponsibility. Something like the wave of panics of 1983–85 probably would have occurred regardless of which party held the White House. The anxieties and fears were already there, waiting to become the foundations for political action. Regardless of the election outcome, the year 1980 would be remembered as marking a significant shift away from social liberalism, away from the 1960s.

On December 8, 1980, a nation already accustomed to shocks heard that former Beatle John Lennon had been shot dead in New York City. The assassination, which so closely fitted the pattern familiar from recent years, was the work of a disturbed loner obsessed with the novel *Catcher in the Rye*. Like the hero of that book, with whom he identified mystically, assassin Mark Chapman was deeply worried about threats to children. He wanted to serve as a protector, a catcher, who could save children from dangers and from phoniness—in this case, from the cultural sellout that Lennon symbolized. As Chapman wrote, his crime was a message from Holden Caulfield to Holden Caulfield. For the baby boom generation, though, many of whom were already troubled by the nation's new political direction, the murder was a catastrophe, all the more so because the violence contradicted all the ideas that Lennon represented. Few commentators could resist the cliché: this was the day the music died. Coming at the end of the dreadful year, at a turning point in the history of American liberalism, the murder served as another painful symbol of the end of the 1960s.[54]

7

Into the Reagan Era

He was our oldest president, but he made America young again.
—John Kerry

Ronald Reagan's election left liberals stunned and alarmed at the prospects for American politics and for global peace. The nation's nuclear arsenal was now in the hands of a president who sincerely and vociferously believed that Communism represented an evil force. Watching the growing crisis in El Salvador, liberals drew immediate analogies with the early stages of U.S. involvement in Vietnam, which had likewise begun with the arrival of American weapons and advisers. Domestically, Reagan's economic policies seemed absolutely out of tune with reality, and a sense of economic disaster was affirmed by the steep downturn of 1981–82. Seemingly, just as radicals had warned, a conservative administration was at once bringing in militarism, class war, and economic depression. On the positive side for liberals—assuming the world survived—was the belief that Republican rule would not last beyond one wretched term.[1]

In retrospect, both liberal pessimism and optimism were baseless. Reagan achieved much of his agenda at home and abroad, and his time in office so changed American politics that all subsequent administrations shared many of his assumptions, including a number that seemed outlandish at the time. To use a word coined by another two-term incumbent, many contemporaries badly misunderestimated Ronald Reagan.

The extent of popular affection and gratitude to Reagan was evident following his death in 2004, when so many ordinary people recalled him as the leader who had restored America and ended the long national nightmares of the 1970s. Crucially, many Americans were willing to share his vision of a nation threatened by enemies, at home and overseas, who had grown dangerously strong because of American decadence and indecision, but who could now at last be defeated. For many—by no means all—the Reagan presidency stands in popular memory as a time of national salvation.[2]

But apart from his personal abilities, Reagan also benefited from some powerful historical trends, above all the serious undermining since the mid-1970s of key national institutions—the presidency itself, but also Congress, the federal courts, and the news media. While the times demanded strong activist leadership, most of the obvious challengers to a renewed imperial presidency were themselves discredited. In addition, through the early 1980s, changes in American social and economic structure provided a basis for Reaganite attempts to reverse the 1960s—but also limited what could be achieved in some areas.

Reaganomics

Revolutions occur not because people want them to happen but because the old order is broken so definitively that it is impossible to move in any direction except forward. That observation would certainly apply to America at the start of the 1980s, following the credit crunch and the frightening brush with serious inflation. In retrospect, we know that Carter-era Federal Reserve policies had already begun the process of healing, but at the time, matters looked desperate. In January 1981, *Time* warned, "For starters, [Reagan] faces an economic situation growing more frightening by the moment." The prime rate remained between 18 and 20 percent from December 1980 through October 1981, and not until late 1982 did it fall below 12 percent.[3]

The failure of recent economic policies allowed Reagan Republicans to advance a radical new vision based on deregulation and tax cutting. In their election materials, Republicans mocked the regulations that, they argued, had hobbled America's natural tendency toward expansion and enterprise, independence and initiative. At every stage, the goal was to restore the centrality of individual moral choice, in economic matters as in personal conduct. As so often in later years, Western imagery was much in evidence. One commercial showed a cowboy tying a portable toilet to his horse before setting off to ride the range, the point being that workplace regulations set wildly unrealistic standards for the provision of sanitary facilities and for so much else. Throughout such rhetoric, we see a gender appeal, rejecting the coddling maternal state that restrains male freedoms. Environmental regulation was condemned because it interfered with property rights and the rights of individuals to pursue their own destinies. Excessive taxes thwarted growth and innovation and had the potential for selective politicized application.[4]

Reagan offered a bold new economic approach, so radical that his rival in the primaries, George Bush, had dismissed it as "voodoo economics." (This remark was embarrassing once Bush accepted Reagan's vice presidential slot.) Somehow, Reagan was planning to cut taxes while launching a huge expansion of military expenditures, all without bankrupting the nation. Basic to the new economics were dramatic tax cuts, and the Economic Recovery Tax Act of 1981 offered across-the-board cuts, together with a cut in the top marginal rate from 70 to 50 percent. Tax cutting was made possible by substantial cuts in public spending, with Great Society–inspired anti-poverty programs taking much of the damage: Medicaid, food stamps, and Aid to Families with Dependent Children all suffered. Even with these cuts, so radically did the administration slash taxes that tax increases were needed the following year, under the euphemism "revenue enhancements." Booming defense expenditures threatened larger and larger deficits. Reagan lived up to his principle that "defense is not a budget issue. You spend what you need." The 1986 budget offered a record deficit of $226 billion. Reagan's anti–New Deal was made possible by the loyal votes of conservative Democratic congressmen, mainly southerners, the so-called boll weevils.[5]

Fundamental to the new administration was the reduction of federal intervention in society, and not just in the economic realm. Across the board, agencies reduced the scope of regulation, generating controversy quite as intense as the tax fights. Justifying the weakening of environmental regulation, the new secretary of the interior, James Watt, appeared to believe that long-term environmental protection was scarcely needed when the Second Coming of Christ might not be too far removed. Watt was so outrageously conservative that he famously denounced the Beach Boys as the kind of hell-raising rock band that would attract the "wrong element" to a public celebration. Another demon figure for liberals was William Bradford Reynolds, the new assistant attorney general for civil rights and a forthright enemy of affirmative action programs.[6] The ideal of the "progressive administrative" state crumbled.

The American economy changed rapidly in the early 1980s, as many traditional industries entered a period of terminal decline. One painful area of transformation was the steel industry, which only recently had been such a symbol of economic power and virility. By 1979, U.S. Steel was suffering massive losses, and the corporation lost $561 million in a single quarter of 1980. Cutbacks and layoffs began in earnest at legendary works such as Youngstown and Homestead. In the Pittsburgh area, the number of steelworkers fell from ninety thousand in 1980 to only forty-four thousand by 1984. Once-booming steel towns now tried to rescue themselves from the worst social crisis since the Great Depression. Damage was almost as great in the auto industry. In 1979–80, the Chrysler Corporation had been rescued by a $1.5 billion federal bailout, while Ford lost over $1 billion in 1980. Severe cutbacks were needed to save the car industry from collapse. General Motors, which employed 600,000 workers in 1979, today has a U.S. workforce of only 125,000.[7]

By weakening established centers of heavy industry, the economic shakeout devastated the labor unions that had formed so critical a part of the New Deal coalition. The proportion of unionized workers fell steadily from the 1970s through the 1990s. The administration accelerated this process when in 1981 the federal air traffic controllers planned an illegal strike. Reagan ordered the dismissal of all striking members of their union, the Professional Air Traffic Controllers Association (PATCO). Among other effects, the PATCO shock deterred unionizing activity among the growing army of clerical and service workers. By the end of the century, the number of temporary, on-call, and contract workers in the United States was roughly equal to the combined membership of the nation's labor unions. The familiar American economy, with its established political assumptions, was quickly becoming the "old economy." Worst hit of all, perhaps, was the oldest economy—agriculture—as the credit crisis ruined farms across the Midwest.[8]

America began the 1980s facing a recession of dire proportions. Observers cited with alarm the Kondratieff cycles that some traced in modern world history, fifty-two-year periods that separated peaks and troughs in economic activity. If that view was correct, then notionally 1981 could see a replay of 1929, the start of the Great Depression. The official unemployment rate rose from 6 percent in 1978–79 to almost 10 percent in 1982–83, affecting some twelve million people. The number officially classified as living below the poverty level rose by some 25 percent between 1979 and 1983, to exceed thirty-five million individuals. Economic miseries were naturally blamed on the administration, and particularly on Reagan's apparent bias toward the rich, the military, and corporate America.[9]

Liberals found many opportunities to condemn the apparent war on the poor. One trivial but memorable symbol was the decision in September 1981 to classify ketchup as a vegetable, to ensure that school meal programs provide the required nutritional allowance while coping with stringent budget cuts. Reagan associates could demonstrate a Marie Antoinette—like insouciance. Presidential aide Edwin Meese commented, "I don't know whether these [accounts of hunger] are anecdotal things from which some members of the press and political opponents are generalizing or whether there are genuine pockets of hunger." In popular memory, this was summarized as a callous dismissal of hunger as "anecdotal," a word often quoted alongside "ketchup" to damn the Reagan presidency, especially its perceived neglect of children. In the summer of 1981, liberals pointed to unprecedented rioting in British cities as an ugly foretaste of what the United States might expect if the government pursued its class war policies. While the administration hoped that wealth would trickle down to the poor, perhaps economic resentment and despair would trickle up, to provoke open revolution. The battered forces of organized labor rallied, and in September 1981 a Solidarity Day attracted 400,000 to Washington, D.C., to march for workers' rights. The name was a clever appropriation of contemporary right-wing rhetoric, since "Solidarity" implied a connection with the union federation challenging the repressive Communist government of Poland. Some religious groups, including Catholic activists, expressed strongly liberal views on labor rights and welfare while challenging the administration on the nuclear arms race and Central America. Briefly, it seemed as if the old left-liberal coalition might be reconstituting.[10]

The president's approval rating slid disastrously. From 68 percent in May 1981, it fell to 42 percent in May 1982 and to a horrendous 37 percent by February 1983, a level almost as low as Carter's. Democrats tried to use Reagan's own powerful Western symbolism against him. At the 1984 Democratic convention, Mario Cuomo complained that "the Republicans believe that the wagon train will not make it to the frontier unless some of the old, some of the young, some of the weak are left behind by the side of the trail."[11]

Recovery

Yet economic discontent did not translate into mass support for Democrats, who won no Senate seats in the 1982 midterm elections, although they strengthened their hold on the House. Even in the depths of a vicious recession, the 1970s still cast a frightening shadow. Also, Reagan's position steadily improved, with an economic revival at home and marked foreign policy successes abroad. In November 1982, the U.S. economy began one of its longest and most triumphant periods of growth and expansion, a trend scarcely broken until 2000 (the painful recession of 1990–92 was relatively short). It was a major cause of celebration in late 1980 when the Dow Jones index rose above 1,000; it topped 2,000 for the first time ever in 1987, and crested 3,000 in 1991. Meanwhile, inflation was purged from the system. Inflation rates, which had approached 13 percent in 1980, fell below 4 percent in 1982. The prime rate was down to 11 percent through 1983. The National Mortgage Contract Rate—an average of rates reported by a sample of various lenders—reached a high of 15.57 percent in May 1982 but fell to 11.61 percent in April 1984 and remained in single digits from 1986 through 1988. Across the board, the years 1983–84 marked a welcome return to economic optimism.

The administration benefited enormously from changes in the oil market and the steadily dropping price of crude. During the height of the Iranian revolution and the ensuing crisis, oil prices had risen from $14 a barrel in 1978 to $35 in 1981. The price fell below $30 in 1983 and below $15 by 1985, sinking at one point to $10. The price remained between $15 and $20 through most of the next decade. At the same time, Carter-sponsored measures to improve energy efficiency reduced reliance on foreign oil. The overall official mileage of new American cars grew from 14 miles per gallon in the late 1970s to 22 in 1987. As a wonderful political bonus for Reagan-era hawks, low oil prices seriously undermined the Soviet economy. Meanwhile, impressive international cooperation stabilized currency markets. In 1985, the United States and other leading industrial nations intervened decisively to bring down a perilously high dollar, effecting a sizable controlled drop in its international value.[12]

Domestically, the new prosperity was based on quite different economic foundations. Hard though it was to imagine a U.S. economy not dominated by cars and steel production, the impact of the economic crisis was softened by the growth of major new sectors, including defense and aerospace. The military buildup reinforced the prosperity and population of the South and West, which was good news for faith-and-flag Republicanism. In a powerful symbolic gesture, the American space program resumed with the successful launch of the shuttle *Columbia* in April 1981.

Employment in the financial and service sectors boomed, as the United States transformed into an information economy. Again, the growth of financial services had its roots in the 1970s, with the development of instruments intended to counter the effects of inflation, such as mutual funds and money market funds, which tempted more ordinary citizens to explore the world of investment. As Joseph Nocera has described, the middle class was joining the money class.

An atmosphere of deregulation, beginning in the Carter era, fostered growth and diversification. Already in 1975, stock exchanges were forbidden to fix brokerage commissions, increasing competition and opening the way for discount brokerages. In 1978, the U.S. Supreme Court ruled that banks issuing credit cards could charge any rate prevailing in their home states of operation, leading issuers to set up shop in states with little regulation, such as South Dakota and Delaware. This change suddenly made the credit card industry lucrative and highly competitive, beginning a plastic boom that encouraged the use of credit throughout society. To take another visible sign of well-being, the effects of airline deregulation after 1978 made air travel much cheaper and more generally available, in effect democratizing the older notion of the jet set. One token of unprecedented competition was the appearance of frequent flier programs, created in 1981 to promote passenger loyalty. In 1980, Congress deregulated both the rail freight and trucking industries. Contrary to Democratic warnings, the shift away from heavy industry did not transform the United States into a proletarianized "nation of hamburger flippers."[13]

Economic growth in the early 1980s further undermined the anti-business attitudes of the Watergate years, not to mention ideas of regulation. If the Reagan presidency did nothing else, it restored the belief in free enterprise capitalism in a way that shaped the policies of all subsequent administrations of whatever party. Complain as they might that tax cuts did not really boost the economy, few critics have dared suggest a return to the stifling tax rates of the pre-Reagan years. By the fall of 1983, Reagan's approval rating was approaching 50 percent, and it topped 60 percent by October 1984.[14]

Entering the 1984 election season, Reagan enjoyed inexorable momentum. He campaigned on an anti-malaise platform, reminding people what they had faced four years previously. In a sense, he was campaigning against the year 1980, or rather against the stereotypes associated with that era. One Reagan commercial recalled, "This was America in 1980. A nation that wasn't working. Huge government spending gave us the worst inflation in 65 years. . . . People were losing faith in the American dream." Such rhetoric reinforced the popular perception of the 1970s as an era of confusion, disorder, and weakness, in obvious contrast to the strength and confidence of the 1980s, with the revolutionary turning point the 1980 election. Reagan explicitly recalled Carter's "malaise" theme. "From Washington we heard only an elaborate and disheartening series of excuses about our national and international problems. We were told these problems were basically insoluble and that we had to accommodate ourselves to stagflation, to limitations on growth, to living with less. . . . And, worse, some said all of this was the fault of the American people, who, we were told, suffered from a crisis of confidence."[15]

On the other side, the Democratic left, buoyed by the upsurge of popular activism since 1981, was suffering from overconfidence and saw no point in making centrist compromises. The party almost willfully provoked disaster by choosing as their presidential candidate Walter Mondale, a figure associated with the horrible last year of the Carter regime. In the name of honesty, moreover, Mondale made a campaign pledge to raise taxes. The Democrats' best-known public face was probably that of Jesse Jackson, who recalled for many all the worst nightmares of 1960s turmoil while symbolizing pervasive urban ills.[16]

The overwhelming Reagan election victory in 1984 (49 states and 60 percent of the popular vote) goes far to confirming that the conservative agenda did command widespread public support. In this election, a quarter of all registered Democrats actually voted for Reagan. Based on a case study of Baltimore, Kenneth Durr suggests that it is this election, far more than 1980, that marked "the definitive end of the Democratic New Deal Coalition." At the state level too, Republicans consolidated their hold on most of the South.[17]

Gains and Losses

So striking and complete were Reagan's victories in some areas—notably the economy and foreign policy—that we might overlook the lack of progress made by conservatives in other key matters, especially the morality issues that had aroused such fervor in the late 1970s and which had contributed so much to his electoral triumph. The lack of success by morality advocates surprised not just liberals but also more mainstream conservatives. One foe of the moral conservatives was Reagan's budget director, David Stockman, who later apostatized and wrote a dyspeptic memoir of his time in the administration. In his view, once in office, the Reagan camp had "opened its doors and let in every crazy who knocked." Yet the "crazies," if so they were, won few victories.[18]

At least in 1981, moral conservatives had high hopes of reversing liberal gains in matters of sexuality and gender. Some hoped to use national victories to pursue their agendas at state and local levels in debates over school prayer, textbook censorship, gun control, and gay rights. In 1980 and 1981, twenty-three states debated bills demanding balanced treatment of evolution and creationism in the public schools, leading to a series of brushfire legal battles with the ACLU. Ultimately, all these attempts were ruled unconstitutional. Another failure was the proposed federal amendment permitting school prayer, which went down to defeat in 1984, although it attracted the support of no less than fifty-six U.S. senators.[19]

Abortion was the touchstone issue, the area in which liberal gains could be reversed only by action at the federal level. Reagan himself spoke repeatedly against abortion. In his Evil Empire speech of 1983, he complained, "Abortion on demand now takes the lives of up to one and a half million unborn children a year." In 1981, Congress considered the proposed Hatch Amendment, which would have declared that "a right to abortion is not secured by this Constitution," that is, stressing states' rights rather than the much more contentious issue of deciding when human life begins. Liberals and feminists warned not just of setbacks but of the imminent rise of a patriarchal theocratic state of the sort later imagined in Margaret Atwood's dystopian novel *The Handmaid's Tale*. Attempting to confirm such fears, liberal propaganda made much use of religious hate figures such as Pat Robertson, Jerry Falwell, and James Watt.[20]

Obviously, such a scenario did not emerge, and moral and religious conservatives lost most of their battles, including those over abortion. Reagan's first nominee to the U.S. Supreme Court was Sandra Day O'Connor, who was distinctly moderate on abortion issues and who favored the ERA. Meanwhile, the Hatch Amendment met heavy public opposition, running at over 75 percent in one 1982 poll (though as always in such matters, much depends on the phrasing of the survey question). The amendment eventually passed the Senate by a vote of 50–49 the following year, far short of the two-thirds majority required to change the Constitution. If moral conservatives could not even win on something as broadly phrased as this, they were not going to win any more ambitious gains in other matters. It was a token of its frustration that beginning in the mid-1980s, the pro-life movement developed its strategy of direct action against abortion facilities, including physical attacks by extremists. Anti-abortion violence escalated sharply in 1984–85, including dozens of arson and bomb attacks, and the militant Operation Rescue emerged in 1986. The movement justified its existence by effecting the kind of "rescues" that the government refused to do. By the late 1980s, religious activists expressed their disillusion with the administration, complaining that they had been treated as electoral foot soldiers by a regime that abandoned them once in power. The Moral Majority dissolved in 1989, little mourned.[21]

Given the strength of the Reagan victory in 1980, the relative failure of moralistic policies may seem surprising, but Republicans had triumphed with the support of a large and often inconsistent coalition of regions, economic interests, and moral attitudes. Also, the rapid pace of technological innovation during the decade after 1975 caused far-reaching social and demographic changes. In some ways, these developments worked against moral conservatives: in a world in which women were increasingly critical to the economy, feminist gains were unlikely to be reversed. At the same time, though, the emerging politics both of gender and of generations raised the potential for new kinds of political movement, the manipulation of social fears, and ultimately a new kind of law-and-order politics.

Engines of Creation

New technologies made a far more obvious impact on everyday life in the post-1975 decade than at any other time since the coming of television, as venture capital moved decisively into computing and electronics. This was the decade of home computers, video games, video cameras and recorders, and cable television, with all the last implied for standards of news presentation. And although the high-tech boom is closely associated with the "Reagan eighties," in technology matters at least, the formal division of decades makes no sense: the Carter-Reagan transition was quite seamless. This might seem remarkable in light of the anti-science ideas that we have seen to characterize the mid-1970s, the protests against space travel and nuclear energy, but the rising generation of entrepreneurs and pioneers succeeded thoroughly in portraying their endeavors as creative and democratizing, as play rather than soulless research. New breakthroughs seemed, in fact, to represent science fiction made manifest.

The arrival of personal computers was a critical social development that advanced at an amazing rate. Just how rapidly electronic technology was moving can be appreciated by watching a film such as 1973's *Soylent Green*, a dystopian nightmare about a grossly overcrowded Manhattan in the year 2022. Among the squalor, the privileged super-rich survive, and they while away their idle hours by playing games that the filmmakers obviously thought would represent the cutting-edge technology of the coming century. In one scene, a woman plays an extremely simple kind of video tennis, in which a dot bounces off crude lines that signify rackets. In the context of 1973, the technology seemed impressive, though it would be laughably outdated within just four or five years, never mind fifty. The futuristic dreams of the early 1970s came nowhere near grasping the realities that were so close at hand.

We can find any number of powerful symbolic moments in the post-1975 decade. In 1975, Bill Gates coined the name *Microsoft* (microcomputer software); in 1976, Steve Jobs and Steve Wozniak founded the Apple Computer Company; Oracle emerged in 1977. The Apple II was introduced in 1977, the first personal computer to offer color graphics. The IBM PC appeared in

1981, and the personal computer was *Time*'s Man of the Year for 1982. In 1982, Apple became the first PC maker to top a billion dollars in sales. In 1984, computers became massively more accessible to ordinary consumers when the Macintosh popularized the principle of WIMP, with the now all-but-universal elements of windows/icons/mouse/point. In 1977, the introduction of the Atari Video Computing system brought video games into the American home, and in 1980, Atari began offering familiar arcade games such as Space Invaders for home consumption, unleashing a consumer boom. The United States led a new era of technological innovation. From 1978, an optimistic and youth-oriented high-tech culture found a popular platform in the science-fact-and-science-fiction magazine *Omni*.[22]

The world of communications that we know today appeared in these years, as American homes acquired that harbinger of greater changes yet to come, the modem. Though the World Wide Web would not appear until the Clinton era, the development of Usenet in 1979 gave grassroots users access to a kind of pre-Web in the form of a distributed bulletin board system. Intolerably clunky by modern standards, bulletin boards and newsgroups marked a stunning breakthrough in global communication. There were four hundred Usenet sites by 1982, and many millions today. Also in 1979, CompuServe gave ordinary subscribers access to email, and by 1985, America Online and CompuServe were competing for a swelling market fascinated by the potential of Internet culture. (On the dark side of that culture, the first spam e-mail was sent as early as 1978.) The TCP/IP protocol that allows computers to communicate with each other was developed in 1974 and massively improved by the end of the decade. In 1980, Tim Berners-Lee's program Enquire pioneered a new means of organizing and accessing data through hypertext links, which ultimately became the foundation of the Web. One of the few moments when Reagan-era laissez-faire ideas contributed directly to these developments came in 1983, when the FCC forbade phone companies from levying charges on data transmission, as opposed to voice communications. This paved the way for all later Internet development.[23]

But computers were not the only area of dizzying advance, as other communication technologies were also revolutionized. Fiber-optic technology entered boom years after 1977, when U.S. phone companies began using the medium for transmitting telephone traffic. In 1978, the first GPS satellite was launched. And though invented long previously, the cell phone was first practically applied in the early 1980s. The FCC authorized cellular service in 1982, and the first commercial service began the following year. By 1987, the United States had over a million cell phone subscribers. Taken alongside expanding computer use and the growth of e-mail, the arrival of the cell phone heralded the radical shift in the definition of work and the workplace that has reshaped American life over the past quarter century. As people could accomplish far more away from their desks and offices, the boundaries between home and office and between work and leisure time were eroded, if not obliterated.

Repeatedly, technological progress seems concentrated in the late 1970s, years when political confusion and uncertainty coincided with sweeping social and cultural advance. Corporate America now applied the insights of artificial intelligence research, while the publication of Douglas R. Hofstadter's book *Gödel, Escher, Bach* inspired a new generation of AI explorers. The modern discipline of materials science and engineering is commonly dated to the 1974 publication of the study *Materials and Man's Needs*. As so often before in history, science fiction writers helped stir the dreams of real-world scientists about the directions that current developments might take. One visionary work was Arthur C. Clarke's *Fountains of Paradise* (1979), with its dazzling description of how superstrong crystalline carbon nanofiber could be used to build a "space elevator," potentially opening the solar system to human exploration. In 1986, Eric Drexler's *Engines of Creation* heralded the emerging age of nanotechnology.[24]

These years also witnessed epoch-making expeditions into inner space, the realm of the human body and mind. Partly driving these changes were breakthroughs in noninvasive imaging, with the invention of the CAT scan (the first whole-body image was produced in 1977) and magnetic resonance imaging, while PET scanning offered unprecedented information about the functioning of the brain. The chemistry of the brain was far better understood by the late 1970s with the discovery of endorphins and new insights into the workings of neurotransmitters such as serotonin and dopamine. Medical developments had a vast economic impact, as whole new fields of expertise and employment opened up and new technologies demanded significant investment. Through the 1980s, the health care industry was by far America's biggest producer of new jobs. Also, advances in neurochemistry raised the prospect of new drugs that could regulate mood and emotion, and some would make serious profits. Prozac was patented in 1974, though it did not enter general use until the late 1980s. Through the 1980s, pharmaceutical companies would be the most profitable sector of the U.S. economy.

Helping this growth was the Bayh-Dole Patent Act of 1980. By permitting academic institutions to exploit patents for products developed under their auspices, this measure radically changed the social organization of scientific research. Discoveries made at universities thus became proprietary, rather than entering the public domain, and offered the potential for commercial exploitation. University-based researchers were encouraged to establish private companies, as universities and industry worked closely together. The measure stimulated the growth of research parks around academic institutions, thus making college towns vigorous centers of new urban development. Changes of the Reagan years certainly benefited Big Pharma, not least the very generous revisions of patent law under the 1984 Hatch-Waxman Act, but as with electronics, the boom was foreseeable before the 1980 election.

The controversial new industry of genetic engineering enjoyed growth quite as explosive as personal computing. (This industry also benefited greatly from Bayh-Dole.) Though recombinant DNA research had been under way for some years, a momentous turning point occurred in 1977 when the newly founded company Genentech first used a synthetic recombinant gene to manufacture a human protein, somatostatin. In 1980, the U.S. Supreme Court ruled in *Diamond v. Chakrabarty et al.* that newly developed organisms could be patented, giving a legal foundation to what would soon be a lucrative commercial enterprise. When Genentech went public in 1980, its stock established a record for an initial public offering. In 1982, the company produced a form of human insulin that became the world's first genetically engineered drug to be approved by the U.S. Food and Drug Administration. Other discoveries followed rapidly in what was plausibly described as a biotechnological revolution: polymerase chain reaction techniques and DNA fingerprinting were both in place by the mid-1980s. And in vitro fertilization now became possible: Britain produced the first test-tube baby in 1978, and another was born in the United States in 1981.[25]

Though ordinary lay observers might have little detailed knowledge of developments in biotechnology, it was widely appreciated that a revolution was in progress. Much of the initial excitement—and concern—focused on the possibility of human cloning, which at this stage was of course a distant prospect. By 1977, though, awareness of cloning reached a mass audience when a well-publicized photograph showed thirty cloned frogs, arousing speculation as to when the technology would be extended to mammals. In 1978, David Rorvik's highly suspect book *In His Image* claimed that human cloning had already been accomplished. Films such as *The Boys from Brazil* and even *Sleeper* made the idea of cloning a mainstay of popular culture, and the first *Star Wars* film recalls the bloody Clone Wars. Even if these stories remained in the realm of the fantastic, the prospect of cloning served to focus national debate over the ethics of biotechnology.

Though seemingly exploring such very different matters, new developments in electronics and biology had many themes in common—enough, in fact, to cause thoughtful observers to ask worrying questions about the limits and definition of humanity. As the power of computing increased, the frontiers separating human and machine intelligence eroded; advances in neurochemistry and the localization of function caused the brain to be understood as a material system, which could be altered by appropriate chemicals and nutrients. If pleasure, misery, or exaltation could all be seen as neurochemical states, notions of an extraphysical "mind" looked increasingly implausible. Also, human capacities to alter or improve the body were suggested by trends in biomechanics, cosmetic surgery, and reproductive technology. Taking these currents together, it was easy to envisage close future interactions between brain and computer, a union of the biological and electronic. Such visions were explored in popular culture in films such as *Blade Runner, Tron,* and *The Terminator,* in novels such as William Gibson's *Neuromancer* (1984), and in countless science fiction books. Fears of the sinister effects of unchecked technology resonated in political life through the popular image of illicit demon drugs turning innocent users into atavistic monsters or robotic killers. Such was the rhetoric directed against PCP and crack cocaine, and Frankenstein mythology permeated the designer drug scare of 1984–85.

Visions of robots, machine-human hybrids, and synthetically created life were familiar enough in human culture, but as fairy tales or metaphors. What was different about the post-1975 decade was that such beings suddenly came closer to plausibility than ever before.

Masters of the Universe

Technological change reverberated through society, with a special impact on the gender balance of the workplace. Employment swelled in high-tech industries such as computing, pharmaceuticals, and biotech, all of which set a premium on intelligence and creativity, rather than physical strength or endurance. In the service sector too, new access to computers brought ever more women into the workplace, increasing the number of two-income households and expanding consumer purchasing power. Moreover, the huge presence of women in the workplace meant that any attempt to reverse feminist gains would be limited. Feminists succeeded in projecting their belief that women's economic success depended upon their control of their reproductive freedoms, ensuring that far-reaching anti-abortion measures would fail.[26]

The electronic revolution helped transform values in other ways. Since the 1950s, youth cultures had defined themselves against the perceived ethos of corporate America, which was seen as hierarchical, stuffy, and authoritarian. The shift to new technologies made business and profit attractive to educated young people who some years earlier might have rejected the corporate world. In newer and more successful businesses, individualism and imagination were highly valued, and a willingness to flout rules was actively praised. Computer hackers might make excellent designers. By 1983–84, the media were publicizing the new phenomenon of the yuppie, the young urban professional, highly oriented to success and enterprise, display and excess. To adapt the slogan popularized by a fictional corporate buccaneer, greed was now good.[27]

In many ways, countercultural values were effectively channeled into what was fast becoming the corporate mainstream, the now-fashionable pursuit of wealth. The cultural shift was reflected in a transformation of personal appearance that is obvious from any films or news footage of the era. Young men were wearing much shorter hair and generally adopting a less epicene appearance: even ties made a comeback. Young women returned to more elaborate hairstyles and makeup. If not exactly a return to the 1950s world of the organization man (or woman), at least the idea of dressing for success was definitely in vogue. By the mid-1980s, young adults were being satirized for their obsessive materialism, ceaseless quest for wealth, and hedonism. These themes, so startling in light of the assumptions of the mid-1970s, were central to best-selling novels such as Jay McInerney's *Bright Lights, Big City* (1984), Bret Easton Ellis's *Less than Zero* (1986), and Tom Wolfe's *Bonfire of the Vanities* (1987). And while accounts of yuppie life adopted a tone of fascinated horror, they attracted a mass audience, often from readers who wished to copy those styles.[28]

At the same time, advances in technology further discredited ideas of state intervention and regulation. Of course, the computer industry worked closely with government and the military and borrowed their innovations: the Internet had its origins in a defense-oriented project. And the drug and biotech patents secured by universities under Bayh-Dole were commonly the outcome of government funding, through research grants from the National Institutes of Health or similar taxpayer-supported agencies. In the context of the 1980s, though, the flourishing technology industries—especially computing—looked like wonderful commercials for decentralization and deregulation, entrepreneurship and risk taking, heroic private enterprise and free trade. These developments consigned to political obsolescence familiar liberal assumptions about unions, tariffs, taxes, and welfare. The conspicuous success of technology lent credence to Reagan's repeated use of frontier rhetoric and his optimistic sense that America had nearly infinite room to grow.

Generation X

The economic shift drew ever-sharper generational lines between the younger generation and the baby boomers, whose sixties values seemed increasingly irrelevant. In this context, the "young" meant those born after 1963, who were children and teenagers as the boomers were settling down into adult life. (Though the definition of Generation X is flexible, I include those Americans born between 1963 and 1979.) Their elders saw these young people as undisciplined and dangerous, much as every other American generation had viewed its own adolescents. In 1977–78, it was children of thirteen and fourteen who were at the center of the new anti-drug panics, presumed to be the targets of underage vice rackets; the pressing criminal danger was believed to be remorseless violent offenders of fifteen or sixteen. In 1979, the release of the gang film *The Warriors* aroused fears that teen viewers would imitate it, spawning further urban violence, and tales of *Warriors*-inspired murders did wonders for the film's advertising campaign. Many of those alarmed by such dangers ignored the irony that they themselves had been defined as teenage menaces in earlier decades, and in almost identical terms.[29]

These generational gulfs raised political issues. As they became politically aware, children born in the mid-1960s had a very different set of memories and expectations than their elders. As far as they knew, abortion and easy contraception had always been available, while racial segregation had never existed outside the history books. Homosexuality had always been legal. Those battles were long since won and finished, and no realistic prospect existed that older restrictions might be reintroduced. They had never faced a real military draft, as opposed to the notional chore of Selective Service registration. Generation X grew up in a racially different America. While previous generations knew a world of black and white, the young recognized a polychrome society that included Latinos and East and South Asians, a world in which continuing immigration constantly changed ethnic realities.[30]

In other matters too, the question of memory radically divided the generations. Boomers shared a common set of historical memories of the 1960s, however they might interpret them. Images of Vietnam and racial violence loomed large, providing a powerful motive to avoid any similar disasters in the future. By the mid-1980s, such events were passing into history for a newer generation, which had more immediate nightmares of national chaos and humiliation—the Iran hostages, gasoline crises, aggressive Soviet conduct around the world. They had grown up in a world in which Soviets, Islamists, and terrorists always had been the enemy, in which anti-Communist rhetoric was not risible. Neither the military nor intelligence agencies were automatically suspect, nor was big business. Technology and science were both exciting and enticing and were symbolized by enviable young entrepreneurs. By the time Gen Xers could first vote in a presidential election, in 1984, they could recall just one confident and successful national leader, namely, Ronald Reagan. As Bob Greene complained, "To them Lyndon Johnson is as distant a figure as FDR was to us."[31] Appeals to the political values of the 1960s lost force.

Technological change reinforced cultural and political divisions. Not least, being computer-savvy helped teenagers assert their independence from their uncomprehending parents. Boomers in their thirties were shocked to learn that they no longer represented a cultural cutting edge.

Developments in popular music also illustrate the culture clash. Through the mid-1970s, the most successful acts were either veterans of the 1960s or obviously grew out of that era, including Led Zeppelin, Rod Stewart, and Pink Floyd. Most appealed to an audience with a taste for a mellower and less radical sound than during the era of the British invasion or flower power. Artists, like their fans, had aged, and they explored more mature themes. The Age of Mellow culminated in 1976–77 with the release of several albums that for many defined the sound of the seventies: Peter Frampton's *Frampton Comes Alive, Hotel California* by the Eagles, Fleetwood Mac's *Rumors*, and Jackson Browne's *Running on Empty*. Also from 1976 was Led Zeppelin's concert film, *The Song Remains the Same*.[32]

In the late 1970s, though, popular music was experiencing one of its periodic returns to roots in the form of new wave and the punk explosion of 1976–77. U.S. groups formed between 1974 and 1977 included the B-52's, the Ramones, Blondie, the Cars, and Talking Heads, and all were achieving hit status by the end of the decade. On the independent fringes of the rock world, punk inspired violent and anarchic bands such as the Dead Kennedys and Black Flag. Richard Hell's anthem "Blank Generation" appeared in 1976. In 1978, Van Halen's debut album created the mold for later hard rock and heavy metal. Another innovation from 1977–78 was urban rap culture: the first national hit was "Rapper's Delight," released by the Sugar Hill Gang in late 1979. Like new wave, this music delighted listeners born in the mid-1960s as much as it baffled those born ten or fifteen years previously. No less puzzling to adults was the enthusiastic youth response to the film *The Rocky Horror Picture Show*, which came to be known for its audience participation. The rituals made little sense to most born before 1960. In popular music, as in politics, few of the assumptions of 1975 still made sense in 1979.[33]

The newer bands and their fans specialized in boomer-baiting, with more sedate groups such as Fleetwood Mac and the Bee Gees as the ultimate "corpo-rock" enemy. Even bands themselves made up of boomers deliberately exploited this youthful image for their younger fans. The Dead Kennedys could scarcely have chosen a name better calculated to shock boomers, while the Ramones affected a staunch working-class anti-Communism. As part of the reaction against mellow middle age, new wave and metal bands commonly espoused aggressively macho styles, replete with leather and studs.[34]

Inevitably, though, new wave and heavy metal themselves became mainstreamed. These movements coincided with fundamental changes in the corporate structure of the music business, resulting from the wave of mergers and acquisitions that were transforming the U.S. business world. The result was a much greater centralization, together with a new integration of media products. Music sales had suffered a sharp decline at the end of the 1970s, but salvation came to hand in the form of new technologies and attractive new commodities. More reliable audiotape made possible the individual music player, the Sony Walkman (1979), while the compact disc debuted in 1982. And as we will see, mergers in the media business created giant networks with stakes in music, film, television, news media, and information services.

The popularization of music video both symbolized and encouraged such crossovers. The video genre was not entirely new, in the sense that most music video style can be traced to the 1965 Beatles film *Help!*, and was developed through the 1970s by groups such as Queen. In 1981, the new channel MTV debuted. MTV and its imitators ensured the rapid spread of a series of new genres, including heavy metal and hair metal bands oriented strictly to younger teens. It also created a new age of teen-targeted global pop idols, including Madonna and Michael Jackson. The music industry focused its attention on promoting megastars, encouraging albums that were commercially risk-free and rarely adventurous.

Films and television presented a new stereotype of the generation gap, in which the Beatles and the Byrds epitomized the taste of the parents rather than the children. In 1981, the television comedy series *Family Ties* depicted a family in which unreconstructed hippie parents fail to understand their conservative teenage children. The young Alex P. Keaton has a poster of

Richard Nixon on his wall, and he dreams of making millions on Wall Street. Of course, many Generation Xers scarcely fitted this conservative mold, and teenage rebellion often took radical forms, denouncing Reaganism in violent and obscene terms. Even so, the parental generation against whom they were rebelling was still the boomers, with their attendant assumptions. Teenagers were listening to music their parents would scarcely acknowledge as music, and spending long hours in their rooms working with computers their parents found intimidating. When not apparently wasting time on computer games, teens were risking life and limb on skateboards. It was during these years that the more perceptive boomers realized that they were indeed dinosaurs, that they were becoming their own parents. Soon, the young and the less young could not even agree on which was the real *Star Trek* (*Star Trek: The Next Generation* debuted in 1987).[35]

So enormous was the generational gulf that by the mid-1980s, even many boomer parents were prepared to believe that their offspring were being assailed by a rock music culture awash with images of rape, violence, and devil worship, very much like the devil music that they had been accused of listening to twenty years before. As teenagers tried to shock their elders by adopting the gothic symbols of satanism and the occult, this gave credence to advocates of a satanic cult menace in contemporary America. Through the 1980s, teenagers found themselves the subject of parental campaigns to regulate their behavior, to restrict the influence of gratuitous sex and violence. One suggestive token of changing attitudes was the steep decline of hitchhiking, long a standard form of youth transportation. In the early 1980s, though, fears about threats to the young forced a definitive cultural change, ordained by families and enforced by police.

The Spectacle of News

The mass media were also undergoing speedy transformation about 1980, in a way that changed the making and consumption of news and the marketing of social problems. In 1976, Rupert Murdoch's purchase of the *New York Post* marked the beginning of his American media empire, which would be characterized by a sensational and tabloid approach to social issues. Murdoch also bought Twentieth Century Fox, which in 1985 allowed him to launch the Fox Broadcasting Corporation, the long-awaited fourth network. In order to carve out a distinctive niche, Fox specialized in sensational news programs, together with comedy shows that pushed the boundaries of television standards. Meanwhile, the presentation of broadcast news placed a new premium on immediacy, as satellite, video, and other new technologies allowed immediate access to news sites, without the need for traditional bulky film cameras and their attendant crews. Electronic news-gathering radically changed both the operations of journalism and the expectations of viewers. In 1980, public demand for news of ongoing crises led to the creation of ABC's *Nightline*, a direct outgrowth of the Iran hostage coverage. The same year, Ted Turner created his all-news network, CNN.[36]

Together, these developments marked a trend toward sensational coverage, immediate presentation of news (especially in visual terms), and simplistic stories that could be encapsulated within a short time frame. If Americans of Marshall McLuhan's generation thought they lived in a media-saturated world, in which reality and illusion merge into each other, they would be still more startled by the standards prevailing in the early 1980s. The classic postmodern film *Videodrome* dates from 1981. Still more prescient was Gibson's *Neuromancer*, which explored the incredible potential of interlinked computers and media offering sensory illusions, and accurately prophesied many aspects of the later Web. Gibson even coined the term *cyberspace*.

The new channels transformed the standards and behavior of the three main networks, who now had to deal with these competitors, in addition to cable networks such as HBO. The Big Three could not compete in terms of nudity or profanity-laced comedy shows, but they could still try to match their rivals through spectacle and sensation. The hit show *Miami Vice* (1984–89) dripped with the techniques and images of music video. Reflecting a new social ethos, though the show often carried liberal messages, *Miami Vice* was a hymn to glamour, consumption, and wealth. These particular gritty street cops wore outrageously priced designer clothes.

News programming was similarly transformed. In 1982, Gannett Corporation launched *USA Today*, with a design targeted for visually oriented readers with limited attention spans. Through the 1980s, television news and documentary programs across the board moved steadily toward fast-paced reality shows, immediate and sensational reporting, and manipulative coverage of social problems. In 1986, CBS presented *Forty-eight Hours on Crack Street*, in which several different reporters around the country offered highly colored reports on the problem of crack cocaine. Though individual reports were accurate, the total effect was to produce a vastly exaggerated picture of what at that stage was still a strictly limited danger. Such reporting, however, helped ensure that crack soon reached all parts of the country. Greater sensationalism transformed the traditional flagship news programs such as *20/20* and its rivals (NBC's *1986* and CBS's *West 57th*), which showed a distressing taste for outlandish productions about child abuse and kidnapping, serial murder, poorly substantiated drug menaces, and even satanism. In 1984, *20/20* perpetrated a credulous account of the mass abuse allegations concerning southern California's McMartin preschool. Stories such as these—and they proliferated—were targeted at the large female audience, working women with discretionary income, who were presumed to be concerned with stories about threats to women and children.[37]

As the decade progressed, virtually nothing in the satirical film *Network* looked like parody anymore: even the most outrageous stunts were being transmitted daily on multiple networks. Television talk shows entered a daring new age of vulgar sensationalism, following the trail blazed by *20/20* veteran Geraldo Rivera. These productions showed little regard for distinctions between fact and fiction, provided the menace on offer was sufficiently terrifying. As in the true crime shows, the programming staple was sensational predatory crime, especially multiple murder and child victimization. Some shows enlisted viewers to combat crime and abuse, with phone-ins providing a sense of interactive immediacy.[38]

Developments in presenting news had a political impact, placing a high premium on the management and manipulation of information and images. These skills were well mobilized by White House media strategist Michael Deaver. Under Deaver, presidential press conferences were usually photo opportunities, while remarks were suitably packaged as sound bites (a term that now entered general usage). U.S. officials were impressed by how effectively the British government and armed forces manipulated their own news media in their victorious Falkland Islands war of 1982, when the media were offered only triumphant or patriotic images, while troubling or bloody pictures were withheld. This offered a powerful contrast to the U.S. experience in Vietnam, when popular support of the war had been badly shaken by images from television news. Aware of the new immediacy of newsgathering, the Reagan administration tried to replicate the Falklands experience, especially in the Grenada invasion of 1983. Initially, this even extended to caution about showing U.S. troops in their newly redesigned helmets, which uncomfortably recalled World War II-era German coal-scuttle helmets.[39]

Mark Hertsgaard argues in *On Bended Knee* that the media readily accepted the restrictions imposed by the Reagan administration. That charge is somewhat unfair, since observers of the 1980s were comparing their own time with the much more hostile reporting environment of the Vietnam and Watergate years. The press was no more docile under Reagan than it had been under John Kennedy or Dwight Eisenhower. Still, we can see a marked change from the 1970s, partly because network executives sensed a public reaction against the nihilistic attacks on administrations over the past decade. Particularly from 1983 onward, Americans showed great confidence in Reagan and were less willing to tolerate media criticism. Young adult Americans were much less tolerant of disrespect toward the president than were their elders.[40]

Corporate changes and mergers had their effect on the styles and standards of news reporting, much as they were transforming popular music. Films, television shows, news programs, and records all came from the same few stables. In 1982, for instance, Columbia Pictures was bought by Coca-Cola, which in 1986 sold the business to Sony. Also in 1986, General Electric acquired RCA, the parent company of NBC. Paramount was already a wholly owned subsidiary of Gulf and Western. The more complex such networks became, the more they resembled Japanese *keiretsu*, great extended families of firms. In the U.S. case, some of the parent companies of the media firms dealt closely with government, often through the lavish defense contracts of the era: General Electric was a huge beneficiary of such favors. In such a setting, corporate leaders would be less willing to offend the government, with all its power to reward friends and punish critics.[41]

Teenage Dreams

New commercial and corporate values can also be seen in the world of cinema. Of course, filmmaking has always been a strictly commercial enterprise, with a strong preference for uncontroversial ventures that would maximize profit. In the late 1970s, though, trends in Hollywood encouraged the making of bigger and more simplistic films, often with conservative social messages.

At the start of the 1970s, Hollywood studios had been in near-terminal crisis, having overinvested in expensive failures while failing to accommodate the tastes of younger film-goers. However, two sensational successes suggested a program for future success. *Jaws* (1975) and *Star Wars* (1977) pioneered a new generation of crowd-pleasing blockbuster films targeted at teenage and young adult audiences, their release dates closely tied to particular holidays or seasons. Other films in these years suggested the profits that could be won by appealing to teen markets, whether in slasher films *(Halloween)* or slob comedies *(Animal House)*. At the same time, the growth of multiplex cinemas allowed much greater flexibility in programming, with the chance of reaching larger audiences. *Star Wars* showed the potential of merchandising, while the integration of Hollywood studios into media empires enhanced sales through related music and soundtrack albums. The soundtrack of *Saturday Night Fever* enjoyed a global triumph.[42]

Accelerating developments in computer technology permitted ever more spectacular special effects: George Lucas's Industrial Light and Magic was founded in 1975. Though the original *Star Wars* astonished audiences by its technical innovation, by 1983 the effects in *Return of the Jedi* made the original film look like a magic lantern show. New cinematic techniques revolutionized the horror and fantasy genres, and the transformation scenes in the 1981 films *The Howling* and *American Werewolf in London* would have seemed inconceivable five years before. The pace of innovation gave rich opportunities to filmmakers while vastly raising public expectations about the spectacles that films could and should offer.

Still, these technological advances carried a significant economic downside. As the cost of filmmaking grew, new films required huge corporate investments and had to offer enough mass appeal for investors to make profits. The catastrophic failure of a few megaprojects at the end of the 1970s served notice that in the future, even the most brilliant directors would have to pay close attention to the commercial needs of the studios. Debacles such as *1941, Heaven's Gate, Popeye*, and *The Blues Brothers* (all released 1979–80) were object lessons to a generation of studio executives. In consequence, the 1980s would be a decade of safe, profitable films.[43]

The most successful films of the early 1980s were aimed at a much younger audience than hitherto, especially teenagers. This included blockbusters such as *Raiders of the Lost Ark, ET, Poltergeist, Ghostbusters*, the later Star Wars films, and *Aliens*, as well as whole new genres of teen movies represented by *Risky Business* and *Fast Times at Ridgemont High*. Slasher films proliferated in these years, though virtually all the individual entries were forgettable. All successful titles generated multiple sequels. The series spawned by *Halloween, Nightmare on Elm Street*, and *Friday the 13th* included a combined total of twenty movies by the early 1990s, and equally prolific were teen-oriented comedies such as *Police Academy* and *Porky's*.

The triumphant success of formula movies made studios cautious about more subversive or experimental fare or films aimed directly at an adult audience. Glamour and romance dominated even those films that did claim a social message, such as *Nine to Five* (1980), with its improbably glamorous working secretaries. In *Reds* (1981), a story of early Bolshevik politics, long creative disputes ensured that the main focus of the story shifted to the romance between the superstar principals. With some notable exceptions, films were expected to offer straightforward heroes and villains, morally unambiguous happy endings, and usually the triumph of the young. Most of the leading screen idols were themselves Generation Xers, including the heavily overpublicized Brat Pack. In *All the Right Moves,* the question is not how a declining steel town will solve its social problems but whether Tom Cruise's character will escape to sports stardom. Blatant teenage wish fulfillment could also be seen in films that addressed still weightier matters. *War Games* (1983) presented an anti-war and anti-nuclear message firmly at odds with the policies of the Reagan administration at this time. Even so, the film is the story of a brilliant young hacker who outsmarts every adult, whose brilliance at video games amply equips him to save the world, and who—of course—gets the girl.

Though *War Games* was liberal and anti-war in tone, many of the most successful films of the Reagan era were powerfully conservative. This was less a calculated strategy of propaganda by the studios than a shrewd assessment of what themes were likely to appeal to a young male audience with a taste for action sequences. Stories of struggle and combat demanded villains, the more egregiously evil the better. Indiana Jones uncontroversially combats Nazis in *Raiders of the Lost Ark,* while *The Terminator* was an android engaged in a war of machine civilization against all humanity. Many films, though, drew strictly on modern enemies, and in the context of the early 1980s, that meant either Communists or terrorists, the latter usually Middle Eastern. By mid-decade—the era of *Rambo, Missing in Action,* and *Top Gun*—Hollywood's imagery of good and evil had achieved a stark us-and-them contrast scarcely seen since John Wayne's much-mocked *The Green Berets* (1968) and before that the golden age of anti-Communist cinema in the mid-1950s. *Top Gun,* the highest-earning film of 1986, was made with the active cooperation of the U.S. Navy. Commercial and demographic considerations gave an unabashedly propagandist tone to popular cinema. Almost certainly, these pressures would have produced similar results even if Carter rather than Reagan had won in 1980.[44]

Clean and Sober

When recent films reconstruct modern American history, both drug use and sexuality symbolize a sharp and clear distinction between the 1970s and 1980s. In both areas, the 1970s appear hedonistic and carefree, the 1980s conservative and timorous. For many today, the transition from the 1970s is commemorated by the arrival of AIDS and Reagan, with crack cocaine as an additional symbol of a new era. In both cases, though, those memories oversimplify the transition between decades. In fact, a new cultural conservatism is apparent well before the arrival of AIDS and crack, and indeed even before the 1980 election.

In drug matters, the incoming Reagan administration benefited from an existing willingness to recognize the harm done by substance abuse, broadly defined. Greater personal responsibility was expected and was to be enforced by law where necessary. In the post-1975 decade, changing attitudes sharply affected tobacco use, a sensitive issue given the industry's economic importance for the U.S. South. Starting in the mid-1970s, though, policy makers increasingly accepted the arguments that smoking posed a health risk to nonsmoking bystanders and that the passive smoking threat demanded public intervention. In 1977, the American Cancer Society held the first Great American Smokeout, to help smokers mend their ways. The following year, Joseph Califano, secretary of health, education, and welfare, declared smoking public health enemy number one. Through the late 1970s, attempts to regulate smoking in public places stirred controversy, as pro-tobacco groups funded by the industry ran up against organizations pledged to defend the rights of nonsmokers. The anti-tobacco lobby won ever more victories, as courts ruled that nonsmokers had the right to a smoke-free workplace, and states and local authorities restricted the right to smoke in restaurants and other public places. By the mid-1980s, the battle against public smoking was largely won, and smokers increasingly found themselves excluded from buildings, literally out in the cold.[45]

Anti-tobacco activism set a powerful precedent for official regulation, as the United States entered one of its recurring eras of concern about physical and dietary purity. In 1977, a Senate committee led by George McGovern used (and exaggerated) questionable scientific evidence to present red meat and high cholesterol as deadly threats to national health. The committee launched "the first comprehensive statement by any branch of the federal Government on risk factors in the American diet. The simple fact is that our diets have changed radically within the last 50 years, with great and often very harmful effects on our health. These dietary changes represent as great a threat to public health as smoking . . . these and other changes in the diet amount to a wave of malnutrition—of both over and under consumption— that may be as profoundly damaging to the nation's health as the widespread contagious diseases of the early part of the century." These ideas remained orthodox until they were undermined, indeed reversed, by the Atkins fad of the new century.[46]

Substance abuse was all the more reprehensible when it victimized children, and again, this rhetoric had its origins in the Carter years. Child protection themes pervaded the anti-smoking crusade, as activists denounced tobacco companies for targeting children as potential smokers. By the early 1980s, the populist activism of the parents' anti-drug movement found a formidable voice in the National Federation of Parents. In 1981, Keith Schuchard boasted that parent activism had progressed "from a handful of scattered individuals and groups to an increasingly cohesive, articulate, and powerful national movement."[47]

Parents' rights rhetoric motivated another enormously successful movement, Mothers Against Drunk Driving. MADD began in response to two tragic accidents caused by drunk drivers, both notorious repeat offenders: one in 1979 left a baby girl a quadriplegic, while another in 1980 killed a thirteen-year-old girl. MADD (originally Mothers Against Drunk Drivers) had seventy chapters nationwide by 1982, and the showing of the television movie *The Candy Lightner Story* in early 1983 boosted the total to two hundred. In attacking substance abuse, the group initially avoided the openly moralistic or religious rhetoric of the older temperance movement, focusing instead on the practical harm that was done by drunkenness, especially to children. Such immoral behavior demanded not therapy or treatment but draconian criminal punishment. The movement's gender component was always overt. This was a movement of women directed against uncontrollable men, and the stereotypical drunk driver featured in publicity materials was invariably male.[48]

The obvious appeal of a mothers' movement gave it political momentum: what legislator wanted to vote against motherhood or for drunk drivers? During the 1980s, most states soon accepted its basic demands, dramatically raising the penalties for drunk driving, lowering blood alcohol limits, and ensuring a de facto national minimum age for consuming alcohol. Legislators competed with each other to offer the harshest legislation aimed at the users and suppliers of alcohol. Civil courts reinforced the new social crusade by extending the concept of liability in DUI cases, making it very much in the financial interest of bar owners and liquor companies to enforce safe drinking habits. MADD succeeded thoroughly in changing behavior, and among other things introduced the concept of the designated driver. So radical were the effects that founder Candy Lightner resigned from the organization, deploring its neo-prohibitionist agenda.[49]

The anti-drink movement had an acute impact on the young, as it redefined the limits of adulthood. Access to alcohol had long been a symbolic marker of coming of age, and as in matters of sexuality, concepts of appropriate age limits shifted over time. During the 1960s, many states had reduced their minimum drinking ages below the familiar twenty-one, some as low as eighteen. Partly, this was a response to the Vietnam-era draft and the argument that a person old enough to fight and die was old enough to drink beer. Between 1976 and 1983, though, a reaction set in, as sixteen states restored the twenty-one limit. In 1984, the U.S. Congress passed a Uniform Drinking Age Act, demanding that states accept the higher limit as a condition for receiving federal highway funds, and all states soon complied. Immediately affected by the new law were those born in the mid-1960s, who suddenly found their legal coming of age postponed for several years.[50]

Child protection rhetoric reversed the laissez-faire attitudes to alcohol that had prevailed since the end of Prohibition. In popular culture, drunkards and drunkenness ceased to be the source of easy humor and instead became associated with addictive alcoholism or dangerous anti-social behavior. Not long after Dudley Moore played the title role in the film *Arthur* in 1981, the funny drunk slouched into history. At the same time, films and television succumbed to heavy pressure not to depict smoking except as a warning sign that a given character was wicked or irresponsible. If not yet prepared for a full-scale war against illicit drugs of all kinds, Americans were willing to see the legal suppression of substances that caused major social harm, especially when that harm was framed as a threat to children.

More than AIDS

In the area of sexuality too, social attitudes were in transition at the end of the 1970s. Watching *Summer of Sam*, the modern audience is startled to see the abandon with which characters in 1977 visit the sex club Plato's Retreat to engage in casual unprotected sex with multiple partners. In *Forrest Gump*, the transition between decades comes, unsurprisingly, when sexually liberated Jenny announces that she has AIDS. With the devastating penalties it imposed on irresponsible sexual behavior, AIDS declared a sudden end to the sexual revolution. Casual sex was again seen as potentially lethal in a way it had not been since the worst ravages of syphilis in the early twentieth century. But without denying the social effects of AIDS, we can also see other signs of widespread nervousness about sexual excess, and those were very marked well before the horrendous new disease made any significant impact on the social mainstream. Though AIDS transformed sexual attitudes, it was not the only force driving change.

Quite apart from the cost in lives, the social consequences of AIDS were massive. Given its close linkage to homosexual subcultures, the disease threatened to wreck advances in gay rights. Matters would have been still worse if, as nearly happened in 1982, it had come to be known as gay-related immune deficiency syndrome (GRID); in the early days of the disease it was commonly described as "gay cancer." Yet even without this ominous label, the arrival of AIDS decimated gay communities and changed their political concerns from generalized activism on liberal and radical issues to a single-minded focus on the question of survival. For conservatives, the disease substantiated their gravest warnings about homosexuality and sexual promiscuity—indeed, the whole moral inheritance of the 1960s. Evangelicals pointed to biblical texts warning that homosexuals and the sexually immoral would be punished with bodily plagues. But even for moderates not hitherto alarmed about homosexuality, the rapid growth of AIDS was terrifying.

AIDS activists faced an impossible dilemma. In order to attract public concern and win resources, they had to make the disease sound as threatening as possible and to stress how rapidly it could spread outside the gay community. However, such hyperbole faced the danger of a panic reaction, which might take the form of quarantining existing patients.[51] Expert medical opinion was long divided about just how contagious AIDS might be: while a consensus held that it could probably not be transmitted by casual contact with a sufferer, this was far from certain. By mid-decade, commentators were speculating that a global AIDS epidemic might revolutionize society in ways not seen since the plagues of the Middle Ages.

But AIDS was only one factor in a much broader conservative reaction in sexual matters. This is evident if we look at the chronology of the disease, which did not develop its full social impact until mid-decade. Only at the start of 1981 did medical authorities identify the first cases of what looked like a disturbing new phenomenon, and not until May 1982 did an AIDS story reach the front page of a major newspaper, the *Los Angeles Times*. In 1984, the crisis found an appealing human face in teenager Ryan White, who was driven from his school because of his infection, while the following year, popular actor Rock Hudson died of the disease. These events in 1984–85 marked the point at which mainstream Americans understood that something was happening beyond a localized outbreak of a mysterious gay plague. Also in 1985, the television movie *An Early Frost* offered a wrenching portrait of AIDS sufferers. Thereafter, the epidemic became a familiar part of social discourse, with its distinctive forms of activism and commemoration: the AIDS Memorial Quilt began in 1985.[52]

Well before mainstream America discovered AIDS, we see signs of growing alarm about recent changes in sexual conduct. The sheer amount of casual sexual contact in the 1970s spread diseases, most of which could be cured. In the late 1970s, though, the problem of genital herpes emerged and swiftly became a major focus of media reporting. Obviously herpes was not vaguely comparable to AIDS in its gravity, but the extensive coverage of the disease stressed themes of incurability and pervasive menace, and urged the need for safe sex or abstinence. The malady attracted some media attention in 1979, but it fueled a national panic in 1981 and 1982. Years before AIDS entered the public consciousness, news magazines were offering headlines such as "Is Herpes Quelling the Sexual Revolution?" "Herpes: The VD of the 80s," and "Battling an Elusive Invader." In 1982, *Time* devoted most of an issue to the menace, claiming that "herpes, an incurable virus, threatens to undo the sexual revolution." "Suddenly, the old fears and doubts are edging back. So is the fire and brimstone rhetoric of the Age of Guilt." The disease had "exploded into a full-fledged epidemic," hitting twenty million Americans. Soon, "a veritable herpes industry [had] grown up to care for the traumatized: herpes resource centers, herpes hotlines, herpes therapists, and group sessions with other herpes victims." *Ebony* termed herpes "the scourge of the 80s."[53]

The "epidemic" contributed to the cause of sexual restraint and temperance. Above all, claimed *Time*, the disease demonstrated the irresponsible foolishness of sixties sexual attitudes, the age of "the Pill, Penthouse Pets and porn-movie cassettes." News stories told how younger people were renouncing casual sex and seeking deeper and more lasting relationships. Herpes was "delivering a numbing blow to the one night stand. The herpes counter-revolution may be ushering a reluctant, grudging chastity back into fashion . . . many swingers have dropped out because of herpes." The disease would help end the "era of mindless promiscuity." *Christianity Today* noted, "In its efforts to legislate morality, herpes . . . has encountered considerably less resistance than the New Right." The *New Republic* suggested that "if herpes did not exist, the Moral Majority would have had to invent it." So frightening was the disease that some suggested, semi-seriously, that sufferers should be forced to wear a tattooed scarlet letter *H*, again exactly foreshadowing the later rhetoric of AIDS. Though none of these herpes stories drew comparisons with that then-obscure medical phenomenon, they certainly used what would become the familiar AIDS script.[54]

Just as something much like the crack cocaine panic was well under way several years before crack achieved any kind of mass popularity, so the nightmare of sexual disease preceded the recognition of AIDS. The media were already commenting on the decline of the sexual revolution and the arrival of a new age of caution and responsibility. The AIDS issue gave a dramatic new urgency to such calls, but it did not create them.

In retrospect, the inauguration of Ronald Reagan in January 1981 seems like an obvious hinge between two very different eras. For both political sides, such a night-and-day contrast between decades is convenient, allowing the right to take credit for bringing morning to America while permitting liberals to avoid blame for trends they dislike in the Reaganaut eighties. A more plausible account would see both parties responding, quite similarly, to major social changes under way about that time, many of which had little to do with what we conventionally think of as mainstream politics.

8

Evil Empires

In large measure, Ronald Reagan became president because a majority of Americans saw him as the candidate who would stand up to foreign enemies without surrender or compromise. During his long and quotable political career, perhaps the most famous single phrase associated with Reagan was his description of the Soviet Union as an "evil empire." Though his characterization was mocked by Western liberals, the moral clarity of the words had an enormous impact in the Eastern bloc. Both officials and dissidents correctly understood that a new and quite radical attitude now dominated American foreign policy. The administration that took power in 1981 was determined to restore U.S. military power and to stand up against Communist power in a way that Jimmy Carter had conspicuously failed to do.

Yet for all the obvious national hostility to détente policies during the 1970s, the American public gave Reagan no blank check for military revival. The new president encountered real difficulties in persuading Americans to support active confrontation, and not just where it stood a good chance of provoking open war with the Soviets. Throughout his administration, Reagan met serious opposition to new weapons systems and to his interventionist policies in Central America, while the anti-war nuclear freeze campaign became a forceful mass movement. His administration's victories owe much to Reagan's personal determination, rhetorical skills, and ability to keep on framing the conflict in comprehensible moral and often religious terms of good and evil. More than once, his efforts were aided by the Soviet tendency to act in ways that confirmed the most damning American charges. And though nervous about the military risks involved, most Americans ultimately supported both his moral vision and its political consequences. Having said this, the single-minded focus on the evils of Communism, to the neglect of other dangers, also led the United States to suffer some political disasters of its own.

Confronting Evil

From the beginning of his presidency, Reagan's critics complained about his apparent obsession with Soviet Communism, "his simplistic anti-Soviet patter." The *New Republic* argued in 1981, "In foreign affairs a red thread runs through everything the Reagan administration undertakes. . . . There is a disturbing tendency to treat every foreign development as an extension of Soviet aggression." Reagan's anti-Communism was integrated into an ambitious vision of the United States and its historic role. Reagan himself made little use of domestic conspiracy theories, remarkably so in view of the commonplaces of the political right in his day: "the paranoid style was not really Reagan's style." Instead, the real threat from the forces of evil came in the international realm, from the forces of global Communism. As Hugh Heclo remarks, this focus on external menace was "an inherent component of the vision, whereby the nation's 'chosenness' stood against outside powers of darkness."[1]

Reagan believed certain things that resonated mightily with a popular audience, as much as they appalled many sophisticated observers. He believed in a straightforward confrontation between good and evil: "There are no easy answers, but there are simple answers. We must have the courage to do what we know is morally right." Communists were not a rival ideology or a competing political force, they were evil, "the most evil enemy mankind has known in his long climb from the swamp to the stars." Particularly important for understanding his anti-Communism of the era was the analogy to Nazism, a parallel that liberals saw as hysterical and inflammatory. Reagan, however, meant it literally, declaring in his "Time for Choosing" speech in 1964, "We will preserve for our children this, the last best hope of man on earth, or we will sentence them to take the first step into a thousand years of darkness." The reference is to the thousand-year Reich. If this analogy was reasonable, then it was approaching blasphemy for Jimmy Carter to speak of an "inordinate fear of Communism." If he had lived in 1938, would he have spoken of an "inordinate fear of Nazism"? And if

Communism really was such an unmitigated evil, there could be only one goal, as Reagan announced: "We win and they lose."[2]

But as liberals noted, Nazism had not vanished without a last-ditch struggle, and neither, it seemed, would Communism. The USSR would not evaporate without a major war that could threaten the human race. After a 1982 visit to Moscow, historian Arthur Schlesinger Jr. declared, "Those in the U.S. who think the Soviet Union is on the verge of economic and social collapse, ready with one small push to go over the brink, are . . . only kidding themselves." If the United States had to live with the Soviets, it was foolish to antagonize them. Only ideologues such as Reagan believed that Communism was a transient phenomenon, "a temporary aberration which will one day disappear from the earth because it is contrary to human nature."[3]

Reagan's vision became even starker and more religious after the attempt on his life in 1981, when he concluded that God had preserved him in order to accomplish a special destiny. In June 1982, Reagan visited London to address the British Parliament. The setting was significant because Britain had just fought a successful war against Argentina, which had briefly occupied the Falkland Islands. Closely watched in the United States, the Falklands conflict showed that Western powers could successfully humble Third World dictators. He denounced "totalitarian forces in the world who seek subversion and conflict around the globe to further their barbarous assault on the human spirit," and asked, "Must freedom wither in a quiet, deadening accommodation with totalitarian evil?"[4]

Just as uncompromising was Reagan's attack on Communism in March 1983 in a speech delivered to the National Association of Evangelicals in Orlando, Florida. Not only did he speak directly of an "evil empire," but he did so in the context of references to Satan and absolute spiritual evil. Quoting Whittaker Chambers, Reagan described Marxism-Leninism as "the second oldest faith, first proclaimed in the Garden of Eden with the words of temptation, 'Ye shall be as gods.'" He charged that "while they preach the supremacy of the state, declare its omnipotence over individual man, and predict its eventual domination of all peoples on the earth, they are the focus of evil in the modern world." Moving directly from C. S. Lewis's *Screwtape Letters*, the famous account of demonic evil and temptation, Reagan urged his audience "to beware the temptation of pride—the temptation of blithely declaring yourselves above it all and label both sides equally at fault, to ignore the facts of history and the aggressive impulses of an evil empire, to simply call the arms race a giant misunderstanding and thereby remove yourself from the struggle between right and wrong and good and evil."[5]

Liberals were appalled by the religious and moralistic quality of Reagan's views. Anthony Lewis termed the Orlando speech "primitive: that is the only word for it," while historian Henry Steele Commager denounced it as "the worst presidential speech in American history, and I've read them all. No other presidential speech has ever so flagrantly allied the government with religion." Still worse, from this point of view, Reagan's actions showed that his concept of "evil empire" was by no means empty rhetoric. In a series of national security directives in 1982–83, the administration described a plan not just to contain the Soviet empire but to disrupt and destabilize it. NSDD 32 proposed to neutralize Soviet control over Eastern Europe through various forms of covert action and planned aid to dissident groups, above all in Poland. In November 1982, NSDD 66 envisaged the disruption of the USSR itself through a "strategic triad," limiting Soviet access to financial credit, high technology, and natural gas. Most ambitiously, in January 1983, NSDD 75 renounced the aim of coexisting with the Soviet Union in anything like its existing form, seeking rather to change it fundamentally, to defeat "Soviet imperialism."[6] These new strategic goals represented a massive departure from U.S. policies over the past three decades.

Rearmament

Between 1981 and 1984, Reagan launched a program of military modernization and revitalization that would have been hard to justify except against a background of imminent hostilities with an aggressive and expansionist Soviet empire. The message of urgency was inspired by disastrous memories of 1980 and the Soviet pressures on Afghanistan and Poland. Through 1981, it was widely feared that the Soviets would intervene militarily in Poland, and in December, the Polish army tried to stave off such a disaster by launching an internal coup aimed at suppressing the Solidarity movement.[7]

Military spending surged. The U.S. Defense Department budget rose from $136 billion in 1980 to $244 billion in 1985, and that figure takes no account of related expenditures tucked away in the spending of other units such as the Department of Energy. The administration financed its defense buildup by means of deficit spending on a scale unprecedented in peacetime. Even at the height of the Vietnam War, the U.S. government had only rarely run up a deficit of some $25 billion in a single year, or 3 percent of GNP. Under Reagan, however, previous restraints were abandoned, and annual deficits of $200 billion were common through the mid-1980s, around 5 or 6 percent of GNP. Total public debt doubled between 1980 and 1985, and in 1987 the U.S. budget finally exceeded $1 trillion.[8]

Central to the rearmament program was the new generation of nuclear missiles and weapons. For years, the United States had depended upon a strategic triad of land-based ballistic missiles, submarine-launched missiles, and manned bombers. The new administration proposed to modernize each aspect of this system, with the new MX ballistic missile, the Trident submarine, and the B-1 bomber, respectively. Especially controversial was the deployment of new intermediate-range missiles. These were seen as a necessary response to new Soviet missile deployments in Europe, which had destabilized the existing military balance. In the late 1970s, the Soviets introduced a new class of intermediate-range SS-20 missiles that could destroy targets in Western Europe, though they could not touch the United States. Though the Soviets portrayed them as a timely updating of older weapons, anti-Soviet critics saw a more devious strategy. In this view, the Soviets planned to use these weapons to pressure Western European states without overtly threatening the United States, thereby detaching the NATO allies from Washington. Would the United States really risk annihilation in order to save Germany or Italy?

From 1979 onward, U.S. administrations proposed to match the SS-20s with their own intermediate-range Pershing and cruise missiles, which were to be deployed in Western Europe. Again, this was a policy that originated in the Carter years but came to be associated with the Reagan administration's hard line. Reagan pressed ahead with the new deployment, which would take place in the fall of 1983. The new U.S. missiles were designed to promote what the European allies themselves originally termed the zero option, the removal of intermediate missiles by both sides. Either the Soviets would dismantle their SS-20s or they must accept new U.S. missiles targeted at their population centers. Reagan wanted to replace SALT—mere arms limitation—with START, strategic arms reduction talks.[9]

In both Europe and America, the left denounced U.S. deployment as a wanton escalation of the arms race. Just as troubling, the new weapons were so accurate that they appeared to be intended for fighting a nuclear war, rather than merely deterring a potential enemy. Their presence might force the Soviets to launch a nuclear strike in order to prevent the destruction of their command-and-control facilities. The Soviets were alarmed, and an even tougher line emerged from the Kremlin when Brezhnev was succeeded by former KGB chief Yuri Andropov. Following Reagan's evil empire speech, the Soviet news agency, TASS, described the president as inspired by "bellicose lunatic anti-communism," which was roughly the view of many liberal media outlets in the West. The new weapons systems spurred a massive anti-war movement in Britain, West Germany, Italy, and other nations, which had no wish to serve as the European theater in a potential cataclysm. The anti-war movement attracted a broad range of supporters, motivated by sincere and quite realistic fears about the growing likelihood of annihilation. Among the broad coalition, though, a pro-Soviet faction used the cynical slogan "No new missiles in Europe," the implication being that existing missiles—such as the recently installed SS-20s—were quite acceptable. They weren't even technically in Europe, as it was then defined: they were on Soviet soil, in the Ukraine or Byelorussia.[10]

Particularly infuriating the European left was the rhetoric used by the Americans to justify their new weapons. The U.S. administration drew heavily on the language of the Old West, with its frank symbolism of gender and masculinity. The proposed MX missile was the Peacekeeper, recalling the legendary Colt revolver of the West; cruise missiles were Tomahawks. European critics—and American liberals—mocked the Western overtones, describing the Tomahawks as suitable for a childish fantasy of cowboys and Indians rather than a dangerous and well-armed real world.[11]

Yet for all these cavils, the transatlantic alliance held firm, to a degree that might astonish modern observers accustomed to gaping U.S.-Europe tensions. During 1983, European allies accepted the new missiles, if only after searing debates, and also supported U.S. policies in other delicate policy areas. When U.S. forces entered Lebanon in 1982–83, they were accompanied by British, French, and Italian allies. While the strength of Atlantic ties in these years owed much to shrewd U.S. diplomacy, the fact of Soviet power persuaded Europeans not to stray too far from the Western alliance. Whatever doubts Europeans harbored about Reaganism, aggressive Soviet conduct through the 1970s had been genuinely terrifying, and there was no doubt about the need for a response. For whatever reasons, then, the United States won its point.

Our Guerrillas and Their Guerrillas

In other ways too, the new administration aimed to reverse what it saw as the disastrous weakening of the United States during the 1970s. By 1980, the political right held that terrorism had been an effective tactic to destabilize Western powers. The Soviet connection with terrorism was publicized anew in congressional hearings through 1981 and 1982, as committees heard lengthy testimony on themes such as "Terrorism: The Role of Moscow and Its Subcontractors" and "The Historical Antecedents of Soviet Terrorism." The terror network idea remained in the headlines as conservative journalists investigated the alleged Soviet and Eastern-bloc connections involved in the assassination attempt directed against Pope John Paul II. Once again, Claire Sterling was a prominent advocate of Soviet complicity.[12] The Soviet linkage served as a multipurpose form of stigmatization, allowing activists to discredit their enemies by association. Pro-Israel advocates used the Soviet connection to attack radical Arab states, and friends of the white South African regime attacked that nation's guerrillas for their Moscow ties.[13]

For the administration, the implications were still more sweeping. If the Soviets deployed their terror machinery against the West, then the United States should reply in kind, by supporting clandestine wars in countries at the margins of Soviet power. This theory was formulated by Reagan's old friend Laurence W. Beilenson and was restated in popular terms in *The Spike*. After a thinly disguised Senator Moynihan finds himself directing U.S. policy, he warns the Soviet president, "We've put up with your sort of liberation movements around the world for quite a few years now. . . . It's about time you learned to put up with pro-Western guerrillas." The Reagan Doctrine advocated the rollback of Communism at its margins. As Charles Krauthammer wrote in 1985, the doctrine "proclaims overt and unabashed American support for anti-Communist revolutions" based on principles of "justice, necessity and democratic tradition." During the decade, the Reagan Doctrine would justify campaigns as far afield as Afghanistan, Nicaragua, Angola, Mozambique, Ethiopia, and Cambodia.[14]

U.S. intervention had its most immediate effects in Central America. The United States supported anti-Communist regimes in El Salvador and Guatemala, despite abundant evidence of their misdeeds, and launched a proxy guerrilla war against the Sandinista regime of Nicaragua, undertaken by counterrevolutionary fighters known as contras. None of these situations involved direct combat activity by U.S. military forces, but by 1982, U.S. intelligence agents and advisers were deeply involved in all these insurgencies. For a while, the American public could experience a sense of doing something positive against the Soviet empire without suffering combat losses. A gradual process of desensitization allowed the possibility of U.S. military intervention to be contemplated in a way that had not happened since the fall of Saigon.[15]

The public remained skittish about the prospect of actual combat. Compounding the obvious Vietnam syndrome—heavily exploited by leftist opponents of intervention—was the intense Catholic concern with Central American matters. Many American Catholics had a broad sympathy for Latin American liberation movements and were outraged by rightist attacks on the Church. In 1980, El Salvador's archbishop, Oscar Romero, had been murdered by pro-government paramilitary forces, as had four American churchwomen. In the spring of 1982, polls suggested heavy public opposition to the direct use of U.S. troops in El Salvador, even if that was the only means of preventing a victory by the leftist guerrilla movement, the Farabundo Martí National Liberation Front (FMLN).[16]

Congressional Democrats took advantage of public nervousness about intervention and attempted to limit U.S. intervention as effectively as they had in Angola in the 1970s. In December 1982, the Boland Amendment prohibited the use of U.S. funds to promote the overthrow of the Nicaraguan regime, while a congressional spending cap was intended to shut down the contras altogether by mid-1984. Congress was further provoked by a CIA operation that mined Nicaraguan harbors, risking confrontation with the Soviets. Later in 1984, a second and more comprehensive Boland Amendment prohibited any U.S. support for the contras, using any funds whatever that were "available to the Central Intelligence Agency . . . or any other agency or entity of the United States involved in intelligence activities." Shortly afterward, the revelation of a CIA-sponsored training manual suggested that Nicaraguan contras were being trained in assassination, that nightmare from the mid-1970s. The president failed to calm concern by denying that discussions of removing Sandinista officials from office necessarily implied assassination ("You just say to the fellow that's sitting there in the office, 'You're not in the office anymore' "). Even after the 1984 election triumph, Reagan could only gradually induce Congress to restore any kind of contra funding, even when it was strictly earmarked for non-military uses.[17]

Even so, U.S. policy maintained severe pressure on the targeted regimes, as Reagan mobilized all his rhetorical skills to present the Central American leftists as a pressing danger to the United States, using the most effective cultural and political analogies. The Sandinistas, obviously, were Communists of the darkest Stalinist dye, and their opponents must of necessity be heroic revolutionaries. In 1984, Reagan made his case for helping the anti-Communist contras: "The Sandinista rule is a Communist reign of terror. Many of those who fought alongside the Sandinistas saw their revolution betrayed. They were denied power in the new government. Some were imprisoned, others exiled. Thousands who fought with the Sandinistas have taken up arms against them and are now called the Contras. They are freedom fighters." The Sandinista danger was perilously close to the United States, placing aggressive Communism a mere two days' drive from Harlingen, Texas. In 1985, he proclaimed the contras "the moral equivalent of our Founding Fathers."[18]

Though Reagan never convinced Congress to restore full contra funding, the administration kept the operation alive through some ingenious expedients, as the United States sought surrogate aid and training from Israel, Saudi Arabia, South Africa, and many private sources. The administration deliberately promoted the idea that critical funding was coming from an assortment of international ultra-right groups such as the World Anti-Communist League, in order to divert attention from clandestine U.S. involvement. Following the second Boland Amendment, though, such desperate measures increasingly ran the danger of flouting the law, especially when administration officials were forced to lie directly about the extent of U.S. support; the resulting crisis would ultimately endanger the presidency. But the contras survived and in the end would force the Sandinistas to come to terms. Meanwhile, seemingly inevitable revolutions elsewhere in Latin America, especially in El Salvador and Guatemala, were likewise stemmed. Far more successfully than might have been imagined in the mid-1970s, the United States helped suppress leftist insurgencies, partly through prolonged involvement by the CIA.[19]

Middle Eastern Encounters

In the Middle East, likewise, the United States initially appeared to be winning significant victories, again without losses. The Tehran hostages were released on the day of Reagan's inauguration, for reasons that remain unclear. Undoubtedly, the United States did make substantial concessions to Iran, but at the time, most Americans believed that the ending of the crisis showed that Iran was deeply worried about the consequences of provoking a tough new president. Iran already had been invaded the year before by the Iraqi regime of Saddam Hussein, who received steadily more U.S. aid and intelligence, and the Reagan administration kept up that clandestine pressure.[20]

Later in 1981, the United States engaged in a standoff with the dictatorship of Libya's Muammar Qaddafi, who in the late 1970s had become for Americans a demon figure second only to the Ayatollah Khomeini. Qaddafi had extended his nation's territorial waters while producing bizarre rhetoric about confronting the United States and provoking a Third World War. The Libyan stance collapsed in the face of a huge show of U.S. naval force and the downing of some Libyan aircraft. Just as Reagan could stand up to the Soviets, it seemed, so he could put Third World despots in their place. Despite a no-nonsense attitude toward Middle Eastern affairs, the United States suffered no retaliation in terms of oil cuts or price hikes. In fact, gas prices tumbled and there were no gas lines, and at least in popular thought this was largely due to a well-justified fear of how Reagan might respond. These apparent successes retroactively cast a still more damning light on the Carter administration, which had failed to act comparably toward Iran. The point was unfair, since the situations were so different in many ways, but in the popular mind, the comparison was inevitable, as was the basic lesson: toughness paid off.[21]

In the aftermath of these symbolic triumphs, another Middle Eastern crisis allowed the actual introduction of U.S. combat troops, through political accident rather than geopolitical design. Though the Lebanese situation was complex, the immediate crisis began in the spring of 1982 when the Israelis invaded the nation and besieged PLO forces in Beirut. Seeking to avoid massive civilian casualties, the United States negotiated an agreement whereby the PLO evacuated Lebanon under the supervision of U.S. Marines. In the circumstances, few Americans objected to a military presence that was clearly aimed at temporary peacekeeping and saving the civilians of Beirut. Some months afterward, though, the U.S. deal was grossly violated when Lebanese forces allied to Israel massacred hundreds of Palestinian civilians. To protect the Palestinians, and to salvage U.S. honor, the Marines returned that fall with a mission that was poorly defined in terms of goals or guidelines.[22]

Over the following months, though, the Lebanese venture seemed to be yet another demonstration that a determined U.S. policy would produce results. Admittedly, U.S. troops were in direct combat with Arab or Muslim forces for the first time since the early nineteenth century. U.S. Marines were fighting a guerrilla war against local militias, and unfamiliar groups such as Shi'ites and Druzes joined the national demonology, often as joke figures mocked by television comedians and vulgar T-shirts. ("Hey, I just stepped in some Shi'ite" was one gruesome example.) Also, the crisis inspired daring new tactics of unconventional warfare, as both American and Israeli forces first encountered suicide bombers driving bomb-laden trucks or cars. One catastrophic attack in April 1983 destroyed the United States embassy in Beirut, in the process killing many of the CIA officials who were closely familiar with the Middle East. The bombing destroyed the last vestiges of what had only recently been a strong U.S. intelligence operation in the Middle East. The loss of the Tehran embassy in 1979 had closed that once critical center of activity, compromising many sensitive documents, while the PLO's evacuation of Beirut ended a fruitful working relationship between the CIA and the Palestinians. The destruction of the Beirut embassy left the United States with little useful intelligence in the region, except for scraps thrown by the Israelis and other allied governments. Henceforward, Americans in Lebanon were flying blind.

But this peril was not apparent at the time. In the short term, Lebanon offered a training ground for U.S. forces, including finding a role for the nation's newly recommissioned battleships, and enthusiastic commentators discovered a retroactive justification for the U.S. presence. In this view, pushed hardest by pro-Israel media, Shi'ites and other leftist forces were proxies of the Soviets just as much as the Sandinistas were, so that even in Lebanon, the United States was fighting the Cold War. Marines on the ground were convinced that they were defending "the government" (which scarcely existed) against pro-Soviet "rebels" (who generally loathed Communism).[23]

Crescendo

By 1983, the various global confrontations were creating an atmosphere of acute crisis. Looking back at the half century of the Cold War, three moments emerge when the world truly stood on the brink of nuclear war: the Cuban missile crisis of 1962, the Yom Kippur War of 1973, and the fall crisis of 1983, the last little less dangerous than the more notorious Cuban events. This sobering reality illustrates how thoroughly the Reagan administration had projected its sense of being in an apocalyptic struggle, as well as the dangers of that message.

Tensions grew in March when President Reagan made a speech advocating his Strategic Defense Initiative, a space-based program to defend the United States and its allies from missile attack. The program—which critics promptly christened Star Wars, for its fanciful and science-fiction quality— had immediate real-world consequences. If built, such a U.S. space-based system would also be able to dominate the entire planet, while the challenge of countering it would demand that the Soviets spend vast sums, which their failing economy could not afford. Also, the Star Wars speech came just two weeks after Reagan's "evil empire" remarks. Putting that evidence together with the imminent arrival of new U.S. missiles in Europe, the Soviet leadership began to suspect a threat far more immediate and lethal than anything yet imagined. In September, the dying Andropov warned that the United States had fallen prey to "outrageous military psychosis."[24]

In this view, the United States, inspired by religious and apocalyptic ideas, was preparing a nuclear first strike on the USSR, a danger that the Soviets understood as parallel to Hitler's surprise attack on their nation in 1941. In their different ways, both the U.S. and Soviet leaderships were now using the Nazi framework as a means of conceptualizing their Cold War enemies, a pattern that boded poorly for peace. As both sides knew from historical experience, the Nazi menace had to be destroyed, and negotiation could never offer more than a temporary truce.

Tensions grew that September when the Soviets shot down a Korean airliner that penetrated its Far Eastern airspace, close to sensitive strategic sites. Two hundred sixty-nine civilians were killed, including Larry MacDonald, a strongly right-wing U.S. congressman from Georgia. The incident provoked popular outrage and patriotic fervor in the United States, with boycotts of Soviet products. Though it is no defense of the crime to point this out, the shootdown illustrated the extreme fear then prevailing among the Soviet leadership, and the worry that Western forces were probing Soviet defenses preparatory to an open attack.[25] Both sides remained perilously sensitive to a possible surprise assault. On September 26, Soviet early warning systems announced a U.S. missile launch, demanding an urgent decision about retaliation: after intense debate, Soviet commanders correctly decided that the alert was false, and civilization survived.

Meanwhile, in Lebanon, U.S. armed forces were fighting on a scale not seen since Vietnam. On October 23, what had seemed like a one-sided police operation went catastrophically wrong when a suicide truck bomber destroyed a U.S. barracks in Beirut, killing 240 Marines and effectively ending the U.S. mission. U.S. forces were soon withdrawn from combat and pulled out of the country in a humiliating withdrawal, which Reagan described as merely a "redeployment of the Marines from Beirut airport to their ships offshore." The barracks attack caused by far the largest number of combat deaths of U.S. forces since the Vietnam War.[26]

But events elsewhere meant that the administration escaped the worst consequences of the Beirut disaster. A leftist coup had overthrown a radical regime on the tiny Caribbean nation of Grenada. Citing the danger to U.S. citizens, the United States ordered a military intervention, which led to fighting with Cuban forces and advisers. Since American forces had so often intervened in Caribbean nations—dozens of times since the Civil War—the Grenada affair seems quite unexceptional. At the time, though, Grenada enjoyed a symbolic significance far beyond its military importance, as a deliberate attempt to cure Vietnam syndrome and to accustom the American people once more to the prospect of direct confrontation with Communist forces, even if that meant U.S. casualties. Justifying the invasion in terms of a rescue of threatened Americans allowed the administration to boast of averting a new hostage crisis. Secretary of State George Shultz recorded that after Grenada, "suddenly, I could sense the country's emotions turn around."[27] Nicaragua and Cuba now remained the only leftist havens in the hemisphere, and conservatives pressed for one of those nations to be the next item on the U.S. military agenda.

By the start of November, global affairs were more threatening than they had been since the Cuban missile crisis. The Doomsday Clock maintained by the *Bulletin of the Atomic Scientists* had been moved to a perilous four minutes to midnight in late 1980, suggesting the nearness of annihilation. At the end of 1983, it was moved forward still further, to just three minutes, the closest to midnight since 1953. As the *Bulletin* remarked, "There has been a virtual suspension of meaningful contacts and serious discussions. Every channel of communications has been constricted or shut down; every form of contact has been attenuated or cut off. And arms control negotiations have been reduced to a species of propaganda."[28]

Matters came to a head that November when NATO organized the huge ABLE/ARCHER exercises, which would mobilize forces from Norway to Turkey. This came at a time when the United States was intervening around the world, fighting in Lebanon and the Caribbean and deploying new missiles in Europe. The Soviets now intensified their Operation RYAN, collecting information about the imminent nuclear surprise attack supposedly planned by Reagan (the term is an acronym for *raketno-yadernoye napadenie*, "nuclear missile attack"). Soviet forces were alerted to expect a nuclear war within days and, by some accounts, to prepare to launch their own attack as a means of preserving some of their military capacity before it was annihilated by a preemptive assault. Not until months afterward, when defectors let it be known just how serious the menace had been, did a puzzled President Reagan ask how the Soviets could have been so misled about Western intentions. How could they have thought the United States would launch a surprise attack? That was the sort of thing the Nazis would do, and it was the Soviets, not the Americans, who were self-evidently the Nazis of the modern world.[29]

Red Dawns

By 1980, commentators were speaking of a "new Cold War," and there was real fear that it would soon turn hot. In late 1981, an NBC/Associated Press survey found that over 75 percent of Americans expected a nuclear war within a few years. In response, an anti-nuclear campaign became the flagship issue for the political left, and in June 1982, the nuclear freeze movement attracted 750,000 demonstrators to New York City, the largest protest in the city's history. The anti-nuclear movement found its manifesto in the work of Jonathan Schell, whose 1982 essay "The Fate of the Earth" urged the absolute moral necessity of preventing nuclear annihilation. The following year, the anti-nuclear movement attracted the powerful support of the Roman Catholic bishops, whose pastoral letter "The Challenge of Peace" advocated an end to nuclear weapons. One potent new argument for peace was the nuclear winter theory, the idea that nuclear war of any scale would irrevocably ruin the climate, causing human extinction in "a cold dark apocalypse." Right-wing apocalypticism was thus countered by a left-liberal version, quite as religious in tone and implications. The religious analogy became explicit as environmentalists influenced by the Gaia hypothesis argued that nuclear annihilation threatened nothing less than deicide. In the first Reagan term, probably half a million young men refused to follow the new law requiring draft registration, though only a token handful were prosecuted.[30]

Anti-war and anti-nuclear rhetoric was expressed in a series of strongly liberal films. The television miniseries *The Day After* depicted the horrors of a nuclear attack on the U.S. heartland and attracted the largest audience ever recorded for a television movie. Unknown to the audience, the miniseries was shown only a few days after the ABLE/ARCHER crisis actually had come close to detonating a clash infinitely more destructive than the limited war depicted in the film. Another portrayal of nuclear warfare on American soil was *Testament*. Appropriately, given the emphases of the time, the film stressed the horrifying effects of nuclear war on families, with the main theme being the death of children: the bomb was the ultimate form of child abuse. Left and liberal voices were also expressed in films such as *Under Fire* and *Salvador,* both about Central America, while *Daniel* linked the familiar left-wing mythology of the Rosenberg case to the contemporary anti-nuclear movement. Less overtly political, but quite frightening, were television miniseries such as *World War III*, while the television movie *Special Bulletin* was a faux news reportage of the nuclear destruction of the city of Charleston by terrorists. Anti-nuclear themes reached the musical hit parade, with songs such as "Safety Dance," "Enola Gay," and "99 Red Balloons." Pink Floyd's 1983 album *The Final Cut* ends with a vision of nuclear holocaust, as a newsreader forecasts high temperatures of around 4,000 degrees Celsius.

But in light of the obvious fears of nuclear war, it is remarkable how much of popular culture demonstrated support for the military and national defense while portraying Communism in quite as villainous a way as the president could have wished. In Hollywood productions, pro-military views first surfaced in nonpolitical films such as the romantic drama *An Officer and a Gentleman*, which resembled a World War II-era film in showing how military training turned an undisciplined civilian into a navy pilot, a true man. Already in 1982, Clint Eastwood's *Firefox* deployed familiar Cold War themes in an account of how an American pilot steals a supercharged Soviet fighter.

By 1984, popular patriotism became more aggressive. Patriotic expressions were much in evidence during the red-white-and-blue television coverage of the Los Angeles Olympics, an event boycotted by the Soviet bloc.[31] Cold War themes continued to dominate popular fiction. One of the best-selling books of the decade was Tom Clancy's 1984 submarine saga, *The Hunt for Red October*, which inspired many imitators. Clancy followed his triumph with *Red Storm Rising* (1986), a fictional account of a U.S.-Soviet war in Europe, while he explored the terror network in *Patriot Games* (1987). Frederick Forsyth's *Fourth Protocol* (also 1984) imagined an attempted Soviet overthrow of the West by means of covert nuclear terrorism, combined with subversive penetration of Western political systems. However much they feared East-West confrontation, millions wanted to read about it, and they expected the West to emerge victorious.

By 1984, Hollywood films were depicting Communist villains little different from the most grotesque Nazi caricatures of the World War II years. This new Cold War spirit was manifested in films such as *Red Dawn*, showing a Soviet-Cuban invasion of the American heartland, and *Rocky IV*, in which Rocky defends American honor against the robot-like Soviet fighter Drago. For all its apparent use of the anti-CIA conspiracy genre, *No Way Out* revived the 1950s nightmare of the Soviet sleeper agent placed within the United States, waiting for an opportunity to betray his country. *Heartbreak Ridge* also reverted to an older genre, involving a platoon of Marines being readied for combat by a tough but well-meaning sergeant, but this time the enemies they confront are Cuban combat troops in Grenada. The 1987 miniseries *Amerika* devoted fourteen prime-time hours to depicting a United States under Soviet occupation; reportedly, the series was designed as a riposte to *Testament*.[32]

Consistently, such films won audience sympathy by portraying Americans and particularly American soldiers as outnumbered and outgunned by hostile forces, which historically has not been a common feature of U.S. wars. In film, though, Americans have to be the underdog, whether they are the teenage anti-Communist partisans of *Red Dawn* or the abused prisoners of many productions of the mid-1980s. The genre of Vietnam fantasy films about prisoner rescue missions began in 1983 with *Uncommon Valor* and continued with the *Missing in Action* series (three parts released between 1984 and 1988). The most successful contribution was *Rambo*

(1985), in which the hero frees U.S. prisoners from their Vietnamese and Soviet Communist captors. By the time *Rambo III* was released in 1988, John Rambo was massacring Soviet invaders in Afghanistan.[33]

After the Empire

Given the obvious popular fears of nuclear war, one might have expected an anti–Cold War groundswell to have caused grave problems for Reagan and perhaps to have displaced him that November. Yet, obviously, nothing of the sort happened. For all the war fears, most Americans rallied to the president in a time of crisis, their patriotism reinforced by events such as the Grenada invasion and the Korean airliner shootdown. Also, the sharp economic improvement that began at the end of 1983 vastly improved the public mood and encouraged confidence in the administration. Moreover, Reagan benefited from his enemies' mistakes. Anti-nuclear activists over-stated their cause by presenting the cruise and Pershing missile deployments as an inevitable trigger for war. As 1984 dawned with the planet still intact, Reagan could claim to have successfully offered a powerful bargaining chip that would sooner or later force Soviet concessions, and back-channel negotiations did indeed get under way. Later that year, the Democrats' choice of Walter Mondale as presidential candidate suggested that party's total lack of connection with the new political realities.

Cold War passions cooled after the near-catastrophe of late 1983. The longer U.S. missiles were deployed in Europe, the more obvious it became that a preemptive attack was not a prospect, and the Soviets were increasingly distracted by their own internal crises. Reagan caused a minor scare in the summer of 1984 when a joke of his was accidentally broadcast. He was heard to proclaim, "My fellow Americans, I am pleased to tell you today that I've signed legislation that will outlaw Russia forever. We begin bombing in five minutes." (The sound bite was mockingly adapted as a hit dance record under the title "Five Minutes.") Fortunately, though, the incident scarcely upset the general trend to warmer relationships.

In March 1985, Mikhail Gorbachev secured the leadership of the USSR. Desperately worried by the growing economic gulf with the West, Gorbachev initiated a period of extensive reform at home and new relations abroad. Undoubtedly, U.S. economic and military pressure did much to motivate these changes. In 1986, Gorbachev told the Soviet Politburo, "Our goal is to prevent the next round of the arms race. If we do not accomplish it, the threat to us will only grow. We will be pulled into another round of the arms race that is beyond our capabilities, and we will lose it, because we are already at the limit of our capabilities. . . . If the new round begins, the pressure on our economy will be unbelievable." Crippling the Soviet economic position was the near-collapse of world oil prices: from 1986 through 1988, prices were around $10 a barrel.[34]

Reagan, in his second term, also had powerful motives for making peace, as he looked to a grand political settlement that would ensure his place in history. In late 1985, Reagan and Gorbachev met at a summit in Geneva and delighted observers by their apparently warm relationship and their willingness to engage in serious discussions—though no formal agreement was concluded. This was the point at which the worst nuclear terrors lifted, on both sides of the Atlantic. Reagan even had visions of an extraordinary global deal that would abolish the nuclear arsenals of both sides, and these sweeping proposals surfaced briefly at the Reykjavik summit meeting of 1986. Although the Reykjavik meeting failed, the international political mood shifted, as Reagan felt that Gorbachev really did have the potential to transform Soviet Communism.[35]

The virulent anti-Communism of the early 1980s faded. In 1987, the United States and the USSR signed the Intermediate Range Nuclear Forces Treaty, which ordered the dismantling of long- and short-range missiles in Europe. This was the first U.S.-Soviet treaty actually to provide for the destruction of nuclear weapons, and also the first arms control agreement to receive Senate approval since SALT I in 1972. Though the American right denounced the treaty, it represented an enormous U.S. diplomatic victory, effectively granting Reagan his long-mocked zero option. The Soviet Union, meanwhile, staggered on to fresh disasters until it was forced to relinquish control of eastern Europe, evacuate Afghanistan, and, ultimately, abandon Communism. The Cold War faded as one party to it was slipping into oblivion.

Some have seen Reagan's new willingness to compromise as a reversal of his earlier stance, a desperate response to the growing political crisis at home. Sidney Blumenthal, for instance, sees the new openness to disarmament as the key moment when "Reagan ditched the right" in "the U-turn that saved the Gipper." For all Reagan's anti-Communist bluster, Blumenthal suggests, common sense and moderation eventually triumphed. In fact, Reagan was much more consistent than critics claim, and 1986 does not represent such a dramatic demarche. Reagan forced his opponents to negotiate on the terms and issues as he defined them, and ultimately the Soviets gave him what he had always wanted.[36]

Though always accepting the principle of "better dead than Red," Reagan never believed that those could or should be the only options. In order to preserve the America that he believed had a divine mission, he had to resist external menaces, but that did not mean accepting commonplace wisdom about the best means of fighting Communism. Reagan was genuinely appalled by the prospect of nuclear war and was moved by syrupy productions such as *The Day After* and *War Games*. His rejection of mutual assured destruction led him to seek alternatives, either in anti-missile defense or in the still more fundamental abandonment of nuclear weapons as such. He wanted to render nuclear weapons "impotent and obsolete." He was as devoted to avoiding war as the most pragmatic of arms control experts but was simply more prepared to try truly radical expedients. In Gorbachev, he thought he had found a suitable partner for peacemaking, and his judgment proved right.[37]

So complete was the Western victory that Reagan's many enemies refused to credit either him or his policies, preferring to attribute the collapse of the USSR to Gorbachev's moderation or to inevitable forces in Soviet society. In support of this, they often quote the remarks of Gorbachev himself, who has said that the Cold War ended without any winners—though Gorbachev is probably the worst witness in the world to evaluate these epochal events with any degree of objectivity. At least Walter Mondale never claimed that no real winners had emerged from the 1984 presidential contest. However much it may gall, no account of the collapse of the Soviet empire can ignore the vision of Ronald Reagan, who had correctly predicted in the face of all skepticism that we would win and they would lose.

Supping with the Devil

Just as the Soviet menace was apparently fading, so another was gaining strength, and fears about terrorism surged in the mid-1980s. In this area, though, realistic interpretations of the problem were severely distorted by the power of stereotypes, at least some arising from the concentration on Soviet Communism as the absolute source of evil in the world.[38]

Throughout the decade, U.S. administrations identified certain enemies as the symbols and sources of evil, and the public largely accepted those identifications. The Soviets were the primary enemies, and terrorism, while highly dangerous, was a subset of the larger Communist threat. This linkage was reinforced when, following the twin events in Lebanon and Grenada, the administration immediately presented these as fights against one common menace. Reagan declared that these conflicts, "though oceans apart, are closely related. Not only has Moscow assisted and encouraged the violence in both countries, but it provides direct support through a network of surrogates and terrorists." This one speech referred ten times to "terrorism." Framing the struggle in this way was meant to appeal to a U.S. public still hesitant about warfare with the Soviets but quite willing to fight terrorists. The more closely the twin menaces could be contextualized together, the more success the administration would have in its aggressive anti-Communist agenda. The problem was that the focus on Soviet Communism precluded deeper analysis of terrorism or Islamist extremism and ensured that a great many political lessons about the Middle East would go unlearned.[39]

The decision to see the terrorist threat as secondary has caused much retroactive blame. In the aftermath of September 11, 2001, it seems incredible that the United States should once have supported Islamist forces in Afghanistan, including (indirectly) Osama bin Laden. Through the 1980s, the United States actively favored the teaching of Saudi-style Wahhabi Islam as a bastion against both Communism and Iranian Khomeinism. Equally, given the nation's later conflicts with the Iraq of Saddam Hussein, some find it embarrassing to recall that this same regime was once regarded as a close ally. Watching *Fahrenheit 911*, modern audiences are startled to see Saddam receiving visits from distinguished U.S. politicians, including arch-hawk Donald Rumsfeld. By 1987, the U.S. Navy was patrolling the Persian Gulf, ostensibly to preserve oil supplies without taking sides between Iran and Iraq, though there was never the slightest doubt that U.S. forces were primarily there to help Saddam.[40]

Many retroactive criticisms of such U.S. policies are ill-placed. In the context of the 1980s, it was anything but irrational to give full priority to the Soviet danger: one, and only one, nation posed a sufficient threat to the United States to end its existence, and weakening Soviet power in Afghanistan was an overarching goal. Only in hindsight do foreign policy experts confidently assert that the Soviet Union was on the verge of collapse regardless of what the West did. At the time, in fact, the perception of Soviet vulnerability was largely confined to controversial anti-Communists such as Ronald Reagan, who was dismissed as a harebrained ignoramus. But even Reagan never believed that Soviet Communism would simply vanish: the USSR could and should be driven to defeat, but only if the West made a decisive push.

Nor were U.S. officials under any illusions that bin Laden and their other de facto allies on the ground were just heroic anti-Communist nationalists. If the United States had waited to find democratic-minded secular liberals to form the core of an Afghan resistance, then the Soviets might well have overwhelmed that nation and avoided the massive strain on their resources. As late as 1986, many Western experts felt that the Soviets were on the verge of suppressing the Afghan guerrillas. Without the Afghan cancer, the Soviet Union might have endured for decades longer, and conceivably Russians would still be occupying Kabul today. This is not to deny that U.S. administrations erred by arming particular forces or by trusting Pakistani and Saudi intelligence agencies to select the Islamist militants to whom aid should be channeled. But if the same U.S. officials had been granted a crystal ball that allowed them to witness the later rise of al-Qaeda, they would not have acted very differently, in Afghanistan or elsewhere.

For similar reasons, supporting Saddam made excellent sense when he was a bulwark preventing the expansion of the Iranian revolution, not to mention helping the United States avenge Iranian assaults such as the embassy takeover. The Iran-Iraq War ended when the Islamist regime was forced to accept a peace that Khomeini himself described as drinking poison, and all this was achieved with limited involvement by U.S. combat forces. When we also recall the war's effect on oil prices, we can scarcely deny that the main victor of the Iran-Iraq confrontation was the United States. In historical context too, the support of Saddam scarcely seems shocking. Franklin Roosevelt's reputation has survived the fact that in World War II the United States allied with Stalin's frightful regime, a fact that throws the nation's later diplomatic dalliances into a much more balanced perspective.[41]

Lords of Terror

But in other ways, the selective U.S. identification of villains and evil enemies in the Reagan years definitely did twist its policies, with damaging results. While the U.S. administration understood the need to fight terrorism, it made some questionable choices in identifying the main culprits and in almost willfully ignoring some of the worst perpetrators. Commonly, practical constraints prevented the United States from pursuing the logic of implacable war against evildoers that presidential rhetoric seemed to demand.

This kind of distortion was evident during the global terrorist crisis that erupted unexpectedly in the mid-1980s. The previous spasm of international terrorism had calmed down by 1977, but beginning in 1984, a series of spectacular attacks hit the headlines, mainly assaults against airliners and airports. These attacks included the bombing and hijacking of airliners, the simultaneous massacres of passengers at airports in Rome and Vienna in December 1985, and a bloody series of bombings directed against civilian targets in Paris in 1986. A singularly vicious attack involved the hijacking of the cruise ship *Achille Lauro* in October 1985, when Palestinian terrorists murdered an elderly wheelchair-bound American Jew, Leon Klinghoffer.

Most of the attacks had clear Middle Eastern connections, and the Abu Nidal group and Islamic Jihad became notorious. At the same time, the remnants of the old European domestic terror networks revived, under titles such as Action Directe and the Red Army Fraction.[42]

Middle Eastern politics went far toward explaining why this terror wave occurred when it did. Partly, these campaigns were an outgrowth of conflicts within the Palestinian movement, which was deeply divided over the prospect of peace talks with Israel. Each faction, and the state that backed it, used what military force it possessed in order to show its effectiveness and its revolutionary militancy. But the main reason for the violence was the Iran-Iraq War, which lumbered on from 1980 through 1988. Despite international arms embargoes, each side desperately needed advanced weapons, which they obtained from shady and semi-legal transactions in a dozen European nations. When conflicts arose, such deals could not be enforced in court, but terrorist violence could be used as a means of extortion or of pressuring reluctant suppliers. Both sides used their proxies and front groups: Iraq had its Abu Nidal group, while Iran had both its own Islamic Jihad and the various networks that operated through Iran's ally Syria. Sometimes, the connections with sponsor states were quite clear. The Paris bombings of 1986 were firmly attributed to Iranian embassy officials, while Abu Nidal's outrages could generally be linked to Iraqi diplomats or intelligence agents. The terror wave of the 1980s ended abruptly in 1988, just as peace was concluded in the Persian Gulf. Terrorist attacks stopped not because they were prevented or deterred but because they were no longer necessary.[43]

How the United States in the mid-1980s saw the terrorist menace is suggested by some of the fictional productions of this time, as stereotypical terrorists became a mainstay of American popular culture, no less than the Communists of the recent neo–Cold War productions. Traditional Orientalist stereotypes of fanatical Easterners dating back to the film of *Gunga Din* were compounded by more recent images from America's own domestic cults, with their lunatic leaders and gurus and their robotic killer soldiers. The Klinghoffer murder in particular stirred fury against Middle Eastern radicals. Screen terrorists were always Middle Eastern in character, and best-selling novels about terrorism vary only in the degree of psychopathic evil attributed to Arab or Islamist militants. These books can often be identified from their titles alone, which frequently use words or names implying Arab fanaticism and violence, such as *jihad* or *Saladin*.[44]

Cinematic images were no more subtle. *Delta Force* presented a fantasy of how heroic U.S. soldiers defeat and kill savage Arab hijackers, who are barely human. In the 1985 film *To Live and Die in L.A.*, U.S. Secret Service agents detailed to protect a politician find that a suicide bomber is planning an imminent attack. When the agent confronts the would-be bomber on a hotel roof, his speech fits every known cliché of Middle Eastern fanaticism. He declares, "I am a martyr! Death to America and all the enemies of Islam!" The sequence has next to nothing to do with the main plot of the film, but by 1985, combating Arab terrorists was simply part of the tasks of a fictional hero. Even the teen comedy *Back to the Future* showed Michael J. Fox pursued by a homicidal Libyan terror cell rampaging through American suburbia.

Yet by no means all pop culture treatments offered simplistic stereotypes and heroics, and some responded soberly to the new challenges. American media often echoed the warnings from official agencies that a massive terror attack would almost certainly strike the American homeland. The culprit would most likely be Abu Nidal, who was portrayed quite as lethally as our own generation sees Osama bin Laden. This perception shaped a 1986 television miniseries that in the aftermath of September 11 looks quite prophetic. Co-written by Bob Woodward, *Under Siege* convincingly depicts a terror campaign on U.S. soil, involving multiple suicide truck bombs, a rocket attack on the U.S. Capitol, and random bombings of malls and restaurants. The chief villain is one Abu Ladeen—roughly, *Nidal* spelled backward—who serves as a proxy for Iran, and the plot focuses on the propriety of a U.S. retaliatory strike against that nation. Complicating the debate is the possibility that sinister forces within the U.S. government have provoked or manipulated violence in order to incite international conflict. Such popular-culture treatments indicate how thoroughly the notion of a terror war, rooted in Middle Eastern conditions, had penetrated the national consciousness by mid-decade. Nor was the conspiratorial potential of such a conflict a creation of *Fahrenheit 911*.

Striking Back

The confrontation with terrorism raised critical policy questions. U.S. conservatives demanded a forthright American response to terrorism, military where appropriate, and at first the Reagan administration seemed to exemplify this hard line. At the start of his presidency, in January 1981, Reagan welcomed home the returning Tehran hostages with these words: "Let terrorists be aware that when the rules of international behavior are violated, our policy will be one of swift and effective retribution. We hear it said that we live in an era of limit to our powers. Well, let it also be understood, there are limits to our patience." A new range of clandestine military units was devoted to future anti-terrorist actions, and covert U.S. aid helped free American general James Dozier, kidnapped by the Italian Red Brigades. In 1985, a U.S. military response resulted in the capture of the *Achille Lauro* hijackers, who were seized after their flight was forced down over Italy. The victory provoked Reagan's boast to terrorists: "You can run, but you can't hide."[45]

By this time, though, conservative policy was becoming still more ambitious. Not content with fighting and killing terrorists, governments should retaliate militarily against the states that sponsored terrorism, which Reagan characterized as "outlaw states run by the strangest collection of misfits, Looney Tunes and squalid criminals since the advent of the Third Reich." In 1984, NSDD 138 discussed the menace of state-sponsored terrorism, declaring, "The states that practice terrorism or actively support it cannot be allowed to do so without consequences," and that when other means have been exhausted, "it must be understood that when we are victimized by acts of terrorism, we have the right to defend ourselves—and the right to help others do the same."[46]

The retaliatory doctrine was popularized by hawkish Israelis and pro-Israel writers, especially Benjamin Netanyahu, who in 1986 edited the influential book *Terrorism: How the West Can Win*. (Adding to his credibility, Netanyahu was the brother of the Israeli commando leader killed during the legendary Entebbe raid.) Contributors to the book included George Shultz. Reading Netanyahu today, his dualistic views seem quite familiar, as they became the established orthodoxies of the Bush-era war on terror, but in the mid-1980s, they represented a significant departure. In the view of Netanyahu and his allies, terrorism was not a tactic but a global movement. Terror was dedicated to the destruction of the democratic West, that is, NATO plus Israel. "Spiritually, its values are the direct antitheses of those of terrorism." "The West can and must defeat the forces of terror before they spread further. It must unite and fight to win the war against terrorism. This is the challenge facing the democracies." If it acted with sufficient determination, the West "can stop the forces of world terror in their tracks and root out this malignancy from our civilization." Going beyond simple retaliation, Israel also pioneered the doctrine of armed pre-emption, of doing unto enemies before they succeeded in doing unto you. In 1981, an Israeli air raid had preemptively eliminated Iraq's nuclear capacity.[47]

The rhetoric of aggressive retaliation, of standing tall, demanded action —but against which target? Were all these terrorist movements separate and independent, or were they obeying dictates from one or more "rogue states"? Who decided what terrorist mastermind actually stood behind a given front group? Identifying targets was by no means easy, and the main protagonists in the current terror wave—Iran, Iraq, and Syria—were particularly difficult to deal with, given the overwhelming importance of the U.S.-Soviet relationship. Political considerations demanded that Iraq's role not be emphasized, since that would prevent it from receiving the U.S. aid it so badly needed to resist Iran. In 1982, Iraq was formally removed from the U.S. roster of terrorist sponsor states, and its activities received little attention until after the Kuwait invasion of 1990, when it was retroactively painted as the principal mastermind of global violence. Syria was a sensitive target, as a close ally of the Soviet Union, with Soviet advisers manning its anti-aircraft defenses. A 1983 U.S. raid on that nation resulted in the loss of a fighter aircraft and an embarrassing crisis over the return of the pilot. (In the aftermath of America's wars since 2001, the concern over one pilot may seem surprising, but in the post-Vietnam years, POW issues were explosive.) A direct U.S. attack on Syria was potentially dangerous in terms of international relations, and the same constraint applied to Iran. Attacks on those nations could precipitate full-scale regional wars, which conceivably could draw in the Soviet bloc. Other terrorist sponsor states were well connected diplomatically; Algeria, in particular, received its customary free pass. Largely by default, that left Libya as the major candidate for rogue state.[48]

Libya's role as arch-villain was justified to the extent that the country had been involved in numerous acts of savage violence around the world, but no more so than other powers that were more discreet or better connected. After repeated brushes with the U.S. military, new confrontations occurred in 1986, when the Libyans declared that their territorial sea limits represented a "line of death"—which immediately prompted U.S. naval incursions into the disputed area in the Gulf of Sidra. Matters deteriorated following the bombing of a disco in Berlin, in which two American soldiers were killed. According to contemporary media reports, U.S. intelligence linked the attack to the intelligence services of Libya and Syria, but the Syrian linkage was promptly forgotten, and on April 15, U.S. fighters bombed Libya. Qaddafi's encampment was targeted, but in keeping with recent prohibitions on assassination, the United States ostensibly tried to avoid killing the Libyan leader.[49]

Most Americans celebrated the attack as a blow against international banditry and a reaffirmation of the nation's willingness to stand up for itself and its citizens. The raid even had a suitably cowboy-like title, Operation El Dorado Canyon. When the bombing prompted anti-American demonstrations across Western Europe, that in itself confirmed the rightness of

Reagan's willingness to act unilaterally to defend U.S. interests. The fact that U.S. bombs accidentally hit the French embassy in Libya was widely seen as a bonus, given the strained relationship with that nation, and comedians and television shows celebrated the event. The popularity of the Libyan raid helps explain the massive success of the film *Top Gun*, which depicts a similar action against an unspecified Arab dictatorship, as does the derivative *Iron Eagle*.

How the West Did Not Win

Muammar Qaddafi continued to be the ultimate symbol of the terrorist rogue state, and he was frequently caricatured by cartoonists. But at just the time when it was acting so decisively against this token figure, the U.S. administration was behaving ignominiously in the face of other, far more substantial terrorist activity. It is in these other interactions, above all with the Islamist regime in Iran, that the United States suffered most acutely from misreading its enemies.

The debacle had its roots in Lebanon. Following the Marine barracks bombing of 1983, Lebanese Shi'ite groups systematically attacked U.S. targets, with the support and operational direction of Iranian intelligence. The major activist group was Hizbullah, usually acting under the nom de guerre of Islamic Jihad. This thin disguise allowed Western nations to affect ignorance of the real culprits and to escape public blame for not retaliating. In 1984, Islamic Jihad captured the CIA chief in Beirut, William Buckley, who reputedly died under torture. The group attacked U.S. and NATO targets in Spain and elsewhere, and in June 1985, it hijacked Flight 847 from Athens to Rome, beginning a fifteen-day ordeal publicized daily in the mass media. The hijackers killed an American sailor. U.S. retaliation was at best sporadic and ineffective. Acknowledging the role of Hizbullah in the campaign, in 1985 a car bomb was directed against the group's spiritual leader, Sheikh Fadlallah, but the attack—presumably CIA-inspired—went tragically wrong. Though eighty civilians were killed, Fadlallah survived.[50]

Hizbullah's war against the United States entered a new stage in 1985 when Westerners began to be kidnapped in Beirut. Ultimately, over a dozen victims were taken, some of whom were held for years. Ostensibly, the kidnappers belonged to a variety of mysterious groups, but Hizbullah was chiefly to blame. Following its recent tough rhetoric, the U.S. government might have been expected to refuse any negotiations and to exercise military pressure on the state sponsoring the terrorism, namely, Iran. Publicly, though, the administration never directly connected Iran with the growing hostage crisis and instead began to deal with the radical Iranian regime, which was demanding missiles and other weaponry for the ongoing Gulf War. The United States complied to the extent of sending thousands of anti-tank missiles, often routed through Israel. At a National Security Council meeting in early 1986, Defense Secretary Caspar Weinberger noted, "President decided to go with Israeli-Iranian offer to release our five hostages in return for sale of 4,000 TOWs [U.S. missiles] to Iran by Israel."[51]

Notionally, the policy was justified by the urgent need to compete with the supposedly growing Soviet influence in Iran, though the Iranians had proved more determined in rooting out local Communists than the shah had ever been. Another defense was that arms sales might win the support of more moderate and pro-Western elements in the Iranian political establishment, helping to promote U.S. interests. But the point demands to be noted. For all the contrasts so often made between Jimmy Carter's weakness and Ronald Reagan's staunch determination, it was Carter who at least attempted a rescue mission to save American hostages, while Reagan traded arms for hostages—even though he denied to the last, in the face of overwhelming evidence to the contrary, that this was the nature of the exchange.[52]

The Reagan policy proved disastrous at every turn. Not only were most hostages not freed until years afterward, but the deal generated a political crisis in the United States. The main Iran transaction violated law, and so did the subsidiary deal, in which profits were diverted to support the Nicaraguan contras. The executive branch was thus in the position of setting up both a private alternative fiscal system and an intelligence network to carry on its policies, and illegality was piled upon illegality. After the resulting Iran-contra mess came to light in November 1986, it dominated the headlines for the following two years and came close to causing Reagan's impeachment. In the immediate aftermath of the exposés, Reagan's approval rating dropped by twenty points in a month, less because of public horror at the legal violations—which remained puzzlingly technical—than at the impression that the president had exercised so little control over vital policy issues. The affair seemed to justify the worst charges that Reagan was a genial but uncomprehending figurehead.

Fortunately for the administration, the scandal's long-term public impact was limited. Many ordinary observers broadly sympathized with Reagan's basic goals of combating Communism and freeing the hostages. The scandal remained largely within the Beltway and failed to generate the kind of public alienation or rage that had unseated Richard Nixon. As would again be demonstrated by the financial and sexual scandals surrounding

Bill Clinton a decade later, the public does not become angry enough to support a president's removal while the economy is booming or when oil is $15 a barrel.[53]

The Iran-contra matter even generated a new conservative hero in Oliver North, a Marine colonel who had supervised the capture of the *Achille Lauro* terrorists and who was unabashed in his defense of the contra policy. Testifying to a congressional inquiry in the summer of 1987, dressed in full uniform, he seemed like a real-life manifestation of the heroic American fighters who had featured in recent patriotic films, and political critics soon realized how easily he might become an anti-Communist martyr figure.[54] But though the presidency was saved, the affair made nonsense of Reagan's image as an uncompromising fighter against terrorist violence.

U.S. administrations in the 1980s wished to draw a sharp contrast between their own strength and toughness and the weakness of earlier years, and that demanded visible public action against the demonized figures who represented threats against America. This meant portraying international dangers as the work of identifiable conspiratorial groups or individuals. The United States would react against specific culprits with names and faces, who were constructed according to well-established popular demonologies. Understanding problems in this way made them solvable, given sufficient political will.

This is not to say that conspiratorial interpretations were necessarily wrong. A plausible case can be made that the Soviet Union was indeed an evil empire. But not all problems and conflicts can be understood as the work of malevolent conspirators operating in a vacuum, immune from the influence of changing social and political circumstances. A single-minded focus on a national enemy is an admirable thing— provided that the enemy is indeed the only danger to be faced.

9

Dark Victories

The solution to the crime problem will not be found in a social worker's files, a psychiatrist's notes, or a bureaucrat's budget: it is a problem of the human heart, and it is there we must look for the answer.

—Ronald Reagan

Conservative victories in the Reagan years were most marked when the administration could build upon existing public concern and discontent. This was true of economic policy, in matters of defense and foreign affairs, and, just as strikingly, in the areas of crime, justice, and internal security. During the Reagan presidency, police, prisons, and intelligence agencies regained much of the power and prestige they had lost since the mid-1960s. Repeatedly, this was achieved by a rhetorical tactic of interpreting lesser issues in the light of some major menace universally agreed to be a kind of ultimate evil. Thus public horror at crack cocaine was used to demonize all illicit drugs, and the threat of domestic terrorism helped stigmatize any causes that might loosely be linked to such acts.

More important than any one single reform was a general shift toward ideas of individual responsibility. Reagan himself stressed traditional views of good and evil, of individual moral choice, which were applied to problems of crime and violence as much as economics. Many academics saw his views as simplistic. To quote sociologists Craig Reinarman and Harry Levine: "The most basic premise of social science—that individual choices are influenced by social circumstances—was rejected as left wing ideology. Reagan and the New Right constricted the aperture of attribution for America's ills so that only the lone deviant came into focus. They conceptualized people *in* trouble as people who *make* trouble." But Reagan's familiar rhetoric captured what was evidently a powerful public mood.[1]

In the Reagan view, crime was not a social dysfunction but a conscious moral act, and it had to be treated as such. Speaking in 1984, he said, "The American people are fed up with leniency toward career criminals, and they're fed up with those wrongdoers who are openly contemptuous of our way of justice . . . the American people have lost patience with liberal leniency and pseudo-intellectual apologies for crime. They're demanding that our criminal justice system return to realism; that our courts affirm values that teach us right and wrong matters, and that individuals are responsible for their actions, and retribution should be swift and sure for those who prey on the innocent." Failure to act threatened to license and tolerate the "criminal predators" who had ravaged in the country in the aftermath of 1960s liberalism. Just as moral equivalence had no place in dealings with the USSR or Libya, so it was wrong to balance the interests of ordinary citizens against criminals who assailed them. Listing the reasons for Reagan's victory in 1980, Pennsylvania governor Dick Thornburgh counted "the idea of the toughness of the American fiber, which means a firm line with criminals at home and with our adversaries abroad. . . . Those principles are now a majority view."[2]

The Penal Revolution

New attitudes to crime and deviancy provide an enduring legacy of the Reagan years. Already during the late 1970s, criminal justice policies were becoming much more oriented toward punishment, with the insanity defense as a prime exhibit for the perceived gullibility of liberal models of justice. Hard-line policies became still more marked under the Reagan-era Justice Department, which was headed successively by two of his old California comrades, William French Smith and Edwin Meese. Meese himself epitomized the resistance to the 1960s, having served as Reagan's chief of staff during the legendary controversies of the era, including the battle for Berkeley's People's Park and the controversies surrounding prison martyr George Jackson. For California radicals, Meese was a hate figure almost comparable to Reagan himself.[3]

But quite apart from federal policies, states too continued and accelerated a penal boom quite as striking as the long economic bull market. Taking prisons and jails together, America's inmate population in 1980 was 540,000. The total grew to 743,000 by 1985 and to over a million by 1989. By the start of the new century, the U.S. incarceration rate was six or seven times that prevailing in most of Western Europe, and the nation has long since outpaced Russia. In 1980, about 1.8 million Americans were under the supervision of the state, either through incarceration or by probation or parole. That total grew to 4.4 million by 1990 and to 7 million by 2004. This increase is all the more striking when we realize how starkly it ran against demographic trends. By all expectations, crime of all sorts, and especially violent crime, should have been plummeting during the late 1980s, reflecting the sparse numbers of the baby bust cohort. As for removing minor criminals and morality offenders from the system, again, the results of reform were the opposite of what was hoped. Between 1980 and 2000, the proportion of state inmates serving time only for drug offenses grew from 6.4 to 21 percent. More people were sent to prison for nonviolent offenses, sentences lengthened, and the ability to release inmates before their time was served shrank, as parole was restricted. One landmark measure was the federal Sentencing Reform Act of 1984, which led to severe sentencing guidelines.[4]

The impact is still more obvious when seen at state level. In 1977, California had fewer than 20,000 prison inmates; by 1998, that figure had risen to 160,000, a rate of increase far greater than the growth of population. Two-thirds of those were incarcerated for nonviolent crimes, usually drug-related, or for parole violations. Sex offenders (very broadly defined) represented another booming segment of the prison population. The prisonbuilding boom has become an economic driving force in some regions. Between 1974 and 2000, the number of federal and state prisons grew from 592 to 1,023. Texas alone built six new prisons a year, while Florida and California also invested deeply in prison construction. Building, maintaining, and staffing new prisons gave a strong material incentive to maintaining harsh penal laws, with contractors and unions becoming powerful vested interests. The more prisons were used, the more powerful the impetus for legislators to outdo each other in advocating penal solutions to social problems. Once the spiral began, it is difficult to see how it might be ended.[5]

In the Belly of the Beast

Support for conservative policies was reinforced by a number of sensational crimes, each of which in its way was taken to indicate the bankruptcy of liberalism. I have already suggested that the sensational nature of a crime has to do not so much with any intrinsic qualities of the act itself but rather with how it is reported by the media and how far it resonates with the general public, how far they see it as expressing their concerns. In a different context, a career such as Ted Bundy's could have received little public attention. In the early 1980s, though, a series of spectacular crimes earned just this kind of notoriety, and each in its way carried its distinctive political message.

One involved Jack Henry Abbott, a violent career criminal whose harrowing account of prison life, *In the Belly of the Beast*, won critical acclaim. Abbott's radical politics made him a plausible successor to that earlier convict star, George Jackson, and to Caryl Chessman before him. In 1978, Abbott corresponded with novelist Norman Mailer, who was then writing his book about executed killer Gary Gilmore. Mailer soon became Abbott's highly visible public advocate, seeing in him "an intellectual, a radical, a potential leader, a man obsessed with a vision of more elevated human relations in a better world than revolution could forge." By 1981, Abbott attracted the notice of shell-shocked liberals looking for heroes in the aftermath of the Reagan victory. He won parole, but only weeks later he returned to the headlines when he murdered a waiter at a New York restaurant. He was imprisoned once more, eventually committing suicide in 2002. Media coverage of the case was intense because of its New York location, so close to the headquarters of so many media outlets, while the lengthy trial in 1982 attracted liberal celebrities such as Mailer himself. Susan Sarandon would later name her child Jack Henry. However, in contrast to the widespread support for George Jackson, it was clear to most observers that Abbott was a brutal thug whose supporters were utterly naive. Media response to the case stressed instead the irredeemable evil of the killer, the near-impossibility of rehabilitation, and the gullibility of Abbott's admirers.[6]

Another villain of the time was John Hinckley Jr., who in March 1981 attempted to murder Ronald Reagan. The incident, which was widely televised, was chilling to a nation just recovering from the horrors of 1980 and hoping desperately that Reagan's leadership would mark the start of better times. Reagan recovered, of course, and it was generally assumed that the assassin would receive an efficient trial and a sharp punishment, much as John Lennon's killer had shortly before. In the event, Hinckley's trial was a leisurely affair that did not produce a verdict until mid-1982. The case produced many curious echoes of the 1970s. Hinckley reputedly performed his crime to win the attention of Jodie Foster, who had starred in the film *Taxi Driver*, which was based on the actual career of a true-life assassin. The boundaries between art and life were more porous than ever. Hinckley's bizarre motivation suggested that he was disturbed and dangerous, and the media saw his guilt as a foregone conclusion. In the closing stages of his trial, Hinckley himself had prepared remarks to be delivered to the court following his conviction. To popular disgust, though, the jury found him not guilty by reason of insanity, leading to his commitment in a mental hospital.[7]

Even more than the Dan White verdict, the Hinckley case demonstrated the gulf separating public perceptions of guilt from those of the legal system itself. An ancient legal tradition held that "guilt" implied full responsibility, the capacity to act freely and make moral judgments, which could be impaired by insanity. An insane individual might have committed an act and might be thoroughly dangerous but could not technically be guilty. In practice, the consequence of an insanity verdict might be not too different from that of formal conviction, in that it would usually lead to a hospital stay at least as long as the prison sentence one might otherwise have received. At various times in history, medical treatment for mental illness might be far more intrusive than anything inflicted in the name of punishment. Many years after the event, Hinckley remains in medical custody.

But to the lay observer, the Hinckley verdict came as a shock, and the outcome was taken to mean that a flagrantly guilty assassin was escaping punishment. Surveys showed that over 80 percent of Americans felt that justice had not been done in the case. Aggravating the situation was the fact that the verdict stemmed from a predominantly black jury in the District of Columbia, suggesting that Hinckley had been acquitted by anti-Reagan fanatics. Yet again—it appeared—hyperliberal courts, aided and abetted by hired-gun psychiatrists, were assisting criminals and ignoring the cause of public protection.

For conservatives, such cases indicated the need for punishment rather than correction, for retribution, not rehabilitation, and for acceleration of the movement for mandatory sentencing. In the months following the Hinckley verdict, the national outcry led to a generalized attack on the whole notion of the insanity defense. Many states ended the ability of courts to find someone not guilty by reason of insanity. Instead, the verdict would be "guilty but mentally ill" and would result in a penal sentence for the act committed, followed by psychiatric treatment where appropriate. In terms of legal tradition, such a verdict is problematic. The phrase suggests a real contradiction about the concept of guilt, and some psychiatrists regard it as equivalent to "red but green." In the political circumstances of 1982, though, the attack on the insanity defense represented a reassertion of the ideal of punishment.[8]

Besides the Abbott and Hinckley cases, a series of sensational cases in 1981–82 offered weighty symbolic messages. For Californians, one notorious crime was the Wonderland murders, a drug-related mass killing marked by extreme brutality and which commentators compared to the Manson case. Later investigation implicated adult film star John Holmes in the crime, again suggesting that the pornography industry was by no means the peaceful and "victimless" world that its defenders claimed. Through the winter of 1981–82, the trial of alleged Atlanta child-killer Wayne Williams made headlines repeatedly, reinforcing the lesson that violence was the product of personal evil rather than of social dysfunction or poverty. Also in 1982, a still unidentified individual or group tampered with Tylenol tablets in a number of Chicago stores, causing seven deaths. The poisonings occurred as part of a blackmail effort against the makers of Tylenol, who responded by adopting the kind of elaborate tamper-proof packaging that has since become universal. For years afterward, every time someone struggled with the new packaging, it served as a reminder of the Tylenol case and the personal dangers that Americans might face from homicidal violence.[9]

Public resentment toward criminals and their treatment by lenient officialdom again surfaced in 1984 with the case of subway vigilante Bernhard Goetz. Though accounts vary, Goetz (who is white) was approached on a New York subway train by a group of four black youths, who allegedly planned to rob him. Goetz shot all four, but the jury at his trial effectively exercised their right of nullification, finding him guilty only of less serious weapons violations. They sympathized with his assertion that "when you are surrounded by four people, one of them smiling, taunting, demanding, terrorizing, you don't have a complete grasp or perfect vision." Despite attempts to portray the shooting as racially motivated, many urban dwellers celebrated Goetz's action, undoubtedly recalling notorious crimes such as those of Willie Bosket. Goetz had struck back.[10]

Less immediately threatening than street crime, though ideologically important, was organized crime, which received a new emphasis from the incoming administration. Historically, Americans have often seen gangsters as far less dangerous than street criminals, and gang conflicts enjoy a certain spectator sport appeal. Organized crime of the most traditional kind was firmly in the news, with a bloody gang war in Philadelphia running for several years following the 1980 murder of Mafia don Angelo Bruno. Also, the Reagan-era FBI scored some major successes against Italian-American organized crime families, and in 1984 the administration commissioned a massive official investigation of organized crime, the first systematic effort of its kind since the late 1950s. A commission headed by Judge Irving Kaufman presented a substantial report on organized crime, studying not just Italian-American activities but also Asian-American and Latino syndicates, as well as emerging groups such as biker gangs and prison gangs.[11]

This inquiry was significant because of what it did not say. Unlike its predecessors, the Kaufman commission paid little attention to official or political corruption, still less to mob alliances with police or intelligence agencies, and rather focused on crime as a free-standing institution. Organized crime, it appeared, was a major social menace, yet another of the conspiratorial networks challenging the nation. As with other forms of threat in this era, its existence demanded a forthright justice-oriented solution, a renewed war on crime. Drawing explicit international analogies, Reagan proclaimed that "this administration seeks no negotiated settlement, no détente with the mob."[12]

Ghosts

In the Jack Abbott case, the ghosts of the 1960s had resolutely refused to walk: Abbott did not become a second George Jackson. But ghosts returned en masse in October 1981 following a bloody armored car robbery at Nyack, in New York's Rockland County. Two police officers and a security guard were murdered in a shootout with heavily armed criminals. At first sight, the affair seemed like a straightforward professional crime, one of a series of similar attacks that had occurred over the previous two years. When the culprits were identified, though, a completely different interpretation emerged of the Nyack robbery and its predecessors. The result was a dramatic new concern with domestic terrorism, which could now be plausibly linked with the heritage of 1960s radicalism.

The best-known member of the Nyack group was Kathy Boudin, a former member of the 1960s Weather Underground. She had last been in the public eye in 1970, when she survived an explosion in a Greenwich Village townhouse caused when a bomb-making operation went wrong; three of her comrades were killed.[13] Since 1970, she had been on the run, spending time in Cuba. She linked up with diehard veterans of the BLA and the Weather Underground, and the network carried out a series of armed robberies, allegedly to raise money for revolutionary warfare. Meanwhile, allies in the Puerto Rican FALN continued their campaign in the island itself, as well as on the U.S. mainland. In January 1981, FALN guerrillas blew up eleven jets at an Air National Guard base in Puerto Rico. In 1983, extremists robbed a Wells Fargo truck in Connecticut, stealing $7 million to finance guerrilla operations. Through the early 1980s, Puerto Rican extremists were seen as one of the most dangerous internal security threats, among the most likely to carry out major attacks against strategic targets and energy installations.[14]

The Nyack raid led to the capture of several old Weather Underground and BLA members, and provoked an investigation of the wider linkages in the radical underworld, including old black nationalist groups such as the Republic of New Africa. Another 1960s veteran, Susan Rosenberg, was arrested in 1984 for possession of over seven hundred pounds of explosives. Between 1981 and 1984, the continuing investigation led to the arrest of dozens of radicals. One holdout group carried out a series of bombings in New England and other northeastern states between 1982 and 1984, and they also killed a New Jersey state trooper. Though this group went under several aliases, it was chiefly known as the Sam Melville/Jonathan Jackson group, commemorating respectively a leader of the Attica rising and the brother of Soledad's George Jackson. Connections with the extreme wing of 1960s protest movements could hardly have been more glaring. Conservatives were delighted by the many headlines linking their old enemies with terror and violence. *Newsweek* offered simply, "Radicals: The Hunt Goes On."[15]

Obviously, only a small proportion of 1960s radicals was ever involved in violence, and only a handful joined an urban guerrilla campaign. Through the early 1980s, even the old extremists gradually reentered mainstream society, usually without severe legal consequences. Old firebrands such as Abbie Hoffman and Weather Underground leaders Bernardine Dohrn and Bill Ayers renounced violence and rejoined the world of peaceful activism. But the Nyack raid and its aftermath cast a grim light on sixties radicalism and served as an unpleasant reminder of just how violent and divisive those times had been. These events recalled the 1960s heritage of extremism and disorder, rather than peace and justice. Stories inspired by Nyack surfaced in popular television shows such as *Hill Street Blues*, allowing even these politically liberal programs the opportunity to condemn the kind of violent extremism symbolized by Boudin.[16]

Terror Networks

As we have seen, violent terrorism had been endemic in the mid-1970s. The amount of activity declined substantially by the early 1980s, but it received far more attention in the Reagan years, because federal agencies were more able to focus on these issues, rather than daily defending their very existence against political threats. Also, domestic radicalism was now presented as part of a systematic terrorist assault on the United States. In this view, individual events such as Nyack were not the outcome of misguided idealism but rather formed part of a coordinated movement that was ultimately linked to other global dangers, Communist or Islamist. As readers of *The*

Spike and *The Terror Network* knew, terrorism—whatever its ostensible cause—ultimately served the interests of Moscow.

Still more insidious was the Libyan hit squad story that dominated news reporting through the fall of 1981, in the immediate aftermath of the Nyack arrests. Reportedly, intelligence agencies had received convincing reports that Libyan dictator Muammar Qaddafi had dispatched a team of assassins to kill President Reagan and other leading officials in retaliation for the U.S.-Libyan naval confrontation. The origins of the story are uncertain, but they may have lain with Iranian arms dealer Manucher Ghorbanifar, who would later be pivotal to the Iran-contra affair. Subsequent investigation found no basis for the tale, but at the time, the story seemed plausible, coming as it did so soon after other well-publicized episodes of political murder, including the attacks on the Pope and Reagan himself the previous spring and the murder of Egyptian president Anwar el-Sadat that October.[17] The assassination network of the mid-1970s seemed to be back in operation, this time fighting for America's foreign foes. The hit team made headlines on every evening's national news broadcast over a period of several weeks. We heard when the team had crossed the Canadian border, when they were approaching Washington, and so on. Until the story died away that December, it reinforced the supposed lesson of Nyack: that international terrorism was now to be unleashed on American soil.

Responding to these perceived menaces, the administration justified the restoration of many of the powers removed from intelligence agencies during the mid-1970s, despite robust opposition by civil liberties activists. On December 4, 1981, with Libyan assassins reportedly converging on Washington, the president issued Executive Order 12333, which effectively served as the charter for U.S. intelligence agencies for two decades. The order carefully restricted domestic intelligence gathering, offering a long list of what agencies could not do, in order to avoid a recurrence of anything like the FBI's COINTELPRO scheme. However, exceptions were granted, and these permitted a whole new realm of domestic operations. Agencies could collect and disseminate information on U.S. citizens in certain circumstances, including "information obtained in the course of a lawful foreign intelligence, counterintelligence, international narcotics or international terrorism investigation." The exceptions raise obvious questions. If, as a potent theory held, most or all terrorism had an international dimension, did the clause permit any and all investigations of terrorism? And if so, what exactly was terrorism? Where was the dividing line between preventing an imminent terrorist act and investigating a group or cause that might have some contact with violent groups?[18]

Under the executive order, agencies had a powerful vested interest in arguing that domestic protest or opposition movements were in fact involved in real or potential terrorism or were connected to foreign powers. In addition to permitting intelligence gathering, applying the terrorist label effectively delegitimized any movement so labeled and any cause to which it could be plausibly connected. The order strongly encouraged agencies to speculate about conspiratorial and clandestine connections, especially by groups strongly opposed to U.S. policies.

Through the mid-1980s, the principal liberal complaints against the Reagan administration were its nuclear policies and its conduct of the covert wars in Central America. Activists formed support groups such as the Committee in Solidarity with the People in El Salvador (CISPES), ostensibly a peaceful protest movement. At the same time, the church-related Sanctuary Movement was formed to support Latino refugees, most of whom lacked legal immigrant status. From 1981 through 1984, federal agencies targeted both CISPES and the Sanctuary Movement for their supposed terrorist and subversive links. A widespread official mythology held that leftists were planning to assassinate Reagan at the Republican convention in Dallas, a charge that justified the massive investigation and penetration of the political left. Any association of the words *Dallas* and *assassination* must strike a nerve. By 1984, sixty of the FBI's field offices had as a major focus the investigation of CISPES and cognate groups, all in the name of anti-terrorism.[19] In the Reaganite film *Red Dawn*, Central American "refugees" prepare the way for the Soviet-Cuban invasion of the U.S. heartland. The rhetoric of terrorism permitted the restoration of domestic spying.

Fears of terrorism on U.S. soil reached new heights in the months following the Marine barracks attack in Beirut. It was at this point that the authorities first blocked traffic in front of the White House, fearing a truck bomb assault. Concern became more acute as international terrorism escalated between 1985 and 1988. The nation's nuclear agencies now began exploring the catastrophic consequences of a truck bomb attack on a U.S. nuclear facility.[20]

Though official fears were quite genuine, they were also exploited to justify expanding the government's arsenal of legal powers and to revive old and largely discredited internal security laws. Two major sedition trials charged defendants with plotting or conspiring to overthrow the United States government, an exceptionally serious allegation that had been little used since the height of the McCarthy era. One target was the Melville/Jackson group; the other case indicted ultra-right leaders, whom the government linked to the campaign of the neo-Nazi movement the Order in 1984–85. Though the Order was a genuinely dangerous group that plotted attacks against nuclear power stations and fantasized about obtaining nuclear and biological weapons, the sedition charges proved overly ambitious, and the defendants were acquitted. Nevertheless, the official response to terrorism showed a new official willingness to deploy an expanded legal arsenal against subversives, real or suspected.[21]

Fear and Loathing

Though violent crime and terrorism both made a huge public impact, the centerpiece of Reagan-era law enforcement policy was the war on drugs, a campaign against the primary symbol of the freedom, and excesses, of the 1960s.

When Reagan took office, the most dreaded illegal drugs were PCP and heroin, and the scares surrounding both resemble the later war against crack cocaine. Identical charges were used, focusing on the effects on individuals and the destruction of communities. Renewed concern about heroin, which peaked in 1980–81, stressed the perennial threat that a drug so infamously associated with racial minorities would penetrate the white middle class. Stories about middle-class junkies proliferated in newspapers and television news. The very name *heroin* had such enormous symbolic power that the public needed no convincing about its devastating potential or the failings of a society in which it became popular. *New York* magazine claimed that the city in 1980 was "facing a new heroin epidemic," but this time among the middle class. *Newsweek* used the drug's revived popularity to offer a critique of the 1960s, blaming the problem on "the specific influence of the rock culture [or] the general breakdown of middle class values." And of course it was a threat to children. In 1980, journalist Janet Cooke told of an eight-year-old Washington boy enslaved by heroin. The story was exposed as fictitious, but not before it earned Cooke a Pulitzer Prize.[22]

PCP also continued to serve as an ultimate evil, even in Hollywood cinema, which was otherwise so willing to exploit drug humor. In the 1981 comedy *Trading Places*, a successful lawyer falls victim to a conspiracy intended to ruin his life. He is framed for possession of angel dust, to the horror of a police officer, who angrily asks, "Have you ever seen what this stuff does to kids?" At the time, no other drug would have had such dreadful connotations—not cocaine or marijuana, and probably not even heroin. Also in 1981, the police drama *Fort Apache, the Bronx* used angel dust to symbolize mindless animal savagery. A prostitute carries out a random shooting attack on two police officers: she is "whacked" from smoking angel dust, because "that shit'll make you crazy." In 1984, *The Terminator* portrays a killer android who demonstrates incredible feats of strength and endurance, beyond the capabilities of any normal human being. When a witness claims that this could be no normal man, police officers assure her that he was high on angel dust, which prevented him from feeling pain. PCP made monsters.[23]

Gradually, fear and hatred of drugs moved beyond such demonized substances to cover all illicit chemicals. Partly, this new hostility was a response to the expanding use of cocaine, which was originally advertised as fairly harmless. By 1981, though, millions of users had enough experience with the drug, and had seen enough effects on friends and neighbors, to realize that this simply was not the case. Cocaine could be severely addictive, and its abuse could ruin lives. By 1984, even *Rolling Stone* was running head-lines such as "How to Get Off Cocaine." The dangers of drugs were brought home by some celebrity cases, as in 1982, when comedian John Belushi perished from a heroin-cocaine cocktail. Belushi's death was a powerful symbol for a generation that had loved his appearances in *Saturday Night Live* and *Animal House*. Belushi, age thirty-three, was also a definitive boomer. And since official attitudes toward drug use were becoming much harsher, casual users recognized a much greater danger of detection and the likelihood that arrest would lead to a ruinous prison term. Like drunk driving or smoking, drug use ceased to be funny.[24]

America's Crusade

In 1982, the administration formally declared its war on drugs, in large measure a crisis response to growing evidence that the nation's coasts were wide open to narcotic importation. In the late 1970s, Colombian dealers had ensconced themselves in the Bahamas and used light aircraft to fly enormous quantities of drugs into south Florida. The unprecedented scale of import-ation destabilized existing illicit markets, provoking embarrassingly public gang wars and massacres. Authorities were seizing vast quantities of cocaine —two tons in one 1982 raid alone—but this had no effect on street prices, indicating that official action was scarcely even denting the drug trade.[25]

The administration adopted military-oriented measures to confront the apparent menace. The war became literally a military affair on U.S. soil, as the government weakened the prohibition on military involvement in civilian criminal justice, which dated back to the Posse Comitatus Act of 1878. The first modern departure came in 1977, when the governor of Hawaii mobilized the National Guard against the state's marijuana production. By 1981, the federal government formally permitted military activity against drugs, and several joint police-military operations took place, some using Vietnam-era helicopters. Such activity coincided neatly with the administration's efforts to shore up its southern flank against terrorism and Communist subversion emanating from Central America, and it sent a potent message about the potential challenges from the south. In 1982, Vice President Bush was placed in command of the South Florida Drug Task Force, which aimed to coordinate action by the Drug Enforcement Agency, Customs, the FBI, the Bureau of Alcohol, Tobacco, and Firearms, and the Internal Revenue Service, in addition to the army and navy. At one point, zealous anti-drug interdiction so thoroughly blockaded Key West from the rest of Florida that islanders announced their secession from the United States and the creation of a independent republic.[26] Meanwhile, the United States became heavily involved in the internal affairs of Colombia, trying to seek out and destroy drug laboratories and force the arrest and extradition of drug cartel leaders. The policy enjoyed some success, though at enormous cost to the region's stability: by 1984–85, Colombia was on the verge of civil war.[27]

Domestically too, the administration sought a thorough change of attitudes, to reduce the demand side of the drug trade. Already by 1981, the mass media were cooperating with official pleas to deglamorize drug use, as television shows such as *Family Ties* and *Hill Street Blues* depicted drugs as evil, their users as weak or immoral. The contrast can be seen in the work of the team that from 1978 to 1983 produced the sitcom *Taxi*, in which drug-related humor was commonplace. In 1982, the same group produced the show *Cheers*, which not only was free of drug references but featured as its lead character a recovering alcoholic. Staunch anti-drug attitudes would characterize such popular shows as *Miami Vice*. One music hit of 1984 was "I Want a New Drug," by Huey Lewis and the News, but despite its suggestive title, the song is basically an anti-drug anthem, listing the horrors of various illegal substances. No chemical offers an experience comparable to the feeling when "I'm alone with you." The drug use in films such as *Airplane* and *Poltergeist* was already looking embarrassingly dated.

The parents' anti-drug movement found a public face in First Lady Nancy Reagan, who first encountered the issue of youth drug use in 1980. In June 1982, she opened her well-funded "Just say no" campaign, targeted toward middle-class youngsters. President Reagan announced that "starting today, Nancy's crusade to deprive the drug peddlers and suppliers of their customers becomes America's crusade." The influence of the parents' movement was obvious in her denial of any barrier between hard and soft drugs, any sense that marijuana might be one whit less deadly than PCP or cocaine. From now on, the drug war would target all illicit substances equally. In 1983, the Los Angeles Police Department initiated Drug Abuse Resistance Education (DARE) in association with the Los Angeles school system. DARE carried a propaganda message of the absolute evil of all illegal drugs to schools across the country. The new movement particularly stressed the threat to children and families. As Nancy Reagan declared in a major 1986 speech, "Drugs take away the dream from every child's heart and replace it with a nightmare. . . . For the sake of our children, I implore each of you to be unyielding and inflexible in your opposition to drugs." The enemy was especially targeting children: "Drug criminals are ingenious. They work every day to plot a new and better way to steal our children's lives, just as they've done by developing this new drug, crack."[28]

Like many anti-drug advocates over the following decade, Nancy Reagan's primary exhibit proving the danger to children was the "crack baby," the severely weakened and underweight child supposedly born as a result of maternal drug use. As she remarked, "As a parent, I'm especially concerned about what drugs are doing to young mothers and their newborn children." She cited a case from a Florida hospital, reporting on "a baby named Paul [who] lies motionless in an incubator, feeding tubes riddling his tiny body. He needs a respirator to breathe and a daily spinal tap to relieve fluid buildup on his brain. Only one month old, he's already suffered two strokes." The crack baby idea has been extensively attacked over the years, especially for its failure to distinguish between the effects of drugs and those of the poverty that characterized many urban drug users. At the time, though, the story seemed the perfect illustration of adult irresponsibility harming the very young. As a bonus, it also assisted conservative arguments in debates over abortion. As legislatures strove to protect fetal health and welfare, pro-life arguments became more plausible.[29]

So heinously were drugs viewed that most states passed laws prohibiting the sale of so-called drug paraphernalia, devices or accoutrements designed to assist drug use. Again, these laws grew directly from the local campaigns of the parents' movement in the late 1970s, especially in Georgia and Florida. The laws were questionable, because they were so subjective: who decided whether a small spoon was intended as a cocaine spoon? Also, such statutes used public concern about hard drugs as a means of striking at less harmful substances, especially marijuana. But the federal courts upheld the new laws, in the process banning many surviving manifestations of hippiedom and the old counterculture.[30]

At the same time, private enterprise wholeheartedly supported the anti-drug movement. Beginning with major corporations, businesses demanded that employees submit to drug testing as a condition of employment and to random testing while in the workplace. Initially, these tests were applied to workers in sensitive or dangerous jobs, such as transportation and utilities, but tests increasingly became standard for all categories. In 1982, just 5 percent of Fortune 500 companies required some form of employee drug testing; by 1995, that figure had grown to 95 percent. In 1988, a federal law mandated that corporations receiving federal contracts must maintain a drug-free workplace, and the following year, the U.S. Supreme Court accepted the constitutionality of drug testing. The humiliating practice of "pissing on demand" was accepted with astonishingly little protest. It is difficult to credit that anything of the sort would have been tolerated five or ten years previously, or in a society not convinced that drugs of all kinds represented a pernicious social evil. Drug tests represented one of the many penances necessary to expiate the sins of the 1960s.[31]

Crack Wars

Though derided as clumsy and dated, the "Just Say No" campaign neatly coincided with the existing social trend away from drug use. Despite official charges that drug use was soaring out of control, consumption nationwide now began a steep and general decline among all age categories. The proportion of high school seniors who admitted having tried illegal drugs fell precipitously. By 1992, 3.1 percent of seniors reported using cocaine in the previous twelve months, compared with 12.4 percent in 1981.[32]

But far from stopping the incipient drug war, changing usage patterns actually made it more intense. Declining white and middle-class usage and the withdrawal of casual users permitted the drug problem to be framed as a distinctively urban and minority phenomenon. This change was exaggerated by the growing popularity of crack cocaine, which displaced longer-established drugs. Crack acquired all the stereotypical evils associated with PCP, and before that with older demon drugs such as cocaine and marijuana, stereotypes that drew heavily on images of black primitivism and savagery.[33] By 1985, the media had discovered the crack problem, painting it in the most pernicious terms. In 1986, *Time* magazine declared the crack problem the issue of the year, and *Newsweek* proclaimed it the biggest story since Vietnam and Watergate (bigger, that is, than the 1980 hostage crisis or the nuclear confrontation of 1983). The NBC *Nightly News* remarked how crack was "flooding America" as "America's drug of choice."

Crack was an "epidemic," a phrase that suggested analogies with that other lethal situation, the AIDS epidemic, which some believed might end Western civilization.[34]

The national drug war reached new heights in 1985–86. The new approach emphasized strict repression, with extensive use of paramilitary tactics against a drug underworld seen as an evil empire within America's own frontiers. By 1985, the news media offered their first reports of fortified crack houses, which were scenes of open drug taking and sexual excess, and shortly afterward, police departments were using armored vehicles and battering rams to smash into these premises. Such scenes provided a staple of the true crime and real-life policing shows that proliferated in these years, reinforcing the image of the cities as war zones. And as in the realm of terrorism and subversion, the problem found human faces in conspiratorial elites. The terminology of drug lords and cartels, such as the criminal syndicates of Medellín or Cali, dates from these years.[35]

War rhetoric justified stringent new laws. In 1986, the Anti–Drug Abuse Act specified stern mandatory penalties for drug use or distribution. Mandatory life sentences were provided in some instances, and savage minimum sentences were enforced. Such laws had an untold impact on the correctional system. Sweeping new legislation allowed the military to gather intelligence in the war on drugs. And the expanding scope of criminal forfeiture law came close to making the drug war self-financing. Under a 1970 law, authorities were permitted to seize property connected with drug manufacture or trafficking, a concept extended by the Omnibus Crime Control law of 1984. The new legal apparatus meant that goods could be confiscated through a process in which the accused possessed few rights. As confiscated goods were then used to fund further anti-drug efforts, agencies had a potent incentive to seek out and prosecute drug trafficking. There was an enormous vested interest in adopting the harshest possible view of illicit drugs.[36]

Drug Politics

So familiar has anti-drug rhetoric become in the past two decades that it is difficult to recognize what a transformation the drug war wrought in public attitudes. The range of acceptable opinions about drug policy narrowed frighteningly in these years. It had long been impossible for any but the most courageous (or rashest) politicians or professionals to advocate the kind of tolerance that had been freely advocated in the 1970s, but by the mid-1980s, a like taboo extended to suggestions that treatment for drug addiction might replace warlike criminal justice responses. While the culture of drug experimentation in the 1970s was often irresponsible, the conservative reaction of the following decade also went too far. In recent times, this overreaction extended to the legal prohibition of substances that genuinely can have medical or therapeutic uses. Debates over medical marijuana use are a case in point. Panic responses are also illustrated by the debate over synthetic "designer drugs" in 1985, when the government decided to prohibit the substance MDMA, despite copious evidence of its uses in therapy. Yet MDMA had acquired the nickname Ecstasy, and the America of that time had no wish to promote any chemical associated with pleasure, let alone ecstasy. The dominance of law enforcement perspectives has also limited the use of other useful chemicals that might conceivably have illicit markets, most notably certain painkillers.[37]

By the mid-1980s, drugs had become a domestic hot-button issue quite as potent as Communism in earlier decades, and charges that rivals were soft on drugs flew freely during congressional election campaigns. This in itself represented a major conservative victory, since framing drug issues in terms of a drug war demanded an acknowledgment of themes critical to Reagan administration policy. The drug crisis—and few doubted there was a crisis—resulted from personal immorality, weakness, and criminality. Drug dealers were the epitome of evil. To quote Los Angeles police chief Daryl Gates, "The casual drug user ought to be taken out and shot." Personal depravity was a primary cause of many pressing social failings, and the crack epidemic especially was blamed for the appalling problems facing the inner cities. Poverty, social dysfunction, and the calamitous state of minority youth were all attributed to drugs, rather than to social and economic failings. By the late 1980s, inner-city crises were largely discussed in terms of drugs, with the proper remedies to be found in effective policing and sentencing, coupled with firm border controls. Anti-drug militants adopted wholeheartedly the "broken windows" argument proposed by James Q. Wilson and George Kelling, who suggested that police could effectively promote social order by rigorously enforcing laws against minor nuisance offenders, including vagrants, drunks, and petty drug dealers—exactly the "harmless" deviants whose rights had been assiduously defended by the federal courts in the previous decade.[38]

The criminal justice response to social crisis enjoyed widespread appeal among both political parties. Who needed an urban policy when they had the drug war? These perceptions became quite profitable as developers demolished and rebuilt decaying cities during the 1980s. Activists were less likely to protest when redevelopment was portrayed not as the elimination of poor people's homes but as the draining of noxious moral swamps.

Overseas too, the drug war permitted behavior that would have been political suicide a decade previously. Though the heavy-handed intervention in Colombia may have been necessary, it was still a striking departure for a United States that remained nervous about military interventions overseas. Images of helicopters, advisers, and jungle warfare still triggered understandable flashbacks. Yet the drug war justified massive political and paramilitary intervention in Colombia and other Latin American nations in a way that never would have been tolerated in a struggle ostensibly directed against Communism. U.S. intervention in El Salvador and Nicaragua infuriated congressional leaders and provoked popular demonstrations; intervention in the vastly more consequential nation of Colombia aroused no such passions.[39]

Drugs provided an effective trump card for promoting Third World intervention. In 1984, the drug war obtained one of its most significant allies when cartel pilot Barry Seal secretly defected to U.S. authorities. He then acted as an undercover agent within cartel operations, producing copious intelligence about network activities. In one operation, he landed in Nicaragua, where Sandinista officials were photographed loading the aircraft with cocaine. So politically valuable was this smoking gun that Reagan himself cited it in broadcasts designed to persuade Congress to support the contras. Even for a public unconvinced that the Sandinistas posed any political threat, it was still damning to frame them in terms of other problems that were more immediately convincing, including terrorism, drug dealing, and child endangerment. As Reagan declared, "I know that every American parent concerned about the drug problem will be outraged to learn that top Nicaraguan government officials are deeply involved in drug trafficking." Not only were the Sandinistas running a Communist police state, but "now they're exporting drugs to poison our youth and linking up with the terrorists of Iran, Libya, the Red Brigades, and the PLO." The plea was influential, although the premature exposure of Seal's activities ruined the undercover operation and led to his murder.[40] In the same years, U.S. attacks on Fidel Castro's Cuba cited his regime's involvement in cocaine trafficking as a new reason for wishing to remove him. In the mid-1980s, the administration identified narcoterrorism as a pressing security issue.[41]

So overwhelming was any possible drug connection that Democrats themselves sought to use the same weapon, to outdrug the Republicans. This became a major theme in the Iran-contra scandal, which dominated

Washington politics from 1986 through 1988. The admitted offenses were serious enough, with arms trafficking, financial diversion, and perjury in congressional testimony. For many liberals, though, the real unexploded bomb in the affair was the cocaine connection. Through these years, it was repeatedly charged that the contras were heavily engaged in drug trafficking, with the full consent and acquiescence of the U.S. government, and specifically the CIA. Like many scandals, the charges metastasized in the retelling, and one variant still widely believed in African-American communities holds that the CIA had a double motive in promoting the drug trade: besides trying to fund their paramilitary friends, the agency was deliberately flooding black ghettos with crack cocaine in order to destabilize black America and justify escalating repression. The story is commonly associated with charges that the U.S. government spread AIDS in black communities.[42]

Charges of governmental drug trafficking found an official focus in the Senate Subcommittee on Narcotics, Law Enforcement, and Foreign Policy, chaired by Massachusetts senator John Kerry. In 1989, after the fiercest passions had cooled, the Kerry committee found that the CIA had indeed turned a blind eye to drug dealing by contras and others, while continuing to channel funds to these groups. The findings disappointed conspiracy theorists, because the committee failed to identify high-level participation in drug operations.

Though the events of these years are obscured by so many charges, not to mention instances of deliberate falsification and provocation, we can probably say that both sides, left and right, had some degree of truth on their side. Cuban and Nicaraguan leftist forces were dealing in cocaine, as were rightist forces such as the contras, and some U.S. government agents assuredly dabbled. The potential profits offered a temptation too immense for most to resist. In their different ways, both Reagan and Kerry were reading the situation accurately enough. But what should strike us about these controversies is how totally drug-related American scandals had become. For liberals, the potential gains were obvious enough. If the administration was in fact implicated in cocaine dealing, that not only invalidated all its recent rhetoric but justified a political upheaval at least as thorough as Watergate. And if charges of drug dealing could revive the anti-CIA fervor of the mid-1970s, all the better.

In practice, though, the liberal emphasis on drug politics served only to reinforce the position—stated explicitly by the administration of George H. W. Bush—that drugs, specifically cocaine, were the single most pressing issue facing the United States. Drugs defined social policy, and once Soviet Communism vanished, drugs defined national security. The fizzling of the contra cocaine scandal left Republicans firmly in command of the drug issue, which they presented utterly in their own terms. And as in matters of crime and terrorism, the consequence was an aggressive restoration of the power and prestige of criminal justice agencies as they had operated before the crises of the 1960s.

The Abuse Epidemic

Hell is for children.

—Pat Benatar

Reagan-era concerns about crime, drugs, and terrorism successfully reshaped public policy in broadly conservative ways. Just as effective in changing attitudes was the powerful child protection movement that originated in the late 1970s. During the Reagan years, claims about the scale and severity of child abuse swelled to astonishing proportions, as the villains believed to be threatening American children acquired ever more diabolical qualities. So marked was this escalation that by the mid-1980s, widely credited charges identified literal devil worshipers as leading perpetrators of abuse and molestation. Even if these claims were rejected, the purely secular aspects of the perceived crisis were harrowing enough. Child protection became a national social orthodoxy, a package of basic beliefs and assumptions that permeated discourse on a variety of seemingly unrelated issues. Though child abuse issues rarely surface in conventional histories of the United States in the 1970s and 1980s, they are critical to understanding popular attitudes toward gender and sexuality, as well as toward law enforcement.[1]

Especially when framed in sexual terms, child protection enjoyed a central role in social ideology almost equal to the anti-drug movement. Indeed, the two movements overlapped closely. Anti-drug activists stressed that the substances they were targeting were so evil precisely because they damaged American children and teenagers. Both threats stemmed from conspiratorial rings and cartels. Like the drug war, the effort to protect children gave ammunition to those determined to condemn the libertinism of the 1960s.

Watching the Children

No later than 1981, the sexual revolution was meeting social resistance, as herpes and later AIDS gave a new credibility to the concept of sexual restraint. Contributing to the reaction against sexual excess was the perceived epidemic of child sexual abuse, which was believed to reflect the national quest for hedonistic liberation.

Since 1977, concern about child protection had created an institutional structure dedicated to the investigation and exposure of sexual abuse, as child abuse specialists found institutional homes in universities, charities, and social work agencies. A cascade of works about abuse, incest, and sexual exploitation reached flood proportions by 1983–84.[2] The federal government strongly supported research into child abuse issues through agencies such as the Justice Department, NCCAN, and the National Institute of Mental Health. Federal support intensified under the Reagan administration, at a time when social welfare spending was under wide-ranging attack. In 1984, the new National Center for Missing and Exploited Children (NCMEC) became a leading force in disseminating extreme claims about child endangerment, while issues of investigating and prosecuting child abuse became a funding priority for the National Institute of Justice. In 1986, the Children's Justice Act provided federal grants for programs to improve the prosecution of child abuse cases.[3]

Initially because of the mandatory reporting laws of the mid-1970s, the statistics of child abuse were soaring, though activists asserted that the boom reflected a real change in conduct. In this view, American children were being abused in vastly greater numbers than hitherto. Between 1976 and 1986, reports of child abuse and neglect across the whole United States rose from 669,000 to over 2 million. In the same decade, reports of *sexual* abuse rose eighteenfold. Many spoke of child abuse as an "epidemic," with all that implied for the uncontrollable spread and geometric expansion of a disease—just like AIDS, just like crack cocaine, and similarly the product of the moral swamp of the 1960s and its aftermath.

Still more alarming were the figures for child abuse as determined by self-report studies among adults, who were asked to recall abusive behavior they had suffered in childhood. By the early 1980s, studies were commonly finding a reported incidence of at least 20 percent among girls. Diana Russell's much-quoted research indicated that 38 percent of girls had been abused before the age of eighteen, 28 percent before fourteen. In 1985, the *Los Angeles Times* reported a poll finding that "at least 22 percent of Americans have been victims of child sexual abuse." Media accounts eventually agreed that at some point, abuse affected between 20 and 30 percent of children. All such figures should be taken with caution, since most defined abuse very broadly, often including acts involving no physical contact. In popular retellings, though, these figures were cited for children who fell victim to extreme molestation, such as rape and sodomy.[4]

If true, such findings demanded national soul-searching: what had gone so wrong with American families, and especially American men, that they had unleashed such an epidemic upon their young? These claims also raised critical questions about the workings of the child protection system. Even with the recent upsurge in reported child abuse, the number of abuse victims coming to light was nowhere near what might be expected from self-report studies. Why, it was asked, were the authorities not encountering millions of child victims who represented the tragic dark figure of the abuse statistics? The belief in the vast hidden problem of abuse demanded newer and more proactive methods of interviewing child victims. Above all, investigators must follow the crucial watchwords, "believe the children." No matter how bizarre the charges or the means by which they had been produced, reports of abuse must never be rejected. Activists were determined not to repeat the mistakes of Freud, who had notoriously come to view the many tales of incest and seduction he heard from his female patients as fantasies, rather than actual memories. Childhood trauma was real.[5]

New views of child abuse transformed the therapeutic professions and the related movements promoting self-help and recovery. Through the 1980s, ever more adults, especially women, identified themselves as victims of childhood molestation or incest, with the assumption that these early traumas had shaped their whole lives and lay at the root of every misfortune or problem they had encountered. Sufferers categorized themselves as "survivors," a term borrowed from victims of cancer, suggesting that molestation was a comparably lethal and life-changing affliction. Though expressed in psychological terms, the recovery movement had a powerful religious quality, with its core ideas of the loss of primal innocence through sexual sin and the recovery of an untarnished childlike state. The process by which the incest is recalled and the path to healing begun has much in common with the evangelical language of conversion: to recover is to be born again. Also recalling religious language is the emphasis on unquestioning faith, of belief in the testimony of others, even if it directly contradicts common sense. The children, external or internal, must be believed. By the mid-1980s, pop psychology was acquiring an explicitly religious bent, partly through the influence of Scott Peck, author of the hugely successful *The Road Less Traveled*. Peck's accounts of his patients stressed the objective nature of evil and even praised exorcism techniques. Child abuse was acquiring a demonic quality.[6]

Stories about sexual abuse and violence became part of popular culture. Abuse stories were a major theme for television in 1984, when NBC's highly rated documentary *Silent Shame* offered an alarming exposé of the hazards of child abuse, child pornography, and prostitution. Fictional productions also popularized the concerns of experts and professionals. In October 1983, the television movie *Adam* dramatized the case of six-year-old Adam Walsh, kidnapped and murdered in a sensational 1981 case. In early 1984, *Something About Amelia* depicted incest in an outwardly respectable middle-class family. This made-for-TV movie showed the perpetrator not as a stereotypical sex criminal but as a likable professional played by comedy star Ted Danson. The implication was that abuse could happen to any child, even in the most seemingly normal environment. Critically praised, the film earned some of the highest ratings ever achieved by a television movie, topped only by such recent blockbusters as *The Day After*. Also that year, Farrah Fawcett's appearance in *The Burning Bed* drew national attention to another form of male exploitation, domestic violence and battering.

Conspiracies

Not only was child abuse an epidemic of appalling proportions, but there were worrying signs of criminal organization. In this view, children were being abused, abducted, and murdered by shadowy sex rings. Conspiratorial ideas were rife following the Atlanta murders. One focus of concern was NAMBLA, the pedophile pressure group that since its foundation in 1978 had enjoyed a thorny relationship with the mainstream gay movement. In 1981, some weeks after the arrest of Wayne Williams in Atlanta, several NAMBLA leaders were arrested in New York state. The following year, a number of men and teenage boys were arrested in a Massachusetts house that was described in the media as a safe house, a "sex den," and the headquarters of a sex ring which entrapped boys. The media linked NAMBLA members to one of the most notorious crimes of recent years, the 1979 disappearance of six-year-old Etan Patz in Manhattan, as well as to other kidnappings and disappearances of small children.[7]

NAMBLA was portrayed as an absolute social evil. The organization was depicted as "a group of child kidnappers, pornographers and pimps" and perhaps child-killers, with an "international sex ring" lurking behind the front of the civil rights organization. In 1983, the FBI and other agencies formed a task force to investigate "the kidnapping and selling of children and their use in porn films, the murder of children and adolescents by kidnappers." Though these charges remained in the realm of rumor, the NAMBLA investigation seemed to establish the reality of claims about organized sex rings preying on children.[8]

Claims about organized molestation were boosted by the support of former FBI agent Ted Gunderson, a highly unorthodox source, but one much cited by journalists and authors. (Among other things, Gunderson believes that "the fall of the World Trade Center was executed by Satanists who have infiltrated the Government.") Partly through his influence, child protection activists described syndicated networks of powerful and often lethal molesters. The sex ring theme now entered the realm of mystery and detective novels, as organized and highly placed pedophiles were depicted in Jonathan Kellerman's popular thriller *When the Bough Breaks* (1985) and Andrew Vachss's 1985 novel *Flood*.[9] By the mid-1980s, older claims about child pornography were merging with other terrifying social menaces, including child molestation and abduction. In 1985, an exposé of "the shame of the nation" in a family magazine noted "a dramatic increase in child sexual abuse over the past five years in this country, at least half of them involving children compelled to participate in the making of pornography. According to one Los Angeles Police Department estimate, at least 300,000 children under the age of 16 are involved in the nationwide child pornography racket." This problem was connected with "even more dramatic increases in the number of missing children."[10]

In fact, all the evidence suggests a dramatic decline in overt child pornography manufacture in the United States since the late 1970s; the last major commercial operation based in the United States was closed down in 1982. Child porn activity was not booming, any more than the actual incidence of child abuse was. Nevertheless, the claims gave wonderful ammunition to activists. In 1986, one anti-pornography crusader claimed that "each year, fifty thousand missing children are victims of pornography. Most are kidnapped, raped, abused, filmed for porno magazines and movies and, more often than not, murdered." The Meese Commission on Pornography, which held controversial hearings in 1985–86, gave support to such speculations when it urged the creation of a national task force to examine "possible links between sex rings, child pornography and organized crime . . . [and] possible linkages between multi-victim, multi-perpetrator child sex rings throughout the United States."[11]

If sex rings were out there, then it only remained to catch and convict their members more convincingly than in the recent NAMBLA case. By 1982, prosecutors and therapists were alerted to the likelihood that molestation cases might have complex conspiratorial dimensions that needed to be explored vigorously, and the more strongly people believe in such linkages, the more prone they are to find them. Success was all the more likely when child victims were interviewed by therapists using experimental new techniques predicated on the belief that abuse had occurred and that the child must be weaned away from his or her state of denial. In such circumstances, accusations were readily forthcoming. In Bakersfield, California, a 1982 case began with an accusation that a man had abused his two daughters, but the affair spread to charges that the family was part of a network of adults who exchanged children for sexual purposes. Within two years, seven further "child sex rings" had been alleged in Bakersfield, with stories of satanic rituals and murdered children. Individuals from these cases still remain in prison today, though the affair is widely recognized as a grave miscarriage of justice. At the time, though, the Bakersfield experience convinced investigators of what a serious menace they were facing.[12]

Missing and Murdered

The incessant diet of media horror stories sent a powerful message about how endangered children were in a sick American society. The popular impact of such tales is suggested by the upsurge of news reports during 1982 concerning alleged incidents of Halloween sadism, in which children's treats are said to be poisoned or tampered with. These stories, almost entirely baseless, followed closely after the sensational Tylenol poisonings.[13]

In addition, the public proved willing to accept media statistics about social threats that on the surface should have stirred instant skepticism. One was the panic over missing children that raged from 1982 through 1985 and which occasionally resurfaced for years afterward. Of course, some children do vanish, and some are murdered: Etan Patz and Adam Walsh were two tragic examples. But for several years, activists and bureaucratic agencies were offering incredible figures for just how prevalent this problem had become. Reportedly, fifty thousand children disappeared every year, and 1.5 million in all were now missing; or perhaps 1.5 million went missing every year? Accounts varied. In 1982, acknowledging the national crisis, the U.S. Senate designated May 25 as National Missing Children's Day. The director of NCMEC lent the weight of his office to the claim that "at least twenty to fifty thousand kids are abducted each year in the United States and are never seen again."[14]

Commercial enterprises showed their public spirit by adopting innovative means of finding the legions of the lost. It was in these years that milk cartons began displaying pictures of the missing, bringing the crisis into every home. Just as repackaged medicines were a constant reminder of the criminal forces besieging society, so every kitchen now contained visual symbols of child exploitation. Activists also exploited public fears. Throughout the decade, the huge fund-raising operation of Bruce Ritter's Covenant House suggested the desperate need to "save" runaways, who were depicted as rural or suburban kids lost in the urban jungle and in constant danger from sexual predators. Ritter also vastly exaggerated the scale of the problem by counting as endangered "runaways" every young person who stayed away from home for a night or two.[15]

From first to last, the missing-children crisis was spurious. Most missing children disappear in entirely nonsuspicious circumstances and are soon found again, while longer-term disappearances usually involve noncustodial parents in messy divorce cases. Fewer than a hundred children each year might be kidnapped by strangers—a horrible enough statistic, but not enough to justify the mass panic of the mid-1980s. A little thought should have suggested that if so many children were really going missing, then every neighborhood would be agitated about some recent occurrence in that locality, as obviously was not the case. Abductions remained sufficiently rare to be very noticeable when they really did happen. The missing-children affair was possible only because of the cumulative effects of several years of stories on related dangers to children.[16]

Hunters

The missing-children issue acquired new faces in the form of the sex ring and, even more so, the predatory serial killer. Serial murder had consistently been making national headlines since the mid-1970s, with a new ultimate villain surfacing every few months. Following in the tracks of Harris's *Red Dragon*, serial murder fiction became a whole subgenre located somewhere between horror and mystery, acquainting a mass public with the supposed characteristics of this monstrous type of offender. But the problem leaped to an entirely new plane of seriousness in the fall of 1983, when an arrested criminal named Henry Lee Lucas confessed to several hundred murders committed over the previous decade across the country.[17] Lucas epitomized the worst public fears of the serial killer as an itinerant monster from whom no one was safe. Slasher films, it seemed, were recounting the sober truth.

In his interviews with police and press, the killer calmly and lucidly discussed the most grisly crimes. During 1984 and 1985, interviews were shown on ABC's *20/20* and *Good Morning America* and on CBS' *Nightwatch*.[18]

Lucas was portrayed as a manifestation of a national crisis. A *New York Times* story headlined, "Thirty-five Murderers of Many People Could Be at Large, Says US." (The story appeared on October 26, 1983, at exactly the time of the Grenada invasion, which similarly pointed out the need to stand up against external enemies.) According to this story, and hundreds more that followed over the next two years, the menace—freshly christened "serial murder"—was entirely new in its scale. Following the pattern alleged for Lucas, the new breed of superpredator was a sexually motivated killer, a Ripper mutilating his victims, who were almost always women or children. He roamed the country, killing victims in perhaps dozens of states, thus preventing individual police departments from connecting the individual crimes as part of a murder series. If Lucas was anything to go by, he killed perhaps seventy or a hundred people each and every year, and as the Justice Department now calculated, there might be thirty-five such individuals active at any given time. Together, they killed between four thousand and five thousand victims each year, accounting for between 20 and 25 percent of all homicides. As the *Times* headlined in 1984, it was essential to stop such criminals "before they kill again and again and again." The serial murder scare apparently gave a solid foundation to claims that many of the nation's missing youngsters were victims of grotesque serial killers such as Gacy, Bundy, or now Lucas, and so the missing-children problem segued into the still more frightening issue of "missing and murdered children."[19]

Virtually everything in this account was bogus. Not only was Lucas innocent of most or all of the killings he boasted about, but no serial killer on record has ever committed murders at such a rate. The estimate for the annual number of victims of this type of offender is perhaps 1 or 2 percent, rather than the astronomical figures presented as sober orthodoxy between 1983 and 1985. Particularly rare are sexually motivated killings of children, which in these years were discussed as commonplace.[20]

Treated Like Garbage

But inflated figures achieved credence through the efforts of a core of well-connected child protection advocates, who received a platform from some powerful political leaders. The most important were U.S. senators such as Paul Simon of Illinois, Paula Hawkins of Florida, and above all Arlen Specter of Pennsylvania, whose chairmanship of the active Juvenile Justice Subcommittee of the Judiciary Committee allowed him to mount frequent media spectacles. Obviously, no single political agenda was at work here. Simon was strongly liberal, and while the Republican Specter is a fervent exponent of law-and-order politics, his witnesses often included feminist activists. Not until 1991 would Specter's role in the Clarence Thomas hearings make him an arch-villain for feminists, who were appalled by his adversarial questioning of Anita Hill. For members of both parties, though, claims about child endangerment gave a precious opportunity to show one's determination to safeguard children against abominable predators.[21]

Between 1982 and 1985, a series of federal hearings exposed the supposedly intertwined issues of child pornography, pedophilia, serial murder, and missing children. In 1982, the Juvenile Justice Subcommittee held separate hearings on child pornography and on missing and exploited children. Activities in 1983 included hearings on child abduction and on "patterns of murders committed by one person in large numbers with no apparent rhyme, reason or motivation," that is, on the newly defined menace of serial murder.[22]

For journalists, the successive committee hearings were a goldmine, each guaranteed to produce headlines. Not only were the issues covered sensational in themselves, but the witnesses included a roster of media-savvy activists who could be relied on for quotable remarks. Among the frequent witnesses were John Walsh, father of the murdered Adam Walsh, who was reputedly a victim of Lucas's partner Ottis Toole. Other voices included prolific crime writer Anne Rule, as well as Kenneth Wooden, who in 1977 had produced the pioneering 60 Minutes exposé of "kiddie porn." Over the next decade, Wooden's role as a producer on newsmagazine shows such as 60 Minutes and 20/20 gave him a uniquely powerful platform from which to issue warnings about child murderers and abductors. He would also work with Geraldo Rivera, in 1988 producing Rivera's special Devil Worship: Exposing Satan's Underground, which gave unprecedented visibility to the satanism scare.[23]

Walsh and Wooden presented wrenching testimony about threats to children. Walsh related the issue of missing children to that of multiple sex killers, claiming that "the number of random unsolved murders of women and children in this country rose from 600 in 1966 to 4,500 in 1981." Every hour, he stated, 205 children were reported missing in this country, a figure corresponding to 1.8 million cases per annum, and many would be found murdered. Kenneth Wooden asserted that "children in America are treated like garbage. Raped and killed, their young bodies are disposed of in plastic bags, in trash trucks, and left in city dumps." Specter agreed: "The molestation of children has now reached epidemic proportions."[24]

The Devil Rides In

At just the time that concern over serial murder and child abuse was peaking in 1984, the threat to America's children suddenly become even worse, with new accounts of mass abuse cases that seemed to demonstrate human wickedness at its most extreme. The prototype involved teachers at the prestigious McMartin preschool in Los Angeles, who had allegedly molested hundreds of their young charges over a period of years, threatening them with brutal torture if they spoke out. The case inspired dozens of similar cases around the nation, and increasingly the abuse described took on an explicitly religious coloring. The McMartin affair, it appeared, was the first public exposure of satanic ritual abuse in modern America. Within a few years, tens of thousands of Americans—mainly women—reported having experienced such atrocities in childhood. Hard though it now seems to credit, the most extreme charges were presented regularly not in the marginal tracts of isolated conspiracy cranks but in the main media outlets: television networks and respectable newspapers.[25]

In retrospect, most observers regard the whole satanism scare of the 1980s as a classic example of a great deal of smoke being produced with no fire. Twenty years later, no so-called ritual abuse case has ever produced a shred of evidence to corroborate charges of ritualistic or satanic behavior. Yet however morbid it appears, the satanic affair was an extreme and controversial example of much more general social trends. Quite apart from any satanic elements, it seemed that no charge about conspiratorial threats against children was so extreme, no statistic so ludicrous, that it could not gain immediate acceptance. If generations could have been unaware of the real threat of "regular" child abuse, who was to deny that the modern world was in a comparable state of denial about ritualistic abuse?[26]

The McMartin school case began in 1983 with an accusation from a deranged woman. Unwisely, authorities suggested that worried parents take their children to be interviewed by therapists specializing in child abuse, who soon produced what they thought was abundant evidence that the school had for years been the scene of systematic child abuse. Based on these charges, seven teachers were arrested and charged, and the coverage by respected media outlets such as *20/20* absolutely accepted their guilt. But what kind of crimes had taken place? Based on recent stories, obvious interpretations were offered. For some, the school was a center for making child pornography, or else the children were being exploited by elite pedophiles who could afford to have them flown to remote cities to be molested. Might an organization such as NAMBLA be at work? Gradually, the children's fantasies about stars, animals, and funny clothes were integrated into a new picture of cult abuse, drawn heavily from the 1980 book *Michelle Remembers*. Once that synthesis was complete, it was ready to be applied time and again. One satanic ring had been detected, so perhaps others were still operating behind the cloak of other schools and day care centers. New cases erupted in Minnesota and California, North Carolina and Massachusetts.[27]

Therapists and investigators across the country now knew exactly what questions to ask their young patients and, increasingly, adults seeking to uncover the roots of their troubled lives. As therapists explored the realm of recovered memory, some asked just how those traumatic memories had been suppressed in the first place. The answer seemed to be that cults of the sort denounced through the 1970s had become highly adept in brainwashing and programming. The mid-1970s anti-CIA mythology now returned in full force, with satanic cults as the expert manipulators of memory, the creators of programmed assassins. Whatever their motives, questioners extracted the answers they wanted from their suggestible witnesses.[28]

A growing mythology suggested the practice of widespread human sacrifice. By late 1984, investigators of a ritual abuse case in Jordan, Minnesota, were exploring rumors of ritual murders, and charges proliferated the following year. On television, *20/20* publicized the allegations, with Kenneth Wooden as a prime mover. In 1985, a segment of that show entitled "The Devil Worshipers" argued that satanic cults were widely active in child ritual abuse and human sacrifice. Shortly afterward, national media reported on an Ohio sheriff who attempted to excavate the alleged site of satanic rituals, where dozens of sacrificial murder victims were believed to be buried. In fact, no remains were found. Though this affair was a fiasco, the concept of ritual murder cults was not laid to rest. The idea gained new strength from images of California serial killer Richard Ramirez, known as the Night Stalker. At his arraignment in 1985, he displayed to the court a pentagram drawn on his palm, and shouted, "Hail Satan!" The mythology of contemporary satanism was born. By the end of the decade, thousands of police officers and social workers around the nation had attended seminars warning of the danger from occult crime.[29]

Yet however weird the concocted diabolical claims seem, they were not a whit more outlandish than the conventional orthodoxies of the time concerning child protection. Even those who scoffed at ritual abuse tales— and such individuals were rare—still commonly accepted that a quarter of small girls would be abused at some point in their childhood; that fifty thousand children were abducted each year, and that many or most would be murdered; that conspiratorial pedophile rings were seeking children to abduct and molest; that two million Americans belonged to dangerous and destructive cults, which controlled their members by brainwashing and violence; that child pornography was a multi-billion-dollar industry exploiting hundreds of thousands of American children. In each case, such claims were amply vouched for by official agencies, including the Justice Department and the FBI, whose assertions were supported by politicians of all political shades. In this environment, it hardly seemed fanciful that diabolists might also be contributing to the general mayhem.

Cui Bono?

The perceived threats from abuse and random violence naturally inspired calls for action, in terms of both new laws and more far-reaching social changes. Certainly, no one political cause or faction benefited from the reaction to the child abuse scare, but social conservatives certainly reaped their reward.

Federal law enforcement agencies were among the immediate beneficiaries of the crime panics. As the drug issue was proving, requesting resources to confront a criminal danger encouraged legislators to ease the restrictions placed on federal agencies during the post-Watergate years. Recognizing the serial murder problem as one of roaming killers moved the issue into the federal domain and demanded that the FBI receive additional resources for data collection. After a decade of bitter public hostility toward expanded federal powers in policing, the Justice Department now won support for an enhanced interstate role in fighting the menace from serial killers. By 1985, this led to the creation of a new computer system and the National Center for the Analysis of Violent Crime (NCAVC), which sought to identify and profile violent offenders. The whole modern mythology of criminal profiling grows directly out of the serial murder panic of these years. Though serial killers were the initial targets, FBI officials made it clear that this apparatus would soon be deployed against other violent offenses, including "rape, child molestation, arson and bombing." The new program was the Violent Criminal Apprehension Program (VICAP), and it became operational in spring 1985, exactly the time that journalists were finally demonstrating the massive fictions in the confessions of Henry Lee Lucas, the man whose activities sparked the whole panic. The formation of the NCAVC was regarded as sufficiently important to be announced by President Reagan personally, in a 1984 address to the National Sheriffs Association. This was, after all, a war, and a war needed intelligence. A news account of the inauguration of the NCAVC in 1984 was headlined "FBI Launches Frontal Attack on Serial Killers."[30]

Since the abuse and murder of children was seen as an ultimate evil, any other conduct that could plausibly be linked to this issue received a like stigma. Similar linkages were attempted in moral debates, as when conservatives used the gay-pedophile connection in referendum votes. Through the 1980s and 1990s, anti-gay campaigners repeatedly used news footage of NAMBLA's banner flying at gay pride events. In debates over gay rights, conservatives attacked the official promotion of "homosexuality, pedophilia, sadism or masochism," suggesting a direct relationship between these "perverted" behaviors, and linking homosexuality to violence and to offenses against children. In a time when the gay cause was already so embattled by the AIDS crisis, this was a weighty argument.[31]

Conservatives could also point to other social changes that had made America such a perilous environment for children, especially in the changing role of women. As the day care scandals spread in 1984–85, even traditionally liberal commentators expressed concern about the careless abandonment of children to potentially deadly caregivers. In the *New York Times,* a 1984 story drew heavily on FBI sources to indicate a pervasive day care menace, which grew directly from "the rise in the numbers of single working mothers and working couples [which] may have put more children at risk of abuse," as preschools and day care centers "are being used increasingly by child pornographers and those who desire sexual relations with children." The McMartin horrors, here described uncritically, were directly attributed to the number of two-paycheck families in that locality and, by implication, the irresponsibility of mothers going out to work. One McMartin parent was left to present the moral message: "We were buying freedom. That's what everyone is buying. It allowed us to do other things during the day." This liberation, we are meant to infer, was bought at the price of the rape of their children.[32]

It was in the area of pornography that the child protection issue would demonstrate its greatest symbolic power. In the early 1980s, a number of different political movements wished to reimpose restrictions on pornography. Apart from the obvious conservative and religious objections, feminist groups wanted to destroy what they saw as a leading source of violence against women. From 1982 on, feminists tried to ban pornography through local and city ordinances. Minneapolis passed one such measure in 1983, to combat "a substantial threat to the health, safety, peace, welfare, and equality of citizens in the community." In Cambridge, Massachusetts, a proposed ordinance in 1985 defined pornography as "a systematic practice of exploitation and subordination based on sex which differentially harms women . . . [it] creates public and private harassment, persecution and denigration; promotes injury and degradation such as rape, batter, sexual abuse of children, and prostitution." Ultimately, most such efforts were largely defeated in the courts, and pornography prosecutions continued to be very difficult.[33] Yet bringing in the issue of children did win some legal and judicial victories. By exposing child pornography, activists were trying to stigmatize all pornography and demand a new legal offensive while avoiding libertarian objections. Every new allegation about organized child abuse prompted activists to claim that child porn was at the heart of the matter.

Even a society that largely tolerated the private use of sexually explicit materials showed itself reluctant to accept anything that could be classified as child pornography. In 1977, the federal Sexual Exploitation of Children Act prohibited the manufacture or commercial distribution of obscene material involving subjects under sixteen years of age, and this measure virtually eliminated the open availability of child porn materials in adult stores. By 1982, the courts had interpreted this law to created a much lower standard of condemnation for sexually explicit materials involving youngsters. Where adult subjects were concerned, prosecutors had to establish that materials were obscene, which was next to impossible, but for children, the only question was whether the images were indecent, a much easier matter. In this area too, prosecutors could convict an individual who merely possessed indecent images, rather than as in adult cases, where only manufacturers or distributors were targeted.

Federal actions against child pornography transformed approaches to sexuality not just among children but also among older teenagers. In 1984, the radical Child Protection Act was sponsored by Arlen Specter and publicized once more by sensational hearings before his subcommittee. This law virtually removed the whole category of child pornography from First Amendment protection. Any depiction of sex involving a minor was automatically obscene, making it child pornography and therefore illeg: This law also raised the age of a minor for these purposes from sixtee eighteen, at a stroke extending the status of child to millions of Ar w adolescents, most old enough to marry. The draconian quality o ues laws made filmmakers and television producers reluctant to e for a of youth sexuality, in order to avoid legal conflicts. When t as Folk U.S. audience in 2000, even a television series as liberated ds freely had to avoid the portrayal of a mid-teens gay chara t of strict depicted in the British original. The powerful— concern over child pornography permitted the limits to teenage sexuality.[34]

Guilt by association also had a religious dimension, in justifying attacks on fringe religions and cults. Though such activity declined after the end of the 1970s, some surviving extremist sects were targeted by the new administration. In 1985, the Justice Department secured the deportation of the Indian guru Bhagwan Shree Rajneesh, whose followers had taken over a small Oregon community. In the same year, a confrontation with Philadelphia police resulted in the bloody destruction of the headquarters of the MOVE cult, together with most of the neighborhood in which it stood.[35] But especially for the growing churches of the Christian evangelical and Pentecostal movements, the satanic issue justified a more comprehensive attack on the religious fringe. Many of the new evangelical churches believed that the world would suffer enormous chaos, violence, and injustice before the ultimate triumph of Christ. In this scenario, the end times would be marked by the rise of evil and diabolical forces heralding the coming of the Antichrist. Through the 1980s, one could find in any evangelical bookstore whole shelves of books, tracts, and videos asserting that these conditions were now being fulfilled through the upsurge of ritual abuse and murder.

Concern over satanism spilled over to condemn any other kind of religious or supernatural practice that might be seen as vaguely occult, including astrology, New Age religion, and even the observance of Halloween. All were condemned by televangelists, as well as by the substantial publishing industry that catered to the evangelical subculture. For years, evangelicals had attacked New Age and esoteric dabbling for the way it subverted gender by exalting the role of women prophets and the divine feminine, and for its Asian-inspired ideas. Now, New Age and occult ideas were charged with opening the way to devil worship, which was seen not just as another kind of religious practice but as a form of violent crime lethally dangerous to American children. By the late 1980s, evangelical campaigners against satanism and occult crime acquired a surprising degree of public respectability when media and even police agencies consulted them for their posed expertise in this arcane form of criminality.[36]

Music Wars

Th
clout American history, movements to protect children are often
that with movements to control children, to reimpose discipline
saving eakened in a time of social and political upheaval. The child-
motiv t of the Progressive Era witnessed such an amalgam of
1s, the sense that children were facing massive threats to

and denigration; promotes injury and degradation such as rape, battery, sexual abuse of children, and prostitution." Ultimately, most such efforts were largely defeated in the courts, and pornography prosecutions continued to be very difficult.[33] Yet bringing in the issue of children did win some legal and judicial victories. By exposing child pornography, activists were trying to stigmatize all pornography and demand a new legal offensive while avoiding libertarian objections. Every new allegation about organized child abuse prompted activists to claim that child porn was at the heart of the matter.

Even a society that largely tolerated the private use of sexually explicit materials showed itself reluctant to accept anything that could be classified as child pornography. In 1977, the federal Sexual Exploitation of Children Act prohibited the manufacture or commercial distribution of obscene material involving subjects under sixteen years of age, and this measure virtually eliminated the open availability of child porn materials in adult stores. By 1982, the courts had interpreted this law to created a much lower standard of condemnation for sexually explicit materials involving youngsters. Where adult subjects were concerned, prosecutors had to establish that materials were obscene, which was next to impossible, but for children, the only question was whether the images were indecent, a much easier matter. In this area too, prosecutors could convict an individual who merely possessed indecent images, rather than as in adult cases, where only manufacturers or distributors were targeted.

Federal actions against child pornography transformed approaches to sexuality not just among children but also among older teenagers. In 1984, the radical Child Protection Act was sponsored by Arlen Specter and publicized once more by sensational hearings before his subcommittee. This law virtually removed the whole category of child pornography from First Amendment protection. Any depiction of sex involving a minor was automatically obscene, making it child pornography and therefore illegal. This law also raised the age of a minor for these purposes from sixteen to eighteen, at a stroke extending the status of child to millions of American adolescents, most old enough to marry. The draconian quality of the new laws made filmmakers and television producers reluctant to explore issues of youth sexuality, in order to avoid legal conflicts. When translated for a U.S. audience in 2000, even a television series as liberated as *Queer as Folk* had to avoid the portrayal of a mid-teens gay character, who was freely depicted in the British original. The powerful—and often justified— concern over child pornography permitted the reestablishment of strict limits to teenage sexuality.[34]

Guilt by association also had a religious dimension, in justifying attacks on fringe religions and cults. Though such activity declined after the end of the 1970s, some surviving extremist sects were targeted by the new administration. In 1985, the Justice Department secured the deportation of the Indian guru Bhagwan Shree Rajneesh, whose followers had taken over a small Oregon community. In the same year, a confrontation with Philadelphia police resulted in the bloody destruction of the headquarters of the MOVE cult, together with most of the neighborhood in which it stood.[35] But especially for the growing churches of the Christian evangelical and Pentecostal movements, the satanic issue justified a more comprehensive attack on the religious fringe. Many of the new evangelical churches believed that the world would suffer enormous chaos, violence, and injustice before the ultimate triumph of Christ. In this scenario, the end times would be marked by the rise of evil and diabolical forces heralding the coming of the Antichrist. Through the 1980s, one could find in any evangelical bookstore whole shelves of books, tracts, and videos asserting that these conditions were now being fulfilled through the upsurge of ritual abuse and murder.

Concern over satanism spilled over to condemn any other kind of religious or supernatural practice that might be seen as vaguely occult, including astrology, New Age religion, and even the observance of Halloween. All were condemned by televangelists, as well as by the substantial publishing industry that catered to the evangelical subculture. For years, evangelicals had attacked New Age and esoteric dabbling for the way it subverted gender by exalting the role of women prophets and the divine feminine, and for its Asian-inspired ideas. Now, New Age and occult ideas were charged with opening the way to devil worship, which was seen not just as another kind of religious practice but as a form of violent crime lethally dangerous to American children. By the late 1980s, evangelical campaigners against satanism and occult crime acquired a surprising degree of public respectability when media and even police agencies consulted them for their supposed expertise in this arcane form of criminality.[36]

Music Wars

Throughout American history, movements to protect children are often closely linked with movements to control children, to reimpose discipline that has been weakened in a time of social and political upheaval. The child-saving movement of the Progressive Era witnessed such an amalgam of motives. In the 1980s, the sense that children were facing massive threats to life and limb gave an urgency to official intervention intended to restrain a younger generation seen as flying out of control.

And as so often before, movements to restore discipline focused on symbolic cultural issues, especially rock music. Similar campaigns against immoral music date back at least as far as the ragtime craze of the early twentieth century. Often, the charge was that such new music was inspiring loose sexual morals, or else the damning claim that it was encouraging white people to adopt the ways of blacks and other racial minorities. In the 1980s, though, the child protection movement gave potent new justifications for cultural conservatism. For evangelicals and other conservatives, much rock music was not merely immoral but actively satanic, a charge given credence by the posturings of the heavy metal bands. A fanciful literature even claimed that satanic messages were surreptitiously infiltrated into rock lyrics through the technique of backward masking ("If you play this album backward, it tells you to worship the devil"). As ritual abuse theorists knew, satanic cults were experts at mind control.[37]

But even some responsible observers skeptical of the overt satanic claims themselves became involved in movements to clean up youth culture, trying to recapture the child protection issue for the cause of political liberalism. In the mid-1980s, one visible campaign was led by Tipper Gore, wife of Senator Al Gore, together with the wife of Treasury Secretary James Baker and a number of other political spouses, whose personal connections gave them instant access to well-placed media outlets. Gore herself, with her husband, was one of the many Americans who had been born again since the mid-1970s, and she allied with activist religious groups.

According to Tipper Gore, her quarrel was not with the rock music of her own teenage years in the mid-1960s, but rather with the depraved and violent products of the Gen Xers, among which she included Mötley Crüe, Van Halen, Ozzy Osbourne, Madonna, Cyndi Lauper, Judas Priest, and, incredibly, the saccharine Sheena Easton. The specific detonator for her campaign was Prince's album *Purple Rain,* which contained a song referring to female masturbation.[38] Early in 1985, the new Parents Music Resource Center (PMRC) organized to campaign for decency in music. Through that year, PMRC complaints were heavily reported in the mass media, and congressional hearings followed that fall.

The so-called porn rock hearings produced their share of unintentional farce, with solemn-faced politicians staring in horror at music videos that most fans took to be funny or self-parodying. On the other side, musician Frank Zappa outspokenly condemned the proceedings initiated by the "Mothers of Prevention." He condemned the whole PMRC movement as "a hodgepodge of fundamentalist hogwash and illogical conclusions" and "an ill-conceived piece of nonsense which fails to deliver any real benefits to children, infringes the civil liberties of people who are not children, and promises to keep the courts busy for years." By common consent, Zappa emerged as the hands-down victor of the congressional confrontation, and he later used film of the hearings in his own (funny) music video "Porn Wars." The American Civil Liberties Union mobilized popular recording stars into a "Musical Majority."[39]

But the campaign is significant for the publicity it gave to concerns over uncontrollable youth and for how the satanism issue symbolized other ill-defined fears. For Tipper Gore, rock music and contemporary teen culture created a society in which children were at risk of moral or physical ruin, and she largely accepted the most extreme charges of the contemporary child protection advocates. In modern America, she believed, "nearly two million cases of abuse and neglect were reported in 1985. Some children are lured into cults. Others just go missing, or end up in a simple pauper's grave, never to be identified." Rock music and teen films were blamed for encouraging teen suicide, promoting desensitization to violence and sexual exploitation, and advocating devil worship. For Gore, "the advent of Satanic rock has introduced the accoutrements of Satanism to a generation of kids." Basing herself on the customary range of "cult cops," Gore asserted, "The Satanism that teens toy with is often linked to religious desecration, Satanic graffiti and animal theft and mutilation." These were the views publicized, and accepted, by a group of well-informed and well-connected political figures.[40]

Though the mass abuse cases of the 1980s attracted little direct political attention, they are significant for what they indicate about the public's willingness to believe the unbelievable when claims were framed in terms of social predators and the threat they posed to children. The generation that came of age in the late 1960s was now prepared to believe that America was under assault from armies of nightmare figures. In little over a decade, utopianism and libertarianism transformed into as threatening a social vision as had prevailed in America since the time of Cotton Mather and Jonathan Edwards. The nation moved from the era of Woodstock to that of the witch-hunts.

Wars Without End

This terrible sin took the lives of our American family, innocent children in that building, only because their parents were trying to be good parents as well as good workers . . . one thing we owe those who have sacrificed is the duty to purge ourselves of the dark forces which gave rise to this evil.

—Bill Clinton

However fondly we recall (or imagine) the 1960s, American political culture in the early twenty-first century owes at least as much to the post-1975 decade and its darkening vision of both the personal and political realms. The power of this inheritance is all the more striking considering how messily the Reagan era ended, amidst a welter of political scandals and economic troubles. Despite these setbacks, the rightward shift of the 1980s largely endured, as did the fundamental emphases on themes of conspiracy and evil and the ready use of war analogies.

Evening in America

Several possible dates suggest themselves for the decline of the Reagan era, chiefly in 1986–87. One symbolic turning point occurred in January 1986, when the space shuttle *Challenger* exploded. This event, followed closely by the Chernobyl nuclear disaster in the Soviet Union, reawakened popular concerns about the potential of technology to resolve problems, and gave a new boost to the ecology movement. Reagan himself noted the apocalyptic quality of the Chernobyl affair, since the place name translates to "wormwood," and that word has catastrophic implications in the Book of Revelation.[1]

Domestic setbacks for Reagan-era conservatism accelerated from the end of that year. In November 1986, the Democratic recapture of the U.S. Senate meant that henceforward the administration had to deal with a more stubborn Congress. A few weeks later, Attorney General Meese officially revealed the Iran-contra dealings, initiating a scandal that dominated the remainder of Reagan's term. Ironically, Reagan suffered from his foreign policy successes. The less glaring the Soviet danger, the more public attention turned to missteps and malfeasance at home. Further disasters followed in 1987, including the defeat of Robert Bork's nomination to the U.S. Supreme Court and the dizzying stock market plunge that October. The market meltdown failed to slow economic growth, but multiple business and political scandals provoked an anti-corporate reaction reminiscent of the mid-1970s. The gurus of the once-flourishing mergers and acquisitions world faced a series of criminal trials for insider dealing and stock manipulation, while the nation's savings and loan industry was showing signs of imminent catastrophe.[2] Deregulating the S&Ls had been a proud boast of the Reagan administration, but in practice the policy favored poorly funded and highly speculative institutions. By 1988, the S&Ls began evaporating, leaving the government to face a trillion-dollar cleanup. Southern and western states were hard hit, and the collapse had a domino effect through the real estate market.[3]

At the same time, wide-ranging criminal inquiries exposed other scandals that had their roots in the Reagan years. The Wedtech affair threatened to bring down senior administration officials, including Attorney General Meese, while presidential aide Michael Deaver was prosecuted for influence peddling and perjury. A whole rogues' gallery of cases tainted the defense procurement world of the military buildup years. Also in 1987, sexual and financial scandals destroyed some of the nation's leading televangelists, who had for a decade aspired to offer moral leadership to a troubled America. Other scandals discredited conservative figures who had loudly demanded a new moral rigor, including Charles Keating—implicated in the S&L disaster —and Father Bruce Ritter, subject of allegations concerning misconduct with teenage boys. Keating had been a pioneer of the 1970s anti-pornography movement, and both he and Ritter had served on the staunchly moralistic Meese Commission on Pornography. Liberals made no attempt to hide their hilarity. Films such as *Wall Street* (1987) were already depicting the Reagan years as a bygone Gilded Age of greed and selfishness.[4]

Democratic Revival

Though the Reagan years had shifted the ground of political debate, that did not create a lasting hegemony for the Republican Party. Democrats put up a strong fight in 1988, with Michael Dukakis at one point leading George

H. W. Bush by seventeen points in the polls. Dukakis conceded conservative ground sufficiently to deny that he might be described by a term as nefarious as *liberal*, and he tried to prove his manly credentials by being photographed driving a tank. Unfortunately, the resulting image made him look like a furry cartoon creature. More seriously, emotive issues of crime and race derailed the Dukakis campaign, though he still won 46 percent of the popular vote, more than Mondale or Carter had in their unsuccessful bids. Economic worries brought the Democrats into office in 1992, though Bill Clinton's victory was made possible only by the third-party movement of Ross Perot. Democrats won roughly half the popular vote in 1996, 2000, and 2004, and Clinton even managed to split the southern states.[5]

Prospects for the Clinton era were boosted enormously by the successes of the conservative years and the achievement of victory in the Cold War. Already during Reagan's second term, Americans and Soviets were moving toward better relations. In June 1987, Reagan's speech at the Berlin Wall, when he urged Gorbachev to "tear down this wall," marked a historic moment in the Cold War. The difference from earlier appeals was that this time, change as utopian as this was feasible. Later that year, the two powers signed their historic Intermediate Forces Treaty, providing for the destruction of some nuclear weapons, and over the next two years, the Cold War was effectively wound up. Confrontation with the Soviets failed to produce a nuclear cataclysm, while determined Western policies led directly to the collapse of European Communism in 1989, the fall of the Berlin Wall, and the disintegration of the USSR. By 1991, the famous Doomsday Clock of the *Bulletin of the Atomic Scientists* stood further from midnight than at any time since the device was created in 1947.[6]

Also in the category of doomsdays that did not happen, struggles in Central America resolutely refused to turn into quagmires drawing in thousands of American soldiers. Quite the contrary—U.S. policy succeeded without the necessity of direct involvement, and in 1990 democratic elections ejected Nicaragua's Sandinista regime. In 1991, the U.S.-led assault on Iraq showed that the West was no longer prepared to tolerate the behavior of absurd despots who menaced oil supplies. The Gulf War was a triumph for Reaganite policies, not to mention an advertisement for all the weaponry bought during the recent spending binge. The end of the Iran-Iraq War reduced the incidence of global terrorism, and after the 1988 bombing of Pan Am's flight 103, the United States experienced a lull in serious terrorist attacks. By 1988, the global terror conspiracy receded from the headlines sufficiently to become a source of parody. The comedy film *The Naked Gun* imagines a caricature summit of America's deadliest bogeymen, as

Gorbachev, Castro, Qaddafi, Khomeini, and Idi Amin convene in Beirut and launch ludicrously overheated tirades against the United States. For a modern audience, though, smiles freeze when one of the clique urges a colossal terrorist attack that will lay waste New York and Washington.

At least for a while, neither Communists nor terrorists could any longer be portrayed as ultimate villains. The new world instead demanded an understanding of other conflicts and relationships, not least the North-South division of global wealth and power first publicized by the Brandt Commission of 1980. Also critical in the emerging new world order would be two forces that had arisen in the post-1975 decade: the new economic colossus of China and the ideological strength of radical Islam. In the long term, historians may well regard these two trends as the most important global phenomena of the late twentieth century, and each finds a convenient symbol in 1979, respectively Deng Xiaoping's visit to the United States and the Iranian revolution. For a few years, though, neither of these rising forces posed an imminent military danger to the United States. Taken together, U.S. foreign policy successes meant that a new Democratic president could face an economy far less weighed down by defense spending than any comparable situation in decades past, with the pleasant dilemma of how to deal with the peace dividend. The absence of Communism made it difficult for conservatives to deploy traditional anti-conspiratorial or anti-subversive rhetoric against liberals. There no longer was a Soviet Union to be soft on.[7]

But while Democrats won elections, they won by adopting policies that would have seemed very conservative not too long since. Recognizing a new public mood, the Democratic Party accepted the politics of "realism," which meant taking aboard many key points of the Reagan agenda. Following the Mondale disaster of 1984, centrist Democrats formed the Democratic Leadership Council, which played a critical role in shaping the Clinton agenda. Political debates during the Clinton era accepted as axiomatic ideas such as fiscal conservatism, limiting the scope of government, moderate taxes, welfare reform, strong national defense, tough anti-crime policies, and no relaxation of the war on drugs. During the 1992 campaign, Clinton ostentatiously returned to Arkansas to perform his gubernatorial duty of signing an execution warrant. The collapse of his ambitious plan for national health care only reinforced the necessity of avoiding any programs with a Great Society flavor. So strong was the influence of Reagan-era values in the 1994 midterm elections, in which Republicans gained control of both houses of Congress, that they have been aptly described as Ronald Reagan's third election triumph. Thereafter, Clinton adopted ever more neo-Democratic economic policies.[8]

Also, even under a popular Democratic president, the Democratic Party continued to lose ground at other levels of government, badly so by post–New Deal standards. When the Democrats had lost control of the House in earlier decades, it had usually been for only one election, but 1994 marked the beginning of a still-enduring minority status. The Democratic decline was especially marked in state legislatures and governors' mansions. By many measures, the 1990s were the party's worst decade since the 1920s. By 2009, Republicans will have held the White House for twenty-eight out of the previous forty years.

The Triumph of God

Of course, achieving consensus over some issues, particularly economic, does not mean that partisan divisions faded away. Rather, the substance of debate shifted, to emphasize gender, family, sexuality, and morality, and demographic facts underlay political changes. For one thing, America was aging. The median age of the U.S. population jumped from thirty in 1980 to thirty-six in 2005, and the rise is more marked if we consider just non-Latino whites, with their disproportionate wealth and political involvement. The relative number of those over age sixty grew, while the ranks of those under eighteen fell, with all that implies for fear of crime and delinquency, public willingness to support public education, and sympathy for youth rights rhetoric.

But the process of aging and the declining number of children did not occur in all regions at the same pace. Other demographic factors—reflecting attitudes toward family and children—have done much to determine partisan divisions. Following the 2004 election, much ink was spilled determining why given states tinted red or blue, and factors commonly cited included income, level of religious practice, and degree of urbanization. But one solid predictor was the total white fertility rate, the number of children that a white woman could expect to bear during her lifetime. George W. Bush won twenty-five of the twenty-six states with the highest white fertility rates—states in which white couples were most likely to be concerned about "family values," variously defined, and probably to support community-affirming institutions such as churches. Conversely, John Kerry won the sixteen states with the lowest white fertility rates and more laissez-faire attitudes toward sexual expression. Kerry's own state, true-blue Massachusetts, was also the only one of the fifty states to record a net population loss in 2004.[9]

In the post-1975 decade, the whole raison d'être of America's political parties changed. Comparing the political parties of the early 1970s to what they would become ten or twenty years later, the most obvious difference is how crucially questions of morality and identity defined political orthodoxy. Just to take abortion, a pro-life Democrat was as unlikely to win national office as a pro-choice Republican. Looking back as recently as 1976, it seems incredible that Ronald Reagan could even have thought of balancing his ticket with a social liberal. From 1992, prominent Democrats with strong liberal credentials were excluded from speaking at their party's convention if they were visible pro-lifers.[10]

Polarization increased during the 1980s, in part as conservatives recognized the power of religiously oriented voters. By the end of the decade, some 40 percent of Americans described themselves as born again in Christ. Another sign of evangelical activism was the boom in megachurches, each claiming at least two thousand worshipers weekly: around a thousand such institutions exist today, up from just fifty in 1980. Moreover, the failure of the Moral Majority showed conservatives that political involvement must continue after election day. The centrality of cultural and religious politics was suggested by the powerful support for confrontational figures such as Pat Buchanan, who in 1992 famously told the Republican convention, "There is a religious war going on in our country for the soul of America. It is a cultural war, as critical to the kind of nation we will one day be as was the Cold War itself." By the end of the 1980s, exponents of culture war politics were delighted to find that the president's own son, George W. Bush, shared most of their views and rejected compromise on moral and religious issues.[11]

On many issues, obviously, liberals consistently won key debates, preserving the continued legality of abortion. Though the Supreme Court came close to weakening this right in 1992, abortion remained legal, and through the 1990s, gay rights causes also survived and thrived. One reason for this success is that Democrats themselves often succeeded in speaking the language of religion and morality at least as convincingly as Republicans, and southern politicians such as Bill Clinton did a spectacular job of rooting themselves in religious thought and rhetoric. Clinton's abilities in this area won the hearts of many who would have looked dimly on his liberal record in the 1960s, his opposition to the draft, and his marijuana experimentation.

Any observer who complains that George W. Bush has presented terrorism in unprecedented religious and even dualistic terms has forgotten the emotive speeches that Clinton gave after the Oklahoma City bombing of 1995. Clinton was thoroughly comfortable with the language of evil and sin, especially as they threatened children. As an Arkansan speaking to Oklahomans, how could he be otherwise? In a commemorative service a year after the attack, he stated that Christians would "bear witness to our faith that the miracles of Jesus and the miracles of the human spirit in Oklahoma City only reflect the larger miracle of human nature, that there is something eternal within each of us, that we all have to die and that no bomb can blow away even from the littlest child, that eternity which is within each of us." Not just among African-Americans, Clinton succeeded largely because he spoke directly to the values of religious believers. But is it conceivable that any president in the pre-Carter generation would have used such language? If a Republican spoke like this today—if President Bush called for a purging of the dark forces that had caused a terrible sin—he would be accused of preaching theocracy.[12]

While evangelical Protestantism was the commonest point of reference for such language, other Democrats spoke from other faith traditions. John Kerry evoked liberal Catholicism when he claimed in 2004 that "my faith affects everything that I do, in truth," while 2000 vice presidential candidate Joe Lieberman ostentatiously affirmed his Orthodox Judaism. In 2000, Al Gore told a *60 Minutes* interviewer that his born-again Christian beliefs were the "core of my life. It is—it's the foundation of my other beliefs, my political philosophy." He denounced the "arrogant" and "intimidating" anti-religious view that scorned beliefs such as his. The question was not whether personal morality or religion should play a defining role in politics, but how those attitudes should be applied to specific questions. With both parties freely speaking the language of God and religion, popular expectations about public rhetoric shifted. As late as 1984, only 22 percent of Americans surveyed believed that presidential candidates should discuss the role religion played in their lives; by 2004, that figure had grown to 42 percent. No less than in economic matters, post-1985 Democrats and Republicans shared many assumptions about the proper place of religion, however much they disagreed on the practical policy consequences. In the Clinton years, the issue of international religious freedom brought evangelical groups into the diplomatic arena more directly than any time since the nineteenth-century heyday of missionary endeavor.[13]

Don't Stop Believing

Both political sides deployed the language of religion and sin, and to that extent we can trace a continuity of rhetoric from the Reagan years through subsequent presidencies. In other ways too, ideas and themes that emerged in the early 1980s survived and flourished long after the Reagan presidency ended, especially in the personification of social threats through monstrous predators.

This theme emerged strongly in the continuing child protection move-ment. Under the Clinton administration, the rhetoric of children and children's rights became central to public discussion of social and economic topics. Hillary Rodham Clinton, of course, laid out her social agenda in her 1995 book, *It Takes a Village,* which borrowed its title from the African proverb "It takes a village to raise a child." And we have already seen how the new vice president's wife, Tipper Gore, had used her attack on teenage culture and music to spread charges about child endangerment.[14]

The campaigning and (often) scare-mongering of the post-1975 decade has shaped debate over social problems up to the present day. By the mid-1980s, public fears about children were far too well established to be dispelled, but they might instead be redirected to other forms of the issue. Ritual abuse fears reached their height in the early 1990s before being debunked in mid-decade. But even then, the new nightmare involved predators and kidnappers, of the sort made famous by the notorious cases of Polly Klaas and Megan Kanka, the inspiration for various forms of Megan's Law nationwide. During the 1990s, the language of sexual "predators" moved from the pages of sensational true crime books to the formal titles of state and federal laws. Clearly, the term *predator* is a metaphor—a predatory animal is one that survives by hunting and eating other animals, and only by analogy is this compared with the pursuit and sexual exploitation by humans of less powerful strangers. But the concept of sexual predators was increasingly associated with sexual violence and stalking, the other mon-strous hunting metaphor that entered the legislative code in these years. (The concept first entered the popular consciousness in 1989, and California passed the first anti-stalking law a year later.) Between 1989 and 1992, a num-ber of sensationalized cases revived the older panic about monstrous serial killers, with Jeffrey Dahmer as its new symbol. Hollywood helped publicize the revived fears, most spectacularly in the film *The Silence of the Lambs,* the title itself suggesting images of predation.[15]

Such fears had policy consequences. In 1990, a sexual predator law passed by Washington state revived the idea of indeterminate sentencing in its most punitive form. Even after a sex offender served the criminal sentence for a given act, the state was empowered to detain him pending a hearing on civil commitment. Laws of this kind proliferated through the early 1990s, despite complaints that they threatened to hold individuals in prison for life on the basis of what someone thought they might do at some future date. Was this not double jeopardy? In 1997, however, the U.S. Supreme Court upheld predator laws, which are now a familiar part of U.S. criminal practice. Existing imagery about predators entangling children in webs of abuse meshed perfectly with the new technological realities of the Internet and the

World Wide Web and provided the basis for new panics about stalkers and child pornographers.[16]

President Clinton himself appropriated these predatory images, citing the Polly Klaas case in his 1994 State of the Union address and deploying the story in campaign commercials. He also favored creating a national registry of sex offenders so that police and local communities would know the whereabouts of each and every "dangerous sexual predator." Using such a scarlet letter approach meant abandoning hopes for rehabilitation, but as Clinton said, "Nothing is more important than keeping our children safe. . . . We respect people's rights. But there is no right greater than a parent's right to raise a child in safety and love."[17] When Clinton himself faced sex scandals, political conservatives turned his rhetoric back on him, accusing him of being the nation's most egregious sexual predator. More recently, a few notorious instances of child murder have resurrected the most pernicious stereotypes of sex offenders, inducing state legislatures to pass ever more draconian sanctions.[18]

The Branch Davidian siege at Waco in 1993 demonstrated the enduring strength of allegations about the cult abuse of children. The disaster occurred when federal agents convinced themselves, all evidence to the contrary, that the residents of a "cult compound" were being held prisoner by an evil mastermind and that urgent action was necessary to prevent child molestation. The resulting actions by the FBI led to the massacre of the Davidians, which in turn enraged far-right "patriot" groups and militias, and ultimately led to the Oklahoma City bombing. The affair added a new and deadly stigma to cult stereotypes, reinforcing the poisoned Kool-Aid associations of Jonestown.[19]

Also during the 1990s, concern about child protection developed another kind of conspiratorial focus, with the damaging exposé of abuse by the nation's Catholic clergy. Though cases had surfaced over the years, a major boom occurred in 1992, during the more general scare over sexual violence and sexual predators. While there is no evidence that Catholic clergy are or were any more likely to be engaged in abuse than any other professionals closely involved with children, clergy abuse scandals conformed to powerful ideas about the conspiratorial nature of child endangerment. As the new century began, the resulting scandals devastated what had been one of the nation's most powerful political institutions.[20]

The Punishment Drug

In the area of drug abuse likewise, fears aroused in the post-1975 decade have continued to shape politics and social affairs. The incessant diet of horror stories about cocaine had its impact during the 1980s, with the proportion of Americans citing drug abuse as the nation's most important problem soaring from 3 percent in 1986 to 64 percent in 1989. Under the first Bush administration, the drug war became the central front in U.S. social policy, with a potent influence on international affairs. By 1989, with the Soviet menace collapsing almost hourly, international drug cartels emerged as a new evil empire to focus American policies. That September, President Bush declared, "All of us agree that the gravest domestic threat facing our nation today is drugs . . . our most serious problem today is cocaine and in particular crack . . . it is turning our cities into battle zones, and it is murdering our children. Let there be no mistake, this stuff is poison." In Panama shortly afterward, the drug menace was used to justify the invasion of an independent state. Though even conservative hard-liners of the late 1970s had never proposed resolving the Panama Canal debates by invasion, the drug issue allowed this outcome to take place with minimal public criticism. By 1989, congressional committees were claiming that the Colombian drug cartels were "far more dangerous than any criminal enterprise in history."[21]

The mass media uncritically reported official claims that one or another substance was "as addictive as crack cocaine" and was about to sweep the nation, destroying a new generation of American youth. In the face of such a menace, no expenditure seemed too great, and the drug war vastly expanded the resources available to criminal justice agencies to fight narcotics: the Drug Enforcement Administration boomed. In 1988, the administration created the imposing new office of drug czar, with all that term implied about the sweeping emergency powers that were required to combat the national evil, and several states appointed regional counterparts. Under the Clinton administration too, the czar's office continued to represent the symbolic center of federal anti-drug policy, the bully pulpit from which the latest menaces could be condemned.

The anti-drug movement made a seamless transition to the new political order. The drug war had created a network of well-funded agencies with an overwhelming vested interest in constantly discovering and drawing attention to new chemical dangers. Once the worst phase of the crack epidemic receded, we see a series of attempts to sustain public concern by focusing on new substances. Particularly powerful was the anti-methamphetamine movement that reached its apogee in the mid-1990s, with its heavily racialized rhetoric. Also called "redneck cocaine," speed allegedly threatened to introduce white suburban youngsters to black urban dysfunctions, to remove their social and sexual inhibitions. Clinton himself warned that the drug might soon become "the crack of the 1990s." More recently, the same rhetoric has been directed powerfully against club drugs, especially Ecstasy.[22]

During the 1990s, ever harsher penal laws were justified by a bleak vision of the danger posed by various types of irredeemable deviant. In each case, the solution was to be found in prisons and punishment rather than in policies of rehabilitation, drug treatment, psychiatric care, or any form of community alternative to corrections. States multiplied mandatory sentencing, and in 1994 California's "three strikes" law imposed a twenty-five-years-to-life prison sentence for anyone found guilty of three felonies. We have already seen the quantitative effects of such measures, making the United States distinctive among Western societies in its heavy reliance on imprisonment. At the time of writing, around 2.2 million Americans are in prisons or jails. Perhaps 3 percent of the population is directly in the hands of the state, whether through imprisonment, incarceration in a juvenile institution, or probation and parole. The proportion of minority populations is of course far higher: around 10 percent of African-American men ages twenty-five to twenty-nine are currently in prison. Mass incarceration also has a far-reaching political impact. Today, state laws that strip felons of voting rights affect some five million people, with a particular impact on black and Hispanic populations. In nine states, including Florida, disenfranchisement is lifelong. In 2000, when the presidency was decided by a few hundred votes in Florida, felony convictions excluded around a half million state residents from the ballot.[23]

Not only were Americans much more likely to be in the hands of the criminal justice system, but that experience would entail far fewer rights than in earlier years. One of the battlefronts for legal reform in the 1960s had been the rights of prisoners and others involuntarily committed to state custody, in mental institutions or juvenile reformatories. Underlying such activism was a sense that inmates met their fate through social and economic pressures, through the fact of poverty and social injustice. Beginning in the 1980s, the more general assumption was that criminals were personally wicked and undeserving of special rights. In 1996, the Prison Litigation Reform Act was intended to limit frivolous lawsuits by inmates, but in practice, the law made it difficult for inmates to resort to the courts, even when suffering gross physical or emotional abuse. Prison conditions deteriorated sharply.

Also suggesting a changed attitude to punishment, capital punishment became routine once more during the 1980s. In 1977, the execution of Gary Gilmore was a noteworthy event in popular culture, inspiring not just rock songs but even a Norman Mailer novel, *The Executioner's Song*, which won a Pulitzer Prize. By the 1990s, few Americans living in death penalty states could name any of the last few people executed in those jurisdictions, unless they had some personal connection to the cases.

Wars on Terror

In foreign policy too, much of the post-1993 story can be traced to the Reagan years. Arguably, many of the key strands in modern American politics—the terrorist crisis, September 11, the Iraq war—can be linked to U.S. obsessions with a particular set of enemies, or rather, to how those villains are perceived.

In the aftermath of September 11, liberal critics of U.S. policy charged that the Reagan administration had been so fixated on Soviet Communism that it failed to recognize the importance of other deadly threats, especially from radical Islamism. As we saw earlier, underplaying some of these enemies was by no means foolish in the context of the time, but some aspects of U.S. policy in the 1980s would raise real difficulties during the later confrontation with terrorism. Following the bomb attack on U.S. Marines in Beirut, the Reagan administration decided that Lebanon served no vital interests in the wider struggle with the Soviets, and U.S. forces were precipitously withdrawn. To Islamist militants, this resounding victory sent a dual message: unconventional warfare could overcome a nation with vastly superior forces and weaponry, and the United States had a low tolerance for casualties. In their efforts to explain the disaster, U.S. officials themselves offered a powerful advertisement for the most radical tactics. As Defense Secretary Weinberger explained helpfully, "Nothing can work against a suicide attack like that, any more than you can do anything against a kamikaze flight." Meanwhile, Osama bin Laden claimed that his plan to attack the World Trade Center was a direct response to the savagery inflicted on Beirut during the 1982–83 war: "As I was looking at those towers that were destroyed in Lebanon, it occurred to me that we have to punish the transgressor with the same, and that we had to destroy the towers in America, so that they taste what we tasted."[24]

Nor were these the last lessons from Beirut. By 1985, the Lebanese war was already in its tenth year, and hostage taking was commonplace, as was natural in any society founded upon kinship and clan ties. Militants were amazed to see the political impact of kidnapping Westerners and specifically Americans, even among those not directly connected to the victims. This again suggested a powerful new form of pressure, one that was applied with devastating effect. When dealing with Americans, clandestine tactics such as kidnapping and suicide bombing worked in a way that conventional weapons did not. In 1993, confused and indecisive Clinton administration policies in Somalia faithfully followed Reagan's Beirut script. For Islamists, this proved once again that terrorism worked and that the Americans had no stomach for casualties. All America's later experiences with Middle Eastern radicalism have been shaped by those encounters, up to and including the Iraqi insurgencies since 2003, in which kidnapping has been used to such effect.[25]

The American encounter with Iraq represents another example of continuity in the rhetoric of terrorism and external threat. Encouraged by the United States to confront Iran, Saddam Hussein became ever more ambitious, with aspirations toward nuclear, biological, and chemical weapons. Saddam's invasion of Kuwait in 1990 began a chain of events that culminated in both the first Gulf War of 1991 and the U.S.-led occupation of Iraq in 2003. Between the two spasms of overt violence, leading U.S. pundits and policy makers included much the same cohort that had urged resistance to the Soviets in the late 1970s, with figures such as Richard Perle, Paul Wolfowitz, and Dick Cheney—the group James Mann has called the Vulcans.[26] Calls for militant action against the Soviet Union in the late 1970s closely foreshadow the anti-Saddam movement of the last decade, and in neither case would the more extreme claims about the strengths of the adversary hold up to subsequent examination.

In both cases too, activist rhetoric stressed the immediate threat posed to the United States and the West by clandestine attacks and terrorism. Between 1979 and 1981, Communist-bloc sponsorship of the terror network was a mainstay of anti-Soviet politics and a justification for covert support for anti-Communist movements around the globe. Since 2001, the intelligence community has been riven over charges that Iraq was directly involved in some of the leading terrorist attacks against the United States, including the World Trade Center attack of 1993 and—of course—the catastrophic assault of 2001.

To point out these similarities is not necessarily to cast doubt on the accuracy of specific claims. The Soviets certainly did support terrorist movements, Saddam did so on an impressive scale, and an Iraqi linkage to at least the 1993 World Trade Center attack is conceivable. But the resemblances do suggest the continuing power of a particular kind of rhetoric, with its themes of conspiracy, clandestine manipulation of violence, and ultimately the masterminds lurking at the center of a global web. In 2002, President George W. Bush bracketed together Iran, Iraq, and North Korea under a phrase soon to become legendary: "States like these, and their terrorist allies, constitute an axis of evil, arming to threaten the peace of the world." The original draft had denoted them merely as an "axis of hatred," but the notion of evil had moved powerfully to the forefront of administration thinking. Recalling the World War II Axis centered on Nazi Germany, the term harked back to Reagan's view of Soviet Communism and of course the evil empire.[27]

On the eve of the 2003 Iraq war, the theme of the terrorist mastermind was explicitly stated by arch-Vulcan Douglas Feith, the undersecretary of defense: "One of the principal . . . thoughts underlying our strategy in the war on terrorism is the importance of the connection between terrorist organizations and their state sponsors. Terrorist organizations cannot be effective in sustaining themselves over long periods of time to do large-scale operations if they don't have support from states." To which the obvious retort must be made: what about the IRA? The organization has been helped sporadically by various foreign regimes, including the USSR and Libya, but it would be absurd to see such help as sustaining or driving the movement. The same point could be made about other long-lived movements such as the Basque ETA. Any analysis of terrorist campaigns must distinguish carefully between assistance or support, often given and taken in an opportunistic fashion, and outright control, but this critical distinction is lost in the rigid emphasis on rogue states masterminding global terror networks. Terrorism represents a tactic rather than a movement, and a tactic that in appropriate circumstances can be employed by exponents of virtually any political or religious ideology.[28]

Cult of Evil

After 2001, U.S. relations with Osama bin Laden and Saddam Hussein—those two revenants from the 1980s—dominated world affairs, and in both instances, the U.S. response was thoroughly shaped by the culture and politics of the Carter-Reagan era. In the case of bin Laden, there was no need to invent a far-reaching global conspiracy, since one certainly did and does exist, in the form of the murderous al-Qaeda network. But having said this, a particular version of conspiratorial thought has shaped interpretations of the enemy. However much it resembles one of the world domination syndicates familiar from James Bond books, al-Qaeda is not a monolithic organization in which all supporters carry party membership cards; rather, it is a federation of separate militant organizations allied to other groups more or less directly involved in the movement's ongoing affairs. We might draw a parallel with the radical and democratic movements of nineteenth-century Europe, which had multiple organizations and symbolic leaders but little in the way of a nerve center. (Obviously, I suggest no moral equivalence between those movements and modern-day Islamist extremism.) We need not presuppose a center for global terrorism, any more than state support.

Nor is al-Qaeda necessarily the most powerful or threatening such network with the potential for global action: Hizbullah may be still more significant.

Even well-informed Americans imagine Osama bin Laden as the spider in the center of a global web; that clichéd image is often used, but the metaphor is harmful in its simplistic portrait of the enemy. In practical terms, it demands that the United States seek out enemy leaders and hierarchies, concepts that are becoming less and less relevant in a world of decentralized organization, lateral communication, and leaderless resistance. This kind of focus, this quest for kingpins and conspiracies, explains why U.S. authorities find it next to impossible to come to terms with the dangers of Internet crimes such as cyberterrorism, fraud, and child pornography. To doubt the evil empire model of terrorism is in no sense to advocate weakness or surrender—by all means, let us pursue bin Laden to his grave—but we should at the same time devise more precise and better-targeted strategies against his supporters.[29]

If America's terrorist enemy was as easily identifiable as the administration claimed, then the national response was predictable. From the first days after September 11, the Bush administration spoke consistently of a struggle against evil, with bin Laden as the principal evildoer. Two weeks after the attack, the president told an audience of FBI employees, "The people who did this act on America, and who may be planning further acts, are evil people. They don't represent an ideology, they don't represent a legitimate political group of people. They're flat evil. That's all they can think about, is evil. And as a nation of good folks, we're going to hunt them down." He told a commemorative service at the Pentagon, "The hijackers were instruments of evil who died in vain. Behind them is a cult of evil which seeks to harm the innocent and thrives on human suffering. . . . We cannot fully understand the designs and power of evil. It is enough to know that evil, like goodness, exists. And in the terrorists, evil has found a willing servant." Like Clinton, he invoked the threat to the young, asking the country to pray "for the children whose worlds have been shattered, for all whose sense of safety and security has been threatened."[30]

Bush's language appealed precisely to the national mood and helped rally massive domestic support behind what had hitherto been seen as a weak and ineffectual presidency. According to the new national doctrine, bin Laden was the national foe in a global war on terror, apparently designed to combat all forms of terrorism wherever they surfaced—an amazingly ambitious notion, and a misleading one for policy making. But as the president said starkly, this was a straightforward conflict between good and evil, and all nations had to choose the side they were on: either you are with us or you are against us. Before acknowledging the word's sensitivity in the Muslim world, Bush spoke of a crusade. The language of evil has characterized his presidency.

Such dualistic language, with its absolute implications of religious and moral evil, alienated other nations. Increasingly, the use of religious concepts divides the United States from Western Europe, the other component of the traditional Western alliance of the Cold War years. In attitudes toward the Middle East conflict, for instance, Americans naturally sympathize with the biblically based justifications for the existence of the state of Israel, claims Europeans regard as cynical or deluded. For Europeans, claims to religious authority betoken hypocrisy or insanity; for most Americans, however, such religious themes remain pervasive.[31]

The Spirit of '76

Political opponents denounced what they saw as the simplistic rhetoric of the Bush-era war on terror. Yet, looking at the post-1986 era, it is difficult to tell which political side was more prone to speak the language of conspiracy, of wars against evildoers. In fact, much political debate in modern America revolves around notions of conspiracy; the question is which of the competing conspiracies is more plausible. One of the most successful television shows of the Clinton era was *The X-Files*, which regularly mocked conspiracy paranoia but also gave a national platform to its most grotesque manifestations.

While conservatives had their distinctive conspiracies and evildoers, so did liberals. Liberal campaigns against alleged CIA drug dealing segued into allegations that the 1980 Reagan campaign conspired with Iran to delay the release of the embassy hostages until after Jimmy Carter was safely defeated.[32] Leftist and anti-CIA conspiracy theories received a massive boost from Oliver Stone's 1991 movie *JFK*, a nostalgic revival of the radical thought-world of the mid-1970s. One veteran of that era was Sidney Blumenthal, editor of the 1976 assassination theory potpourri *Government by Gunplay*. In the Clinton years, he preached that the administration was under attack from what Hillary Clinton termed a "vast right-wing conspiracy." Suspicion of the intelligence agencies remained an enduring component of liberal ideology. In 1995, Congress placed strict limits on the CIA's ability to use human intelligence, as opposed to electronic sources, for intelligence gathering, for fear of supporting human rights violations. After September 11, of course, Congress would criticize the CIA for its failure to investigate terrorism proactively.[33]

Through the liberal Clinton years, the quest for evil enemies remained an ineradicable part of our political life. The controversial rhetoric of the post-9/11 war on terror grows directly from these roots, and ultimately from the older terrorist crises. At issue is not the notion of the war against evil, since that is a given, but rather a debate over which particular evil empire is to be blamed. If conservatives defined themselves and their values against hostile terror networks, so did liberals. As the horrendous bombing at Oklahoma City demonstrated, the United States did and does have an alarming strain of violent extremism. Yet much of the response to that event was wildly disproportionate and ill-focused, and can best be understood in terms of the nightmare images from the early 1980s. Far from being the work of a few isolated figures, something like Oklahoma City had to be portrayed as the tip of a vast iceberg, the work of a vast national conspiracy, members of which might be our next-door neighbors.

Oklahoma City generated a full-scale militia panic in 1995–96, when activists tried to demonstrate not just the enormous scale of the threat but how directly relevant it was to their particular issues. We find countless books with titles such as *America's Militia Threat, Terrorists Among Us,* and *Gathering Storm: America's Militia Threat.* Militia members also appeared as villains in countless television series and police shows. The film *Arlington Road* offered all the conspiracy and subversion clichés of the McCarthy years or of the early 1980s, except now the terrorists next door belong to the far right. They hold membership cards in "patriot" militias rather than Communist cells.[34]

Also in 1996, scattered instances of fires at rural churches were tendentiously constructed as a national epidemic of arson attacks against black churches, supposedly committed by the same ultra-right racist fanatics who supported the militias. So seriously was the issue taken that the president formed a National Church Arson Task Force. As a political bonus, this spurious wave of violence represented a direct attack by the far-right terror network against religion, especially churches of an evangelical bent. The perceived upsurge of racist and far-right violence did much to taint by association the vociferous conservative politicians who had won such a resounding victory in the 1994 midterm elections.[35]

In the summer of 1996, the United States experienced a terrorist crisis on a scale not witnessed since the Reagan years. Public fears were aroused by two seemingly connected episodes: a bomb at the Atlanta Olympic games, and the crash of a Paris-bound airliner over Long Island Sound. Though both events were at the time linked to Middle Eastern violence, in neither case has this interpretation been upheld (the airliner crash is now attributed to accident, the Olympic bomb to a domestic right-wing loner). These disasters were, however, used to justify passage of a sweeping anti-terrorist law, much of which in fact had little to do with combating terrorism. It was instead general-purpose anti-crime legislation, a package of measures that had for some time been on the wish list of the federal justice agencies, and it closely foreshadowed the controversial Patriot Act of 2001. Neither political party has a monopoly on exploiting public fears of the "terrorists among us."[36]

More recently, liberal and left versions of conspiracy theories have played a prominent role in national political debate. Kevin Phillips has traced the deep roots of evil underlying the Bush dynasty, which he links to the Nazis. Michael Moore's wildly tendentious documentary *Fahrenheit 911* popularized sinister theories linking the Bush family to the Saudi regime and suggested that the administration exploited the September 11 attacks for the benefit of U.S. corporations and political factions.[37] However outlandish such polemics might be, they follow closely the radical exposés of the mid-1970s. Jimmy Carter professed to regard *Fahrenheit 911* as one of his two favorite films, alongside *Casablanca,* and he invited Moore to share his box at the 2004 Democratic convention. Also in 2004, the classic conspiracy thriller *The Manchurian Candidate* was remade, complete with its deep-cover penetration agents and programmed assassins, though this time the puppet masters were not the KGB but (domestic) corporate malefactors of great wealth. And terrorism is just one of the bogeymen the corporate plotters use to arouse public fear for their own purposes. As much as Stone's *JFK,* such productions perfectly manifest the spirit of '76.

The degree to which both liberals and conservatives have adopted a worldview based on fears of subversion and predation shows that the rhetoric of the post-1975 years is unlikely to fade away in the foreseeable future. These themes mold the way we think and speak; they shape the outlook of political parties. They condition how we see problems, and constrain our options in dealing with them, whether dealing with issues of crime or drugs, terrorism or international conflict. The idea of evil flourishes in American public discourse.

To remark this is not to suggest that the language of morality or religion has no place in political language. In some circumstances, the terminology of evil seems appropriate, even unavoidable: perhaps evil empires really did, and do, exist. But looking at public policy over the past thirty or forty years, we see how thoroughly ideas of personal moral evil have replaced alternative interpretations and driven out other possible approaches to social problems at home and abroad. While nobody wants a return to the starry-eyed nonjudgmental optimism of the 1960s, the reaction of the post-1975 decade went too far in its way, with the thorough demonization of criminals, drug users, and social deviants, the quest for conspiracies, and the abandonment of solutions that did not mesh easily with military metaphors. Just to take criminal justice, the area that most directly affects the largest number of Americans, perhaps we should reopen some of the debates that were effectively closed off in the late 1970s, to consider once more issues of overcriminalization, the excessive use of purely penal sanctions, and overreliance on prisons. We might even find new roles for treatment and rehabilitation. But in order to do this, we would have to debate theories of social versus individual causation of crime, and even jettison well-established images of the criminal as monster or predator. We would have to move beyond the endemic metaphor of the "war" against a given problem.

Early in the life of the American nation, John Quincy Adams famously boasted that his country "goes not abroad, in search of monsters to destroy." America's problems today are plentiful enough without having to conjure up monsters at home.

Notes

Abbreviations

GPO   U.S. Government Printing Office
NYT   *New York Times*

Introduction

1. The lyrics are from David Crosby's "Wooden Ships," recorded by Jefferson Airplane on their 1969 album *Volunteers.*
2. Godfrey Hodgson, *More Equal than Others* (Princeton: Princeton University Press, 2004).
3. As Austin Powers was shocked to find, this is anything but a society in which "people are still having promiscuous sex with many anonymous partners without protection, while at the same time experimenting with mind-expanding drugs in a consequence-free environment." *Austin Powers: International Man of Mystery* (New Line Cinema, 1997).
4. Van Gosse, "Postmodern America," and Richard Moser, "Was It the End or Just a Beginning?" in Van Gosse and Richard Moser, eds., *The World the Sixties Made* (Philadelphia: Temple University Press, 2003); Daniel Marcus, *Happy Days and Wonder Years* (New Brunswick, NJ: Rutgers University Press, 2004). Though see Leo P. Ribuffo, "Will the Sixties Never End?" in Peter J. Kuznick and James Gilbert, eds., *Rethinking Cold War Culture* (Washington, DC: Smithsonian Institution Press, 2001).
5. For the "spirit of 1968" in the United States, see William L. O'Neill, *Coming Apart* (Chicago: Quadrangle, 1971); Charles Kaiser, *1968 in America* (New York: Weidenfeld and Nicolson, 1988); Irwin Unger and Debi Unger, *Turning Point, 1968* (New York: Scribner's, 1988); David Caute, *The Year of the Barricades* (New York: Harper and Row, 1988); Robert V. Daniels, *Year of the Heroic Guerrilla* (New York: Basic Books, 1989); Todd Gitlin, *The Sixties*, rev. ed. (New York: Bantam, 1993);

Jules Witcover, *The Year the Dream Died* (New York: Warner, 1997); Alexander Bloom, ed., *Long Time Gone* (New York: Oxford University Press, 2001); Mark Kurlansky, *1968* (New York: Ballantine, 2004).

6. Steve Fraser and Gary Gerstle, eds., *Rise and Fall of the New Deal Order* (Princeton: Princeton University Press, 1990); Godfrey Hodgson, *The World Turned Right Side Up* (Boston: Houghton Mifflin, 1996).

7. Tony Kushner, *Angels in America*, rev. ed. (New York: Theatre Communications Group, 1993–96); Lee Edwards, *The Conservative Revolution* (New York: Free Press, 1999).

8. For 1974 as a critical turning point in modern history, see, for instance, James T. Patterson, *Grand Expectations* (New York: Oxford University Press, 1996); Mark Lytle, *America's Uncivil Wars* (New York: Oxford University Press, 2005). For the beginning of the 1960s era, see Bruce Bawer, "The Other Sixties," *Wilson Quarterly*, spring 2004.

9. Bruce J. Schulman, *The Seventies* (New York: Free Press, 2001), 1.

10. Though any list of the best films of an era must be subjective, some of the major U.S. productions between 1975 and 1986 must include:

Taxi Driver	*Being There*	*True Confessions*
One Flew Over the Cuckoo's Nest	*Atlantic City*	*The Right Stuff*
Network	*All That Jazz*	*Star 80*
Annie Hall	*Raging Bull*	*Tender Mercies*
Days of Heaven	*Heaven's Gate*	*Amadeus*
The Deer Hunter	*The Shining*	*My Favorite Year*
Apocalypse Now	*Reds*	*The Terminator*
A Wedding	*Videodrome*	*Blood Simple*
The Idolmaker	*Raiders of the Lost Ark*	*Blue Velvet*
Mikey and Nicky	*Blade Runner*	*Platoon*
Melvin and Howard		

David A. Cook, *Lost Illusions* (New York: Scribner's, 2000); Robert Kolker, *A Cinema of Loneliness*, 3rd ed. (New York: Oxford University Press, 2000). In the realm of fiction, this period produced key works by Robert Coover, William Kennedy, Robert Stone, Saul Bellow, Joan Didion, E. L. Doctorow, Joyce Carol Oates, Don DeLillo, John Updike, William Gibson, and Bret Easton Ellis. The era was especially rich in minority voices, and any list of the most important writers would include Alice Walker, Leslie Marmon Silko, Ishmael Reed, and John Edgar Wideman. Joseph Dewey, *Novels from Reagan's America* (Gainesville: University Press of Florida, 1999); Kathryn Hume, *American Dream, American Nightmare* (Urbana: University of Illinois Press, 2000).

11. J. David Hoeveler, *The Postmodernist Turn* (New York: Twayne, 1996). Some of the influential works on theory published in this period would include Michel Foucault, *Discipline and Punish* (New York: Pantheon, 1977) and *The History of Sexuality*, 3 vols. (New York: Pantheon, 1978–86); Jacques Derrida, *Writing and Difference* (Chicago: University of Chicago Press, 1978); Edward W. Said, *Orientalism* (New York: Pantheon, 1978); Jean-François Lyotard, *La Condition Postmoderne* (Paris: Editions de Minuit, 1979); Stanley Fish, *Is There a Text in This Class?* (Cambridge, MA: Harvard University Press, 1980); Terry Eagleton, *Literary Theory* (Oxford: Basil Blackwell, 1983). The postmodern journal *Social Text* was founded in 1979.

12. David Frum, *How We Got Here* (New York: Basic Books, 2000); Schulman, *The Seventies*.

13. Other important studies of the decade include Peter N. Carroll, *It Seemed Like Nothing Happened* (New York: Holt, Rinehart and Winston, 1982); Hodgson, *The World Turned Right Side Up*; Stephanie A. Slocum-Schaffer, *America in the Seventies* (Syracuse: Syracuse University Press, 2003).

14. Carroll, *It Seemed Like Nothing Happened*; Rolling Stone, *The Seventies* (Boston: Little, Brown, 2000).

15. Richard Linklater, Denise Montgomery, and friends, *Dazed and Confused* (New York: St. Martin's, 1993); Rob Owen, *Gen X TV* (Syracuse: Syracuse University Press, 1997); Josh Ozersky, *Archie Bunker's America* (Carbondale: Southern Illinois University Press, 2003).

16. Stephen Feinstein, *The 1980s from Ronald Reagan to MTV* (Berkeley Heights, NJ: Enslow, 2000). The film *Party Monster* is more concerned with the early 1990s than the eighties as commonly defined.

17. Sidney Blumenthal, *The Rise of the Counter-Establishment* (New York: Times Books, 1986); William C. Berman. *America's Right Turn* (Baltimore: Johns Hopkins University Press, 1994); Mary C. Brennan, *Turning Right in the Sixties* (Chapel Hill: University of North Carolina Press, 1995); John Ehrman, *The Rise of Neoconservatism* (New Haven: Yale University Press, 1995); Rebecca E. Klatch, *A Generation Divided* (Berkeley: University of California Press, 1999); Jonathan M. Schoenwald, *A Time for Choosing* (New York: Oxford University Press, 2001); David Farber, *Taken Hostage* (Princeton: Princeton University Press, 2005); Michael Lind, "Conservative Elites and the Counterrevolution Against the New Deal," in Steve Fraser and Gary Gerstle, eds., *Ruling America* (Harvard University Press, 2005).

18. Thomas Byrne Edsall with Mary D. Edsall, *Chain Reaction* (New York: Norton, 1991). The quote "Pitting those . . ." is from p. 3. See also Thomas Byrne Edsall, "The Changing Shape of Power," in Fraser and Gerstle, eds., *Rise and Fall of the New Deal Order*, 269–93.

19. Thomas Frank, *What's the Matter with Kansas?* (New York: Metropolitan, 2004). "The culture wars . . ." is quoted from Frank, "Why They Won," *NYT*, November 5, 2004. Compare Dan T. Carter, *From George Wallace to Newt Gingrich* (Baton Rouge: Louisiana State University Press, 1999).

20. Edsall and Edsall, *Chain Reaction*, 102, mentions the rise of "covert and explicit hostility towards Third World countries." Foreign policy disasters of the Carter years—including the Iran hostage crisis—receive glancing attention: ibid., 135.

21. David H. Bennett, *The Party of Fear*, 2nd ed. (New York: Vintage, 1995); Richard Hofstadter, *The Paranoid Style in American Politics and Other Essays*, reprint ed. (Harvard University Press, 1996); Daniel Pipes, *Conspiracy* (New York: Free Press, 1997); Mark Fenster, *Conspiracy Theories* (Minneapolis: University of Minnesota Press, 1999); Peter Knight, *Conspiracy Culture* (New York: Routledge, 2001); Peter Knight, ed., *Conspiracy Nation* (New York: New York University Press, 2002); Michael Barkun, *A Culture of Conspiracy* (Berkeley: University of California Press, 2003); Corey Robin, *Fear* (New York: Oxford University Press, 2004).

22. Philip Jenkins, *Images of Terror* (Hawthorne, NY: Aldine de Gruyter, 2003).

23. Lawrence M. Friedman, *Crime and Punishment in American History* (New York: Basic Books, 1993); Samuel Walker, *Popular Justice*, 2nd ed. (New York: Oxford University Press, 1998).

24. Paul Boyer, *When Time Shall Be No More* (Cambridge, MA: Belknap, 1992). For "cosmic war," see Mark Juergensmeyer, *Terror in the Mind of God*, 3rd ed. (Berkeley: University of California Press, 2003).

25. Joel Best, *Threatened Children* (Chicago: University of Chicago Press, 1990).

26. Philip Jenkins, *Moral Panic* (New Haven, CT: Yale University Press, 1998), 214–38; Judith Levine, *Harmful to Minors* (Minneapolis: University of Minnesota Press, 2002).

27. Richard Wirthlin is quoted in Edsall and Edsall, *Chain Reaction*, 178.

28. Philip Jenkins, *Using Murder* (Hawthorne, NY: Aldine de Gruyter, 1994).

29. Gary M. Fink and Hugh Davis Graham, eds., *The Carter Presidency* (Lawrence: University Press of Kansas, 1998); W. Elliot Brownlee and Hugh Davis Graham, eds., *The Reagan Presidency* (Lawrence: University Press of Kansas, 2003).

30. Bernard Headley, *The Atlanta Youth Murders and the Politics of Race* (Carbondale: Southern Illinois University Press, 1998). The Atlanta affair receives substantial treatment in Gil Troy, *Morning in America* (Princeton: Princeton University Press, 2005), 86–88.

31. Francis Fukuyama, *The Great Disruption* (New York: Simon and Schuster, 1999).

32. Rowland Evans and Robert Novak, *The Reagan Revolution* (New York: Dutton, 1981); Daniel Patrick Moynihan, *Came the Revolution* (San Diego, CA: Harcourt Brace Jovanovich, 1988); B. B. Kymlicka and Jean V. Matthews, eds., *The Reagan Revolution?* (Chicago: Dorsey Press, 1988); Martin Anderson, *Revolution: The Reagan Legacy*, rev. ed. (Stanford, CA: Hoover Institution Press, 1990).

33. Andrew Adonis and Tim Hames, eds., *A Conservative Revolution?* (Manchester: Manchester University Press, 1994); Bruce J. Schulman, "The Reagan Revolution in International Perspective," in Richard S. Conley, ed., *Reassessing the Reagan Presidency* (Lanham, MD: University Press of America, 2003).

34. Philip Jenkins, *Intimate Enemies* (Hawthorne, NY: Aldine de Gruyter, 1992); Philip Jenkins, "How Europe Discovered its Sex Offender Crisis," in Joel Best, ed., *How Claims Spread* (Hawthorne, NY: Aldine de Gruyter, 2001), 147–67.

35. Annie Gottlieb, *Do You Believe in Magic?* (New York: Times Books, 1987).

36. Susan Jeffords, *The Remasculinization of America* (Bloomington: Indiana University Press, 1989); Richard Slotkin, *Gunfighter Nation* (New York: Atheneum, 1992).

37. Donald A. Downs, *The New Politics of Pornography* (Chicago: University of Chicago Press, 1989).

38. Grace Davie, *Religion in Britain Since 1945: Believing Without Belonging* (Oxford: Blackwell, 1994); Grace Davie, *Religion in Modern Europe* (New York: Oxford University Press, 2000); Andrew M. Greeley, *Religion in Europe at the End of the Second Millennium* (New Brunswick, NJ: Transaction, 2003).

39. Troy, *Morning in America*; John Ehrman, *The Eighties* (New Haven, CT: Yale University Press, 2005).

40. For arguments about the nature of the "Reagan revolution," see, for instance, Dilys M. Hill, Raymond A. Moore, and Phil Williams eds., *The Reagan Presidency* (New York: St. Martin's, 1990); Larry M. Schwab, *The Illusion of a Conservative Reagan Revolution* (New Brunswick, NJ: Transaction, 1991).

Chapter 1

1. Peter Braunstein and Michael William Doyle, eds., *Imagine Nation* (New York: Routledge, 2002).

2. Alice Echols, *Shaky Ground* (New York: Columbia University Press, 2002).

3. Charles A. Reich, *The Greening of America* (New York: Random House, 1970); Annie Gottlieb, *Do You Believe in Magic?* (New York: Times Books, 1987); Douglas T. Miller, "Sixties Activism in the 'Me Decade,' " in Elsebeth Hurup, ed., *The Lost Decade* (Aarhus, Denmark: Aarhus University Press, 1996); Thomas Frank, *The Conquest of Cool* (Chicago: University of Chicago Press, 1997); Stephen A. Kent, *From Slogans to Mantras* (Syracuse: Syracuse University Press, 2001).

4. Matty Simmons, *If You Don't Buy This Book, We'll Kill This Dog!* (New York: Barricade, 1994).

5. Thomas Byrne Edsall with Mary D. Edsall, *Chain Reaction* (New York: Norton, 1991), 17.

6. The definitive parody of cultural trends in this era remains Cyra McFadden, *The Serial* (New York: Knopf, 1977), together with the resulting film, *Serial*. For Des Moines, see Robert Reinhold, "Changes Wrought by 60s Youth Linger in American Life," *NYT*, August 12, 1979. See also Beth Bailey, *Sex in the Heartland* (Cambridge, MA: Harvard University Press, 1999).

7. Charles Murray, *Losing Ground*, 2nd ed. (New York: Basic Books, 1995).

8. Barbara Jordan and Shelby Hearon, *Barbara Jordan* (Garden City, NY: Doubleday, 1979); Chandler Davidson and Bernard Grofman, eds., *Quiet Revolution in the South* (Princeton: Princeton University Press, 1994).

9. Cheryl Russell, *Racial and Ethnic Diversity*, 4th ed. (Ithaca, NY: New Strategist Publications, 2002).

10. Toni Carabillo, Judith Meuli, and June Bundy Csida, *Feminist Chronicles, 1953–1993* (Los Angeles: Women's Graphics, 1993); Ruth Rosen, *The World Split Open* (New York: Viking, 2000); Sara M. Evans, "Beyond Declension," in Van Gosse and Richard Moser, eds., *The World the Sixties Made* (Philadelphia: Temple University Press, 2003); Sherrie A. Inness, ed., *Disco Divas* (Philadelphia: University of Pennsylvania Press, 2003). For *Time*, see http://www.time.com/time/poy2000/archive/1975.html.

11. Marilyn French. *The Women's Room* (New York: Summit, 1977); Alice Echols, *Daring to Be Bad* (Minneapolis: University of Minnesota Press, 1989).

12. Avery Corman, *Kramer Versus Kramer* (New York: New American Library, 1977); Susan Jeffords, *The Remasculinization of America* (Bloomington: Indiana University Press, 1989).

13. Anne Enke, "Taking Over Domestic Space," in Van Gosse and Richard Moser, eds., *The World the Sixties Made* (Philadelphia: Temple University Press, 2003); Kitty Krupat, "Out of Labor's Dark Age," in Van Gosse and Richard Moser, eds., *The World the Sixties Made* (Philadelphia: Temple University Press, 2003). See also Susan M. Hartmann, "Feminism, Public Policy and the Carter Administration," in Fink and Graham, eds., *The Carter Presidency*, 224–43. For new views of rape and sexual violence, see Noreen Connell and Cassandra Wilson, eds., *Rape* (New York: New American Library, 1974); Andra Medea and Kathleen Thompson, *Against Rape* (New York: Farrar, Straus, and Giroux, 1974); Diana E. H. Russell, *The Politics of Rape* (New York, Stein and Day, 1974); Susan Brownmiller, *Against Our Will* (London: Secker and Warburg, 1975); Laura Lederer, ed., *Take Back the Night* (New York: Morrow, 1980); Susan Brownmiller, *In Our Time* (New York: Dial Press, 1999).

14. Andrea Dworkin, *Right-Wing Women* (New York: Coward-McCann, 1983).

15. Rob Hall, *Rape in America* (Santa Barbara, CA: ABC-CLIO, 1995).

16. Toby Marotta, *The Politics of Homosexuality* (Boston: Houghton Mifflin, 1981); John D'Emilio and Estelle B. Freedman, *Intimate Matters* (New York: Harper and Row, 1988); Jonathan Ned Katz, *Gay American History*, rev. ed. (New York: Meridian, 1992); John D'Emilio, *The World Turned* (Durham, NC: Duke University Press, 2002); Jeffrey Escoffier, "Fabulous Politics," in Van Gosse and Moser, eds., *The World the Sixties Made*.

17. "Gays on the March," *Time*, September 8, 1975; Edward Alwood, *Straight News* (New York: Columbia University Press, 1996), 134 for the *Los Angeles Times* story; Vito Russo, *The Celluloid Closet* (New York: Harper and Row, 1981). For changing standards in broadcast television, see Josh Ozersky, *Archie Bunker's America* (Carbondale: Southern Illinois University Press, 2003).

18. Andrew Holleran, *Dancer from the Dance* (New York: Morrow, 1978); Larry Kramer, *Faggots* (New York: Random House, 1978); Armistead Maupin, *Tales of the City* (New York: Harper and Row, 1978), and its sequels. For New York's gay subcultures, see Escoffier, "Fabulous Politics," 199; Jeffery Escoffier, ed., *Sexual Revolution* (New York: Thunder's Mouth, 2003); Patrick Moore, *Beyond Shame* (Boston: Beacon Press, 2004); Doug Ireland, "Rendezvous in the Ramble," *New York*, July 24, 1978.

19. Albert Goldman, *Disco* (New York: Hawthorn, 1978); Tim Lawrence, *Love Saves the Day* (Durham: Duke University Press, 2003).

20. Ray C. Rist, *The Pornography Controversy* (New Brunswick, NJ: Transaction, 1974); Samuel Walker, *In Defense of American Liberties*, 2nd ed. (Carbondale: Southern Illinois University Press, 1999). For changing mores, see Bailey, *Sex in the Heartland*.

21. Larry Flynt with Kenneth Ross, *An Unseemly Man* (Los Angeles, CA: Dove, 1996).

22. Richard Pryor with Todd Gold, *Pryor Convictions* (New York: Pantheon, 1995).

23. Will McBride, *Show Me!* (New York: St. Martin's, 1975); Philip Jenkins, *Moral Panic* (New Haven: Yale University Press, 1998).

24. Philip Jenkins, *Beyond Tolerance* (New York: New York University Press, 2001).

25. Parker Rossman, *Sexual Experience Between Men and Boys* (New York: Association Press, 1976); Thomas Kiernan, *The Roman Polanski Story* (New York: Random House, 1980); *A Report on the Crisis in the Catholic Church in the United States* (Washington, DC: United States Conference of Catholic Bishops, 2004).

26. Lloyd D. Johnston, Jerald G. Bachman, and Patrick M. O'Malley, *Drug Use Among American High School Students, 1975–1977* (Rockville, MD: National Institute on Drug Abuse, 1977), and *Highlights from Drugs and the Class of '78* (Washington, DC: GPO, 1979); David Musto, *The American Disease,* 2nd ed. (New Haven: Yale University Press, 1987); Jill Jonnes, *Hep-Cats, Narcs and Pipe Dreams* (New York: Scribner's, 1996); Richard Davenport-Hines, *The Pursuit of Oblivion* (New York: Norton, 2002).

27. *Sourcebook of Criminal Justice Statistics*. Compare Lloyd D. Johnston, Patrick M. O'Malley, and Jerald G. Bachman, *Drugs and American High School Students 1975–1983* (Washington, DC: GPO, 1984;) Lloyd D. Johnston, Patrick M. O'Malley, and Jerald G. Bachman, *Drug Use Among High School Seniors, College Students and Young Adults 1975–1990* (Washington, DC: GPO, 1991); Larry Sloman, *Reefer Madness* (New York: St. Martin's Griffin, 1998); Philip Jenkins, *Synthetic Panics* (New York: New York University Press, 1999).

28. The *Newsweek* article is quoted in Jill Jonnes, *Hep-Cats, Narcs and Pipe Dreams* (New York: Scribner's, 1996), 304–8; Lester Grinspoon and James B. Bakalar, *Cocaine* (New York: Basic Books, 1985); William Grimes, *Straight Up or on the Rocks* (New York: Simon and Schuster, 1993).

29. Peter Biskind, *Easy Riders, Raging Bulls* (New York: Simon and Schuster, 1998).

30. Bill Zehme, *Lost in the Funhouse* (New York: Delacorte Press, 1999); Tom Shales and James Andrew Miller, *Live from New York* (Boston: Little, Brown, 2002).

31. *Marijuana Decriminalization: Hearing Before the Subcommittee to Investigate Juvenile Delinquency of the Committee on the Judiciary, U.S. Senate* (Washington, DC: GPO, 1977).

32. Philip Jenkins, *Mystics and Messiahs* (New York: Oxford University Press, 2000).

33. Robert M. Pirsig, *Zen and the Art of Motorcycle Maintenance* (New York: Morrow, 1974). For the vast interest in UFOs and extraterrestrials, see, for example, David Michael Jacobs, *The UFO Controversy in America* (Bloomington: Indiana University Press, 1975); Coral Lorenzen and Jim Lorenzen, *Encounters with UFO Occupants* (New York: Berkley, 1976); Brad Steiger, ed., *Project Blue Book* (New York: Ballantine, 1976); Charles Berlitz and William L. Moore, *The Roswell Incident* (New York: Grosset and Dunlap, 1980). Fritjof Capra, *The Tao of Physics* (New York: Random House, 1975); Gary Zukav, *The Dancing Wu Li Masters* (New York: Morrow, 1979).

34. William Proxmire, *The Fleecing of America* (Boston: Houghton Mifflin, 1980); Thomas Raymond Wellock, *Critical Masses* (Madison: University of Wisconsin Press, 1998); Harry C. Boyte, *The Backyard Revolution* (Philadelphia: Temple University Press, 1980).

35. W. French Anderson, "Human Gene Therapy: The Initial Concepts," at http://www.frenchanderson. org/docarticles/pdf/hgt_initial.pdf; Ullica Segerstråle, *Defenders of the Truth* (Oxford: Oxford University Press, 2000).

36. Tom Wolfe, *Mauve Gloves and Madmen, Clutter and Vine* (New York: Farrar, Straus and Giroux, 1976); Edwin Schur, *The Awareness Trap* (New York: Quadrangle/New York Times Book Co., 1976); Christopher Lasch, *The Culture of Narcissism* (New York: Norton, 1978); Aaron Stern, *Me: The*

Narcissistic American (New York: Ballantine, 1979); Steven M. Tipton, *Getting Saved from the Sixties* (Berkeley: University of California Press, 1982); Kent, *From Slogans to Mantras.*

37. Jenkins, *Mystics and Messiahs.*

38. J. D. Lorenz, *Jerry Brown, the Man on the White Horse* (Boston: Houghton Mifflin, 1978); Robert Pack, *Jerry Brown, the Philosopher-Prince* (New York: Stein and Day, 1978).

39. Theodore Roszak, *Unfinished Animal* (New York: Harper and Row, 1975); Carol P. Christ and Judith Plaskow, eds., *Womanspirit Rising* (San Francisco: Harper and Row, 1979); Margot Adler, *Drawing Down the Moon* (New York: Viking, 1979); Elaine H. Pagels, *The Gnostic Gospels* (New York: Random House, 1979); Marilyn Ferguson, *The Aquarian Conspiracy* (Los Angeles: Tarcher, 1980); Shirley MacLaine, *Out on a Limb* (New York: Bantam, 1983); Starhawk, *The Spiral Dance*, 10th anniversary ed. (San Francisco: Harper San Francisco, 1989); Michael J. Harner, *The Way of the Shaman*, 10th anniversary ed. (San Francisco: Harper San Francisco, 1990).

40. Carter Heyward, *A Priest Forever* (New York: Harper and Row, 1976); Anne Marie Gardiner, *Women and Catholic Priesthood* (New York: Paulist Press, 1976); George A. Kelly. *The Battle for the American Church* (Garden City, NY: Doubleday, 1979); Mark Chaves, *Ordaining Women* (Cambridge, MA: Harvard University Press, 1997).

41. Kirkpatrick Sale, *The Green Revolution* (New York: Hill and Wang, 1993); Samuel P. Hays, *A History of Environmental Politics Since 1945* (Pittsburgh: University of Pittsburgh Press, 2000). For Love Canal, see *Love Canal, Public Health Time Bomb* (Albany: State of New York, Dept. of Health, 1978). The PBS series *Nova* dealt with the story in the documentary *A Plague on Our Children* (1979). Daniel F. Ford, *Three Mile Island* (New York: Viking, 1982); J. Samuel Walker. *Three Mile Island* (Berkeley: University of California Press, 2004). For Seveso, see John G. Fuller, *The Poison That Fell from the Sky* (New York: Random House, 1977).

42. Edward Abbey, *The Monkey Wrench Gang* (New York: Avon, 1975); J. E. Lovelock, *Gaia* (New York: Oxford University Press, 1979); Bill Devall and George Sessions, *Deep Ecology* (Salt Lake City: G. M. Smith, 1985).

43. *Tennessee Valley Authority v. Hill et al.*, 437 U.S. 153 (1978) (emphasis added); William Bruce Wheeler and Michael J. McDonald, *TVA and the Tellico Dam, 1936–1979* (Knoxville: University of Tennessee Press, 1986); Jeffrey K. Stine, "Environmental Policy During the Carter Presidency," in Fink and Graham, eds., *The Carter Presidency*, 179–201.

44. Bob Woodward and Scott Armstrong, *The Brethren* (New York: Simon and Schuster, 1979).

45. Samuel Walker, *Popular Justice*, 2nd ed. (New York: Oxford University Press, 1998).

46. Samuel Walker, Cassia Spohn, and Miriam Delone. *The Color of Justice*, 3rd ed. (Belmont, CA: Wadsworth Thomson Learning, 2004).

47. Howard S. Becker, *Outsiders* (London: Free Press of Glencoe, 1963); Joseph R. Gusfield, *Symbolic Crusade* (Urbana: University of Illinois Press, 1966); Kai T. Erikson, *Wayward Puritans* (New York: Wiley, 1966); Troy Duster, *The Legislation of Morality* (New York: Free Press, 1970); David J. Rothman, *The Discovery of the Asylum* (Boston: Little, Brown, 1971) and *Conscience and Convenience* (Boston: Little, Brown, 1980); Ian Taylor, Paul Walton, and Jock Young, *The New Criminology* (London: Routledge and Kegan Paul, 1973).

48. William J. Chambliss and Robert B. Seidman. *Law, Order, and Power* (Reading, MA: Addison-Wesley, 1971); Edwin M. Schur and Hugo Adam Bedau, *Victimless Crimes* (Englewood Cliffs, NJ: Prentice Hall, 1974); William J. Chambliss and Milton Mankoff, eds., *Whose Law? What Order?* (New York: Wiley, 1976); Gilbert Geis, *Not the Law's Business* (New York: Schocken, 1979 [1972]).

49. Sanford Kadish, "The Crisis of Overcriminalization," *The Annals of the American Academy* 374 (1967), 158–70.

50. American Friends Service Committee, *Struggle for Justice* (New York: Hill and Wang, 1971); Jessica Mitford, *Kind and Usual Punishment* (New York: Knopf, 1973).

51. Francis T. Cullen and Karen E. Gilbert, *Reaffirming Rehabilitation* (Cincinnati: Anderson, 1982).

52. Robert Martinson, "What Works?" *The Public Interest* 10 (1974): 22–54. Martinson's argument was nothing like as stark as is suggested by that simple negative, but this was widely taken as the message of the article. Andrew T. Scull, *Decarceration* (Englewood Cliffs, NJ: Prentice-Hall, 1977); Jerome G. Miller, *Last One over the Wall*, 2nd ed. (Columbus: Ohio State University Press, 1998).

53. Andrew Von Hirsch, *Doing Justice* (New York: Hill and Wang, 1976).

54. *Determinate Sentencing: Reform or Regression?* (Washington, DC: U.S. Dept. of Justice, 1978); Alfred Blumstein et al., eds., *Research on Sentencing* (Washington, DC: National Academy Press, 1983).

55. Erving Goffman, *Asylums* (Garden City, NY: Doubleday, 1961); Thomas S. Szasz, *Law, Liberty and Psychiatry* (New York: Macmillan, 1963) and *Ideology and Insanity* (Garden City, NY: Anchor, 1970).

56. Nicholas N. Kittrie, *The Right to Be Different* (Baltimore: Johns Hopkins University Press, 1971).

57. Fred Cohen, ed., *The Law of Deprivation of Liberty* (St. Paul, MN: West, 1980).

Chapter 2

1. Bob Woodward, *Shadow* (New York: Simon and Schuster, 1999); David Greenberg, *Nixon's Shadow* (New York: W. W. Norton and Company, 2003).

2. George S. McGovern, "The State of the Union 1975," *Rolling Stone*, March 13, 1975; David Wise. *The American Police State* (New York: Random House, 1976); Morton H. Halperin et al., *The Lawless State* (New York: Penguin, 1976).

3. Thurston Clarke and John J. Tigue Jr., *Dirty Money* (New York: Simon and Schuster, 1975); Bob Woodward, *The Secret Man* (New York: Simon and Schuster, 2005).

4. Bob Woodward and Carl Bernstein, *The Final Days* (New York: Simon and Schuster, 1976); Richard Nixon, *RN* (New York: Grosset and Dunlap, 1978).

5. Anthony Sampson, *The Sovereign State of ITT* (New York: Stein and Day, 1973); Anthony Sampson, *The Arms Bazaar* (New York: Viking, 1977).

6. *Korean Influence Investigation* (Washington, DC: GPO, 1977–78); *Korean Influence Inquiry* (Washington, DC: GPO, 1978); Robert Boettcher and Gordon L. Freedman, *Gifts of Deceit* (New York: Holt, Rinehart and Winston, 1980).

7. William Ashworth, *Under the Influence* (New York: Hawthorn/Dutton, 1981).

8. Howard Kohn, *Who Killed Karen Silkwood?* (New York: Summit, 1981); Richard Rashke, *The Killing of Karen Silkwood* (Boston: Houghton Mifflin, 1981); David Vogel, *Fluctuating Fortunes* (New York: Basic Books, 1989). For racketeering scandals, see Martin Tallberg, *Don Bolles* (New York: Popular Library, 1977); Michael F. Wendland, *The Arizona Project* (Kansas City: Sheed, Andrews and McMeel, 1978); Dan E. Moldea, *The Hoffa Wars* (New York: Grosset and Dunlap, 1978).

9. John J. McCloy, Nathan W. Pearson, and Beverley Matthews, *The Great Oil Spill* (New York: Chelsea House, 1976); George C. S. Benson and Thomas S. Engeman, *Amoral America* (Stanford, CA: Hoover Institution Press, 1975); Frank Pearce, *Crimes of the Powerful* (London: Pluto Press, 1976); John E. Conklin, *"Illegal but Not Criminal"* (Englewood Cliffs, NJ: Prentice Hall, 1977); Penny Lernoux, *In Banks We Trust* (Garden City, NY: Anchor Press/Doubleday, 1984).

10. Paul Brodeur, *Outrageous Misconduct* (New York: Pantheon, 1985).

11. The civil application of RICO was upheld in *Sedima, SPRL v. Imrex Co., Inc.*, 473 U.S. 479 (1985).

12. Peter Huber, *Liability* (New York: Basic Books, 1988); Walter K. Olson, *The Litigation Explosion* (New York: Dutton, 1991); Philip Jenkins, *Pedophiles and Priests* (New York: Oxford University Press, 1996).

13. Nelson Blackstock, *COINTELPRO* (New York: Vintage, 1975); Thomas Powers, *The Man who Kept the Secrets* (New York: Knopf, 1979) and *Intelligence Wars* (New York: New York Review Books, 2002); Ward Churchill and Jim Vander Wall, *The COINTELPRO Papers*, 2nd ed. (Cambridge, MA: South End Press, 2002); John Prados, *Lost Crusader* (New York: Oxford University Press, 2003).

14. *Report to the President by the Commission on CIA Activities Within the United States* (Washington, DC: GPO, 1975).

15. *Alleged Assassination Plots Involving Foreign Leaders* (New York: Norton, 1976); John D. Marks, *The Search for the "Manchurian Candidate"* (New York: Times Books, 1979); Warren Hinckle and William W. Turner, *The Fish Is Red* (New York: Harper and Row, 1981); John Ranelagh, *The Agency*, rev. ed. (New York: Simon and Schuster, 1987); David Corn, *Blond Ghost* (New York: Simon and Schuster, 1994); Kathryn S. Olmsted, *Challenging the Secret Government* (Chapel Hill: University of North Carolina Press, 1996).

16. Van Gosse, "Unpacking the Vietnam Syndrome," in Van Gosse and Richard Moser, eds., *The World the Sixties Made* (Philadelphia: Temple University Press, 2003); Philip Agee, *Inside the Company* (New York: Stonehill, 1975); Philip Agee and Louis Wolf, eds., *Dirty Work* (New York: Dorset Press, 1978).

17. Ranelagh, *The Agency*; Bob Woodward, *Veil* (New York: Simon and Schuster, 1987).

18. Steve Weissman, ed., *Big Brother and the Holding Company* (Palo Alto, CA: Ramparts Press, 1974); James McKinley, *Assassination in America* (New York: Harper and Row, 1977); James W. Clarke, *American Assassins* (Princeton: Princeton University Press, 1982).

19. William C. Sullivan with Bill Brown. *The Bureau* (New York: Norton, 1979); William Klaber and Philip H. Melanson, *Shadow Play* (New York: St. Martin's, 1997).

20. James Rosen, "Nixon and the Chiefs," *Atlantic Monthly*, April 2002.

21. *The Final Assassinations Report: Report of the Select Committee on Assassinations* (New York: Bantam, 1979); G. Robert Blakey and Richard N. Billings, *The Plot to Kill the President* (New York: Times Books, 1981); "Assassination: An Endless Nightmare," *U.S. News and World Report*, October 6, 1975, 17–21.

22. From a vast literature on assassinations from this period, see Michael Canfield and Alan J. Weberman, *Coup d'Etat in America* (New York: Third Press, 1975); Jim Garrison, *The Star Spangled Contract* (New York: McGraw-Hill, 1976); Robert D. Morrow, *Betrayal* (Chicago: H. Regnery, 1976); Peter Dale Scott, Paul L. Hoch, and Russell Stetler, eds., *The Assassinations* (New York: Random House, 1976); Arthur H. Bremer, *An Assassin's Diary* (New York: Pocket, 1973); Stephen Paul Miller, *The Seventies Now* (Durham: Duke University Press, 1999); Mark Feeney, *Nixon at the Movies* (Chicago: University of Chicago Press, 2004).

23. "The Hollywood blacklist . . ." is from Richard Gid Powers, *Not Without Honor* (New York: Free Press, 1995), 351. See also Joy James, ed., *Imprisoned Intellectuals* (Lanham, MD: Rowman and Littlefield, 2003).

24. Philip Jenkins, *Images of Terror* (Hawthorne, NY: Aldine de Gruyter, 2003).

25. Ron Jacobs, *The Way the Wind Blew* (New York: Verso, 1997); Assata Shakur, *Assata* (Westport, CT: Lawrence Hill, 2001); Akinyele Omowale Umoja, "Repression Breeds Resistance," in Kathleen Cleaver and George Katsiaficas, eds., *Liberation, Imagination, and the Black Panther Party* (New York: Routledge, 2001); Jeremy Varon, *Bringing the War Home* (Berkeley: University of California Press, 2004).

26. Clark Howard, *Zebra* (New York: Berkley, 1980); Peter N. Carroll, *It Seemed Like Nothing Happened* (New York: Holt, Rinehart and Winston, 1982), 215.

27. Donald Freed and Fred Landis, *Death in Washington* (Westport, CT: Lawrence Hill, 1980).

28. Joseph C. Goulden, *The Death Merchant* (New York: Simon and Schuster, 1984); Peter Maas, *Manhunt* (New York: Random House, 1986). For Iraqi death squads on U.S. soil, see Kanan Makiya, *Republic of Fear*, updated ed. (Berkeley: University of California Press, 1998).

29. Marilyn Baker with Sally Brompton, *Exclusive!* (New York: Macmillan, 1974); John Bryan, *This Soldier Still at War* (New York: Harcourt Brace Jovanovich, 1975); Vin McLellan and Paul Avery, *The Voices of Guns* (New York: Putnam, 1977); Patricia Campbell Hearst with Alvin Moscow, *Every Secret Thing* (Garden City, NY: Doubleday, 1982).

30. Frank Snepp, *Decent Interval* (New York: Random House, 1977); Ralph Wetterhahn, *The Last Battle* (New York: Carroll and Graf, 2001); Peter A. Huchthausen, *America's Splendid Little Wars* (New York: Viking, 2003).

31. William A. Au, *The Cross, the Flag, and the Bomb* (Westport, CT: Greenwood Press, 1985); Powers, *Not Without Honor*, 355.

32. Keith L. Nelson, *The Making of Détente* (Johns Hopkins University Press, 1995); Dale Carter, "The Crooked Path," in Elsebeth Hurup, ed., *The Lost Decade* (Aarhus, Denmark: Aarhus University Press, 1996), 103–32; Henry Kissinger, *Years of Renewal* (New York: Simon and Schuster, 1999); Stephanie A. Slocum-Schaffer, *America in the Seventies* (Syracuse: Syracuse University Press, 2003); Jussi M. Hanhimaki, *The Flawed Architect* (New York: Oxford University Press, 2004). For the Apollo-Soyuz program, see Edward Clinton Ezell and Linda Neuman Ezell, *The Partnership* (Washington, DC: GPO, 1978).

33. Dan Caldwell, *The Dynamics of Domestic Politics and Arms Control* (Columbia: University of South Carolina Press, 1991).

34. Steven F. Hayward, *The Age of Reagan, 1964–1980* (Roseville, CA: Prima, 2001), 434; Elmo R. Zumwalt Jr., *On Watch* (New York: Quadrangle/New York Times Book Co., 1976). Even at the height of the anti-CIA fervor, exposés of the KGB had continued; see, for instance, John Barron, *KGB* (New York: E. P. Dutton, 1974).

35. Hayward, *The Age of Reagan*, 427; Caldwell, *The Dynamics of Domestic Politics and Arms Control*; Archie Robinson, *George Meany and His Times* (New York: Simon and Schuster, 1981).

36. Hayward, *The Age of Reagan*, 419; Jesse W. Lewis Jr., *The Strategic Balance in the Mediterranean* (Washington, DC: American Enterprise Institute for Public Policy Research, 1976).

37. Thomas Kiernan, *Arafat, the Man and the Myth* (New York: Norton, 1976); Daniel Patrick Moynihan, "Speech Before the United Nations in Response to 'Zionism Is Racism,'" in Mark Gerson, ed., *The Essential Neoconservative Reader* (Reading, MA: Addison-Wesley, 1996).

38. David Leigh, *The Wilson Plot* (New York: Pantheon, 1988); Stephen Dorril and Robin Ramsay, *Smear!* (London: Grafton, 1991); Rudolf L. Tőkés, ed., *Eurocommunism and Detente* (New York: New York University Press, 1978).

39. Hayward, *The Age of Reagan*, 421; Robert W. Herrick, *Soviet Naval Theory and Policy* (Newport, RI: Naval War College Press, 1988).

40. John Stockwell, *In Search of Enemies* (New York: Norton, 1978); Jorge I. Domínguez, *To Make a World Safe for Revolution* (Cambridge, MA: Harvard University Press, 1989); Chester A. Crocker, *High Noon in Southern Africa* (New York: W. W. Norton, 1992); Fernando Andresen Guimarães, *The Origins of the Angolan Civil War* (New York: St. Martin's, 1998); Piero Gleijeses, *Conflicting Missions* (Chapel Hill: University of North Carolina Press, 2002).

41. Carter, "The Crooked Path."

42. Francis Fukuyama, *The End of History and the Last Man* (New York: Free Press, 1992).

43. Fred C. Allvine and James M. Patterson, *Highway Robbery* (Bloomington: Indiana University Press, 1974); Anthony Sampson, *The Seven Sisters* (New York: Viking, 1975); Robert Sherrill, *The Oil Follies of 1970–1980* (New York: Doubleday Anchor, 1984); Allen J. Matusow, *Nixon's Economy* (Lawrence: University Press of Kansas, 1998).

44. Owen Bowcott, "Heath Feared US Plan to Invade Gulf," *Guardian* (UK), January 1, 2004; Miles Ignotus, "Seizing Arab Oil," *Harper's Magazine*, March 1975.

45. Edward Friedland, Paul Seabury, and Aaron Wildavsky, *The Great Détente Disaster* (New York: Basic Books, 1975). See also Natasha Zaretsky, "In the Name of Austerity," in Van Gosse and Richard Moser, eds., *The World the Sixties Made* (Philadelphia: Temple University Press, 2003). The quote is from a memo from Robert Teeter to Richard Cheney, December 24, 1975, at http://www.fordlibrarymuseum.gov/library/exhibits/polls.htm.

46. Philip Jenkins, "The Post-Industrial Age 1950–2000," in Randall M. Miller and William A. Pencak, eds., *Pennsylvania* (University Park: Pennsylvania State University Press, 2002), 317–70; E. J. McMahon and Fred Siegel, "Gotham's Fiscal Crisis," *Public Interest*, winter 2005.

47. Ronald P. Formisano, *Boston Against Busing* (Chapel Hill: University of North Carolina Press, 1991); Michael Patrick Macdonald, *All Souls* (Boston: Beacon Press, 1999); Thomas J. Sugrue, "Carter's Urban Policy Crisis," in Fink and Hugh Davis Graham, eds., *The Carter Presidency*, 137–57.

48. William K. Tabb, *The Long Default* (New York: Monthly Review Press, 1982); Martin Shefter, *Political Crisis, Fiscal Crisis* (New York: Basic Books, 1985); Jonathan Mahler, *Ladies and Gentlemen, the Bronx Is Burning* (New York: Farrar, Straus and Giroux, 2005).

49. "The Crime Wave," *Time*, June 30, 1975, 10–24.

50. "Gays on the March," *Time*, September 8, 1975; Robin Lloyd, *For Money or Love* (New York: Vanguard Press, 1976); Nik Cohn, "24 Hours on 42nd Street," *New York Magazine*, March 6, 1978, 38–48; Jack McIver Weatherford, *Porn Row* (New York: Arbor House, 1986); Josh Alan Friedman, *Tales of Times Square* (New York: Delacorte, 1986); Samuel R. Delany, *Times Square Red, Times Square Blue* (New York: New York University Press, 1999); Philip Jenkins, *Beyond Tolerance* (New York: New York University Press, 2001); *NYC Sex* (New York: Distributed Art, 2002); Peter Braunstein, "Adults Only," in Beth Bailey and David Farber, eds., *America in the Seventies* (Lawrence: University Press of Kansas, 2004); James Traub, *The Devil's Playground* (New York: Random House, 2004); Anthony Bianco, *Ghosts of 42nd Street* (New York: Morrow, 2004); Mahler, *Ladies and Gentlemen, the Bronx Is Burning*.

51. Lawrence W. Sherman, *Scandal and Reform* (Berkeley: University of California Press, 1978); Gary Marx, *Undercover* (Berkeley: University of California Press, 1988).

52. Lou Sahadi, *Steelers!* (New York: Times Books, 1979).

53. Peter Applebome, *Dixie Rising* (New York: Times Books, 1996); Robert Matej Bednar, "Searching for an Old Faithful America," in Elsebeth Hurup, ed., *The Lost Decade* (Aarhus, Denmark: Aarhus University Press, 1996), 53–78; John G. Cawelti, "That's What I Like about the South," in Hurup, ed., *The Lost Decade*, 11–40. For southernization, see Bruce J. Schulman, *The Seventies* (New York: Free Press, 2001).

54. Dick Dabney, *A Good Man* (Boston: Houghton Mifflin, 1976); Dan T. Carter, *The Politics of Rage*, 2nd ed. (Baton Rouge: Louisiana State University Press, 2000). Charles Bussey, "Jimmy Carter: Hope and Memory Versus Optimism and Nostalgia," in Hurup, ed., *The Lost Decade*. The "stranger in a strange land" quote is from William E. Leuchtenburg, "Jimmy Carter and the Post New Deal Presidency," in Fink and Graham, eds., *The Carter Presidency*, 11.

55. Paul R. Ehrlich, *The Population Bomb* (New York: Ballantine, 1968); William and Paul Paddock, *Famine, 1975!* (Boston: Little, Brown, 1967); Donella H. Meadows et al., *The Limits to Growth* (New York: New American Library, 1974).

56. Harry Harrison, *Make Room! Make Room!* (Garden City, NY: Doubleday, 1966); John Brunner, *Stand on Zanzibar* (Garden City, NY: Doubleday, 1968) and *The Sheep Look Up* (New York: Harper and Row, 1972); Paul M. Sammon, *Future Noir* (London: Orion Media, 1996).

57. Robert L. Heilbroner, *An Inquiry into the Human Prospect* (New York: Norton, 1974); Stewart Udall, Charles Conconi, and David Osterhout, *The Energy Balloon* (New York: McGraw-Hill, 1974); Paul R. Ehrlich and Anne H. Ehrlich, *The End of Affluence* (New York: Ballantine, 1974); L. S. Stavrianos, *The Promise of the Coming Dark Age* (San Francisco: W. H. Freeman, 1976); Paul E. Erdman, *The Crash of '79* (New York: Simon and Schuster, 1976); Stephen H. Schneider with Lynne E. Mesirow, *The Genesis Strategy* (New York: Plenum Press, 1976). Heilbronner is quoted from Colin Campbell, "Coming Apart at the Seams," *Psychology Today*, February 1975, 99.

58. Isaac Asimov, "The Nightmare Life Without Fuel," *Time* April 25, 1977.

59. *The Global 2000 Report to the President* (Washington, DC: GPO, 1980–81).

60. "Toward a Troubled Twenty-first Century," *Time*, August 4, 1980, 54; "A Grim Year 2000," *Newsweek*, August 4, 1980, 38.

61. Ernest Callenbach, *Ecotopia* (New York: Bantam, 1975); Gerald Vizenor, *Bearheart: The Heirship Chronicles* (Minneapolis: University of Minnesota Press, 1990).

62. Larry Niven and Jerry Pournelle, *Lucifer's Hammer* (Chicago: Playboy Press, 1977).

63. James Coates, *Armed and Dangerous* (New York: Hill and Wang, 1987); James W. Gibson, *Warrior Dreams* (New York: Hill and Wang, 1994).

64. Timothy Miller, *The Sixties Communes* (Syracuse: Syracuse University Press, 1999); Eleanor Agnew, *Back from the Land* (Chicago: Ivan R. Dee, 2004).

65. Christopher Capozzola, "It Makes You Want to Believe in the Country," in Beth Bailey and David Farber, eds., *America in the Seventies* (Lawrence: University Press of Kansas, 2004).

Chapter 3

1. "Reagan for President?" *New Republic*, July 2, 1966.

2. In 1936, Alf Landon sank as low as 37 percent of the popular vote.

3. David W. Reinhard, *The Republican Right Since 1945* (Lexington: University Press of Kentucky, 1983); Mary C. Brennan, *Turning Right in the Sixties* (Chapel Hill: University of North Carolina Press, 1995) and "Winning the War, Losing the Battle," in David Farber and Jeff Roche, eds., *The Conservative Sixties* (New York: Peter Lang, 2003); Kurt Schuparra, *Triumph of the Right* (Armonk, NY: M. E. Sharpe, 1998); Rick Perlstein, *Before the Storm* (New York: Hill and Wang, 2001); Lisa McGirr, *Suburban Warriors* (Princeton: Princeton University Press, 2001).

4. Jerome L. Himmelstein, *To the Right* (Berkeley: University of California Press, 1990); George H. Nash, *The Conservative Intellectual Movement in America Since 1945*, reprint ed. (Wilmington, DE: Intercollegiate Studies Institute, 1996); Jonathan M. Schoenwald, *A Time for Choosing* (New York: Oxford University Press, 2001); H. W. Brands, *The Strange Death of American Liberalism* (New Haven: Yale University Press, 2001).

5. Steven F. Hayward, *The Age of Reagan, 1964–1980* (Roseville, CA: Prima, 2001).

6. James Q. Wilson, "A Guide to Reagan Country," *Commentary*, May 1967. Moynihan is quoted in Hayward, *The Age of Reagan*, xxxi. Of course, this does not mean that earlier administrations had not been concerned with issues of family, though these were mainly viewed in economic terms; see Elaine Tyler May, *Homeward Bound* (New York: Basic Books, 1988).

7. Jonathan Rieder, "The Rise of the Silent Majority," in Steve Fraser and Gary Gerstle, eds., *Rise and Fall of the New Deal Order* (Princeton: Princeton University Press, 1990), 242–68; Dan T. Carter, *The Politics of Rage*, 2nd ed. (Baton Rouge: Louisiana State University Press, 2000).

8. Lewis Gould, *Grand Old Party* (New York: Random House, 2003).

9. John Egerton, *The Americanization of Dixie, the Southernization of America* (New York: Harper's Magazine Press, 1974); Kirkpatrick Sale, *Power Shift* (New York: Random House, 1975); Carl Abbott, *The New Urban America* (Chapel Hill: University of North Carolina Press, 1981); Peter Applebome, *Dixie Rising* (New York: Times Books, 1996).

10. Alan Crawford, *Thunder on the Right* (New York: Pantheon, 1980), 78–110; Jeff Roche, "Cowboy Conservatism," in Farber and Roche, eds., *The Conservative Sixties*.

11. Jack Bass and Walter De Vries, *The Transformation of Southern Politics* (New York: Basic Books, 1976); Earl Black and Merle Black, *The Rise of Southern Republicans* (Cambridge, MA: Belknap, 2002).

12. Robert Sherrill, *The Saturday Night Special* (New York: Charterhouse, 1973); *A Shooting Gallery Called America?* NBC documentary, 1975, directed by Tom Priestley; Joseph D. Alviani and William R. Drake, *Handgun Control* (Washington, DC: U.S. Conference of Mayors, 1975); Barry Bruce-Briggs, *The Great American Gun War* (Washington, DC: National Rifle Association of America, 1976); Nancy Loving, Stephen Holden, and Joseph Alviani, *Organizing for Handgun Control* (Washington, DC: U.S. Conference of Mayors, 1977); Edward F. Leddy, *Magnum Force Lobby* (Lanham, MD: University Press of America, 1987).

13. Quoted in Gould, *Grand Old Party*, 427.

14. William Martin, *With God on Our Side* (New York: Broadway, 1996).

15. Kenneth D. Durr, *Behind the Backlash* (Chapel Hill: University of North Carolina Press, 2003); Wyatt C. Wells, *American Capitalism, 1945–2000* (Chicago: Ivan R Dee, 2003); Jefferson Cowie, "Vigorously Left, Right, and Center," in Beth Bailey and David Farber, eds., *America in the Seventies* (Lawrence: University Press of Kansas, 2004).

16. John T. McGreevy, *Parish Boundaries* (Chicago: University of Chicago Press, 1998); Gerald H. Gamm, *Urban Exodus* (Cambridge, MA: Harvard University Press, 2001).

17. Eugene Kennedy, *Himself!* (New York: Viking, 1978); S. A. Paolantonio, *Frank Rizzo* (Philadelphia: Camino, 1993). Los Angeles's Democratic mayor Sam Yorty represented a comparable white ethnic politics.

18. Kenneth A. Briggs, *Holy Siege* (San Francisco: Harper, 1992).

19. Ben Armstrong, *The Electric Church* (Nashville, TN: Thomas Nelson, 1979); Steve Bruce, *Pray TV* (London: Routledge, 1990); Roger Finke and Rodney Stark, *The Churching of America 1776–1990* (New Brunswick, NJ: Rutgers University Press, 1992); Lynne Hybels and Bill Hybels, *Rediscovering Church* (Grand Rapids, MI: Zondervan, 1995); Martin, *With God on Our Side*; Donald E. Miller, *Reinventing American Protestantism* (Berkeley: University of California Press, 1997); Randall Balmer, *Mine Eyes Have Seen the Glory* (New York: Oxford University Press, 2000); Jon Butler, Grant Wacker, and Randall Balmer, *Religion in American Life* (New York: Oxford University Press, 2003).

20. Nancy Tatom Ammerman, *Baptist Battles* (New Brunswick: Rutgers University Press, 1990); Michael W. Cuneo, *American Exorcism* (New York: Doubleday, 2001). Billy Graham, *Angels: God's Secret Agents* (Garden City, NY: Doubleday, 1975); Malachi Martin, *Hostage to the Devil* (New York: Bantam, 1976).

21. Francis A. Schaeffer. *How Should We Then Live?* (Old Tappan, NJ: F. H. Revell, 1976); Paul Boyer, *When Time Shall Be No More* (Cambridge, MA: Belknap, 1992); Bernard McGinn, *Antichrist* (San Francisco: HarperSanFrancisco, 1994); Robert C. Fuller, *Naming the Antichrist* (New York: Oxford University Press, 1995).

22. Samuel S. Hill and Dennis E. Owen, *The New Religious Political Right in America* (Nashville: Abingdon, 1982); Steve Bruce, *The Rise and Fall of the New Christian Right* (New York: Oxford

University Press, 1988); Matthew C. Moen, *The Transformation of the Christian Right* (Tuscaloosa: University of Alabama Press, 1992); Oran P. Smith, *The Rise of Baptist Republicanism* (New York: New York University Press, 1997); Scott Flipse, "Below-the-Belt Politics," in Farber and Roche, eds., *The Conservative Sixties.*

23. Crawford, *Thunder on the Right;* Burton Yale Pines, *Back to Basics* (New York: Morrow, 1982); Mel Gabler and Norma Gabler with James C. Hefley, *What Are They Teaching Our Children?* (Wheaton, IL: Victor, 1985); Ira Shor, *Culture Wars* (Boston: Routledge and Kegan Paul, 1986); Walter H. Capps, *The New Religious Right* (Columbia: University of South Carolina Press, 1990).

24. Carol Felsenthal, *The Sweetheart of the Silent Majority* (Garden City, NY: Doubleday, 1981); Hayward, *The Age of Reagan*, 309.

25. Phyllis Schlafly, *A Choice Not an Echo* (Alton, IL: Pere Marquette Press, 1964); Phyllis Schlafly and Chester Ward, *Kissinger on the Couch* (New Rochelle, NY: Arlington House, 1974); Phyllis Schlafly and Chester Ward, *Ambush at Vladivostok* (Alton, IL: Pere Marquette Press, 1976); Felsenthal, *The Sweetheart of the Silent Majority;* Donald T. Critchlow, "Conservatism Reconsidered," in Farber and Roche, eds., *The Conservative Sixties;* Michelle Nickerson, "Moral Mothers and Goldwater Girls," in Farber and Roche, eds., *The Conservative Sixties.* For the anti-ERA campaign, see Pamela Johnston Conover and Virginia Gray, *Feminism and the New Right* (New York: Praeger, 1983); Andrea Dworkin, *Right-Wing Women* (New York: Coward, McCann, 1983); Gilbert Y. Steiner, *Constitutional Inequality* (Washington, DC: Brookings Institution, 1985); Mary Frances Berry, *Why ERA Failed* (Bloomington: Indiana University Press, 1986); Rebecca E. Klatch, *Women of the New Right* (Philadelphia: Temple University Press, 1987) and *A Generation Divided* (Berkeley: University of California Press, 1999).

26. George F. Gilder, *Sexual Suicide* (New York: Quadrangle, 1973). "There are no human beings . . ." is p. 43; "The feminist program . . . ," 13; "Will the scientists and women's liberationists . . . ," 262; "still instinctively recognize . . . ," 131. See also George Gilder, *Naked Nomads* (New York: Quadrangle/ New York Times Book Co., 1974).

27. Richard N. Ostling and Joan K. Ostling, *Mormon America* (San Francisco: HarperSanFrancisco, 2000); George A. Kelly, *The Battle for the American Church* (New York: Doubleday Image, 1981) and *The Battle for the American Church Revisited* (San Francisco: Ignatius Press, 1995); Patrick Allitt, *Catholic Intellectuals and Conservative Politics in America 1950–1985* (Cornell University Press, 1993).

28. Francis A. Schaeffer and C. Everett Koop, *Whatever Happened to the Human Race?* (Old Tappan, NJ: F. H. Revell, 1979); Dallas A. Blanchard, *The Anti-Abortion Movement and the Rise of the Religious Right* (New York: Twayne, 1994); Rickie Solinger, ed., *Abortion Wars* (Berkeley: University of California Press, 1998).

29. For the obscenity campaigns, see "The Porno Plague," *Time*, April 5, 1976, which is the source for the Brownmiller quote; Larry Flynt with Kenneth Ross, *An Unseemly Man* (Los Angeles: Dove, 1996); Samuel Walker, *In Defense of American Liberties*, 2nd ed. (Carbondale: Southern Illinois University Press, 1999). For snuff films, see Beverley LaBelle, "Snuff," in Laura Lederer, ed., *Take Back the Night* (New York: Morrow, 1980); Scott Aaron Stine, "The Snuff Film," *Skeptical Inquirer* May/June 1999, http://www.csicop.org/si/9905/snuff.html.

30. Richard Gid Powers, *Not Without Honor* (New York: Free Press, 1995).

31. Ben Kiernan, *The Pol Pot Regime*, 2nd ed. (New Haven: Yale University Press, 2002); Aleksandr I. Solzhenitsyn, *The Gulag Archipelago, 1918–1956*, vol. 1 (New York: Harper and Row, 1974) and *Détente* (New Brunswick, NJ: Transaction, 1976).

32. Peter Steinfels, *The Neoconservatives* (New York: Simon and Schuster, 1979); John Ehrman, *The Rise of Neoconservatism* (New Haven: Yale University Press, 1995); Mark Gerson ed., *The Essential Neoconservative Reader* (Reading, MA: Addison-Wesley, 1996); Robert G. Kaufman, *Henry M.*

Jackson (Seattle: University of Washington Press, 2000); Murray Friedman, *The Neoconservative Revolution* (New York: Cambridge University Press, 2005). For the rightward shift of disaffected leftist radicals, see Peter Collier and David Horowitz, eds., *Second Thoughts* (Lanham, MD: Madison, 1989).

33. Tom Wolfe, *Radical Chic and Mau-Mauing The Flak Catchers* (New York: Bantam Doubleday, 1999); Godfrey Hodgson, *The World Turned Right Side Up* (Boston: Houghton Mifflin, 1996); Collier and Horowitz, eds., *Second Thoughts*.

34. Peter Novick, *The Holocaust in American Life* (Boston: Houghton Mifflin, 1999).

35. William Stevenson, *90 Minutes at Entebbe* (New York: Bantam, 1976).

36. Daniel Patrick Moynihan with Suzanne Weaver, *A Dangerous Place* (Boston: Little, Brown, 1978); Godfrey Hodgson, *The Gentleman from New York* (Boston: Houghton Mifflin, 2000).

37. Leo P. Ribuffo, *Right Center Left* (New Brunswick: Rutgers University Press, 1992); *United States National Security Policy Vis-à-Vis Eastern Europe* (Washington, DC: GPO, 1976).

38. Henry Kissinger, *Years of Renewal* (New York: Simon and Schuster, 1999).

39. Hayward, *The Age of Reagan*, 423–24; Hodgson, *The World Turned Right Side Up*; John Prados, *Lost Crusader* (New York: Oxford University Press, 2003); James Mann, *Rise of the Vulcans* (New York: Viking, 2004).

40. Ehrman, *The Rise of Neoconservatism*, 111–13; Richard Pipes, ed., *Soviet Strategy in Europe* (New York: Crane, Russak, 1976); Dan Caldwell, *The Dynamics of Domestic Politics and Arms Control* (Columbia: University of South Carolina Press, 1991); Anne H. Cahn, *Killing Détente* (University Park: Pennsylvania State University Press, 1998).

41. Powers, *Not Without Honor*, 369; Norman Podhoretz, *Breaking Ranks* (New York: Harper and Row, 1979) and *The Present Danger* (New York: Simon and Schuster, 1980); Walter Laqueur, *The Political Psychology of Appeasement* (New Brunswick, NJ: Transaction, 1980); Jerry W. Sanders, *Peddlers of Crisis* (Boston: South End Press, 1983); Charles Tyroler II, ed., *Alerting America* (Washington, DC: Pergamon-Brassey's, 1984).

42. Richard Reeves, *A Ford, Not a Lincoln* (New York: Harcourt Brace Jovanovich, 1975); Robert T. Hartmann, *Palace Politics* (New York: McGraw-Hill, 1980); A. James Reichley, *Conservatives in an Age of Change* (Washington, DC: Brookings Institution, 1981).

43. Phillips is quoted from Lee Edwards, *The Conservative Revolution* (New York: Free Press, 1999), 183–84; William A. Rusher. *The Making of the New Majority Party* (New York: Sheed and Ward, 1975); Patrick J. Buchanan, *Conservative Votes, Liberal Victories* (New York: New York Times Book Co., 1975).

44. Richard A. Viguerie, *The New Right*, rev. ed. (Falls Church, VA: Viguerie, 1981); Crawford, *Thunder on the Right*; Jean Stefancic and Richard Delgado, *No Mercy* (Philadelphia: Temple University Press, 1998); Richard A. Viguerie and David Franke, *America's Right Turn* (Chicago: Bonus, 2004).

45. Jules Witcover, *Marathon* (New York: Viking, 1977); Patrick Anderson, *Electing Jimmy Carter* (Baton Rouge: Louisiana State University Press, 1994).

46. Richard Reeves, *Convention* (New York: Harcourt Brace Jovanovich, 1977); http://www. presidency.ucsb.edu/showplatforms.php?platindex=D1976. Carter's speech is quoted from *Time*; see http://www.time.com/time/poy2000/archive/1976.html.

47. "An Explanation of the Reagan Victories in Texas and the Caucus States," May 1976, http:// www.fordlibrarymuseum.gov/library/exhibits/reagan.htm. "The spokesman for a harsh..." is quoted by Hayward, *The Age of Reagan*, 100; "Reagan failed..." is ibid., 478. See also Craig Shirley, *Reagan's Revolution* (Nashville, TN: Nelson Current, 2005).

48. Mark J. Rozell, *The Press and the Carter Presidency* (Boulder, CO: Westview, 1989); Burton I. Kaufman, *The Presidency of James Earl Carter Jr.* (Lawrence: University Press of Kansas, 1993).

49. Peter G. Bourne, *Jimmy Carter* (New York: Scribner's, 1997); David Brian Robertson, ed., *Loss of Confidence* (University Park: Pennsylvania State University Press, 1998); W. Carl Biven, *Jimmy Carter's Economy* (Chapel Hill: University of North Carolina Press, 2002); Robert M. Collins, *More* (New York: Oxford University Press, 2002); Gregory Paul Domin, *Jimmy Carter, Public Opinion, and the Search for Values, 1977–1981* (Macon, GA: Mercer University Press, 2003).

50. I am very grateful to my colleague Alan Derickson for discussions on this topic. Alan Derickson, *Health Security for All* (Baltimore: Johns Hopkins University Press, 2005); Joseph A. Califano, *Inside* (New York: Public Affairs, 2004); Charles O. Jones, *The Trusteeship Presidency* (Baton Rouge: Louisiana State University Press, 1988); oral history interview with Joseph Califano at http://www.ssa.gov/history/CALIFANO2.html.

51. Jude Wanniski, *The Way the World Works* (New York: Basic Books, 1978). Also deeply influential on Reagan-era economic policy would be George Gilder, *Wealth and Poverty* (New York: Basic Books, 1981). Caddell is quoted from Peter N. Carroll, *It Seemed Like Nothing Happened* (New York: Holt, Rinehart and Winston, 1982), 325. See also Arthur B. Laffer and Jan P. Seymour, eds., *The Economics of the Tax Revolt* (New York: Harcourt Brace Jovanovich, 1979); Robert Kuttner, *Revolt of the Haves* (New York: Simon and Schuster, 1980); Thomas Byrne Edsall with Mary D. Edsall, *Chain Reaction* (New York: Norton, 1991), 116–36; Daniel A. Smith, *Tax Crusaders and the Politics of Direct Democracy* (New York: Routledge, 1998). "California to liberal government . . ." is quoted from Hayward, *The Age of Reagan*, 527.

52. Hodgson, *The World Turned Right Side Up*, 156; Joel Dreyfuss and Charles Lawrence III, *The Bakke Case* (New York: Harcourt Brace Jovanovich, 1979); Griffin Bell, *Taking Care of the Law* (New York: Morrow, 1986); Howard Ball, *The Bakke Case* (Lawrence: University Press of Kansas, 2000); Eric Porter, "Affirming and Disaffirming Actions," in Beth Bailey and David Farber, eds., *America in the Seventies* (Lawrence: University Press of Kansas, 2004). "Bar like discrimination in the future" is quoted from *Albemarle Paper Co. v. Moody*, 422 U.S. 405 (1975).

53. Quoted in Hodgson, *The World Turned Right Side Up*, 176; Edsall and Edsall, *Chain Reaction*. The private school discrimination case was *Runyon v. McCrary*, 427 U.S. 160 (1976).

54. Steve Bruce, *The Rise and Fall of the New Christian Right* (New York: Oxford University Press, 1988).

55. Carl J. Friedrich and Zbigniew K. Brzezinski, *Totalitarian Dictatorship and Autocracy* (Cambridge, MA: Harvard University Press, 1956); Zbigniew Brzezinski, *Ideology and Power in Soviet Politics*, reprint ed. (Westport, CT: Greenwood Press, 1976) and *Power and Principle* (New York: Farrar, Straus, Giroux, 1983); Stephanie A. Slocum-Schaffer, *America in the Seventies* (Syracuse: Syracuse University Press, 2003). "We can no more stop . . ." is quoted from Powers, *Not Without Honor*, 354; Cyrus R. Vance, *Hard Choices* (New York: Simon and Schuster, 1983); Donald S. Spencer, *The Carter Implosion* (New York: Praeger, 1988); David Skidmore, *Reversing Course* (Nashville: Vanderbilt University Press, 1996); Robert A. Strong, *Working in the World* (Baton Rouge: Louisiana State University Press, 2000).

56. SALT II "will mean the permanent surrender . . ." is quoted from Crawford, *Thunder on the Right*, 54. See also Strobe Talbott, *Endgame* (New York: Harper and Row, 1979) and *The Master of the Game* (New York: Knopf, 1988); Stansfield Turner, *Secrecy and Democracy* (Boston: Houghton Mifflin, 1985); Joseph C. Goulden, *The Death Merchant* (New York: Simon and Schuster, 1984).

57. Moynihan is quoted from Ehrman, *The Rise of Neoconservatism*, 94. See also Sherri L. Wasserman, *The Neutron Bomb Controversy* (New York: Praeger, 1983); Vincent A. Auger, *The Dynamics of Foreign Policy Analysis* (Lanham, MD: Rowman and Littlefield, 1996); James Mann, *About Face* (New York: Vintage, 2000).

58. William Stueck, "Placing Jimmy Carter's Foreign Policy," in Fink and Graham, eds., *The Carter Presidency*, 244–66; Gaddis Smith, *Morality, Reason, and Power* (New York: Hill and Wang, 1986).

59. Jeane J. Kirkpatrick, *Dictatorships and Double Standards* (New York: Simon and Schuster, 1982).

60. Allen Weinstein, *Perjury* (New York: Knopf, 1978); Allen Weinstein and Alexander Vassiliev, *The Haunted Wood* (New York: Random House, 1999). In 1983, Ronald Radosh and Joyce Milton confirmed that the Rosenbergs had in fact been Soviet spies; see their *The Rosenberg File* (New York: Holt, Rinehart, and Winston, 1983).

61. Hayward, *The Age of Reagan*, 544.

62. Walter Lafeber, *The Panama Canal* (New York: Oxford University Press, 1978); George D. Moffett, *The Limits of Victory* (Ithaca, NY: Cornell University Press, 1983).

63. Susan Jeffords, *The Remasculinization of America* (Bloomington: Indiana University Press, 1989).

64. Lawrence M. Baskir and William A. Strauss, *Chance and Circumstance* (New York: Knopf, 1978); Ron Kovic, *Born on the Fourth of July* (New York: McGraw-Hill, 1976); Jeremiah A. Denton Jr. with Ed Brandt, *When Hell Was in Session* (New York: Readers Digest Press, 1976); Philip Caputo, *A Rumor of War* (New York: Holt, Rinehart and Winston, 1977); Guenter Lewy, *America in Vietnam* (New York: Oxford University Press, 1978); Michael Herr, *Dispatches* (New York: Knopf, 1977); Mark Baker, *Nam* (New York: Morrow, 1981); Al Santoli, *Everything We Had* (New York: Random House, 1981); Wilbur J. Scott, *The Politics of Readjustment* (New York: Aldine de Gruyter, 1993) and *Vietnam Veterans Since the War* (Norman: University of Oklahoma Press, 2004); James H. Wittebols, *Watching M*A*S*H, Watching America* (Jefferson, NC: McFarland, 1998); Jerry Lembcke, *The Spitting Image* (New York: New York University Press, 2000).

65. Marita Sturken, *Tangled Memories* (Berkeley: University of California Press, 1997); Kristin Ann Hass, *Carried to the Wall* (Berkeley: University of California Press, 1998); Scott, *Vietnam Veterans Since the War*.

66. H. Bruce Franklin, *M.I.A., or, Mythmaking in America* (Brooklyn, NY: L. Hill, 1992); Richard Slotkin, *Gunfighter Nation* (New York: Atheneum, 1992); Susan Katz Keating, *Prisoners of Hope* (New York: Random House, 1994).

67. Lembcke, *Spitting Image*.

68. David A. Stockman, *The Triumph of Politics* (New York: Harper and Row, 1986), 49–50. "Conservative populism . . ." is quoted from Edsall and Edsall, *Chain Reaction*, 165. See also R. Emmett Tyrrell Jr., *The Liberal Crack-Up* (New York: Simon and Schuster, 1984).

Chapter 4

1. Alan Crawford, *Thunder on the Right* (New York: Pantheon, 1980), 53.

2. John T. Noonan Jr., *A Private Choice* (New York: Free Press, 1979); Rickie Solinger, ed., *Abortion Wars* (Berkeley: University of California Press, 1998).

3. Toni Carabillo, Judith Meuli, and June Bundy Csida, *Feminist Chronicles, 1953–1993* (Los Angeles: Women's Graphics, 1993).

4. Rosemary Thomson, *The Price of LIBerty* (Carol Stream, IL: Creation House, 1978); Peter N. Carroll, *It Seemed Like Nothing Happened* (New York: Holt, Rinehart and Winston, 1982).

5. Carroll, *It Seemed Like Nothing Happened*, 268; Phyllis Schlafly, *The Power of the Positive Woman* (New Rochelle, NY: Arlington House, 1977); *The Spirit of Houston* (Washington, DC: GPO, 1978); *What Women Want* (New York: Simon and Schuster, 1979); Rebecca E. Klatch, *Women of the New Right* (Philadelphia: Temple University Press, 1987).

6. Philip Jenkins, *Moral Panic* (New Haven: Yale University Press, 1998).

7. Manfred S. Guttmacher, *Sex Offenses* (New York: Norton, 1951).

8. David Abrahamsen, *The Psychology of Crime* (New York: Columbia University Press, 1960), 161. Pomeroy is quoted in Diana E. H. Russell, *The Secret Trauma* (New York: Basic Books, 1986).

9. Tappan is quoted from Fred Cohen, ed., *Law of Deprivation of Liberty* (St. Paul, MN: West, 1980), 669–70; Alfred C. Kinsey, Wardell B. Pomeroy, Clyde E. Martin, and P. H. Gebhard, *Sexual Behavior in the Human Female* (Philadelphia: W. B. Saunders, 1953), 121.

10. Susan Brownmiller, *Against Our Will* (London: Secker and Warburg, 1975).

11. Judith Levine, *Harmful to Minors* (New York: Thunder's Mouth, 2003); Jenkins, *Moral Panic*. For the changing meaning of child abuse, see C. Henry Kempe et al., "The Battered Child Syndrome," *Journal of the American Medical Association*, 181 (1962), 17–24; *Proceedings of the First National Conference on Child Abuse and Neglect* (Washington, DC: GPO, 1976); Stephen J. Pfohl, "The Discovery of Child Abuse," *Social Problems* 24 (1977): 310–23.

12. Albert E. Wilkerson, ed., *The Rights of Children* (Philadelphia: Temple University Press, 1973); Beatrice Gross and Ronald Gross, eds., *The Children's Rights Movement* (Garden City, NY: Anchor, 1977); Kee MacFarlane and Leonard Lieber, *Parents Anonymous* (Washington, DC: GPO, 1978).

13. Judianne Densen-Gerber, *We Mainline Dreams* (Garden City, NY: Doubleday, 1973); Kenneth Wooden, *Weeping in the Playtime of Others* (New York: McGraw-Hill, 1976); Bruce Ritter, *Sometimes God Has a Kid's Face* (New York: Covenant House, 1988); Charles M. Sennott, *Broken Covenant* (New York: Simon and Schuster, 1992).

14. E. Weber, "Incest," *Ms.*, April 1977, 64–67.

15. Jenkins, *Moral Panic*, 121–25; Philip Jenkins, *Beyond Tolerance* (New York: New York University Press, 2001), 30–40; Ritter, *Sometimes God Has a Kid's Face*, 25, 33. The vice culture of this world received added publicity through the 1980 television movie *Off the Minnesota Strip*. See also Robin Lloyd, *For Money or Love* (New York: Vanguard, 1976); Jonathan Mahler, *Ladies and Gentlemen, the Bronx Is Burning* (New York: Farrar, Straus and Giroux, 2005).

16. The NBC report is quoted in Joel Best, *Threatened Children* (Chicago: University of Chicago Press, 1990), 98. See also "Child's Garden of Perversity," *Time*, April 4, 1977, 55–56; Judianne Densen-Gerber, "What Pornographers Are Doing to Children," *Redbook*, August 1977, 86+; Gloria Steinem, "Pornography," *Ms.*, August 1977, 43–44. The *Chicago Tribune* series ran from May 15–19, 1977, and is reprinted in *Sexual Exploitation of Children: Hearings Before the Subcommittee on Crime of the Committee on the Judiciary. House of Representatives* (Washington, DC: GPO, 1977), 428–41.

17. *Sexual Exploitation of Children*; Lloyd Martin interview in Kathleen Barry, *Female Sexual Slavery* (Englewood Cliffs, NJ: Prentice Hall, 1979), 99–102.

18. *Sexual Exploitation of Children*, 58 (Martin), 74–75 (Leonard).

19. Densen-Gerber is quoted in Ernest Volkman and Howard L. Rosenberg, "The Shame of the Nation," *Family Weekly*, June 2, 1985, 6.

20. Best, *Threatened Children*; Kinsey et al., *Sexual Behavior in the Human Female*.

21. *Barnes v. Costle*, 561 F. 2d 983 (DC Cir. 1977). Lin Farley, *Sexual Shakedown* (New York: McGraw-Hill, 1978); Constance Backhouse and Leah Cohen, *The Secret Oppression* (Toronto: Macmillan of Canada, 1978); Catharine A. Mackinnon, *Sexual Harassment of Working Women* (New Haven: Yale University Press, 1979); *Sexual Harassment in the Federal Government* (Washington, DC: GPO, 1980); Carrie N. Baker, "He Said, She Said," in Sherrie A. Inness, ed., *Disco Divas* (Philadelphia: University of Pennsylvania Press, 2003), 39–55.

22. Ann W. Burgess, A. Nicholas Groth, L. L. Holmstrom, and S. M. Sgroi, *Sexual Assault of Children and Adolescents* (Lexington, MA: D. C. Heath, 1978); Louise Armstrong, *Kiss Daddy Goodnight* (New York: Hawthorn, 1978); Sandra Butler, *Conspiracy of Silence* (San Francisco: New Glide Publications, 1978); David Finkelhor, *Sexually Victimized Children* (New York: Free Press, 1979); Jennifer Barr, *Within a Dark Wood* (Garden City, NY: Doubleday, 1979); Katherine Brady, *Father's Days* (New York: Dell, 1979); Susan Forward and Craig Buck, *Betrayal of Innocence* (New York:

Penguin, 1979); Robert L. Geiser, *Hidden Victims* (Boston: Beacon, 1979); Florence Rush, *The Best-Kept Secret* (Englewood Cliffs, NJ: Prentice Hall, 1980); Judith L. Herman and Lisa Hirschman, *Father-Daughter Incest* (Cambridge, MA: Harvard University Press, 1981). For PTSD, see Allan Young, *The Harmony of Illusions* (Princeton: Princeton University Press, 1995); Wilbur J. Scott, *Vietnam Veterans Since the War* (Norman: University of Oklahoma Press, 2004); Joseph E. Davis, *Accounts of Innocence* (Chicago: University of Chicago Press, 2005).

23. Florence Rush, "The Sexual Abuse of Children," in Noreen Connell and Cassandra Wilson, *Rape* (New York: New American Library, 1974), 73–74; Weber, "Incest."

24. Jonathan Ned Katz, *Gay/Lesbian Almanac* (New York: Harper Colophon, 1983), and *Gay American History* (New York: Meridian, 1992).

25. Parker Rossman, *Sexual Experience Between Men and Boys* (New York: Association Press, 1976).

26. Jeffrey Escoffier, "Fabulous Politics," in Van Gosse and Richard Moser, eds., *The World the Sixties Made* (Philadelphia: Temple University Press, 2003), 199.

27. Anita Bryant, *The Anita Bryant Story* (Old Tappan, NJ: Revell, 1977), 16. Compare Anita Bryant and Bob Green, *At Any Cost* (Old Tappan, NJ: Fleming H. Revell, 1978).

28. Bryant, *The Anita Bryant Story*, 43; ibid., 53 for her use of Gilder; ibid., 42 for "militant homosexuals."

29. "Homosexual acts are not only illegal . . ." is quoted from Escoffier, "Fabulous Politics," 199. "I don't hate the homosexuals! . . ." is from Crawford, *Thunder on the Right*, 52. "Are all homosexuals nice? . . ." is from Bryant, *The Anita Bryant Story*, 90. For scouting scandals, see Patrick Boyle, *Scout's Honor* (Rocklin, CA: Prima, 1994).

30. Perry Deane Young, *God's Bullies* (New York: Holt Rinehart Winston, 1982), 44–46; *Sexual Exploitation of Children*, 433 (*Chicago Tribune*), 205 (Wooden). Compare Bryant, *The Anita Bryant Story*, 119.

31. For the Selma analogy, see Bryant, *The Anita Bryant Story*, 88. "Gay women and men" is quoted from Carroll, *It Seemed Like Nothing Happened*, 291. See also Edward Alwood, *Straight News* (New York: Columbia University Press, 1996), 168–71.

32. "One-third of San Francisco teachers . . ." is quoted in Alwood, *Straight News*, 172.

33. Randy Shilts, *The Mayor of Castro Street* (New York: St. Martin's, 1982). "Resurrected a slumbering activism . . ." is from Robert I. McQueen and Randy Shilts, "The Movement's Born Again," *The Advocate*, July 27, 1977. See also Craig A. Rimmerman, Kenneth D. Wald, and Clyde Wilcox, eds., *The Politics of Gay Rights* (Chicago: University of Chicago Press, 2000).

34. John Mitzel, *The Boston Sex Scandal* (Boston: Glad Day, 1980); Jenkins, *Moral Panic*, 153–60.

35. Frank Rose, "Men and Boys Together," *Village Voice*, February 27, 1978; John Gerassi, *The Boys of Boise* (New York: Macmillan, 1966).

36. Enrique Rueda, *The Homosexual Network* (Old Greenwich, CT: Devin Adair, 1982); John Gallagher and Chris Bull, *Perfect Enemies* (New York: Crown, 1996); Alwood, *Straight News*.

37. Alice Echols, *Shaky Ground* (New York: Columbia University Press, 2002). For the text of the Delineation, see http://members.aol.com/NOWSM/Delineation.html.

38. David Musto, *The American Disease*, 2nd ed. (New Haven: Yale University Press, 1987).

39. "Nor do we, under any conceivable way . . ." is from *Decriminalization of Marihuana: Hearings Before the Select Committee on Narcotics Abuse and Control* (Washington, DC: GPO, 1977), 13. For Bourne, see Jill Jonnes, *Hep-Cats, Narcs and Pipe Dreams* (New York: Scribner's, 1996), 313, 316; Michael Massing, *The Fix* (New York: Simon and Schuster, 1998).

40. Malcolm Gladwell, "Just Say 'Wait a Minute,'" in *New York Review of Books*, December 17, 1998; Massing, *The Fix*; Marsha Keith Schuchard, *Parents, Peers, and Pot II: Parents in Action* (Washington, DC: GPO, 1983), 3.

41. Marsha Keith Schuchard, *Parents, Peers, and Pot* (Washington, DC: GPO, 1979), 1.

42. Philip Jenkins, *Synthetic Panics* (New York: New York University Press, 1999), 54–75; John A. Newmeyer, "The Epidemiology of PCP Use in the Late 1970s," *Journal of Psychedelic Drugs* 12 (1980): 211–15; E. Don Nelson, Leonard T. Sigell, Roger E. Parker, and Janiece Hestness, "Epidemiology of PCP Use," *Journal of Psychedelic Drugs* 12 (1980): 217–22.

43. *PCP, a Killer Drug on the Rise* (Washington, DC: GPO, 1978); Anne J. D'Arcy, *PCP: Angel Dust. Number One Teen Killer* (Centerville, OH: Pamphlet Publications, 1980); Judianne Densen-Gerber and Michael Baden, *The Doctor Talks to You About Cocaine, Angel Dust (PCP) and Other Drugs* (sound recording) (Bayside, NY: Soundwords, 1981).

44. Alice Bonner, "Angel Dust: Schizophrenia Epidemic Here Linked to Youths' Use of PCP," *Washington Post*, June 11, 1977; "PCP: A Terror of a Drug," *Time*, December 19, 1977; P. Chargot, "The Cheap Street Drug PCP," *Detroit Free Press*, January 15, 1978; "Angel Dust: The Devil Drug That Threatens Youth," *Woman's Day*, June 14, 1978; Todd Strasser, *Angel Dust Blues* (New York: Coward, McCann and Geoghegan, 1979); John P. Morgan and Doreen Kagan, "The Dusting of America," *Journal of Psychedelic Drugs* 12 (1980): 195–204; Ronald L. Linder, Steven E. Lerner, and R. Stanley Burns, *PCP, The Devil's Dust* (Belmont, CA: Wadsworth, 1981).

45. The quote about how "PCP can knock out an elephant" is from Robin De Silva, "PCP: Killer Weed Is Status Drug," *Washington Post*, July 3, 1977.

46. For "dynamite," see *Phencyclidine (PCP or Angel Dust): Joint Hearings Before the Subcommittee to Investigate Juvenile Delinquency of the Committee on the Judiciary* (Washington, DC: GPO, 1978), 77. The "King Cobra" quote is from *Abuse of Dangerous Licit and Illicit Drugs—Psychotropics, Phencyclidine (PCP), and Talwin: Hearings Before the Select Committee on Narcotics Abuse and Control* (Washington, DC: GPO, 1979), 2–3. For "death on the installment plan," see Harvey Feldman, Michael Agar, and George Beschner, eds., *Angel Dust* (Lexington, MA: Lexington, 1979), 1. Dupont is quoted from "PCP: A Terror of a Drug," *Time*, December 19, 1977.

47. *Phencyclidine (PCP or Angel Dust)*, 61; Schuchard, *Parents, Peers, and Pot II: Parents in Action*, 6–7.

48. Schuchard, *Parents, Peers, and Pot* and *Parents, Peers, and Pot II: Parents in Action*.

49. Philip Jenkins, *Mystics and Messiahs* (New York: Oxford University Press, 2000), 165–208.

50. Stanley Milgram, *Obedience to Authority* (New York: Harper and Row, 1974); Thomas Blass, *The Man Who Shocked the World* (New York: Basic Books, 2004).

51. Davis is quoted from Ronald Enroth, "The Seduction Syndrome," in Ronald M. Enroth, *Youth, Brainwashing, and the Extremist Cults* (Grand Rapids, MI: Zondervan, 1977), 157. "Since the early 1970s . . ." is from *Transcript of Proceedings: Information Meeting on the Cult Phenomenon in the United States (Dole Hearings)* (Washington, DC: Ace-Federal Reporters, 1979), 25; Rabbi Davis is from ibid., 79.

52. Lee Hultquist, *They Followed the Piper* (Plainfield: Logos International, 1977); John Garvey, ed., *All Our Sons and Daughters* (Springfield, IL: Templegate, 1977); Anson D. Shupe and David G. Bromley, *The New Vigilantes* (Beverly Hills: Sage Publications, 1980); Anson D. Shupe, David G. Bromley, and Donna L. Oliver, *The Anti-Cult Movement in America* (New York: Garland, 1984); James A. Beckford, *Cult Controversies* (London: Tavistock, 1985).

53. Paul Andre Verdier, *Brainwashing and the Cults* (North Hollywood, CA: Wilshire Book Co., 1977); Enroth, ed., *Youth, Brainwashing, and the Extremist Cults*; Flo Conway and Jim Siegelman, *Snapping*, 2nd ed. (New York: Stillpoint, 1995 [1978]); David G. Bromley and James T. Richardson, eds., *The Brainwashing/Deprogramming Controversy* (New York: Edwin Mellen Press, 1983); Anson D. Shupe and David G. Bromley, *A Documentary History of the Anti-Cult Movement* (Arlington: Center for Social Research, University of Texas at Arlington, 1985); Barbara Underwood and Betty Underwood, *Hostage to Heaven* (New York: Clarkson Potter, 1979).

54. *The Challenge of the Cults* (Philadelphia: Jewish Community Relations Council of Greater Philadelphia, 1978); Shea Hecht and Chaim Clorfene, *Confessions of a Jewish Cult-Buster* (Brooklyn, NY: Tosefos Media, 1985); Aidan A. Kelly, ed., *Cults and the Jewish Community* (New York: Garland, 1990).

55. "The Darker Side of Sun Moon," *Time*, June 14, 1976, 50; "Why I Quit the Moon Cult," *Seventeen*, July 1976, 107+; Ann Crittenden, "The Incredible Story of Ann Gordon and Rev. Sun Myung Moon," *Good Housekeeping*, October, 1976, 86+; David Black, "The Secrets of the Innocents," *Woman's Day*, February 1977, 166–75; Christopher Edwards, *Crazy for God* (Englewood Cliffs, NJ: Prentice-Hall, 1979); Allen Tate Wood and Jack Vitek, *Moonstruck* (New York: Morrow, 1979); Steve Kemperman, *Lord of the Second Advent* (Ventura, CA: Regal, 1981).

56. For Scientology, see Russell Miller, *Bare-Faced Messiah* (New York: Henry Holt. 1988). Dederich is quoted from Dave Mitchell, "*Light* to Celebrate 25th Anniversary of Its Pulitzer," *Point Reyes Light*, April 15, 2004, at http://www.rickross.com/reference/synanon/synanon5.html. See also "State of Siege," *Newsweek*, March 27, 1978; Hizkias Assefa and Paul Wahrhaftig, *The MOVE Crisis in Philadelphia* (Pittsburgh: University of Pittsburgh Press, 1990).

57. Dorothy Aldridge, "Are Satan's Phantom Killers Mutilating Cattle?" *Colorado Springs Gazette-Telegraph*, June 13, 1975. See also several articles by Bill Myers: "Theories Abound in Cattle Deaths," *Denver Post*, June 22, 1975; "More Cattle Deaths Reported," *Denver Post*, July 9, 1975; "Sheriff Profiles Cattle Killers," *Denver Post*, July 11, 1975. See also John Makeig, "Trio Bitter That Warnings of Occultist Terror Drive Ignored," *Fort Worth Star Telegram* July 20, 1975.

58. Deborah Layton, *Seductive Poison* (New York: Anchor, 1999).

59. Rabbi Maurice Davis is quoted in T. R. Reid, "Public Relations a Factor as Sen. Dole Opens Session," *Washington Post*, February 6, 1979. See also *Transcript of Proceedings*.

Chapter 5

1. James Q. Wilson, *Thinking About Crime* (New York: Basic Books, 1975), 235–36.

2. Theodore Sasson, *Crime Talk* (Hawthorne, NY: Aldine de Gruyter, 1995); Katherine Beckett and Theodore Sasson, *The Politics of Injustice*, 2nd ed. (Thousand Oaks, CA: Sage Publications, 2004).

3. President's Commission on Law Enforcement and Administration of Justice, *The Challenge of Crime in a Free Society* (Washington, DC: GPO, 1967); Anthony Platt, ed., *The Politics of Riot Commissions, 1917–1970* (New York: Macmillan, 1971); Wilson, *Thinking About Crime*, 5; Michael W. Flamm, "The Politics of 'Law and Order,'" in David Farber and Jeff Roche, eds., *The Conservative Sixties* (New York: Peter Lang, 2003).

4. Wilson's views are further developed in James Q. Wilson and Richard J. Herrnstein, *Crime and Human Nature* (New York: Simon and Schuster, 1985).

5. Stuart Banner, *The Death Penalty* (Cambridge, MA: Harvard University Press, 2002); Michael A. Foley, *Arbitrary and Capricious* (Westport, CT: Praeger, 2003).

6. "Crime Boom," *Time*, April 14, 1975.

7. For how crime "exploded" in 1980, see "The Plague of Violent Crime," *Newsweek*, March 23, 1981. For the "Dodge City" quote, see "Tale of Three Cities," *Newsweek*, August 27, 1979; "Are we not hostages . . ." is quoted from "The Curse of Violent Crime," *Time*, March 23, 1981. See also John Godwin, *Murder USA* (New York: Ballantine, 1978).

8. For crime becoming "more brutal, more irrational," see "The Curse of Violent Crime." See also "The Youth Crime Plague," *Time*, July 11, 1977; Charles E. Silberman, *Criminal Violence, Criminal Justice* (New York: Random House, 1978), 81.

9. The "clockwork riot" is described in "Wild in the Streets," *Newsweek*, August 30, 1976. The "constant urban riot" is from Michael Posner, "My Turn," *Newsweek*, June 27, 1977. See also Joan W. Moore et al., *Homeboys* (Philadelphia: Temple University Press, 1978); R. Lincoln Keiser, *The Vice Lords* (New York: Holt, Rinehart and Winston, 1979).

10. Publicity poster for *The Warriors*, 1979.

11. *Scared Straight!* (1978, directed and produced by Arnold Shapiro); James O. Finckenauer, *Scared Straight! and the Panacea Phenomenon* (Englewood Cliffs, NJ: Prentice Hall, 1982).

12. Dennis Jay Kenney, *Crime, Fear, and the New York City Subways* (New York: Praeger, 1987).

13. Gilmore is quoted in Peter N. Carroll, *It Seemed Like Nothing Happened* (New York: Holt, Rinehart and Winston, 1982), 331; Norman Mailer, *The Executioner's Song* (Boston: Little, Brown, 1979); "The Youth Crime Plague."

14. Fox Butterfield, *All God's Children* (New York: Knopf, 1995).

15. Lucy Freeman, *"Before I Kill More . . ."* (New York: Crown, 1955); Theodore Hamm, *Rebel and a Cause* (Berkeley: University of California Press, 2001).

16. A. M. Rosenthal, *Thirty-Eight Witnesses* (New York: McGraw-Hill, 1964).

17. Marvin E. Wolfgang, Robert M. Figlio, and Thorsten Sellin, *Delinquency in a Birth Cohort* (Chicago: University of Chicago Press, 1972); Mark H. Moore, James Q. Wilson, and Ralph Gants, *Violent Attacks and Chronic Offenders* (Albany: New York State Assembly, 1978); Stephan Van Dine, John P. Conrad, and Simon Dinitz, *Restraining the Wicked* (Lexington, MA: Lexington, 1979); Stuart J. Miller, Simon Dinitz, and John P. Conrad, *Careers of the Violent* (Lexington, MA: Lexington, 1982).

18. Philip Jenkins, *Using Murder* (Hawthorne, NY: Aldine de Gruyter, 1994).

19. Joseph C. Fisher, *Killer Among Us* (Westport, CT: Praeger, 1997); Richard Tithecott, *Of Men and Monsters* (Madison: University of Wisconsin Press, 1997).

20. Mark Fuhrman, *Murder in Spokane* (New York: Cliff Street, 2001).

21. David C. Anderson, *Crime and the Politics of Hysteria* (New York: Times Books, 1995); Samuel Walker, Cassia Spohn, and Miriam Delone, *The Color of Justice*, 3rd ed. (Belmont, CA: Wadsworth Thomson, 2004). Jenkins, *Using Murder*, 160–75.

22. Jack Olsen, *The Man with the Candy* (New York: Simon and Schuster, 1974); Ed Sanders, *The Family* (London: Panther, 1972); Vincent Bugliosi and Curt Gentry, *Helter Skelter* (New York: Norton, 1974).

23. David Abrahamsen, *Confessions of Son of Sam* (New York: Columbia University Press, 1985); Maury Terry, *The Ultimate Evil* (New York: Dolphin Doubleday, 1987).

24. Jenkins, *Using Murder*, 50–57.

25. Ann Rule, *The Stranger Beside Me* (New York: New American Library, 1980); Steven Winn and David Merrill, *Ted Bundy: The Killer Next Door* (New York: Bantam, 1980); Stephen G. Michaud and Hugh Aynesworth, *The Only Living Witness* (New York: Simon and Schuster, 1983) and *Ted Bundy: Conversations with a Killer* (New York: New American Library, 1989).

26. Terry Sullivan and Peter T. Maiken, *Killer Clown* (New York: Pinnacle, 1984); Tim Cahill, *Buried Dreams* (New York: Bantam, 1986); Jason Moss with Jeffrey Kottler, *The Last Victim* (New York: Warner, 1999).

27. David J. Skal, *The Monster Show* (New York: W. W. Norton, 1993); John Kenneth Muir, *Horror Films of the 1970s* (Jefferson, NC: McFarland, 2002).

28. David Rosenthal, "Rated H for Horrors," *New York*, February 18, 1980, 50–54; Robert C. Cumbow, *Order in the Universe*, 2nd ed. (Lanham, MD: Scarecrow Press, 2000); Carol J. Clover, *Men, Women and Chainsaws* (Princeton: Princeton University Press, 1992); Adam Rockoff, *Going to Pieces* (Jefferson, NC: McFarland, 2002).

29. Christopher Sharrett, ed., *Mythologies of Violence in Postmodern Media* (Detroit: Wayne State University Press, 1999); Philip L. Simpson, *Psycho Paths* (Carbondale: Southern Illinois University Press, 2000).

30. Joel Best, *Threatened Children* (Chicago: University of Chicago Press, 1990), 113–23; Skal, *Monster Show*.

31. Michaud and Aynesworth, *Ted Bundy: Conversations with a Killer*.

32. Bundy is used as a major argument for anti-porn polemic in the film *A Drug Called Pornography* (directed by Jonathan Schneider, 2000).

33. Susan Brownmiller, *Against Our Will* (London: Secker and Warburg, 1975); Jane Caputi, *The Age of Sex Crime* (London: Women's Press, 1987); Jill Radford and Diana E. H. Russell, eds., *Femicide* (New York: Twayne, 1992). For Bianchi, see http://www.geocities.com/quietlyinsane5a/angelo.html.

34. Vito Russo, *The Celluloid Closet* (New York: Harper and Row, 1981); Jenkins, *Using Murder*.

35. Thomas Maeder, *Crime and Madness* (New York: Harper and Row, 1985).

36. William Klaber and Philip H. Melanson, *Shadow Play* (New York: St. Martin's, 1997).

37. "The Flick of Violence," *Time*, March 19, 1979.

38. Randy Shilts, *The Mayor of Castro Street* (New York: St. Martin's, 1982); Mike Weiss, *Double Play* (Reading, MA: Addison-Wesley, 1984).

39. Norval Morris is quoted from "The Insanity Plea on Trial," *Newsweek*, May 24, 1982, 60.

Chapter 6

1. Barry Rubin, *Paved with Good Intentions* (New York: Oxford University Press, 1980); Gary Sick, *All Fall Down* (New York: Random House, 1985); James A. Bill, *Eagle and the Lion*, reprint ed. (New Haven: Yale University Press, 1989); Stephen Kinzer, *All the Shah's Men* (New York: John Wiley and Sons, 2003); Kenneth M. Pollack, *The Persian Puzzle* (New York: Random House, 2004); David Harris, *The Crisis* (Boston: Little, Brown, 2004); David Farber, *Taken Hostage* (Princeton: Princeton University Press, 2005).

2. Robin Wright. *The Last Great Revolution* (New York: Random House, 2000); Ofira Seliktar, *Failing the Crystal Ball Test* (Westport, CT: Praeger, 2000). *Time* is quoted from http://www.time.com/time/poy2000/archive/1979.html. See also "The Decline of US Power," *Business Week*, March 12, 1979.

3. *Transcript of Proceedings: Information Meeting on the Cult Phenomenon in the United States* (*Dole Hearings*) (Washington, DC: Ace-Federal Reporters, 1979).

4. Robert Sherrill, *The Oil Follies of 1970–1980* (New York: Doubleday Anchor, 1984).

5. Daniel F. Ford, *Three Mile Island* (New York: Viking, 1982); J. Samuel Walker, *Three Mile Island* (Berkeley: University of California Press, 2004).

6. "Once in office . . ." is quoted from John Mihalic, cited by Susan Jeffords, *The Remasculinization of America* (Bloomington: Indiana University Press, 1989), 10. See also John Orman, *Comparing Presidential Behavior* (New York: Greenwood Press, 1987). Compare Donald T. Critchlow, "Mobilizing Women," in W. Elliot Brownlee and Hugh Davis Graham, eds., *The Reagan Presidency* (Lawrence: University Press of Kansas, 2003), 293–326. For the killer rabbit episode, see Jody Powell, *The Other Side of the Story* (New York: Morrow, 1984); Farber, *Taken Hostage*, 117. See also Charles O. Jones, *The Trusteeship Presidency* (Baton Rouge: Louisiana State University Press, 1988).

7. Christopher Lasch, *The Culture of Narcissism* (New York: Norton, 1978). For the text of the speech, see http://www.usembassy.de/usa/etexts/speeches/rhetoric/jccrisis.htm.

8. Clark R. Mollenhoff, *The President Who Failed* (New York: Macmillan, 1980); Richard E. Burke with William and Marilyn Hoffer, *The Senator* (New York: St. Martin's, 1992). *Time* is quoted from http://www.time.com/time/poy2000/archive/1980.html.

9. Steven F. Hayward, *The Age of Reagan, 1964–1980* (Roseville, CA: Prima, 2001), 563; William M. Leogrande, *Our Own Backyard* (Chapel Hill, NC: University of North Carolina Press, 1998); Robert A. Pastor, *Not Condemned to Repetition*, 2nd ed. (Boulder, CO: Westview, 2002).

10. Marvin E. Gettleman et al., eds., *El Salvador: Central America in the New Cold War* (New York: Grove, 1981); Walter Lafeber, *Inevitable Revolutions*, 2nd ed. (New York: W. W. Norton, 1993).

11. "We stood toe to toe . . ." is quoted in Peter N. Carroll, *It Seemed Like Nothing Happened* (New York: Holt, Rinehart and Winston, 1982), 229. See also Dan Caldwell, *The Dynamics of Domestic Politics and Arms Control* (Columbia: University of South Carolina Press, 1991).

12. Massoumeh Ebtekar, *Takeover in Tehran* (Burnaby, BC: Talonbooks, 2001); Mark Bowden, "Among the Hostage-Takers," *Atlantic Monthly*, December 2004; Farber, *Taken Hostage*. For the alleged MIA link, see Susan Katz Keating, *Prisoners of Hope* (New York: Random House, 1994), 131.

13. Hamilton Jordan, *Crisis* (New York: Putnam, 1982); Cyrus R. Vance, *Hard Choices* (New York: Simon and Schuster, 1983); Warren Christopher, *American Hostages in Iran* (New Haven: Yale University Press, 1985); David Patrick Houghton. *US Foreign Policy and the Iran Hostage Crisis* (New York: Cambridge University Press, 2001).

14. Zbigniew Brzezinski, *Power and Principle* (New York: Farrar, Straus, Giroux, 1983); Steve Coll, *Ghost Wars* (New York: Penguin, 2004).

15. See http://www.jimmycarterlibrary.org/documents/speeches/su80jec.phtml.

16. Quoted at http://www.cnn.com/SPECIALS/cold.war/episodes/20/1st.draft.

17. Midge Decter, *An Old Wife's Tale* (New York: Regan, 2001). Reagan is quoted from Hayward, *The Age of Reagan*, 615.

18. John Powers and Arthur C. Kaminsky, *One Goal* (New York: Harper and Row, 1984). The *New York Times* headlines cited appeared on February 22, 1980.

19. Jordan, *Crisis*; James H. Kyle with John Robert Eidson, *The Guts to Try* (New York: Orion, 1990); Charlie A. Beckwith and Donald Knox, *Delta Force* (New York: Avon, 2000).

20. George Brock et al., *Siege* (London: Macmillan, 1980).

21. Benjamin Netanyahu, ed., *International Terrorism, Challenge and Response* (New Brunswick, NJ: Transaction, 1981); Philip Jenkins, *Images of Terror* (Hawthorne, NY: Aldine de Gruyter, 2003), 36–44.

22. Claire Sterling, *The Terror Network* (New York: Berkley, 1981); Howard Morland, "The H-Bomb Secret," *The Progressive*, November 1979.

23. Arnaud De Borchgrave and Robert Moss, *The Spike* (London: Weidenfeld and Nicolson, 1980), 422–23; Robert Moss, *The Collapse of Democracy* (New Rochelle, NY: Arlington House, 1975) and *Death Beam* (New York: Berkley, 1982); Robert Moss and Arnaud De Borchgrave, *Monimbo* (New York: Pocket, 1984).

24. Andrew J. DeRoche, *Andrew Young* (Wilmington, DE: Scholarly Resources, 2003).

25. Bert Lance with Bill Gilbert, *The Truth of the Matter* (New York: Summit, 1991); *Inquiry into the Matter of Billy Carter and Libya* (Washington, DC: GPO, 1980–81). Billy Carter is quoted from http://www.pbs.org/wgbh/amex/carter/peopleevents/p_bcarter.html. The Billygate affair was complicated by controversial charges that the Republican Party leadership had surreptitiously acquired extra dirt on Billy Carter from the Italian secret service, which had excellent Libyan contacts.

26. General Sir John Hackett et al., *The Third World War* (New York: Macmillan, 1978); Charles McCarry, *The Better Angels* (New York: Dutton, 1979); Michael Kurland and S. W. Barton, *The Last President* (New York: Morrow, 1980).

27. Benjamin Weiser, *A Secret Life* (PublicAffairs, 2004).

28. W. Carl Biven, *Jimmy Carter's Economy* (Chapel Hill: University of North Carolina Press, 2002).

29. For interest rates, see http://www.hsh.com/indices/prime70s.html; http://www.hsh.com/indices/prime80s.html. See also Howard J. Ruff, *How to Prosper During the Coming Bad Years* (New York: Times Books, 1979); Ezra Vogel, *Japan as Number One* (Cambridge, MA: Harvard University Press, 1979).

30. Stephen Chapman, "The Prisoner's Dilemma," *New Republic*, March 8, 1980; W. G. Stone and G. Hirliman, *The Hate Factory* (New York: Dell, 1982); Elizabeth Wheaton, *Codename GREENKIL* (Athens: University of Georgia Press, 1987).

31. Bruce Porter and Marvin Dunn, *The Miami Riot of 1980* (Lexington, MA: Lexington, 1984).

32. David W. Engstrom, *Presidential Decision-Making Adrift* (Lanham, MD: Rowman and Littlefield, 1997).

33. Gigi Mahon, *The Company That Bought the Boardwalk* (New York: Random House, 1980); Robert W. Greene, *The Sting Man* (New York: Dutton, 1981); Ovid Demaris, *The Boardwalk Jungle* (New York: Bantam, 1986).

34. Ron LaBrecque, *Lost Undercover* (New York: Dell, 1987).

35. Jenkins, *Using Murder*, 50–59.

36. Chet Dettlinger and Jeff Prugh, *The List* (Atlanta: Philmay Enterprises, 1983); Bernard Headley, *The Atlanta Youth Murders and the Politics of Race* (Carbondale: Southern Illinois University Press, 1998).

37. James Baldwin, *The Evidence of Things Not Seen* (New York: Holt, Rinehart and Winston, 1985); Maury Terry, *The Ultimate Evil* (New York: Bantam, 1987).

38. For San Francisco, see Larry Kahaner, *Cults That Kill* (New York: Warner, 1988), 16–17; Terry, *The Ultimate Evil*. For the McDonald case, see Joe McGinniss, *Fatal Vision* (New York: Putnam, 1983). For African-American theories of conspiracy, see Patricia A. Turner, *I Heard It Through the Grapevine* (Berkeley: University of California Press, 1993); Toni Cade Bambara, *Those Bones Are Not My Child* (New York: Vintage, 1999).

39. Lawrence Pazder and Michelle Smith, *Michelle Remembers* (New York: Congdon and Lattes, 1980); Kenneth Wooden, *The Children of Jonestown* (New York: McGraw-Hill, 1981); Debbie Nathan and Michael Snedeker, *Satan's Silence* (New York: Basic Books, 1995).

40. Jordan, *Crisis*, 313.

41. *The Global 2000 Report to the President* (Washington, DC: GPO, 1980–81).

42. The speech can be found at http://www.nationalcenter.org/ReaganConvention1980.html.

43. See http://domino.un.org/UNISPAL.NSF/0/5aa254a1c8f8b1cb852560e50075d7d5?OpenDocument.

44. Quotes are from http://www.pbs.org/newshour/debatingourdestiny/80debates/cart2.html.

45. Jack W. Germond and Jules Witcover, *Blue Smoke and Mirrors* (New York: Viking, 1981); Paul T. David and David H. Everson, eds., *The Presidential Election and Transition, 1980–1981* (Carbondale: Southern Illinois University Press, 1983).

46. The *Washington Post* is quoted in Lee Edwards, *The Conservative Revolution* (New York: Free Press, 1999), 223. See also Morton Kondracke, "A Doubtful New Order," *New Republic*, November 15, 1980.

47. John Orman, *Comparing Presidential Behavior* (New York: Greenwood Press, 1987); Matthew Dallek, *The Right Moment* (New York: Free Press, 2000).

48. Paul Kengor, *God and Ronald Reagan* (New York: Regan, 2004).

49. Charles Bussey, "Jimmy Carter: Hope and Memory Versus Optimism and Nostalgia," in Elsebeth Hurup, ed., *The Lost Decade* (Aarhus, Denmark: Aarhus University Press, 1996); James A. Morone, *Hellfire Nation* (New Haven: Yale University Press, 2003); Steven F. Hayward, *The Real Jimmy Carter* (Chicago: Regnery, 2004).

50. "Always believed . . ." is from http://www.reagan.utexas.edu/resource/speeches/1983/91483d.htm. See also Robert Dallek, *Ronald Reagan* (Cambridge, MA: Harvard University Press, 1984); Garry Wills, *Reagan's America* (New York: Doubleday, 1987); Edmund Morris, *Dutch* (New York: Random House, 1999); Kiron Skinner, Annelise Anderson, and Martin Anderson, eds., *Reagan, in His Own Hand* (New York: Free Press, 2001) and *Reagan's Path to Victory* (New York: Free Press,

2004); Peggy Noonan, *When Character Was King* (New York: Viking, 2001); Hugh Heclo, "Ronald Reagan and the American Public Philosophy," in Brownlee and Graham, eds., *The Reagan Presidency*; Richard T. Hughes, *Myths America Lives By* (Urbana: University of Illinois Press, 2003).

51. Compare Godfrey Hodgson, *The World Turned Right Side Up* (Boston: Houghton Mifflin, 1996), 242–43.

52. James M. Scott, *Deciding to Intervene* (Durham, NC: Duke University Press, 1996), 43–46; Jonathan B Tucker, "The Yellow Rain Controversy," *Nonproliferation Review*, spring 2001, 25–29.

53. Quoted in William E. Leuchtenburg, "Jimmy Carter and the Post New Deal Presidency," in Gary M. Fink and Hugh Davis Graham, eds., *The Carter Presidency* (Lawrence: University Press of Kansas, 1998), 16. See also Bruce J. Schulman, "Slouching Towards the Supply Side," in Fink and Graham, eds., *The Carter Presidency*, 51–71; David A. Stockman, *The Triumph of Politics* (New York: Harper and Row, 1986).

54. Fred Fogo, *I Read the News Today* (Lanham, MD: Rowman and Littlefield, 1994).

Chapter 7

1. Laurence I. Barrett, *Gambling with History* (Garden City, NY: Doubleday, 1983); Haynes Johnson, *Sleepwalking Through History* (New York: Anchor, 1992); Michael Schaller, *Reckoning with Reagan* (New York: Oxford University Press, 1994).

2. William Branigin, "Reagan Dies After Long Battle with Alzheimer's Disease," *Washington Post*, June 5, 2004.

3. *Time* is quoted from http://www.time.com/time/poy2000/archive/1980.html. See also Joseph B. Treaster, *Paul Volcker* (Hoboken, NJ: John Wiley and Sons, 2004).

4. Sidney Weintraub and Marvin Goodstein, eds., *Reaganomics in the Stagflation Economy* (Philadelphia: University of Pennsylvania Press, 1983); Benjamin Friedman, *Day of Reckoning* (New York: Random House, 1988).

5. Daniel Wirls, *Buildup* (Ithaca: Cornell University Press, 1992); Hobart Rowen, *Self-Inflicted Wounds* (New York: Times Books, 1994); John W. Sloan, *The Reagan Effect* (Lawrence: University Press of Kansas, 1999).

6. James G. Watt with Doug Wead, *The Courage of a Conservative* (New York: Simon and Schuster, 1985); C. Brant Short, *Ronald Reagan and the Public Lands* (College Station: Texas A&M University Press, 1989). For critical views of the Reagan regime and the political shift it represented, see Gerald R. Gill, *The Meanness Mania* (Washington, DC: Howard University Press, 1980); Jonathan Lash, Katherine Gillman, and David Sheridan, *A Season of Spoils* (New York: Pantheon, 1984); Joan Claybrook and the staff of *Public Citizen*, *Retreat from Safety* (New York: Pantheon, 1984); Raymond Wolters, *Right Turn* (New Brunswick, NJ: Transaction, 1996); Nicholas Laham, *The Reagan Presidency and the Politics of Race* (Westport, CT: Praeger, 1998); Dan T. Carter, *From George Wallace to Newt Gingrich* (Baton Rouge: Louisiana State University Press, 1999).

7. Barry Bluestone and Bennett Harrison, *The Deindustrialization of America* (New York: Basic Books, 1982); Michael Moritz and Barrett Seaman, *Going for Broke* (Garden City, NY: Anchor Doubleday, 1984); John P. Hoerr, *And the Wolf Finally Came* (Pittsburgh: University of Pittsburgh Press, 1988); Maryann Keller *Rude Awakening* (New York: Morrow, 1989); Steven P. Dandaneau, *A Town Abandoned* (Albany: State University of New York Press, 1996); Steven High, *Industrial Sunset* (Toronto: University of Toronto Press, 2003); Philip Jenkins, "The Post-Industrial Age 1950–2000," in Randall M. Miller and William A. Pencak, eds., *Pennsylvania* (University Park: Pennsylvania State University Press, 2002), 317–70.

8. Arthur B. Shostak and David Skocik, *The Air Controllers' Controversy* (New York: Human Sciences Press, 1986); Arch Puddington, *Lane Kirkland* (New York: Wiley, 2005).

9. Frances Fox Piven and Richard A. Cloward, *The New Class War* (New York: Pantheon, 1982); Ken Auletta, *The Underclass* (New York: Random House, 1982); Kevin P. Phillips, *The Politics of Rich and Poor* (New York: Random House, 1990).

10. Physician Task Force on Hunger in America, *Hunger in America: The Growing Epidemic* (Middletown, CT: Wesleyan University Press, 1985); Edwin Meese III, *With Reagan* (Washington, DC: Regnery Gateway, 1992).

11. The quote can be found at http://www.dems2004.org/site/apps/lk/content2.asp?c=luI2LaPYG&b=107052.

12. Robert Mabro, ed., *OPEC and the World Oil Market* (Oxford: Oxford University Press, 1986); Ian Skeet, *OPEC: Twenty-Five Years of Prices and Politics* (New York: Cambridge University Press, 1988); Robert Bartley, *The Seven Fat Years* (New York: Free Press, 1992); Maggie Mahar, *Bull!: A History of the Boom, 1982–1999* (New York: HarperBusiness, 2003).

13. Ivan F. Boesky with Jeffrey Madrick, *Merger Mania* (New York: Holt, Rinehart and Winston, 1985); Joseph Nocera, *A Piece of the Action* (New York: Simon and Schuster, 1994); Richard B. McKenzie, *What Went Right in the 1980s* (San Francisco: Pacific Research Institute for Public Policy, 1994); Bruce J. Schulman, *The Seventies* (New York: Free Press, 2001); Mahar, *Bull!* The decision about credit card rates was *Marquette Nat. Bank v. First of Omaha Corp.*, 439 U.S. 299 (1978).

14. Daniel Yergin and Joseph Stanislaw, *The Commanding Heights* (New York: Simon and Schuster, 1998).

15. "This was America . . ." is from Thomas Byrne Edsall with Mary D. Edsall, *Chain Reaction* (New York: Norton, 1991), 180. "From Washington we heard only . . ." is quoted from "Remarks at the Annual Convention of the Texas State Bar Association in San Antonio" at http://www.reagan.utexas.edu/resource/speeches/1984/70684a.htm. See also Dick Wirthlin and Wynton C. Hall, *The Greatest Communicator* (New York: John Wiley and Sons, 2004).

16. Richard Brookhiser, *The Outside Story* (Garden City, NY: Doubleday, 1986); Steven M. Gillon, *The Democrats' Dilemma* (New York: Columbia University Press, 1992); Kenneth S. Baer, *Reinventing Democrats* (Lawrence: University Press of Kansas, 2000).

17. Earl Black and Merle Black, *The Rise of Southern Republicans* (Cambridge, MA: Belknap, 2002); Kenneth D. Durr, *Behind the Backlash* (Chapel Hill: University of North Carolina Press, 2003), 202.

18. Richard Reeves, *The Reagan Detour* (New York: Simon and Schuster, 1985); David A. Stockman, *The Triumph of Politics* (New York: Harper and Row, 1986); Thomas Ferguson and Joel Rogers, *Right Turn* (New York: Hill and Wang, 1986); Sidney Blumenthal, *The Rise of the Counter-Establishment* (New York: Times Books, 1986) and *Our Long National Daydream* (New York: Harper and Row, 1988).

19. Edward F. Leddy, *Magnum Force Lobby* (Lanham, MD: University Press of America, 1987); Osha Gray Davidson, *Under Fire* (Iowa City: University of Iowa Press, 1998); Samuel Walker, *In Defense of American Liberties*, 2nd ed. (Carbondale: Southern Illinois University Press, 1999), 342.

20. Robert Zwier, *Born-Again Politics* (Downers Grove, IL: Intervarsity Press, 1982); Flo Conway and Jim Siegelman, *Holy Terror* (New York: Doubleday, 1982); Perry Deane Young, *God's Bullies* (New York: Holt Rinehart Winston, 1982); Phillip Finch, *God, Guts, and Guns* (New York: Seaview Putnam, 1983); Pamela Johnston Conover and Virginia Gray, *Feminism and the New Right* (New York: Praeger, 1983). For abortion issues, see Andrew H. Merton, *Enemies of Choice* (Boston: Beacon Press, 1981); Gloria Feldt with Laura Fraser, *The War on Choice* (New York: Bantam, 2004).

21. Dallas A. Blanchard, *The Anti-Abortion Movement and the Rise of the Religious Right* (New York: Twayne, 1994); Clyde Wilcox, *Onward Christian Soldiers?* 2nd ed. (Boulder, CO: Westview, 2000); Orrin Hatch, *Square Peg* (New York: Basic Books, 2002).

22. Tracy Kidder, *The Soul of a New Machine* (New York: Avon, 1981); James Wallace, *Hard Drive* (New York: HarperBusiness, 1993); Paul Freiberger and Michael Swaine, *Fire in the Valley*, 2nd ed. (New York: McGraw-Hill, 1999); Wyatt C. Wells, *American Capitalism, 1945–2000* (Chicago: Ivan R Dee, 2003); Andy Hertzfeld, *Revolution in the Valley* (Sebastopol, CA: O'Reilly, 2004); Timothy Moy, "Culture, Technology, and the Cult of Tech in the 1970s," in Beth Bailey and David Farber, eds., *America in the Seventies* (Lawrence: University Press of Kansas, 2004); John Markoff, *What the Dormouse Said* (New York: Viking, 2005).

23. For the "pre-Internet" of bulletin boards, see Mike Cane, *The Computer Phone Book*, rev. ed., 2 vols. (New York: New American Library, 1986); Michael Hauben and Ronda Hauben, *Netizens* (Los Alamitos, CA: IEEE Computer Society Press, 1997); Christos J. P. Moschovitis, Hilary Poole, Tami Schuyler, and Theresa M. Senft, *History of the Internet* (Santa Barbara, CA: ABC-Clio, 1999). The FCC decision cited is *MTS and WATS Market Structure Order*, 97 FCC 2d 682 (1983).

24. Committee on the Survey of Materials Science and Engineering, *Materials and Man's Needs* (Washington, DC: National Academy of Sciences, 1974). The American Association for Artificial Intelligence was founded in 1979. Douglas R. Hofstadter, *Gödel, Escher, Bach* (New York: Basic Books, 1979); K. Eric Drexler, *Engines of Creation* (Garden City, NY: Anchor Press/Doubleday, 1986); Jeff Hecht, *City of Light* (New York: Oxford University Press, 1999); Arthur C. Clarke, *Fountains of Paradise* (New York: Harcourt Brace Jovanovich, 1979).

25. "Biotech Chronicles" at http://www.accessexcellence.org/RC/AB/BC/; Robert Bud, *The Uses of Life* (Cambridge: Cambridge University Press, 1993). The account of the impact of Bayh-Dole is largely drawn from Marcia Angell, *The Truth About the Drug Companies* (New York: Random House, 2004).

26. Donald T. Critchlow, "Mobilizing Women," in W. Elliot Brownlee and Hugh Davis Graham, eds., *The Reagan Presidency* (Lawrence: University Press of Kansas, 2003), 293–326.

27. Bruce J. Schulman, *The Seventies* (New York: Free Press, 2001), 241.

28. Louis Auchincloss, *Diary of a Yuppie* (Boston: Houghton Mifflin, 1986); Bret Easton Ellis, *Less than Zero* (New York: Penguin, 1987).

29. Charles E. Silberman, *Criminal Violence, Criminal Justice* (New York: Random House, 1978); Ralph W. Larkin, *Suburban Youth in Cultural Crisis* (New York: Oxford University Press, 1979); John G. Fuller, *Are the Kids All Right?* (New York: Times Books, 1981); William Straus and Neil Howe, *Generations* (New York: Morrow, 1990); idem, *The Fourth Turning* (New York: Broadway, 1997); Douglas Coupland, *Generation X* (New York: St. Martin's, 1991); *Generation X: Americans Born 1965 to 1976*, 4th ed. (Ithaca, NY: New Strategist Publications, 2004).

30. Robin Bernstein and Seth Clark Silberman, eds., *Generation Q* (Los Angeles: Alyson, 1996).

31. Bob Greene, *Cheeseburgers* (New York: Atheneum, 1985); Michael X. Delli Carpini, *Stability and Change in American Politics* (New York: New York University Press, 1986); Stephen C. Craig and Stephen Earl Bennett, eds., *After the Boom* (Lanham, MD: Rowman and Littlefield, 1997); Richard D. Thau and Jay S. Heflin, eds., *Generations Apart* (Amherst, NY: Prometheus, 1997).

32. For the rock culture of the 1970s, see Stephen Davis, *Hammer of the Gods* (New York: Morrow, 1985); Mick Fleetwood with Stephen Davis, *Fleetwood* (New York: Avon, 1990); Henrik Bødker, "Popular Music into the Seventies," in Elsebeth Hurup, ed., *The Lost Decade* (Aarhus, Denmark: Aarhus University Press, 1996); Shelton Waldrep, ed., *The Seventies* (New York: Routledge, 2000).

33. Jon Savage, *England's Dreaming* (New York: St. Martin's, 1992); Greil Marcus, *Ranters and Crowd Pleasers* (New York: Doubleday, 1993); Clinton Heylin, *From the Velvets to the Voidoids* (New York:

Penguin, 1993); Marc Spitz and Brendan Mullen, *We Got the Neutron Bomb* (New York: Three Rivers, 2001); Michael Nevin Willard, "Cutback," in Bailey and Farber, eds., *America in the Seventies*; Jeff Chang, *Can't Stop Won't Stop* (New York: St. Martin's, 2005).

34. Everett True, *Hey Ho Let's Go* (London: Omnibus, 2002).

35. Rob Owen, *Gen X TV* (Syracuse: Syracuse University Press, 1997).

36. Thomas Kiernan, *Citizen Murdoch* (New York: Dodd, Mead, 1986); Alex Ben Block, *Outfoxed* (New York: St. Martin's, 1990); Hank Whittemore, *CNN, the Inside Story* (Boston: Little, Brown, 1990).

37. Debbie Nathan and Michael Snedeker, *Satan's Silence* (New York: Basic Books, 1995); Craig Reinarman and Harry G. Levine, eds., *Crack in America* (Berkeley: University of California Press, 1997); Todd Gitlin, *Inside Prime Time*, rev. ed. (Berkeley: University of California Press, 2000).

38. Mark Fishman and Gray Cavender, eds. *Entertaining Crime* (Hawthorne, NY: Aldine de Gruyter, 1998); David L. Altheide, *Creating Fear* (Hawthorne, NY: Aldine de Gruyter, 2002).

39. Michael K. Deaver, *A Different Drummer* (New York: HarperCollins, 2001). Robert Harris, *Gotcha!* (London: Faber and Faber, 1983); Valerie Adams, *The Media and the Falklands Campaign* (New York: St. Martin's, 1986); Deborah Holmes, *Governing the Press* (Boulder: Westview Press, 1986).

40. Mark Hertsgaard, *On Bended Knee* (New York: Farrar, Straus, and Giroux, 1988).

41. Stephen Prince, *A New Pot of Gold* (New York: Scribner's, 2000).

42. Les Keyser, *Hollywood in the Seventies* (San Diego, CA: A. S. Barnes, 1981); Seth Cagin and Philip Dray, *Hollywood Films of the Seventies* (New York: Harper and Row, 1984); Peter Biskind, *Easy Riders, Raging Bulls* (New York: Simon and Schuster, 1998); David A. Cook, *Lost Illusions* (New York: Scribner's, 2000); Robert Kolker, *A Cinema of Loneliness*, 3rd ed. (New York: Oxford University Press, 2000); Robin Wood, *Hollywood from Vietnam to Reagan—and Beyond*, rev. ed. (New York: Columbia University Press, 2003); Tom Shone, *Blockbuster* (New York: Free Press, 2004); Dade Hayes and Jonathan Bing, *Open Wide* (New York: Miramax/Hyperion, 2004).

43. Steven Bach, *Final Cut* (New York: Morrow, 1985). For the impact of new technology on filmmaking, see Michael Rubin, *Droidmaker* (Gainesville, FL: Triad, 2005).

44. Susan Jeffords, *Hard Bodies* (New Brunswick, NJ: Rutgers University Press, 1994); Alan Nadel, *Flatlining on the Field of Dreams* (New Brunswick, NJ: Rutgers University Press, 1997).

45. "Reducing Tobacco Use," August 2000, http://www.cdc.gov/tobacco/sgr/sgr_2000; Peter Taylor, *The Smoke Ring* (New York: Pantheon, 1984); Larry C. White, *Merchants of Death* (New York: Beech Tree, 1988); Jacob Sullum, *For Your Own Good* (New York: Free Press, 1998); Mark Wolfson, *The Fight Against Big Tobacco* (New York: Aldine de Gruyter, 2001); Joseph A. Califano, *Inside* (New York: Public Affairs, 2004).

46. Select Committee on Nutrition and Human Needs, U.S. Senate, *Dietary Goals for the United States* (Washington, DC: GPO, 1977); Ruth Clifford Engs, *Clean Living Movements* (Westport, CT: Praeger, 2000); compare R. Marie Griffith, *Born Again Bodies* (Berkeley: University of California Press, 2004).

47. Schuchard is quoted in Malcolm Gladwell, "Just Say 'Wait a Minute,'" in *New York Review of Books*, December 17, 1998; Michael Massing, *The Fix* (New York: Simon and Schuster, 1998).

48. David J. Hanson, "Mothers Against Drunk Driving," http://www.alcoholfacts.org/CrashCourseOnMADD.html#Note4; Joseph Gusfield, *The Culture of Public Problems* (Chicago: University of Chicago Press, 1981).

49. Micky Sadoff, *America Gets MADD!* (Irving, TX: Mothers Against Drunk Driving, 1990).

50. Henry Wechsler, ed., *Minimum-Drinking-Age Laws* (Lexington, MA: Lexington, 1980); Alexander C. Wagenaar, *Alcohol, Young Drivers, and Traffic Accidents* (Lexington, MA: Lexington, 1983).

51. Susan Sontag, *Illness as Metaphor* (New York: Doubleday, 1990); Jacqueline Foertsch, *Enemies Within* (Urbana: University of Illinois Press, 2001).

52. Michelle Cochrane, *When AIDS Began* (New York: Routledge, 2004). D. Keith Mano, "Journal of a Plague Year," *National Review*, July 8, 1983, 836–37; Edward Alwood, *Straight News* (New York: Columbia University Press, 1996), 218 for the *Los Angeles Times*; Randy Shilts, *And the Band Played On* (New York: St. Martin's, 1987); Christopher Capozzola, "A Very American Epidemic," in Van Gosse and Richard Moser, eds., *The World the Sixties Made* (Philadelphia: Temple University Press, 2003).

53. Richard Hamilton, *The Herpes Book* (Los Angeles: Tarcher, 1980); William H. Wickett, *Herpes, Cause and Control* (New York: Pinnacle, 1982); Oscar Gillespie, *Herpes* (New York: Grosset and Dunlap, 1982); Frank Freudberg, *Herpes* (Philadelphia: Running Press, 1982); "Incurable Venereal Disease Epidemic Threatens Blacks of All Classes," *Ebony*, June 1981, 41–42; "Herpes: The VD of the 80s," *Newsweek* April 12, 1982, 75–76; John Leo et al., "The New Scarlet Letter," *Time*, August 2, 1982, 62–66, quotes from 62; "Is Herpes Quelling the Sexual Revolution?" *Christianity Today*, November 12, 1982; "a veritable herpes industry . . ." is from Ezekiel Emanuel, "Harping on Herpes," *New Republic* September 13, 1982, 15; "The New Scarlet Letter," *Time*, August 2, 1982, 62.

54. "The Pill, Penthouse Pets and porn-movie cassettes" is quoted from Leo et al., "The New Scarlet Letter." For *Christianity Today*, see "Is Herpes Quelling the Sexual Revolution?" For the *New Republic*, see Emanuel, "Harping on Herpes."

Chapter 8

1. "The First 100 Days," *New Republic*, May 2, 1981; Hugh Heclo, "Ronald Reagan and the American Public Philosophy," in W. Elliot Brownlee and Hugh Davis Graham, eds., *The Reagan Presidency* (Lawrence: University Press of Kansas, 2003), 25.

2. The "Time for Choosing" speech is at http://www.pbs.org/wgbh/amex/reagan/filmmore/reference/primary/choose64.html. "We win and they lose" is quoted in Hugh Heclo, "Ronald Reagan and the American Public Philosophy," 27. See also Peter Schweizer, *Reagan's War* (New York: Doubleday, 2002).

3. See http://www.dineshdsouza.com/REAGAN_VS_INTELLECTUALS.htm; http://www.claremont.org/weblog/001292.html; Chester J. Pach Jr., "Sticking to His Guns," in Brownlee and Graham, eds., *The Reagan Presidency*, 86.

4. Peggy Noonan, *What I Saw at the Revolution* (New York: Random House, 1990); David Monaghan, *The Falklands War* (New York: St. Martin's, 1998); Michael Weiler and W. Barnett Pearce, eds., *Reagan and Public Discourse in America* (Tuscaloosa: University of Alabama Press, 1992).

5. The quotes is from http://www.ronaldreagan.com/sp_6.html.

6. The directive is at http://www.fas.org/irp/offdocs/nsdd/nsdd-075.htm. See also Christopher Simpson, *National Security Directives of the Reagan and Bush Administrations* (Boulder, CO: Westview, 1995); Alexander M. Haig, *Caveat* (New York: Macmillan, 1984); Peter Schweizer, *Victory* (Atlantic Monthly Press, 1996); Thomas Reed, *At the Abyss* (Presidio Press, 2004).

7. Benjamin Weiser, *A Secret Life* (PublicAffairs, 2004).

8. Daniel Wirls. *Buildup* (Ithaca: Cornell University Press, 1992).

9. Lee Edwards, *The Conservative Revolution* (New York: Free Press; 1999), 251–52; Strobe Talbott, *Deadly Gambits* (New York: Random House, 1984); Ronald E. Powaski, *Return to Armageddon* (New York: Oxford University Press, 2003).

10. The Soviets were right to fear an effective attack, in the sense that defectors had given NATO the locations of the main bunkers in which high-ranked Eastern-bloc military and civilian officials were to take refuge in the event of war: Weiser, *A Secret Life*. See also Robert Scheer et al., *With Enough*

Shovels (New York: Random House, 1982); Brian May, *Russia, America, The Bomb, and the Fall of Western Europe* (London: Routledge and Kegan Paul, 1984); Jeffrey Herf, *War by Other Means* (New York: Free Press, 1991). For the anti-nuclear protest movement, see E. P. Thompson and Dan Smith, eds., *Protest and Survive* (New York: Monthly Review Press, 1981); Stephen Hilgartner, Richard C. Bell, and Rory O'Connor, *Nukespeak* (San Francisco: Sierra Club Books, 1982).

11. E. P. Thompson, *Beyond the Cold War* (New York: Pantheon, 1982).

12. *Historical Antecedents of Soviet Terrorism: Hearings Before the Subcommittee on Security and Terrorism of the Committee on the Judiciary* (Washington, DC: GPO, 1981); *Terrorism, the Role of Moscow and Its Subcontractors: Hearing Before the Subcommittee on Security and Terrorism of the Committee on the Judiciary* (Washington, DC: GPO, 1982); Paul Henze, *The Plot to Kill the Pope* (New York: Scribner's, 1983); Claire Sterling, *The Time of the Assassins* (New York: Holt, Rinehart, and Winston, 1983); Zbigniew Brzezinski, Robert H. Kupperman, and Linnea P. Raine, eds., *The International Implications of the Papal Assassination Attempt* (Washington, DC: Center for Strategic and International Studies, Georgetown University, 1985); Bob Woodward, *Veil* (New York: Simon and Schuster, 1987); Nigel West, *The Third Secret* (London: HarperCollins, 2000).

13. *The Role of Cuba in International Terrorism and Subversion: Hearing Before the Subcommittee on Security and Terrorism of the Committee on the Judiciary* (Washington, DC: GPO, 1982); *The Role of the Soviet Union, Cuba, and East Germany in Fomenting Terrorism in Southern Africa: Hearings Before the Subcommittee on Security and Terrorism of the Committee on the Judiciary* (Washington, DC: GPO, 1982).

14. Laurence W. Beilenson, *Power Through Subversion* (Washington, DC: Public Affairs, 1972); Arnaud De Borchgrave and Robert Moss, *The Spike* (London: Weidenfeld and Nicolson, 1980), 456; Bob Woodward, *Veil* (New York: Simon and Schuster, 1987); James M. Scott, *Deciding to Intervene* (Durham, NC: Duke University Press, 1996); George Crile, *Charlie Wilson's War* (New York: Atlantic Monthly Press, 2003).

15. Thomas Carothers, *In the Name of Democracy* (Berkeley: University of California Press, 1991); Walter Lafeber, *Inevitable Revolutions*, 2nd ed. (New York: W. W. Norton, 1993); Mark Danner, *The Massacre at El Mozote* (New York: Vintage, 1994); Greg Grandin, *The Last Colonial Massacre* (Chicago: University of Chicago Press, 2004).

16. See, for instance, Steffen W. Schmidt, *El Salvador: America's Next Vietnam?* (Salisbury, NC: Documentary Publications, 1983); Karl Grossman, *Nicaragua, America's New Vietnam?* (Sag Harbor, NY: Permanent, 1984). See also the film *El Salvador, Another Vietnam* (1981, directed by Glenn Silber and Tete Vasconcellos). Also, Penny Lernoux, *Cry of the People* (Garden City, NY: Doubleday, 1980); Daniel Berrigan, *Steadfastness of the Saints* (Maryknoll, NY: Orbis, 1985); Donna Whitson Brett and Edward Tracy Brett, *Murdered in Central America* (Maryknoll, NY: Orbis, 1988); Edward Tracy Brett, *The U.S. Catholic Press on Central America* (Notre Dame, IN: University of Notre Dame Press, 2003); Pach, "Sticking to His Guns," 97.

17. Thomas W. Walker, ed., *Reagan Versus the Sandinistas* (Boulder: Westview, 1987); Robert Kagan, *A Twilight Struggle* (New York: Free Press, 1996); http://www.reagan.utexas.edu/resource/speeches/1984/110384e.htm.

18. *Revolution Beyond Our Borders* (Washington, DC: U.S. Dept. of State, 1985); E. Bradford Burns. *At War in Nicaragua* (New York: Harper and Row, 1987).

19. Scott Armstrong et al., *The Chronology* (New York: Warner, 1987); *The Tower Commission Report* (New York: Bantam/Times Books, 1987).

20. Kenneth R. Timmerman, *The Death Lobby* (New York: Houghton Mifflin, 1992).

21. Brian L. Davis, *Qaddafi, Terrorism, and the Origins of the U.S. Attack on Libya* (New York: Praeger, 1990). Complicating the Libyan affair was Qaddafi's extensive use of former U.S. intelligence agents

and arms dealers, leading to speculation about CIA penetration of the Libyan regime. See Joseph C. Goulden, *The Death Merchant* (New York: Simon and Schuster, 1984); Peter Maas, *Manhunt* (New York: Random House, 1986).

22. Jonathan C. Randal, *Going All the Way*, rev. ed. (New York: Vintage, 1984); Robert Fisk, *Pity the Nation* (New York: Thunder's Mouth/Nation Books, 2002).

23. Eric Hammel, *The Root* (San Diego: Harcourt Brace Jovanovich, 1985); Lawrence Pintak, *Seeds of Hate* (London: Pluto, 2003).

24. Frances Fitzgerald, *Way Out There in the Blue* (New York: Simon and Schuster, 2000); Christopher Andrew and Vasili Mitrokhin, *The Sword and the Shield* (New York: Basic Books, 1999), 214.

25. Seymour M. Hersh, *The Target Is Destroyed* (New York: Random House, 1986); R. W. Johnson, *Shootdown* (New York: Viking, 1986).

26. Hammel, *The Root*; Fisk, *Pity the Nation*.

27. Quoted in Pach, "Sticking to His Guns," 101; Gordon K. Lewis, *Grenada: The Jewel Despoiled* (Baltimore: Johns Hopkins University Press, 1987); Peter A. Huchthausen, *America's Splendid Little Wars* (New York: Viking, 2003).

28. For the clock, see http://www.bullatomsci.org/clock/nd95moore3.html.

29. Christopher Andrew and Oleg Gordievsky, *KGB* (New York: HarperCollins, 1990), 592–606. For a less alarmist view of the fall nuclear crisis, see Benjamin B. Fischer, *A Cold War Conundrum* (Washington, DC: Center for the Study of Intelligence, Central Intelligence Agency, 1997), online at http://www.cia.gov/csi/monograph/coldwar/source.htm. Even so, Fischer agrees that in late 1983, "the Soviet media hammered home that the danger of nuclear war was higher than at any time since World War II."

30. For the new Cold War, see William G. Hyland, *Soviet-American Relations: A New Cold War?* (Santa Monica, CA: Rand Corporation, 1981); Noam Chomsky, *Towards a New Cold War* (New York: Pantheon, 1982); Jonathan Schell, *The Fate of the Earth* (New York: Knopf, 1982) and *The Abolition* (New York: Knopf, 1984); Robert F. Drinan, *Beyond the Nuclear Freeze* (New York: Seabury, 1983); Robert C. Aldridge, *First Strike!* (Boston, MA: South End, 1983); Edward Zuckerman, *The Day After World War III* (New York: Viking, 1984); Helen Caldicott, *Missile Envy* (New York: Morrow, 1984); David S. Meyer, *A Winter of Discontent* (New York: Praeger, 1990). For the Catholic response, see National Conference of Catholic Bishops. *The Challenge of Peace* (Washington, DC: United States Catholic Conference, 1983); Jim Castelli, *The Bishops and the Bomb* (Garden City, NY: Image, 1983); William A. Au, *The Cross, the Flag, and the Bomb* (Westport, CT: Greenwood Press, 1985). For nuclear winter, see Mark A. Harwell et al., *Nuclear Winter* (New York: Springer-Verlag, 1984); Lester Grinspoon, ed., *The Long Darkness* (New Haven: Yale University Press, 1986). "A Cold Dark Apocalypse," *Time* November 14, 1983, 43.

31. Bill Shaikin, *Sport and Politics* (New York: Praeger, 1988).

32. Alan Nadel, *Flatlining on the Field of Dreams* (New Brunswick, NJ: Rutgers University Press, 1997).

33. Jack Hunter, ed., *Search and Destroy* (London: Creation, 2002).

34. Gorbachev is quoted in Edmund Levin, "Reagan's Victory?" *Weekly Standard*, November 15, 2004. See also Mark Kramer, "The Collapse of the Soviet Union," *Journal of Cold War Studies* 5, 1 (2003): 3–16; Brian Taylor, "The Soviet Military and the Disintegration of the USSR," *Journal of Cold War Studies* 5, 1 (2003): 17–66.

35. Don Oberdorfer, *The Turn* (New York: Poseidon Press, 1991); Jack F. Matlock Jr., *Reagan and Gorbachev* (New York: Random House, 2004); Richard K. Herrmann and Richard Ned Lebow, eds., *Ending the Cold War* (New York: Palgrave Macmillan, 2004).

36. Sidney Blumenthal, "The U-Turn That Saved the Gipper," *Guardian* (UK), June 10, 2004; Beth A. Fischer, *The Reagan Reversal* (Columbia: University of Missouri Press, 2000).

37. Lou Cannon, *President Reagan* (New York: Simon and Schuster, 1991); Paul Lettow, *Ronald Reagan and His Quest to Abolish Nuclear Weapons* (New York: Random House, 2005).

38. David C. Wills, *The First War on Terrorism* (Lanham, MD: Rowman and Littlefield, 2003).

39. The speech is at http://www.reagan.utexas.edu/resource/speeches/1983/102783b.htm.

40. Kenneth R. Timmerman, *The Death Lobby* (Boston: Houghton Mifflin, 1992); Steve Coll, *Ghost Wars* (New York: Penguin, 2004).

41. Roosevelt is also credited with the statement that though a Central American dictator—either Trujillo or Somoza—was a son of a bitch, he was nevertheless our son of a bitch. The quote may be apocryphal, and is also attributed to Cordell Hull, but it accurately reflects FDR's own views and policy.

42. Philip Jenkins, *Images of Terror* (Hawthorne, NY: Aldine de Gruyter, 2003), 98–104, 167–72; Patrick Seale, *Abu Nidal* (New York: Random House, 1992).

43. Dilip Hiro, *The Longest War* (New York: Routledge, 1991); Jenkins, *Images of Terror*, 167–72; Kenneth M. Pollack, *The Persian Puzzle* (New York: Random House, 2004).

44. Jack G. Shaheen, *Reel Bad Arabs* (New York: Olive Branch Press, 2001); Jenkins, *Images of Terror*, 150–62.

45. The speech is at http://www.reagan.utexas.edu/resource/speeches/1981/12781b.htm. See also Steven Emerson, *Secret Warriors* (New York: Putnam, 1988); Antonio Cassese, *Terrorism, Politics, and Law* (Cambridge: Polity, 1989).

46. Wills, *The First War on Terrorism*; http://www.fas.org/irp/offdocs/nsdd/nsdd-138.htm.

47. Benjamin Netanyahu, ed., *Terrorism: How the West Can Win* (New York: Farrar, Straus, Giroux, 1986): "The West can and must," 6; the West "can stop the forces of world terror," 4. See also Uri Ra'anan et al., *Hydra of Carnage* (Lexington, MA: Lexington, 1986).

48. Jenkins, *Images of Terror*; Patrick Seale, *Asad of Syria* (Berkeley: University of California Press, 1988); Marius Deeb, *Syria's Terrorist War on Lebanon and the Peace Process* (New York: Palgrave Macmillan, 2003).

49. Huchthausen, *America's Splendid Little Wars*; Joseph T Stanik, *El Dorado Canyon* (Annapolis, MD: Naval Institute Press, 2003).

50. Kurt Carlson, *One American Must Die* (New York: Congdon and Weed, 1986).

51. Armstrong et al., *The Chronology*; *The Tower Commission Report*; Caspar W. Weinberger, *Fighting for Peace* (New York: Warner, 1990); Magnus Ranstorp, *Hizb'allah in Lebanon* (New York: St. Martin's, 1997).

52. Emerson, *Secret Warriors*, describes a hostage rescue mission planned by the Reagan administration but never executed.

53. Neil C. Livingstone, *Beyond the Iran-Contra Crisis* (Lexington, MA: Lexington, 1988); William S. Cohen and George J. Mitchell, *Men of Zeal* (New York: Viking, 1988); Michael A. Ledeen, *Perilous Statecraft* (New York: Scribner's, 1988); Lawrence E. Walsh, *Firewall* (New York: Norton, 1997); Robert Busby, *Reagan and the Iran-Contra Affair* (New York: St. Martin's, 1999).

54. Oliver North with William Novak, *Under Fire* (New York: HarperCollins/Zondervan, 1991).

Chapter 9

1. Craig Reinarman and Harry G. Levine, eds., *Crack in America* (Berkeley: University of California Press, 1997), 37. See also http://www.reagan.utexas.edu/resource/speeches/1981/92881a.htm; Daniel S. Claster, *Bad Guys and Good Guys* (Westport, CT: Greenwood Press, 1992).

2. Reagan declared himself "against the idea that the criminal must be protected from society, rather than the other way around," in "Reagan for President?" *New Republic*, July 2, 1966. See also

Ronald Reagan, "Remarks at the Annual Conference of the National Sheriff's Association in Hartford, Connecticut," http://www.reagan.utexas.edu/archives/speeches/1984/62084c.htm, and "Remarks at the Annual Convention of the Texas State Bar Association in San Antonio," http://www.reagan.utexas.edu/archives/speeches/1984/70684a.htm. Thornburgh is quoted from http://www.time.com/time/poy2000/archive/1980.html.

3. Douglas W. Kmiec, *The Attorney General's Lawyer* (New York: Praeger, 1992); Edwin Meese III, *With Reagan* (Washington, DC: Regnery Gateway, 1992).

4. See http://www.ojp.usdoj.gov/bjs/glance/tables/corr2tab.htm; http://www.ojp.usdoj.gov/bjs/glance/tables/corrtyptab.htm.

5. Sarah Lawrence, Jeremy Travis, *The New Landscape of Imprisonment* (2004), at http://www.urban.org/urlprint.cfm?ID=8848.

6. Jack Henry Abbott, *In the Belly of the Beast* (New York: Vintage, 1981), xi; Jack Henry Abbott with Naomi Zack, *My Return* (Buffalo, NY: Prometheus, 1987).

7. Lincoln Caplan, *The Insanity Defense and the Trial of John W. Hinckley, Jr.* (Boston: D. R. Godine, 1984); "The Insanity Plea on Trial," *Newsweek*, May 24, 1982, 56–61.

8. Henry J. Steadman et al., *Before and After Hinckley* (New York: Guilford Press, 1993). Another attack on the insanity defense from this time was Willard Gaylin, *The Killing of Bonnie Garland* (New York: Simon and Schuster, 1982).

9. Joel Best, *Random Violence* (Berkeley: University of California, 1999).

10. Lillian B. Rubin, *Quiet Rage* (New York: Farrar, Straus and Giroux, 1986); George P. Fletcher, *A Crime of Self-Defense* (New York: Free Press, 1988).

11. Ovid Demaris, *The Last Mafioso* (New York: Bantam, 1981); *Report to the President and the Attorney General: President's Commission on Organized Crime* (Washington, DC: GPO, 1986). Some of the individual volumes include *The Impact, The Edge,* and *America's Habit.*

12. See http://www.reagan.utexas.edu/resource/speeches/1984/62084c.htm.

13. Thomas Powers, *Diana* (Boston: Houghton Mifflin, 1971); Ellen Frankfort, *Kathy Boudin and the Dance of Death* (New York: Stein and Day, 1984); John Castellucci, *The Big Dance* (New York: Dodd, Mead, 1986); Ron Jacobs, *The Way the Wind Blew* (London: Verso, 1997); Susan Braudy, *Family Circle* (New York: Random House, 2003).

14. William Sater, *Puerto Rican Terrorists: A Possible Threat to U.S. Energy Installations?* (Santa Monica, CA: RAND Corporation, 1981).

15. "Radicals: The Hunt Goes On," *Newsweek*, November 9, 1981, 44–45.

16. Larry Sloman, *Steal This Dream* (New York: Doubleday, 1998); Bill Ayers, *Fugitive Days* (Boston: Beacon Press, 2001); William Ayers, Bernardine Dohrn, and Rick Ayers, *Zero Tolerance* (New York: W. W. Norton, 2001).

17. Bob Woodward, *Veil* (New York: Simon and Schuster, 1987), 181–87.

18. The quote is from http://www.cia.gov/cia/information/eo12333.html.

19. *The FBI and CISPES: Report of the Select Committee on Intelligence, U.S. Senate* (Washington, DC: GPO, 1989); *CISPES and FBI Counterterrorism Investigations: Hearings Before the Subcommittee on Civil and Constitutional Rights of the Committee on the Judiciary* (Washington, DC: GPO, 1989); *Senate Select Committee on Intelligence: Inquiry into the FBI Investigation of the Committee in Solidarity with the People of El Salvador (CISPES)* (Washington, DC: GPO, 1989); Ross Gelbspan, *Break-ins, Death Threats, and the FBI* (Boston: South End Press, 1991); Susan Bibler Coutin, *The Culture of Protest* (Boulder: Westview Press, 1993).

20. Daniel Hirsch, "The NRC: What, Me Worry?" *Bulletin of the Atomic Scientists*, Jan-Feb 2002, at http://www.thebulletin.org/issues/2002/jf02/jf02hirsch.html.

21. Kevin Flynn and Gary Gerhardt, *The Silent Brotherhood* (New York: Free Press, 1989); James Ridgeway, *Blood in the Face* (New York: Thunder's Mouth, 1990).

22. "Heroin Plague," *Time*, September 10, 1979, 41; Janet Cooke, "Jimmy's World," *Washington Post*, September 29, 1980; "Middle-Class Junkies," *Newsweek*, August 10, 1981, 63–64. The "new heroin epidemic" is described by Janet Bode, "White-Collar Heroin," *New York*, October 13, 1980, 30–34. See also James A. Inciardi, Lana D. Harrison, eds., *Heroin in the Age of Crack-Cocaine* (Thousand Oaks, CA: Sage Publications, 1998).

23. Philip Jenkins, *Synthetic Panics* (New York: New York University Press, 1999), 72–75.

24. For *Rolling Stone*, see Jill Jonnes, *Hep-Cats, Narcs and Pipe Dreams* (New York: Scribner's, 1996), 333; Bob Woodward, *Wired* (New York: Pocket, 1984); Tom Shales and James Andrew Miller, *Live from New York* (Boston: Little, Brown, 2002).

25. Guy Gugliotta and Jeff Leen, *Kings of Cocaine* (New York: Simon and Schuster, 1989); Bruce Porter, *Blow* (New York: HarperCollins, 1993); Eric L. Jensen and Jurg Gerber, eds., *The New War on Drugs* (Cincinnati: Anderson, 1998); Martin Torgoff, *Can't Find My Way Home* (New York: Simon and Schuster, 2004).

26. Richard Duncan Downie, *Learning from Conflict* (Westport, CT: Praeger, 1998); Peter Kraska, "The Military as Drug Police," in Larry K Gaines and Peter Kraska, *Drugs Crime and Justice*, 2nd ed. (Prospect Heights, IL: Waveland Press, 2003), 288–308.

27. Elaine Shannon, *Desperados* (New York: Viking, 1988); Paul Eddy, Hugo Sabogal, and Sara Walden, *The Cocaine Wars* (New York: Norton, 1988).

28. The Reagan quote is from http://www.pbs.org/wgbh/pages/frontline/shows/drugs/archive/stoppingdrugs2.html; on DARE see Darryl F. Gates and Diane K. Shah, *Chief: My Life in the LAPD* (New York: Bantam, 1992); the Nancy Reagan quote is from http://www.dea.gov/speeches/reagan.html.

29. See http://www.dea.gov/speeches/reagan.html; Laura Gomez, *Misconceiving Mothers* (Philadelphia: Temple University Press, 1997); Loren Siegel, "The Pregnancy Police Fight the War on Drugs," in Reinarman and Levine, eds., *Crack in America*, 249–59; Inger J. Sagatun-Edwards, "Crack Babies, Moral Panic, and the Criminalization of Behavior During Pregnancy," in Jensen and Gerber, *New War on Drugs*, 107–21; Mariah Blake, "Crack Babies Talk Back," *Columbia Journalism Review*, September-October 2004, at http://www.cjr.org/issues/2004/5/voices-blake.asp.

30. *Drug Paraphernalia: Hearing Before the Select Committee on Narcotics Abuse and Control* (Washington, DC: GPO, 1980); *Drug Paraphernalia and Youth: Hearing Before the Subcommittee on Criminal Justice of the Committee on the Judiciary* (Washington, DC: GPO, 1980); *Village of Hoffman Estates v. Flipside, Hoffman Estates, Inc.*, 455 U.S. 489 (1982).

31. Kenneth D. Tunnell, *Pissing on Demand* (New York: New York University Press, 2004).

32. Jenkins, *Synthetic Panics*, 95–100.

33. *The Crack Cocaine Crisis: Joint Hearing Before the Select Committee on Narcotics Abuse and Control* (Washington, DC: GPO, 1987); Jimmie Lynn Reeves and Richard Campbell, *Cracked Coverage* (Durham, NC: Duke University Press, 1994); Reinarman and Levine, eds., *Crack in America*.

34. Reeves and Campbell, *Cracked Coverage*; Reinarman and Levine, eds., *Crack in America*; Katherine Beckett and Theodore Sasson in Eric L. Jensen and Jurg Gerber, *The New War on Drugs* (Cincinnati: Anderson, 1998), 25–44.

35. Gugliotta and Leen, *Kings of Cocaine*; Henry Brownstein, *The Rise and Fall of a Violent Crime Wave* (Guilderland, NY: Harrow and Heston, 1996).

36. Henry J. Hyde, *Forfeiting Our Property Rights* (Washington, DC: Cato Institute, 1995).

37. Philip Jenkins, *Synthetic Panics* (New York: New York University Press, 1999).

38. Gates and Shah, *Chief: My Life in the LAPD*; James Q. Wilson and George Kelling, "Broken Windows" (1982) at http://www.theatlantic.com/politics/crime/windows.htm.

39. Mark Bowden, *Killing Pablo* (New York: Atlantic Monthly Press, 2001); Robin Kirk, *More Terrible than Death* (New York: Public Affairs, 2003).

40. See http://www.reagan.utexas.edu/resource/speeches/1986/31686a.htm; *Role of Nicaragua in Drug Trafficking: Hearing Before the Subcommittee in Children, Family, Drugs, and Alcoholism of the Committee on Labor and Human Resources* (Washington, DC: GPO, 1985).

41. *The Role of Cuba in International Terrorism and Subversion: Hearing Before the Subcommittee on Security and Terrorism of the Committee on the Judiciary* (Washington, DC: GPO, 1982); *The Cuban Government's Involvement in Facilitating International Drug Traffic: Joint Hearing Before the Subcommittee on Security and Terrorism of the Committee on the Judiciary and the Subcommittee on Western Hemisphere Affairs of the Foreign Relations Committee and the Senate Drug Enforcement Caucus* (Washington, DC: GPO, 1983). For the emergence of "narcoterrorism," see *Narcoterrorism Information Rewards Act of 1985: Hearing Before the Subcommittee on Crime of the Committee on the Judiciary* (Washington, DC: GPO, 1986); Rachel Ehrenfeld, *Narco Terrorism* (New York: Basic Books, 1990).

42. Leslie Cockburn, *Out of Control* (New York: Atlantic Monthly Press, 1987); Jonathan Kwitny, *The Crimes of Patriots* (New York: Norton, 1987); Jonathan Marshall, Peter Dale Scott, and Jane Hunter, *The Iran-Contra Connection* (Boston, MA: South End, 1987); Peter Dale Scott and Jonathan Marshall, *Cocaine Politics* (Berkeley: University of California Press, 1991); Michael Levine with Laura Kavanau-Levine, *The Big White Lie* (New York: Thunder's Mouth, 1993); Alexander Cockburn and Jeffrey St. Clair, *Whiteout* (New York: Verso, 1998); Gary Webb, *Dark Alliance* (New York: Seven Stories Press, 1998); *Report on the Central Intelligence Agency's Alleged Involvement in Crack Cocaine Trafficking in the Los Angeles Area. Permanent Select Committee on Intelligence* (Washington, DC: GPO, 2000); Patricia A. Turner, *I Heard It Through the Grapevine* (Berkeley: University of California Press, 1993).

Chapter 10

1. Joel Best, *Threatened Children* (Chicago: University of Chicago Press, 1990).

2. From a large literature, see David Finkelhor, *Child Sexual Abuse* (New York: Free Press, 1984); Ruth S. Kempe and C. Henry Kempe, *The Common Secret* (New York: W. H. Freeman, 1984); Diana E. H. Russell, *Sexual Exploitation* (Beverly Hills, CA: Sage, 1984); *Protecting Our Children* (Washington, DC: U.S. Departmen of Justice, 1985). R. Watson, "A Hidden Epidemic," *Newsweek*, May 14, 1984, 30–36; C. O'Connor, "The Chilling Facts About Sexual Abuse," *Glamour*, June 1984, 265; M. Beck, "An Epidemic of Child Abuse," *Newsweek*, August 20, 1984, 44; R. Watson, "Child Molesting," *Reader's Digest*, September 1984, 148–52; C. McCall, "The Cruelest Crime," *Life*, December 1984, 35–42.

3. Philip Jenkins, *Moral Panic* (New Haven: Yale University Press, 1998).

4. Diana E. H. Russell, *Sexual Exploitation* (Beverly Hills, CA: Sage, 1984) and *The Secret Trauma* (New York: Basic, 1986); Best, *Threatened Children*, 72.

5. Jeffrey M. Masson, *The Assault on Truth* (New York: Farrar, Straus and Giroux, 1984); Jeffrey M. Masson, ed., *A Dark Science* (New York: Noonday, 1988); Ellen Bass and Laura Davis, *The Courage to Heal* (New York: Harper and Row, 1988); Joel Best, *Random Violence* (Berkeley: University of California, 1999).

6. For abuse and survivorship, see, for instance, Ellen Bass and Louise Thornton, eds., *I Never Told Anyone: Writings by Women Survivors of Child Sexual Abuse* (New York: Harper and Row, 1983); Christine A. Courtois, *Healing the Incest Wound* (New York: Norton, 1988); E. Sue Blume, *Secret Survivors* (New York: Wiley, 1990); M. Scott Peck, *The Road Less Traveled* (New York: Simon and Schuster, 1978) and *People of the Lie* (New York: Simon and Schuster, 1983); John Bradshaw,

Homecoming (New York: Bantam, 1990). The image of the Holocaust survivor also contributed to the emerging idea of "survivorship."

7. Jenkins, *Moral Panic*, 145–66; David Thorstad, *A Witch-Hunt Foiled* (New York: North American Man-Boy Love Association, 1985).

8. "A New Furor over Pedophilia," *Time*, January 17, 1983.

9. See http://www.tedgunderson.com/911Report/911intro.htm.

10. Ernest Volkman and Howard L. Rosenberg, "The Shame of the Nation," *Family Weekly*, June 2, 1985; Best, *Threatened Children*, 47.

11. *Attorney General's Commission on Pornography, Final Report* (Washington, U.S. Department of Justice, 1986), 688–89. For one of several libertarian responses to this commission, see Philip Nobile and Eric Nadler, *United States of America vs. Sex* (New York: Minotaur Press, 1986). Jenkins, *Beyond Tolerance*, 35–45; David Finkelhor, Linda Meyer Williams and Nanci Burns, *Nursery Crimes* (Newbury Park, CA: Sage, 1988).

12. Jenkins, *Moral Panic*, 165–68; Debbie Nathan and Michael Snedeker, *Satan's Silence* (New York: Basic, 1995). For Bakersfield, see Maggie Jones, "Who Was Abused?" *New York Times Magazine*, September 19, 2004.

13. Best, *Threatened Children*.

14. Philip Jenkins, *Using Murder* (Hawthorne, NY: Aldine de Gruyter, 1994), 57–59, 197–202; Volkman and Rosenberg, "The Shame of the Nation," 4; Best, *Threatened Children*, 134.

15. Charles M. Sennott, *Broken Covenant* (New York: Pinnacle, 1994),

16. Jenkins, *Moral Panic*, 10–11, 132–34, 157–60.

17. Jenkins, *Using Murder*, 64–67; Mike Cox, *The Confessions of Henry Lee Lucas*. (New York: Pocket Star, 1991); Joel Norris, *Henry Lee Lucas* (New York: Zebra, 1991).

18. The Lucas story is the source of the 1989 film *Henry: Portrait of a Serial Killer*.

19. "Thirty-Five Murderers of Many People Could Be at Large, Says US," *NYT*, October 26 1983; Robert Lindsey, "Stopping Them Before They Kill Again and Again and Again" *NYT*, 22 April 1984.

20. Robert K. Ressler and Tom Shachtman, *Whoever Fights Monsters* (New York: St. Martin's, 1992); John E. Douglas and Mark Olshaker, *Mind Hunter* (New York: Pocket, 1995); Joseph C. Fisher, *Killer Among Us* (Westport, CT: Praeger, 1997); Steven A. Egger, *The Killers Among Us* (Upper Saddle River, NJ: Prentice Hall, 1998); Ronald M. Holmes and Stephen T. Holmes, eds., *Contemporary Perspectives on Serial Murder* (Thousand Oaks, CA, Sage, 1998).

21. Paula Hawkins, *Children at Risk* (Bethesda, MD: Adler and Adler, 1986); Arlen Specter with Charles Robbins, *Passion for Truth* (New York: Morrow, 2000).

22. *Teenage Prostitution and Child Pornography: Hearings Before the Subcommittee on Select Education of the Committee on Education and Labor* (Washington, DC: GPO, 1982); *Exploited and Missing Children: Hearings Before the Subcommittee on Juvenile Justice of the Committee on the Judiciary* (Washington, DC: GPO, 1982); *Child Pornography: Hearings Before the Subcommittee on Juvenile Justice* (Washington, DC: GPO, 1983); *Serial Murders: Hearings Before the Subcommittee on Juvenile Justice of the Committee on the Judiciary* (Washington, DC: GPO, 1983); *Hearings on the Missing Children Assistance Act, April 9, 1984.* (Washington, DC: GPO, 1984); *Effects of Pornography on Women and Children: Hearings Before the Subcommittee on Juvenile Justice of the Committee on the Judiciary* (Washington, DC: GPO, 1985); *Child Pornography and Pedophilia: Hearings Before the Permanent Subcommittee on Investigations of the Committee on Governmental Affairs* (Washington, DC: GPO, 1985); *Child Pornography and Pedophilia: Report Made by the Permanent Subcommittee on Investigations of uhe Committee on Governmental Affairs* (Washington, DC: GPO, 1986); *The Federal Role in the Investigation of Serial Violent Crime. Hearings Before a Subcommittee of the Committee on Government Operations* (Washington, DC: GPO, 1986); *Child Protection and Obscenity Enforcement*

Act and Pornography Victims Protection Act of 1987: Hearing Before the Committee on the Judiciary, (Washington, DC: GPO, 1988); *Child Protection and Obscenity Enforcement Act of 1988: Hearings Before the Subcommittee on Crime of the Committee on the Judiciary* (Washington, DC: GPO, 1989);

23. Kenneth Wooden, *Child Lures* (Arlington, TX: Summit, 1995); Kenneth Wooden, "Light Must be Shed on Devil Worship," letter to the editor, *NYT*, November 23, 1988.

24. *Hearings on the Missing Children Assistance Act* (Washington, DC: GPO, 1984).

25. Jenkins, *Mystics and Messiahs*, 208–15; Jenkins, *Moral Panic*, 164–88.

26. Paul Eberle and Shirley Eberle, *The Politics of Child Abuse* (Secaucus, NJ: Lyle Stuart, 1986); Robert D. Hicks, *In Pursuit of Satan* (New York: Prometheus, 1991); Nathan and Snedeker, *Satan's Silence.* For some of the extreme statements of the satanic danger in these years, see John W. De Camp, *The Franklin Cover-up* (Lincoln, NE: AWT, 1991); Linda Blood, *The New Satanists* (New York: Warner, 1994); James R. Noblitt and Pamela Sue Perskin, *Cult and Ritual Abuse* (Westport, CT: Praeger, 1995).

27. Bill Ellis, *Raising the Devil* (Lexington: University Press of Kentucky, 2000) and *Lucifer Ascending* (Lexington: University Press of Kentucky, 2004); Gareth J. Medway, *Lure of the Sinister* (New York: New York University Press, 2001); Malcolm McGrath, *Demons of the Modern World* (Amherst, NY: Prometheus, 2002); Dorothy Rabinowitz, *No Crueler Tyrannies* (New York: Free Press, 2003); Mary De Young, *The Day Care Ritual Abuse Moral Panic* (Jefferson, NC: McFarland, 2004). For continuing belief in ritual abuse, see Chrystine Oksana, *Safe Passage to Healing* (New York: Harper Perennial, 1994); Valerie Sinason, ed., *Treating Survivors of Satanist Abuse* (London: Routledge, 1994); Sara Scott, *The Politics and Experience of Ritual Abuse* (Philadelphia: Open University Press, 2001); Dawn Perlmutter, *Investigating Religious Terrorism and Ritualistic Crimes* (Boca Raton: CRC Press, 2004).

28. For the proliferating genre of "survivor" memoirs, see Laura Buchanan, *Satan's Child* (Minneapolis: Compcare, 1994); Gail Carr Feldman, *Lessons in Evil, Lessons from the Light* (New York: Crown, 1993); Torey L. Hayden, *Ghost Girl* (Boston: Little, Brown, 1991); Judith Spencer, *Suffer the Child* (New York: Pocket, 1989); Lauren Stratford, *Satan's Underground* (Eugene, OR: Harvest House, 1988).

29. Larry Kahaner, *Cults That Kill* (New York: Warner, 1988).

30. See http://www.reagan.utexas.edu/resource/speeches/1984/62084c.htm; Associated Press, "FBI Launches Frontal Attack on Serial Killers," *Centre Daily Times*, State College, PA, July 11, 1984.

31. John Gallagher and Chris Bull, *Perfect Enemies* (New York: Crown, 1996).

32. Robert Lindsey, "Sexual Abuse of Children Draws Experts' Increasing Concern Nationwide," *NYT*, April 4, 1984.

33. See http://www.nostatusquo.com/ACLU/dworkin/other/ordinance/newday/T2a.htm; http://www.nostatusquo.com/ACLU/dworkin/other/ordinance/newday/AppC.htm; Andrea Dworkin and Catharine A. Mackinnon, *Pornography and Civil Rights* (Minneapolis, MN: Organizing Against Pornography, 1988); Donald A. Downs, *The New Politics of Pornography* (Chicago: University of Chicago Press, 1989); Catharine A. Mackinnon and Andrea Dworkin, eds., *In Harm's Way* (Cambridge, MA: Harvard University Press, 1997); Alice Echols, *Shaky Ground* (New York: Columbia University Press, 2002).

34. Jenkins, *Beyond Tolerance*, 35–39.

35. Charles Bowser, *Let the Bunker Burn* (Philadelphia: Camino, 1989).

36. Kenneth V. Lanning, *Investigator's Guide to Allegations of "Ritual" Child Abuse* (Quantico, VA: NCAVC, FBI Academy, 1992); Gail S. Goodman, *Characteristics and Sources of Allegations of Ritualistic Child Abuse* (Washington, DC: GPO, 1995).

37. Ellis, *Raising the Devil* and *Lucifer Ascending*; Dan and Steve Peters with Cher Merrill, *Rock's Hidden Persuader* (Minneapolis, MN: Bethany House, 1985).

38. Tipper Gore, *Raising PG Kids in an X-Rated Society* (Nashville: Abingdon, 1987).

39. Ibid.; Kevin Courrier, *Dangerous Kitchen* (Toronto: ECW Press, 2002); Barry Miles, *Zappa* (New York: Grove Press, 2004). The song "Porn Wars" was from the album "Frank Zappa Meets the Mothers of Prevention."

40. Gore, *Raising PG Kids in an X-Rated Society*, 46.

Chapter 11

1. Gary L. Gregg, "Healer-in-Chief," in Richard S. Conley, ed., *Reassessing the Reagan Presidency* (Lanham, MD: University Press of America, 2003).

2. Jane Mayer and Doyle McManus, *Landslide* (Boston: Houghton Mifflin, 1988); Ethan Bronner, *Battle for Justice* (New York: W. W. Norton, 1989).

3. Stephen Pizzo, Mary Fricker, and Paul Muolo, *Inside Job* (New York: McGraw-Hill, 1989); James Ring Adams, *The Big Fix* (New York: John Wiley and Sons, 1990); Martin Mayer, *The Greatest-Ever Bank Robbery* (New York: Collier, 1992). For Wall Street scandals, see Donna Sammons Carpenter and John Feloni, *The Fall of the House of Hutton* (New York: Henry Holt, 1989); Martin Mayer, *Stealing the Market* (New York: Basic Books, 1992).

4. Dan E. Moldea, *Dark Victory* (New York: Viking, 1986); William Sternberg and Matthew C. Harrison, *Feeding Frenzy* (New York: Henry Holt, 1989); A. Ernest Fitzgerald, *The Pentagonists* (Boston: Houghton-Mifflin, 1989); Jack Newfield and Wayne Barrett, *City for Sale* (New York: Perennial, 1989); Marilyn Thompson, *Feeding the Beast* (New York: Scribner's, 1990); James Traub, *Too Good to Be True* (New York: Doubleday, 1990); Charles M. Sennott, *Broken Covenant* (New York: Simon and Schuster, 1992).

5. Richard Reeves, *The Reagan Detour* (New York: Simon and Schuster, 1985); Thomas Ferguson and Joel Rogers, *Right Turn* (New York: Hill and Wang, 1986); Sidney Blumenthal, *Pledging Allegiance* (New York: HarperPerennial, 1991); Allen D. Hertzke, *Echoes of Discontent* (Washington, DC: CQ Press, 1993); David C. Anderson, *Crime and the Politics of Hysteria* (New York: Times Books, 1995); Jules Witcover, *Party of the People* (New York: Random House, 2003); Lewis Gould, *Grand Old Party* (New York: Random House, 2003).

6. Jack F. Matlock Jr., *Reagan and Gorbachev* (New York: Random House, 2004).

7. Though see John Kenneth White, *Still Seeing Red* (Boulder, CO: Westview, 1997).

8. Daniel Yergin and Joseph Stanislaw, *The Commanding Heights* (New York: Simon and Schuster, 1998); Kenneth S. Baer, *Reinventing Democrats* (Lawrence: University Press of Kansas, 2000); Haynes Johnson, *The Best of Times* (New York: Harcourt, 2001); Bill Clinton, *My Life* (New York: Knopf, 2004). The 1994 result thwarted the hopes of some who had hoped for a long-term pro-Democratic realignment among the middle class; see Kevin Phillips, *Boiling Point* (New York: Random House, 1993); Stanley B. Greenberg, *Middle Class Dreams*, rev. ed. (New Haven: Yale University Press, 1996); Michael Meeropol, *Surrender* (Ann Arbor: University of Michigan Press, 1998). For the continuing influence of Reagan conservatism, see Nina J. Easton, *Gang of Five* (New York: Simon and Schuster, 2000).

9. Steve Sailer, "Baby Gap," *American Conservative*, December 20, 2004, 7–10.

10. Gould, *Grand Old Party*; Philip Jenkins, *The New Anti-Catholicism* (New York: Oxford University Press, 2003).

11. See http://www.buchanan.org/pa-92-0817-rnc.html; Janet Hook, "A Future President's Rebirth," *Los Angeles Times*, July 11, 2004; David Aikman, *A Man of Faith* (Nashville: W Publishing, 2004); John Micklethwait and Adrian Wooldridge, *The Right Nation* (New York: Penguin, 2004).

12. William J. Clinton, "Oklahoma Bombing Memorial Prayer Service Address," at http://www.americanrhetoric.com/speeches/wjcoklahomabombingspeech.htm; "President Clinton Remembers," April 5, 1996, at http://www.pbs.org/newshour/bb/white_house/clinton_4-5.html.

13. Gore is quoted from http://www.americanatheist.org/columns/ontar12-7-99.html. See also Robert Booth Fowler, Allen D. Hertzke, Laura R. Olson, *Religion and Politics in America*, 2nd ed. (Boulder, CO: Westview, 1999); Michael Cromartie, ed., *A Public Faith* (Lanham, MD: Rowman and Littlefield, 2003); Allen D. Hertzke, *Freeing God's Children* (Lanham, MD: Rowman and Littlefield, 2004).

14. Hillary Rodham Clinton, *It Takes a Village* (New York: Simon and Schuster, 1996).

15. Philip Jenkins, *Using Murder* (Hawthorne, NY: Aldine de Gruyter, 1994) and *Moral Panic* (New Haven: Yale University Press, 1998), 196–99; Joe Domanick, *Cruel Justice* (Berkeley: University of California Press, 2004).

16. James L. Nolan Jr., *The Therapeutic State* (New York: New York University, 1998); Duane L. Dobbert, *Halting the Sexual Predators Among Us* (Westport, CT: Praeger, 2004).

17. The Clinton quote is at http://editioncnn.com/US/9606/22/clinton.radio.transcript.html.

18. Katherine Beckett, *Making Crime Pay* (New York: Oxford University Press, 1997).

19. Philip Jenkins, *Mystics and Messiahs* (New York: Oxford University Press, 2000).

20. Philip Jenkins, *Pedophiles and Priests* (New York: Oxford University Press, 1996).

21. See http://bushlibrary.tamu.edu/research/papers/1989/89090502.html; *The Drug War 1989: Taking the Offensive in Boston: Hearing Before the Select Committee on Narcotics Abuse and Control* (Washington, DC: GPO, 1990); Jill Jonnes, *Hep-Cats, Narcs and Pipe Dreams* (New York: Scribner's, 1996), 336; Richard Davenport-Hines, *The Pursuit of Oblivion* (New York: Norton, 2002); Peter A. Huchthausen, *America's Splendid Little Wars* (New York: Viking, 2003).

22. Sam Staley, *Drug Policy and the Decline of American Cities* (New Brunswick, NJ: Transaction, 1992); Eric L. Jensen and Jurg Gerber, eds., *The New War on Drugs* (Cincinnati: Anderson, 1998); Philip Jenkins, *Synthetic Panics* (New York: New York University Press, 1999); Katherine Beckett and Theodore Sasson, *The Politics of Injustice*, 2nd ed. (Thousand Oaks, CA: Sage Publications, 2004).

23. Franklin E. Zimring, Gordon Hawkins, and Sam Kamin, *Punishment and Democracy* (New York: Oxford University Press, 2001); Sasha Abramsky, *Hard Time Blues* (New York: St. Martin's, 2002); Kathleen Auerhahn, *Selective Incapacitation and Public Policy* (Albany: State University of New York Press, 2003); Donald Braman, *Doing Time on the Outside* (Ann Arbor: University of Michigan Press, 2004); Domanick, *Cruel Justice*. For disfranchisement, see *Losing the Vote* (Washington DC: Human Rights Watch and the Sentencing Project, 1998) at http://www.hrw.org/reports98/vote/index.html#TopofPage; Christopher Uggen and Jeff Manza, "Democratic Contraction?" *American Sociological Review* 67 (2002): 777–803.

24. Quoted by James Bovard, "The Reagan Roadmap for Antiterrorism Disaster," at http://www.counterpunch.org/bovard10082003.html.

25. Mark Bowden, *Black Hawk Down* (New York: Penguin, 2000).

26. James Mann, *Rise of the Vulcans* (New York: Viking, 2004).

27. The quote is found at http://www.whitehouse.gov/news/releases/2002/01/20020129-11.html.

28. Joshua Micah Marshall, "Kerry Faces the World," *Atlantic Monthly*, July-August 2004; Philip Jenkins, *Images of Terror* (Hawthorne, NY: Aldine de Gruyter, 2003).

29. Philip Jenkins, *Beyond Tolerance* (New York: New York University Press, 2001).

30. For Bush's FBI speech, see http://www.whitehouse.gov/news/releases/2001/09/20010925-5.html. The Pentagon speech can be found at http://usinfo.org/wf-archive/2001/011011/epf401.htm. The reference to "the children whose worlds have been shattered" is from http://www.freedom.org/

WTC/pres-1st.html. See also Bruce Lincoln, *Holy Terrors* (Chicago: University of Chicago Press, 2003).

31. Anatol Lieven, *America, Right or Wrong* (New York: Oxford University Press, 2004).

32. Gary Sick, *October Surprise* (New York: Times Books/Random House, 1991).

33. Sidney Blumenthal, *The Clinton Wars* (New York: Farrar, Straus and Giroux, 2003); Jenkins, *Images of Terror*, 112–18.

34. Chip Berlet and Matthew N. Lyons, *Right-Wing Populism in America* (New York: Guilford Press, 2000); Steven M. Chermak, *Searching for a Demon* (Boston: Northeastern University Press, 2002); Jenkins, *Images of Terror*, 49–52.

35. Joe Holley, "Anatomy of a Story," *Columbia Journalism Review* 35, 3 (1996): 26–27; *Implementation of the Church Arson Prevention Act of 1996: Hearing Before the Committee on the Judiciary* (Washington, DC: GPO, 1997).

36 Jenkins, *Images of Terror*, 45, 132–33.

37. Kevin Phillips, *American Dynasty* (New York: Viking, 2004).

Index